VOICES OF THE POOR

Crying Out for Change

VOICES OF THE POOR
Crying Out for Change

Deepa Narayan
Robert Chambers
Meera K. Shah
Patti Petesch

Published by Oxford University Press for the World Bank

Oxford University Press

OXFORD   NEW YORK   ATHENS   AUCKLAND   BANGKOK
BOGOTA   BUENOS AIRES   CALCUTTA   CAPE TOWN   CHENNAI
DAR ES SALAAM   DELHI   FLORENCE   HONG KONG   ISTANBUL
KARACHI   KUALA LUMPUR   MADRID   MELBOURNE   MEXICO CITY
MUMBAI   NAIROBI   PARIS   SÃO PAULO   SINGAPORE   TAIPEI
TOKYO   TORONTO   WARSAW

and associated companies in

BERLIN   IBADAN

© 2000 The International Bank for Reconstruction
and Development / The World Bank
1818 H Street, N.W., Washington, D.C. 20433, USA

Published by Oxford University Press, Inc.
198 Madison Avenue, New York, N.Y. 10016

Oxford is a registered trademark of Oxford University Press.

Manufactured in the United States of America
First printing August 2000

The findings, interpretations, and conclusions expressed in this study are entirely
those of the authors and should not be attributed in any manner to the World
Bank, to its affiliated organizations, or to members of its Board of Executive
Directors or the countries they represent. The boundaries, colors, denominations,
and other information shown on any map in this volume do not imply on the part
of the World Bank Group any judgment on the legal status of any territory or the
endorsement or acceptance of such boundaries.

Library of Congress Cataloging-in-Publication Data has been applied for.

*Text printed on paper that conforms to the American National Standard for
Permanence of Paper for Printed Library Materials, Z39.48-1984*

Dedication

*We dedicate this book to
the more than 20,000 poor women, men, youth and children
who took the time to share their lives with us.*

Contents

Foreword xv

Chapter 1: Perspectives of the Poor 1

Summary 1
Introduction 2
Origin of the Study 3
The Study Process 3
    An Evolving Framework 4
    Focus of the Study 4
    Country Selection 5
    Site Selection: Representativeness 6
Experiences in the Field 8
    The Pressure of Time 8
    Establishing Trust 9
    Unprepared to Deal with Loss, Grief and Anger 10
    Participatory Methods: What Worked and What Did Not 11
    Data Analyses 15
    Ethics of Participatory Methods 16
Challenges in Writing This Book 18

Chapter 2: Wellbeing and Illbeing: The Good and the Bad Life 21

Summary 21
Wellbeing Is Multidimensional 22

Part I. Wellbeing: The Good Life 22
How Poor People Put It 22
Materially, Enough for a Good Life Is Not a Lot 24
    Material Wellbeing: Having Enough 25
    Bodily Wellbeing: Being and Appearing Well 26
    Social Wellbeing 26
    Security 27
    Freedom of Choice and Action 28
Diversity by Context and Person 29
Wealth and Wellbeing Are Different 30

Part II. Illbeing: The Bad Life 31
The Multidimensionality of Illbeing 31
    Material Lack and Want 31

Physical Illbeing 34
Bad Social Relations: Exclusion, Rejection, Isolation and Loneliness . . .35
Insecurity, Vulnerability, Worry and Fear 36
Powerlessness, Helplessness, Frustration and Anger 36

Part III. Psychological Experience of Wellbeing and Illbeing 37
The Experience of Wellbeing: Peace of Mind, Happiness and Harmony 37
The Experience of Illbeing: Humiliation, Shame, Anguish and Grief 38
Humiliation, Shame and Stigma 38
Anguish, Loss and Grief 39
The Illbeing of Children 42
Reflections 42

Chapter 3: The Struggle for Livelihoods 46
Summary 46
Poor People's Priority 46
Rural Livelihoods: Producing amid Scarcity 46
Access to Land 47
Diminishing Inputs and Returns 48
Few Institutional Supports 49
Common Property Resources under Stress .50
Migration and Remittances 51
Diversified Livelihoods in Cities and Countryside 53
Getting Hired—Connections Needed 54
Lawlessness on the Job 54
Seasonal Fluctuations 55
Money in Short Supply 56
Informal Credit 56
Formal Credit and Banks 58
Livelihoods That Steal the Future 59
Limited Opportunities 62
Where Life Is Better 63
Individual Breakthroughs 64
The Challenge of Livelihoods 68

Chapter 4: Places of the Poor 71
Summary 71
Introduction 72
The Missing Basics 72
Water—Inadequate and Unsafe 72
Isolation and Poor Access 75

Bad Housing and Shelter 78
Energy Scarcity 78
No Sanitation—Filth and Stench 80
The Politics of Infrastructure and Place 81
Trapped in Poor Places 84
Environmental Risks 84
Seasonal Stress: Worst at Bad Times 85
Insecurity and Stigma 86
Catastrophic for Children 87
The Challenge of Poor Places 88

Chapter 5: The Body *89*

Summary 89
Introduction 90
How the Body Looks and Feels 90
Physical Appearance 91
Hunger 91
Exhaustion: Poverty of Energy and Time 92
Sickness of Body and Mind 93
The Body as an Asset 95
Body Blows: How Injury, Illness and Their
Costs Impoverish 98
Troubles with Treatment 100
Lacking Physical Access and Medicines 101
Time Spent 101
Financial Costs 102
The Behavior of Medical and Health Staff 103
Poor Quality 104
Positive Experiences 105
Private Treatment 107
The Challenge 107

Chapter 6: Gender Relations in Troubled Transition *109*

Summary 109
Introduction 110
Changing Gender Roles and Responsibilities 111
Diversification of Women's Work 111
Increased Work Burden of Women 114
Household Gender Roles: A Blurred Divide 115
Decisionmaking at the Household Level 116

Male Frustration, Anxiety and Sense of Inferiority 118
Domestic Abuse and Violence 119
    Definitions of Domestic Abuse and Violence 120
    Causes of Domestic Abuse and Violence 122
    Changes in Levels of Domestic Violence 124
The Opportunity and Challenge 131

Chapter 7: Social Illbeing: Left Out and Pushed Down *133*
Summary 133
Introduction 134
    Who Is Excluded? 134
    The Bottom Poor 135
The Basis of Social Exclusion 136
    The Stigma of Poverty 136
    Lack of Money and Power 138
    Ethnic, Linguistic, Racial and Cultural Isolation 139
    Physical, Mental and Health Disabilities 140
    Behaviors outside Community Norms 141
    Area Stigma 141
    Self-Exclusion 142
    The Exclusion of Women 143
Changes in Social Cohesion 145
    Strained Social Relations and Reduced Collective Action 146
    What Brings People Together? 147
The Opportunity and Challenge 149

Chapter 8: Anxiety, Fear and Insecurities *151*
Summary 151
Introduction 152
What Does Security Mean to Poor People? 152
Trends and Patterns 153
    Regional Trends in Security 154
    Gender Differences 154
Types of Insecurity 155
    Survival and Livelihoods 156
    Rural: Uncertain Returns to Farming 156
    Urban: Insecure Work, No Bargaining Power 157
    Natural and Human-Made Disasters 158
    Crime and Violence 159
    Persecution by Police and Lack of Justice 162

Civil Conflict and War 167

Macropolicy Stresses and Shocks 168

Social Vulnerability 171

Health, Illness and Death 175

In Search of Security 175

Chapter 9: The Character of Institutions 179

Summary 179

Introduction 180

Quality of Relationships 181

Trust 181

Participation 182

Accountability 185

Unity and Conflict Resolution 187

Valued Behaviors 188

Respect 189

Honesty and Fairness 189

Listening, Caring, Love and Compassion 190

Hardworking Problem-Solvers 191

Institutional Effectiveness 191

Timely, Responsive and Caring Support 192

Access, Closeness and Contact 193

In Search of Character 194

Chapter 10: Governance: Poor People's Scorecards 197

Summary 197

Introduction 198

Institutional Ratings 199

Important Institutions 199

Effective Institutions 200

Ineffective Institutions 200

Governance and Accountability of State Institutions 200

Accountable to Whom? 203

Lack of Responsiveness 205

The Power of Documents 208

Decentralized Governance: Municipalities, Councilors and Mayors . . .209

Empowerment and Partnership 211

Interactions with Private Enterprise 214

The Power of Industry 214

Shops and Moneylenders 216

Governance and Accountability in Civil Society .218
    Community-Based Organizations 219
    Local Leadership 220
    Churches, Mosques, Temples, Shrines, Trees, Stones and Rivers 222
    Nongovernmental Organizations 224
Conclusion 232

Chapter 11: Powerless, Trapped in a Many-Stranded Web 235

Summary 235
Trapped and Tied 236

Part I. Lack of Capabilities 237
Lack of Information 237
    Telephones, Media and Information Technology 239
Lack of Education 240
    The Strain of Costly and Distant Schools 241
    Children's Labor Needed 243
    Problems of Quality and Relevance 244
Lack of Skills 245
Low Self-Confidence and Self-Worth 246

Part 2. Keeping Poor People Powerless: The Many-Stranded Web 247
The Many-Stranded Web 248
Poor People's Descriptions of Linkages 250
Shocks, Stresses and Sequences 252
Agonizing Choices 255
The Challenge of Powerlessness 260

Chapter 12: A Call to Action: The Challenge to Change 263

Summary 263
Introduction 264
The Challenge to Reflect: The Meaning of Development 264
The Challenge of Power: Whose Voice Counts? .265
The Agenda for Change 266
1. From Material Poverty to Adequate Assets and Livelihoods 267
2. From Isolation and Poor Infrastructure to Access and Services 270
3. From Illness and Incapability to Health, Information
   and Education 272
4. From Unequal and Troubled Gender Relations to Equity
   and Harmony 275

5. From Fear and Lack of Protection to Peace and Security 278
6. From Exclusion and Impotence to Inclusion, Organization
   and Empowerment 281
7. From Corruption and Abuse to Honesty and Fair Treatment 284
The Challenge to Change 288

Appendix 1 — Study Team and Acknowledgments *293*

Appendix 2 — Study Countries and Sites *298*

Appendix 3 — Overview of Study Themes and Methods *306*

Appendix 4 — About the Authors *314*

Foreword

This book is the second in a three-part series entitled *Voices of the Poor.* The series is based on an unprecedented effort to gather the views, experiences, and aspirations of more than 60,000 poor men and women from 60 countries. The work was undertaken for the *World Development Report 2000/2001* on the theme of poverty and development.

Crying Out for Change brings together the voices of over 20,000 poor men and women from comparative fieldwork conducted in 1999 in 23 countries. The first volume in the series—*Can Anyone Hear Us?*—brings together the voices of over 40,000 poor people from 50 countries from studies conducted in the 1990s. The final volume, *From Many Lands,* highlights country case studies and regional patterns. The *Voices of the Poor* project is different from all other large-scale poverty studies. Using participatory and qualitative research methods, the study presents very directly, through poor people's own voices, the realities of their lives. How do poor people view poverty and wellbeing? What are their problems and priorities? What is their experience with the institutions of the state, markets, and civil society? How are gender relations faring within households and communities? We want to thank the project team led by Deepa Narayan of the Poverty Group in the World Bank, and particularly the country research teams, for undertaking this work.

What poor people share with us is sobering. A majority of them feel they are worse off and more insecure than in the past. Poor people care about many of the same things all of us care about: happiness, family, children, livelihood, peace, security, safety, dignity, and respect. Poor people's descriptions of encounters with a range of institutions call out for all of us to rethink our strategies. From the perspective of poor people, corruption, irrelevance, and abusive behavior often mar the formal institutions of the state. Nongovernmental organizations (NGOs), too, receive mixed ratings from the poor. Poor people would like NGOs to be accountable to them. Poor people's interactions with traders and markets are stamped with their powerlessness to negotiate fair prices. How then do poor people survive? They turn to their informal networks of family, kin, friends, and neighbors. But these are already stretched thin.

We commend to you the authenticity and significance of this work. What can be more important than listening to the poor and working with our partners all over the world to respond to their concerns? Our core mission is to help poor people succeed in their own efforts, and the book raises major challenges to both of our institutions and to all of us concerned about poverty. We are prepared to hold ourselves accountable, to make the effort to try to respond to these voices. Obviously we cannot do this alone. We urge you to read this book, to reflect and respond. Our hope is that the voices in this book will call you to action as they have us.

CLARE SHORT,
Secretary of State for International
Development, U.K.

JAMES D. WOLFENSOHN,
President, World Bank

Poverty is like heat:
you can not see it, you can only feel it;
so to know poverty you have to go through it.

—A poor man, Adaboya, Ghana

Chapter 1

Perspectives of the Poor

Summary

This book is based on the realities of poor people. It draws upon research conducted in 1999 involving over 20,000 poor women and men from 23 countries. Despite very different political, social and economic contexts, there are striking similarities in poor people's experiences. The common theme underlying poor people's experiences is one of powerlessness. Powerlessness consists of multiple and interlocking dimensions of illbeing or poverty. The organization of this book roughly follows the 10 dimensions of powerlessness and illbeing that emerge from the study. The remainder of the chapter presents the methodology and the challenges faced in conducting the study.

Introduction

Nobody hears the poor. It is the rich who are being heard.
— Participant, discussion group of men and women,
Borg Meghezel, Egypt

When they assist you they treat you like a beggar.
— Participant, discussion group of men and women,
Vila Junqueira, Brazil

There are 2.8 billion poverty experts, the poor themselves. Yet the development discourse about poverty has been dominated by the perspectives and expertise of those who are not poor—professionals, politicians and agency officials. This book seeks to reverse this imbalance by focusing directly on the perspectives and expertise of poor people. It is based on a study that used open-ended participatory methods to engage more than 20,000 poor women and men from 23 countries to express their own perspectives and experiences of poverty, its causes and how it can be reduced.[1]

From poor people's perspectives, illbeing or bad quality of life is much more than just material poverty. It has multiple, interlocking dimensions. The dimensions combine to create and sustain powerlessness, a lack of freedom of choice and action. Each dimension can cause or compound the others. Not all apply all the time or in every case, but many apply much of the time. For those caught in multiple deprivations, escape is a struggle. To describe this trap poor people use the metaphor of bondage, of slavery, of being tied like bundles of straw. The psychological experience of multiple deprivations is intense and painful. Ten interlocking dimensions of powerlessness and illbeing emerge from poor people's experiences:

▶ Livelihoods and assets are precarious, seasonal and inadequate.
▶ Places of the poor are isolated, risky, unserviced and stigmatized.
▶ The body is hungry, exhausted, sick and poor in appearance.
▶ Gender relations are troubled and unequal.
▶ Social relations are discriminating and isolating.
▶ Security is lacking in the sense of both protection and peace of mind.
▶ Behaviors of those more powerful are marked by disregard and abuse.
▶ Institutions are disempowering and excluding.
▶ Organizations of the poor are weak and disconnected.
▶ Capabilities are weak because of the lack of information, education, skills and confidence.

These 10 dimensions of powerlessness and illbeing are examined in the chapters that follow; they form the core organizational structure of the book.

This chapter describes the origins of the study, the methodology and some of the challenges faced, and chapter 2 explores in some detail the multidimensional nature of wellbeing and illbeing. Chapters 3–11 then address the core findings. Chapter 3 focuses on poor people's livelihoods and coping strategies as well as their limited assets. Chapter 4 describes the places where poor people live and work, and how the lack of infrastructure and services adds to their disempowerment and difficulties. Chapter 5 focuses on the body as poor people's most valuable and sometimes only asset; it includes a discussion of poor people's experiences in accessing health services. Chapter 6 turns to changes in gender roles and the stress on gender relations within the household. Chapter 7 focuses on the many different forms of social exclusion. Chapter 8 explores the many meanings of insecurity and related fears and anxieties experienced by poor men and women. Chapter 9 details the behavior and character of institutions, both the qualities cherished by poor people in institutions with which they have contact and the quality of their interaction with these institutions. Chapter 10 describes the most important institutions in poor people's lives and their ratings of effective and ineffective institutions. Chapter 11 brings these dimensions together into a many-stranded web of powerlessness. It particularly focuses on the lack of capability, including lack of information, education, skills and confidence that together with all the other deprivations contribute to poor people's powerlessness. The final chapter is a call to action and dwells on the challenge of change.

Origin of the Study

The *Voices of the Poor* study, also known as the *Consultations with the Poor* study, was undertaken by the World Bank as background for the *World Development Report 2000/01: Attacking Poverty (WDR 2000/01)* and to inform poverty reduction strategies.[2] Its origins lie in the conviction that at the start of the 21st century any policy document on poverty should be based on the experiences, reflections, aspirations and priorities of poor people themselves. The aim of the study was to enable a wide range of poor people—women and men, young and old—in diverse countries and conditions to share their views in such a way that they could inform and contribute to the concepts and content of the *WDR 2000/01*.

The Study Process

The idea of a participatory poverty study to inform the *WDR 2000/01* emerged in the summer of 1998. It became immediately clear that something like this had never been attempted before. It was also clear that such a study would have to be done on a fairly large scale and completed quickly if it was to inform the *WDR 2000/01*. Planning the study brought out many tensions and differences: between those who thought the study should be done in great depth in four to six countries and those who thought the study should be done in at least 20 countries; between carrying out an analysis of existing data and conducting new studies; between using participatory open-ended methods and precoded questionnaires; and between a more flexible research design that gave freedom to country researchers to choose issues and participatory methods and more standardization of the methodology.

An Evolving Framework

The methodological discussions engaged staff within the World Bank and researchers in civil society. Three methodological workshops were held in August and December 1998 and in January 1999. The framework for the study evolved during these meetings. It was decided that a range of participatory methods would be used; that the study would be conducted in 20 countries with the expectation of success in 15 (in the end studies were completed in 23 countries); that the range of issues would be limited and the study undertaken according to a prepared methodology guide with room for local adaptation; and that a systematic review of existing studies would be conducted while the new comparative studies were undertaken.

While the framework for the study was evolving, a draft methodology guide was developed and field tested in November 1998 in Bolivia, India, Thailand and Sri Lanka by local research teams. Based on this experience and advice from participatory specialists, the methodology was refined and the final methodology guide developed by January 1999.[3] This was translated into Spanish as well as Russian, Indonesian, Thai and Vietnamese.

Focus of the Study

After much discussion, the scope of the inquiry concentrated on four themes:

- ▸ *Wellbeing and illbeing,* as defined and experienced by poor people. The study used the local words and concepts of poor people to elicit their ideas about security, risk, vulnerability, opportunities, social exclusion, and crime and conflict; their perception of how their conditions had changed over time; and how households and individuals coped with changes in wellbeing.
- ▸ *Problems and priorities* of different groups and how these had changed. Poor men, women and youth identified priority problems and solutions, and who could play what role in solving the problems.
- ▸ *Role of institutions,* specifically, the role that public, civic and market institutions play in people's lives; the criteria poor people use in evaluating institutions; to what extent they felt they had control or influence over them; and which institutions supported them in coping with crisis.

▶ *Gender relations,* changes in gender relations, roles, decision-making and violence within the household and the community, including whether women were better or worse off than in the past and how women fared as compared with men.[4]

Discussions on these topics were held in small groups of men, women, the elderly, youth and sometimes with groups that included a mix of men and women. A range of participatory methods was used. Participants sometimes prepared drawings as a tool for sharing and deepening their discussion and analyses. The research teams were encouraged to explore other topics as they emerged. Throughout, the intention was to enable poor people to express the realities of their experience in their own words.

Country Selection

Country selection was guided by the need to represent different continents and contexts while finding in-country partners who could undertake the research and follow-up. The study was conducted in 23 countries of Africa and the Middle East, Eastern Europe and Central Asia, Latin America and the Caribbean, and South and East Asia (see table 1.1). Insights into the experiences of those living in countries that have experienced recent civil conflict and war come from poor people in Bosnia and Herzegovina, Ethiopia, Somaliland and Sri Lanka.

To increase the probability of follow-up action, the study proceeded only in countries where a group with capacity for follow-up action at the policy, project, or community level took clear ownership of the study. This was achieved through a negotiated process of cost sharing. The study project was announced widely throughout the World Bank and staff were invited to express interest, identify programs and policies that would be

Table 1.1 Countries Involved in the Study

Africa and the Middle East	Eastern Europe and Central Asia	Latin America and the Caribbean	South and East Asia
Egypt	Bosnia and Herzegovina	Argentina	Bangladesh
Ethiopia	Bulgaria	Brazil	India
Ghana	Kyrgyz Republic	Bolivia	Indonesia
Malawi	Russia	Ecuador	Sri Lanka
Nigeria	Uzbekistan	Jamaica	Thailand
Somaliland			Vietnam
Uganda			
Zambia			

informed by the study, contribute matching funds and seek government interest and ownership. In four countries the study was managed by nongovernmental organizations (NGOs)—Bangladesh, Bolivia, India and Somaliland. In Jamaica, Malawi and Nigeria the study was conducted in close collaboration with the field offices of the U.K. Department for International Development (DFID).

In many areas where the study was associated with NGOs, follow-up action was almost immediate as findings were fed into ongoing programs. In many countries workshops have been held with government, civil society and the private sector, and the study is beginning to influence development strategies.

Site Selection: Representativeness

Given the constraints of time and resources, national research teams purposively selected 8–15 communities (typically neighborhoods in urban areas and villages in rural areas) to be representative of the most prevalent groups of poor people and a diverse range of people and conditions in that country.[5] A typical example of the site selection process comes from Indonesia, where researchers write:

> There was much discussion with the Government of Indonesia, NGO poverty specialists, and World Bank staff before sites could be selected. Since the locations that could be covered were only 10 or 12, a nationally representative sample was clearly out of the question. The consensus to focus on the island of Java emerged from the fact that Java has the largest number as well as the highest concentration of the country's poor and is the region hit the hardest by the economic crisis. In order to have some representation of the rest of the country, the choice fell on the Nusa Tenggara islands, which have livelihood patterns and geo-climatic features very different from Java. The decision was made to select 8 out of 12 sites on Java and 4 sites on the NTB-NTT islands. The final selection of communities was made in consultation with district level government personnel and NGOs to ensure a mix of rural and urban sites, a mix of hilly, coastal, and plain sites and a mix of remote and accessible communities.

The objective of representing significant diversity usually was achieved by sampling to include communities from different agroecological zones and regions of the country as well as to ensure inclusion of minority groups, refugees, or other locally relevant unique conditions. In Bulgaria, for example, researchers sampled both rural and urban areas and tried to get some national distribution. In addition one community was chosen to represent a minority group. The Russian sites included the town of Dzerzhinsk in the Volga region of central Russia, 400 kilometers from Moscow, an area selected for its environmental pollution and known as the "chemical capital of the country and in constant danger of a technical catastrophe." People there said, "We live on pins and needles all the time. If something happens at the chemical plant, it'll be like a hydrogen bomb. Nothing will be left in the whole area." In India two different states were selected, Bihar and Andhra Pradesh, to contrast areas that are very different in terms of government effectiveness.

In some countries the selection of communities was influenced by the presence of World Bank or NGO activities. In Brazil the study was designed to support the formulation of an urban strategy; hence a diverse set of urban sites was selected. In Bangladesh and in India communities were chosen in areas where NGOs were already working to ensure use of local data and to facilitate access to the communities. The data in these two countries may be particularly biased by the concentrated presence of NGO assistance.

Using this sampling process, field studies were conducted and analyzed in 23 countries, in close to 300 communities. In India, Jamaica and Uzbekistan one proposed site had to be abandoned in each country because of hostility or violence, particularly in urban slums. During one discussion group in Brazil, a local drug dealer burst into the room carrying a gun because he felt threatened by reports of groups discussing crime and drugs. Fortunately he left quietly. In another community, youths worried about the safety of researchers because of a killing in the neighborhood, escorted the team out of the community before discussions could be completed.

The diversity of sampling procedures means that not every type of poverty was studied, nor are the data nationally representative. This affects the types of statements that can be made, and that are made, in this book.

Within communities researchers used a variety of techniques to reach poor men and women as well as, where possible, groups of elderly and youth. Research teams did not always have control over who participated in the study. Within each community team leaders relied on different methods in forming groups of poor people to conduct small group discussions. In some cases, community contacts from within the community or outside helped in forming groups. In some cases, "poor" people were identified after a discussion of what is poverty or wellbeing and the characteristics of different wellbeing groups in that community. While every attempt was made to sample poor people, sometimes the less poor were present in group discussions. There is probably an underrepresentation of the very poor in discussion groups, people who are often excluded or exclude themselves from community meetings. In each community research teams held group discussions with men, women and youth as well as individual interviews focusing on life stories or case studies of those who had escaped poverty and those who were always poor or were once better off but had become poor.[6]

Experiences in the Field

Fieldwork never proceeds according to the researcher's wishes and plans. This study is no exception. In Ecuador, for example, the fieldwork started just as the country plunged into financial crisis and all bank accounts were frozen. In all countries the methodology had to be constantly adapted to field conditions: compromises were made, challenges faced and solutions generated. The quotations in this section represent the voices of the local researchers who conducted the research in the 23 countries.

The Pressure of Time

On average each research team member worked 14–15 hours per day. Long hours working, excessive heat at daytime, and walking long distances to reach the village made one team member sick.
—Research team, Gowainghat, Bangladesh

The extreme poor are also often hidden.
—Research team, Jamaica

All research teams felt the time crunch. While the rapid completion of the country studies is a tribute to the in-country researchers' commitment, it was not without impact on the quality of the data. Even though researchers worked long hours, they sometimes had to make compromises in numbers of people and whom they reached, depth of probing, depth of the analyses and feedback to communities.

When time is short, it is easier to conduct discussion groups or hold interviews with those present. In Sri Lanka, for example, research teams in many places found it sometimes difficult to schedule meetings with villagers when it was "convenient to them and without any hindrance to their normal day-to-day work." This problem was particularly acute in villages where beedi (leaf-rolled cigarettes) manufacturing was the main source of income and payment was on a piece-rate basis: "The villagers were very particular about the number of hours they work. They do not even spare the time to attend the 'Samurdhi meetings.' The time they reluctantly spared for us was limited, and sometimes we had to get information from them while they were at work. This also in a way affected our survey."

Similarly in Bangladesh, researchers found it difficult to reach men during the day. As in other countries, this was overcome by scheduling late-night meetings well in advance.

In one community in Malawi only five of the eight scheduled discussion groups could be held. The team leader notes:

This situation came because it was rather difficult to mobilize men who spend most of the day at work and only come home

in the evening. According to our contact person, the chief him-
self, most men do not stay home even on Saturdays because
they use their time to do other activities to supplement their in-
come. Secondly, on the scheduled dates, there were funerals in
the neighborhood such that the chief excused himself from our
team to facilitate and organize the funeral ceremony. Thirdly,
on the rescheduled date, three of the facilitators had diarrhea
and could not join the team to the field. This, however, did not
affect the process because the people did not turn up either.
The research team did not therefore prepare a date for feed-
back on the research to the community.

While in some places the very poor people, those most marginalized in society, were included in the study, these people were often absent from or silent during group discussions. Still, in some places, as will be seen, glimpses were obtained about the realities of their lives. In Indonesia, for example, researchers systematically scheduled meeting times two days in advance with people from poorer parts of communities. In Dmitrovgrad, Bulgaria researchers spent time with children from residential institutions for the retarded. They write, "Few of the students were actually retarded, the overwhelming majority being either abandoned or orphaned children who ended up at this institution since they had nowhere else to go." In Moscow teams met with Tajik refugees and in Bulgaria with Roma groups.

The study was conducted during only one season of the year. In Sredno Selo, Bulgaria the researchers write, "Spring had come in full force by the time fieldwork began, 12 April. The villagers had pressing seasonal tasks to perform: raking of meadows, building fences around them, grazing livestock before a communal cowherd and shepherd have been hired, preparing the ground for planting onions, garlic, and potatoes." In Bangladesh it was the rainy season and heavy rains made some urban slums mud holes, which were very difficult to get to. In Vietnam, in Ha Tinh Province, it was the hottest and driest period of the year. The seasonal effect of the 1998 World Cup football in France was not anticipated and affected the first round of fieldwork, as many people watched football matches during late night and early morning hours.

In some countries, particularly in Latin America and the Caribbean, researchers paid people small amounts of money for participation in discussion groups. In other countries, snacks, coffee, or tea served halfway through or at the end of discussions were greatly appreciated by participants.

Establishing Trust

There was an element of suspicion among the villagers. It was
hard to explain the study objectives to all the villagers in an
equal manner during a short period of time.
                                        —Research team, Elhena, Sri Lanka

Local authorities did not trust our explanation about the purposes and security of results of our investigations. That is why they warned the group participants about the necessity to remember the proverb, "Talking men will die without a disease." It was not a threat of homicide, but was notice of possible troubles.

—Research team, Takhtakupyr, Uzbekistan

This was our very first site. We wanted it to succeed.

—Research team, Kajima, Ethiopia

Research teams knew well the critical importance of establishing trust. A variety of methods was used to build rapport. Most teams included men and women researchers so as to ease the approach to both men and women. In many countries, teams entered communities with written permits from the government and after briefing local government authorities. The Somaliland report describes one common approach used by the research teams:

Each team leader was responsible for establishing contact with the village or site committee, elder, or headman. It was agreed that at least one respected person from the village should accompany the team to perform the initial introductions, even though most of the team members were not strangers in these villages.

When the teams arrived at the site they requested a meeting with the village elders to explain the purpose of their visit. Individual members would also visit the public places (tea shops, mosques and grocery stores) to establish rapport and familiarize themselves with the community. The first morning of the visit was generally spent in getting acquainted....

The meeting with the elders provided the background of the village and primary information about its people and livelihoods. This meeting also produced suggestions for possible times and places to meet with various community groups.... After initial introductions, all teams reported pastoral people were easy to get along with and their famous hospitality was evident throughout their stay in the village.

In order to learn more about the community and improve acceptance by the community, study team members participated in the community activities, such as watering livestock or collecting wild berries. They also attended social functions like marriage sermons and evening prayers in the mosque.

In many countries, including Indonesia and Jamaica, researchers started their work with a "transect walk," simply walking through a community, stopping to greet people along the way, introducing themselves and learning about the community. Researchers in Bower Bank, Jamaica write:

> *On the first day, all team members walked slowly across through the only road leading in and out of Bower Bank....The team conducted a transect accompanied by Janet, the community representative...it was a public holiday, Labor Day, and a very good day for a transect as almost everyone was involved in a Labor Day project....*

> *As the week progressed the women participated willingly in our discussion. In contrast the men, especially the young, appeared to be distrustful of our presence and remained skeptical. One young man recalled an incident where his friend had participated in a previous interview and was later assassinated, as a result of his picture being made public.... In order to gain their attention they had to be coaxed and interviewed at their place of relaxation, i.e., on the street, at the domino table, or their smoking corner, unlike the women, who led their own sessions inside the central office.... Interviews were carried out in competition with the surrounding noise, hindrances from passing cars, construction work, children playing, inquisitive passersby, and interruptions by the mentally unstable who are often found wandering through the community.*

In some places, despite the best intentions, establishing trust proved harder than was at first apparent as researchers stumbled into local politics and power rivalries. In Kajima, Ethiopia one of the first things that researchers learned was that the community was the result of a merger three years previously of three different communities. The significance of this fact struck the researchers when they realized that the current leader had invited participants only from his part of the community, excluding the other two leaders and their communities. Hence there were not enough people to form eight discussion groups. To correct this problem, researchers decided to return later. They write, "When we went back two days later...we didn't like the atmosphere. Word had gone out that the current Chair of the association had included only his people in the consultations. There was some tension as a result. We thought it would be better to leave and settle with six [eight were planned] discussion groups in the community than to stay and further aggravate the situation."

The difficulties in establishing trust were fiercest in the Eastern Europe and Central Asia sites. In Bulgaria researchers write, "During the preliminary research, the team had experienced some difficulties in gathering focus groups; we were suspected to be either an American religious sect or spies; so we decided to change tactics and to rely on traditional Bulgarian ways of contacting people: ...through previous contacts, friends, and during informal evening discussions and social gatherings."

In the refugee camp of Bratunac, Bosnia and Herzegovina research teams found, "Gaining the confidence and willingness of camp residents to participate [took] more effort than normal, as residents were highly suspicious toward outsiders, particularly toward anyone associated with international organizations, as many people have been through the camp and made promises that nothing ever came of."

The most extreme suspicion was experienced in Uzbekistan, not by community people, but by local authorities. In one community, the team reports:

> *After discussion of the causes of poverty, some people were frightened by their own frank words, and gave notice to the local militia that the* vakhhabtists *(revolutionaries) are visiting their aul, asking questions about rich and poor people, about reasons for poverty and sources of poverty and agitating poor people about rich people and authorities. On April 7th our house was encircled by a group of soldiers with automatic guns. They took our passports and documents and arrested us, and the next day the whole group was evicted from the district. After examination of our documents, and determining that we were not* vakhhabtists, *two weeks later our group was allowed to continue work in the same site.*

Unprepared to Deal with Loss, Grief and Anger

> *When pursuing the case study, participants were asked to relive painful memories, which resulted in one respondent crying as his memory unfolded. This was painful to both him and the team member.*
> —Research team, Bower Bank, Jamaica

All research teams received field-based training in participatory research methods. One major oversight was the psychological preparation of the teams themselves to deal with the emotional intensity of being with poor people for a month or more while facilitating free-flowing discussions about their lives. In addition, researchers felt they were not equipped to deal with the emotional stress, grief and despair that was sometimes unleashed among participants as a result of questions about poverty.

In Bosnia and Herzegovina, the team leader writes, "Two of our note-takers, young men, were strongly affected by the process. Milos crying silently while taking notes during one discussion group, and Dado having nightmares and tension headaches after fieldwork."

In Takhtakupyr, Uzbekistan groups included very poor people who became upset during discussions of criteria of poverty, problems, priorities and cause-impact analysis of poverty. To them, "methods of analysis of their own 'bad life' looked like a forgotten dusty mirror. People were so busy looking for food that they did not have time to look at the mirror. Our visit compelled them to wipe the dust and to look into the mirror and answer the question 'Why are we poor?'" Sometimes this upset the participants very much. Participants remembered:

- The absence of bread and the necessity to send the children to the neighbor, since they had already gone to ask for bread several times before and hesitated to go again.
- The relative who died in the hospital because they could not buy the required medicine in time.
- Their children had forgotten the taste of sugar and meat.
- Their children could not go to school due to the absence of clothes and shoes.

"All this caused tears of despair, and the members of the investigation group had depressing feelings of helplessness which had broken the dynamic of the group and made it impossible to concentrate on the cause-impact analysis of poverty."

Security concerns added to the psychological stress among researchers. In Ecuador, the lead researcher received late night calls from field team members frightened by street gangs and drug dealers.

Participatory Methods: What Worked and What Did Not

Informants discussed gender relations with great interest.
—Research team, Bashi, Kyrgyz Republic

Goat droppings, pebbles, small cards with pictures made by the people themselves were used for scoring and ranking.
—Research team, Daanweyne, Somaliland

There was much debate and disagreement between the women regarding the importance of the institutions, and it was difficult to gain consensus.
—Research team, Adaboya, Ghana

For most of the fieldworkers, but particularly for those from government institutions, it was the first time for training in participatory methodology, involving interactive learning instead of lecture-style passive learning.... A longer training with more fieldwork and practice must be considered essential.
—Research team, Ha Tinh, Vietnam

The study methods are rooted in the open-ended tradition of participatory and qualitative research inquiry. The study methodology guide states, "This approach explicitly encourages study teams to explore key issues that emerge by country, culture, social group, gender, age, occupation, or other dimensions of difference of local importance. New and old study tools will be used to uncover and understand the perspectives and insights of the poor, enabling them to express and analyze their realities, with outsiders playing a facilitating role."

Participatory methods, both verbal and visual and including drawing, scoring, ranking and mapping, were used through nondominating behaviors by the researchers. Some of the country research teams were familiar with these approaches and all research teams were trained in participatory research tools.

Researchers changed the sequencing of methods as needed. In Bangladesh, for example, the teams found that starting the work with discussions of "wellbeing" raised expectations of relief and, hence, after the first day the team decided to start with "problems and priorities." Almost everywhere researchers struggled to find simple local terms for words in the methodology guide. Words that were particularly difficult included *well-being, poverty, crisis, household, risk, vulnerability, institutions* and *social exclusion.*

Out of these struggles much was learned. In the Kyrgyz Republic the discussion of gender relations was introduced using a press clip that focused on domestic abuse to try to break the code of silence surrounding the issue. In Argentina sociodrama—enactment of gender roles—was used. In Jamaica role-playing, an activity called "a turned-over tortilla," was developed whereby men enacted women's lives and vice versa. In Bulgaria a focus on the functions of institutions emerged as the most effective strategy to get the institutions discussion started. In Vietnam all team members were requested to note five or more quotations per day that surprised and impressed them. In Bangladesh team members took on specialized roles each day: a lead facilitator, cofacilitator, content recorder, environment setter and process recorder.

While all researchers experienced some difficulties with some methods, the overall experience is summarized in the Jamaica National Report: "It is important to underline the high acceptance of the methodology by the people in the various locations in which we work. It also contributed to strengthening relations between investigators and participants."

Being asked to describe their lives, being heard and engaging in discussion proved to be a novelty and a big draw in many countries. In Indonesia research teams note:

> *The interest generated was overwhelming. The researchers*
> *found people turning up in much larger-than-expected numbers*
> *and staying on to talk past midnight. Additional groups had to*
> *be conducted at times in order not to disappoint those who*

*came. The visual tools helped generate much interest and deep-
er insight, as people lost their self-consciousness and got involved in drawing, sorting, scoring, and diagramming."*

Despite many problems, the overall feeling among researchers, many of whom had never used participatory methods before, was that it was a "fantastic experience." In Uzbekistan the researchers write that participation in the study helped them see their own country with new eyes: "honestly speaking, the sympathy and sense of sharing the destiny of each person encountered which arose during the research process was an experience never achieved in any of our previous studies, either qualitative or quantita- tive…The sensation of insight and sympathy for our own people is the most important finding of this study."

The reflections of the researchers in Vietnam capture well the sentiments of the research teams who participated in this study:

> *Given an opportunity to speak with people ready to listen, poor
> women, men, boys, and girls were ready, willing, and capable
> of discussing, analyzing, and articulating a wide range of issues
> related to poverty and the ways and means of overcoming it.
> An initial hesitation disappeared easily into passionate and often
> heated discussions and deliberations. Initially it was found to
> be very difficult for PPA [Participatory Poverty Assessment]
> fieldwork staff to listen to poor people mainly because they
> thought that poor people knew little and had very little to say.
> Basic mistakes that were made during the first round of the
> PPA were not taking comprehensive notes, lacking patience
> to wait for and listen to people's replies, and guessing answers
> to questions posed to informants. However, these mistakes were
> less in evidence during the PPA's second round.*

Data Analyses

> *Notes were written up every day, often until dawn.*
> —Research team, Jamaica

> *At the end of each day, the team sat together to analyze the
> day's activities and study findings. Strategies for the next day
> were also discussed and planned.*
> —Research team, Somaliland

> *There was a constant tension between the need to present and
> represent the diversity of views and opinions of poor people
> and the need to have a sharp, focused, and message-loaded pre-
> sentation of findings.*
> —Research team, Ha Tinh, Vietnam

In almost every country researchers wrote, analyzed and discussed findings and interpretations at the end of the day. In some areas where this was not possible they went back to communities to cross-check information as necessary. As elsewhere, in Vietnam the team held daily reviews and wrote fieldwork reports. The entire team in a given district attempted to meet every two days to share experiences and make tactical decisions about what was working and what was not. In Ghana the teams met every evening. In most site reports, researchers were careful to distinguish between their own opinions and interpretations and what was actually said.

The aggregation of data first from different groups within a community, then from several communities into district reports, and finally into national reports proved to be a painful process. Four hurdles emerged. First, there was the challenge of not losing poor people's voices and realities while imposing some organization. Second, it was important not to lose diversity while still grouping by commonalities. Third, suggestions for quantification—or even identification of frequencies especially in priority problems—became cumbersome and began to take precedence over documentation of what was said in poor people's own words. Fourth, fieldworkers were often reluctant to spend time analyzing across communities and writing reports. Time shortages and lack of experience in synthesizing qualitative reports further aggravated the research process in some countries.

After fieldwork was completed national workshops to collate and compare findings were held in several countries, including Argentina, Bangladesh, Ecuador, Nigeria and Vietnam. This led to the preparation of National Synthesis Reports. The teams and project staff shared draft country studies and other insights at an international workshop in New Delhi, India in June 1999, which also marked the beginning of the global synthesis. Three months later in September 1999 a preliminary global synthesis was completed, which provides the foundation for this book.[7]

Ethics of Participatory Methods

It may be that the villagers were not interested in providing information, as they saw no direct benefit for them of this study.
—Research team, Elhena, Sri Lanka

A lot of people secretly tried to ask us to solve their problems; we couldn't do that.
—Research team, Turtkul, Uzbekistan

People were busy in the fields. People were also expecting us to take relief food to them. This made the study difficult. People were also fed up with meetings with NGOs due to empty promises.
—Research team, Muchinka, Zambia

[Village] people were particularly interested to hear about the problems and priorities...they thanked the study team for the work done and said that the work had made them think of possible ways to resolve their problems.
—Research team, Ak Kiya, Kyrgyz Republic

The field research posed four continuing ethical challenges that can apply to all research with poor people—and not only research that uses participatory approaches and methods. They arise especially when the prime objective is not to directly empower and benefit the participants, but to help outsiders learn about the experience and realities of poor people, and then to influence policy and practice.

Taking People's Time. The time of poor people is valuable. The challenge here is to try to ensure at least commensurate benefits. In a few cases participants were remunerated for their time and trouble. In others, forms of hospitality were given. Perhaps more important, when poor people express and analyze their realities, they often themselves learn and gain satisfaction from the experience, enjoy it and develop solidarity with others. The process can lead not only to enhanced awareness, but also to taking action.

Raised Expectations. It was stressed to the research teams that they should clearly and repeatedly say they could not promise any assistance. Nevertheless, it was recognized as unavoidable that to some degree expectations would be raised. While follow-up action is taking place at the community level in some countries, the need remains urgent overall.

Feedback. The methodology guide and the terms of reference for the country studies say that researchers would feed information back to the communities before leaving them or upon return. Despite time constraints, many country teams shared the initial findings with community groups. Feedback meetings were held in community halls, libraries, council meeting rooms, garages and private homes, and under trees. This generated much excitement, pensiveness, sometimes sorrow and requests for information, contacts and assistance to solve problems. Often the findings on problems and priorities and on institutions generated the most interest.

In Brazil and Ecuador written copies of the community report were sent back to communities. In Brazil this process resulted in one community leader requesting multiple copies of the report, which he is using to lobby the municipality for improvements in services. He also sent a copy of the report to the president of the country. However, overall, the process of feedback is far from complete.

Follow-up Action. In some areas where the study was undertaken by NGOs working in the community areas, as in Bangladesh and Vietnam, or by community-based organizations, such as in Somaliland, there was scope for follow-up action, with findings feeding immediately into ongoing programs. At the Khaliajuri site in Bangladesh, for example, Concern Bangladesh at once undertook a program to help villagers improve their damaged and dilapidated housing. All this said, ethical issues remain that demand sustained efforts to ensure follow-up at all levels.

Challenges in Writing This Book

Writing this global synthesis has not been simple. Not only has there been much material—close to 10,000 pages of field notes and national synthesis reports coming from 23 countries—we have also faced a struggle between the voices of those who experience deprivation and poverty and our own training, which drives us to categorize and use words that fit into the current development discourse. Our effort should be viewed as a stage in the search for understanding.

Problems of Language and Syntax. In seeking to enable poor people to express their realities, we have tried not to impose our words, constructs and concepts. In writing, we have had little option, most of the time, but to use words and concepts in English. We sometimes use the phrase "the poor" to refer to poor men and women to avoid endless repetition of the same phrase "poor people" or "poor women and men," often several times in one paragraph or one page. It neither signifies disrespect, nor does it imply that poor people form a homogeneous group.

Generalizations: What Can and Cannot Be Said. The generalizations have emerged from a systematic process of content analysis. From this process, crosscutting themes have emerged, some of which are summarized in the headings of chapters and sections. However, these themes are not necessarily universal. We cross-checked the conclusions we drew by going back to country reports and site reports. In two cases—the analysis of trends in domestic violence and the institutional rankings by community groups—because of the importance of the findings and to ensure that we were not overgeneralizing, we went back and checked every discussion group in every site report and analyzed data for frequency of occurrence. Finally, we also quantified data from mini–case studies on triggers for upward and downward mobility.

Our generalizations are not meant to apply to any country as a whole. In the interests of readability, we chose not to qualify every general statement by saying that it was "based on the communities and people who took part in this study." The reader should keep this in mind when she or he reads, for example, "In Nigeria women say...." We communicate the key themes that have emerged from the analyses through the words of poor people themselves. Their voices are more direct, vivid, powerful and authentic than ours. We use their voices to echo themes that emerged over and over in very different contexts. Finally, although the fieldwork was conducted in 1999, we convey the findings often in present tense to close the distance between the reader and poor people and to add immediacy to what they expressed.

Our hope is that positive changes will result from the enormous efforts of the more than 20,000 poor people who participated in the study.

Notes

[1]Appendix 1 identifies the leaders and members of the national research teams and many, many others who contributed to the study.

[2]*Voices of the Poor* is based on the voices of over 60,000 poor women and men. The research consists of two parts. The first is a systematic review of 81 Participatory Poverty Assessments prepared primarily for the World Bank in the 1990s. These studies reached over 40,000 poor men and women in 50 different countries. The review is entitled *Voices of the Poor: Can Anyone Hear Us?* by Deepa Narayan, with Raj Patel, Kai Schafft, Anne Rademacher and Sarah Koch-Schulte (New York: Oxford University Press, 2000). A review of participatory poverty studies involving 50 focus groups conducted by NGOs and bilateral organizations was prepared in parallel by Karen Brock with the Institute of Development Studies, University of Sussex, entitled "It's Not Only Wealth That Matters—It's Peace of Mind Too: A Review of Participatory Work on Poverty and Illbeing." This was published in an informal publications series for the Global Synthesis Workshop, Consultations with the Poor, World Bank, PREM, Poverty Group, Washington, D.C., September 1999.

The second part of the *Voices of the Poor* study, of which this book is a part, is new comparative research conducted in 23 countries in early 1999 and involving over 20,000 poor women and men. The Process Guide, which contains the methodology used during the fieldwork, was published as *Methodology Guide: Consultations with the Poor.* The findings from 21 countries are available in the National Synthesis Reports from Argentina, Bangladesh, Bolivia, Bosnia and Herzegovina, Brazil, Bulgaria, Ecuador, Ethiopia, Ghana, India, Indonesia, Jamaica, Kyrgyz Republic, Malawi, Nigeria, Russia, Somaliland, Thailand, Uzbekistan, Vietnam and Zambia. Initial global findings were summarized in *Global Synthesis: Consultations with the Poor* by Deepa Narayan, Robert Chambers, Meera Shah and Patti Petesch. The *Global Synthesis,* National Synthesis Reports and the *Methodology Guide* were also published in the informal series for the Global Synthesis Workshop: Consultations with the Poor, World Bank, PREM, Poverty Group, Washington D.C., September 1999. A final book in the *Voices of the Poor* series, *Voices of the Poor: From Many Lands* edited by Deepa Narayan and Patti Petesch (Oxford University Press, forthcoming), draws upon the 23 country studies and presents country case studies as well as regional patterns. For further information on the research project and its reports, see http://www.worldbank.org/poverty/voices.

[3]For the full *Methodology Guide,* see www.worldbank.org/poverty/voices.

[4]See appendix 3 for further information on the study themes.

[5]Appendix 2 summarizes the criteria for selecting sites and lists the communities visited in each country.

[6]Pseudonyms have been used throughout the book to protect the identity of the study participants.

[7]A three-day workshop was held in Washington, D.C. which brought together all the country research teams, 70 development practitioners and the *WDR 2000/01* team. Country research team leaders interacted with Bank staff and others in a series

of half-day workshops hosted jointly with the Bank's regional departments and a day was spent with members of the *WDR 2000/01* team. Twenty-five reports of country findings, secondary reviews, global syntheses and a methodology guide were published and distributed at this workshop. All reports are available from the *Voices of the Poor* Web site indicated in endnote 2.

Chapter 2

Wellbeing and Illbeing: The Good and the Bad Life

Summary

Despite the diversity of poor participants, their ideas of wellbeing and the good life are multidimensional and have much in common. Enough for a good life is not a lot, and for those with little, a little more can mean a great deal. Across continents, countries, contexts, and types of people, a good quality of life includes material wellbeing, which is often expressed as having enough; bodily wellbeing, which includes being strong, well and looking good; social wellbeing, including caring for and settling children; having self-respect, peace and good relations in the family and community; having security, including civil peace, a safe and secure environment, personal physical security and confidence in the future; and having freedom of choice and action, including being able to help other people in the community. Wealth and wellbeing are seen as different, and even contradictory.

Descriptions of illbeing are also multidimensional and interwoven. Experiences of illbeing include material lack and want (of food, housing and shelter, livelihood, assets and money); hunger, pain and discomfort; exhaustion and poverty of time; exclusion, rejection, isolation and loneliness; bad relations with others, including bad relations within the family; insecurity, vulnerability, worry, fear and low self-confidence; and powerlessness, helplessness, frustration and anger.

Wellbeing and illbeing are states of mind and being. Wellbeing has a psychological and spiritual dimension as a mental state of harmony, happiness and peace of mind. Illbeing includes mental distress, breakdown, depression and madness, often described by participants to be impacts of poverty. Children have a distinct view of the bad life. An overarching issue is how to enable poor people to diminish illbeing and enhance wellbeing, gaining for themselves more of the good life to which they aspire.

Wellbeing Is Multidimensional

A better life for me is to be healthy, peaceful and to live in love without hunger. Love is more than anything. Money has no value in the absence of love.

— A 26-year-old woman, Dibdibe Wajtu, Ethiopia

The starting question posed by the researchers to the small group discussions with poor women and poor men is, "How do you define wellbeing or a good quality of life, and illbeing or a bad quality of life?" From these discussions emerge local people's own terminology and definitions of wellbeing, deprivation, illbeing, vulnerability and poverty. The terms wellbeing and illbeing were chosen for their open-ended breadth, so that poor people would feel free to express whatever they felt about a good life and a bad life. "We are trying to present a new way of seeing wellbeing," notes a researcher. It is the way poor people see it themselves.

Poor people's ideas of a good quality of life are multidimensional. As explored in part I of this chapter, they cluster around the following themes: material wellbeing, physical wellbeing, social wellbeing, security, and freedom of choice and action. All of these combine pervasively in states of mind as well as body, in personal psychological experiences of wellbeing. Much of illbeing was described as the opposite of these. Part II examines these dimensions in turn: material deprivation; physical illbeing; bad social relations; vulnerability, worry and fear, low self-confidence; and powerlessness, helplessness and frustration. Part III describes the psychological dimensions of wellbeing and illbeing. In describing the conditions of their lives, poor children especially express resentment.

Part I. Wellbeing: The Good Life

How Poor People Put It

Ideas of wellbeing are strikingly similar across the range of participants. Despite differences of detail, and contexts that are diverse, complex and nuanced, the commonalities stand out. The same dimensions and aspects of wellbeing are repeatedly expressed, across continents, countries and cultures, in cities, towns and rural areas alike. And they are expressed by different people—women and men, young and old, children and adults.

For women in Tabe Ere in rural Ghana wellbeing means security: being protected by God, having children to give you security in old age, having a peaceful mind (*tieru villa*), patience (*kanyir*, meaning not holding a grudge against anyone), and plenty of rain.

To have most, if not all, of the necessary basics of life is *umoyo uwemi* and *umoyo wabwino*, wellbeing as described by different groups in Malawi.

These basics include certain assets, adequate food, decent medical care, constant and regular sources of income, nice clothes, good bedding, a house that does not leak, a toilet, a bathroom, a kitchen, healthy bodies, couples being respectful of each other, being God-fearing, having well-behaved children who are not selfish, and having peace of mind.

For those in Khaliajuri in rural Bangladesh having a good quality of life means having employment for the whole year, a good house, four or five cows, a fishing net, good clothes to put on, food to eat to one's heart's content, and being able to protect one's house from flood erosion. Middle-aged women say that for a good quality of life there should be a male member of the household earning money, a son for every mother, and no husbands pursuing polygamy.

A participant from Renggarasi in rural Indonesia considers a person to be living well who can secure his family's needs with produce from his livestock and who is able to help others who need material and nonmaterial things or advice.

In Nigeria wellbeing is described by different people as being a responsible person who has a pleasurable life, peace of mind, security and independence, and who is popular with the people, is able to marry easily, is able to educate children, is able to patronize private clinics and schools, and who has money, land, a house and good clothes.

In Bulgaria the major distinctive feature of wellbeing is stable employment, which means having money as well as security. The National Synthesis Report notes that the family is another important aspect, along with being able to socialize and being in harmony with oneself. The wealthy, seen as those who have and flaunt money and power, do not necessarily have the respect and security that the community considers essential parts of wellbeing.

In the Kyrgyz Republic, "informants understand wellbeing as good life and wealth; however, they do not think that wellbeing is limited to these tangible components, and believe that wellbeing is impossible without tolerance, peace, family and children. The informants think that the basis of wellbeing is good health, peace in the family and in the society; in their opinion, wealth, which is an important component of wellbeing, can only be gained if these conditions are present." From the Kyrgyz Republic it is also reported that most of the informants define wellbeing as "stability on a household and society level and ability to satisfy one's material and spiritual needs."

In Barrio Las Pascuas in urban Bolivia, a group of youths say that those who have a good life are "those who do not lack food," and those "who are not worried every day about what they are going to do tomorrow to get food for their children. They have secure work, and if the husband does not work, the wife does." In Nuestra Señora de Guadalupe in another part of urban Bolivia young men say that, besides having adequate food and work, wellbeing is to be friendly and to have friends, to have the support of family and society, and "to be patient, and above all happy."

Materially, Enough for a Good Life Is Not a Lot

I would like to live simply. I don't like houses with too much inside. To have a bit more comfort. Nothing big...I would like a simple house...not big, or luxurious...a simple house with a floor.

—A 21-year-old man, Esmeraldas, Ecuador

It is perhaps part of the human condition to aspire not for the moon, but for imaginable improvements. Participants were clear that enough materially for a good life for them was not excessive or unrealistic (see box 2.1). They hope for moderate, not extravagant, improvements. They do not see substantial wealth as necessary for wellbeing. Rather, they express the material dimension of life in terms of having enough for a reasonable level of living. And the material is only one dimension among others.

It is not just that poor people's material aspirations are modest. It is also that the worse off they are, the more a small improvement means. A little then means a lot. This may apply especially with women who so frequently have so little. For women in two Malawi rural sites part of a good life is having adequate utensils, especially pails for drawing water and a rack for drying plates. To a discussion of wellbeing in Bangladesh, a group of older women add, "Those who could pass time for the prayer of God after taking a full meal and could sleep on a bamboo-made platform live a good quality of life."

Box 2.1 The Good Life, Caring for Children

To be well is when you have money, and you have a family and children. You need to have savings in order to be able to support your children till later on in life.
—A young man, Bulgaria

A good life is to have enough food and clothing for my children. To educate them to be self-reliant when we get retired.
—A man, Mitti Kolo, Ethiopia

The rich manage to send their children to school and also...to take their children to the clinic.
—A man, Musanya, Zambia

To be well means to see your grandchildren happy, well-dressed and to know that your children have settled down; to be able to give them food and money whenever they come to see you, and not to ask them for help and money.
—An old woman from rural Bulgaria

None of this justifies modest ambitions in development, accepting the horizons of poor people where these are limited, or restraining efforts to help them and to help them help themselves. To the contrary, it hugely reinforces the case for giving overwhelming priority to their wellbeing as they envisage it. Gains by poor people should come first. When the objective is to enhance the wellbeing to which poor people aspire, the benefits from small changes can be large indeed.

Material Wellbeing: Having Enough

> *But at least for each child to have a bed, a pair of shoes, a canopy over their heads, two sheets—not to sleep like we do on the ground.*
> —Ana Maria, a poor woman, Esmeraldas, Ecuador

> *A poor person is a person who does not own anything that provides him with a permanent source of living. If a person has a permanent source of income, he will not ask for other people's assistance.*
> —A poor woman from Sidkia, Egypt

Three aspects of material wellbeing that are repeatedly mentioned are food, assets and work.

Food. Adequate food is a universal need. In Malawi hunger is ranked as the number one problem by nearly every discussion group in the three urban and seven rural communities participating in the study. Elsewhere—across the range of countries—enough to eat every day is again and again stressed as a feature of wellbeing. In contexts as different as Bangladesh, Bulgaria and Zambia wellbeing included being able to have three meals a day, all year round. Food security too is a critical component, with the number of months of food security given frequently as a criterion for ranking wellbeing, particularly in Vietnam.

Assets. For those living in rural areas secure tenure of adequate resources, especially land, is another nearly universal criterion of wellbeing. This often includes ownership of livestock. In urban areas the parallel needs are savings and capital, and access to consumer goods. In urban Ghana wellbeing is identified with capital to start a business. The need for housing—as well as furniture, utensils and tools—is also a virtually universal aspect of wellbeing and sometimes poor people describe a "house that should not let in the rain."

Work. Work to gain a livelihood is a nearly universal aspiration among participants. Money itself is mentioned less frequently than one might expect and, when mentioned, it is implied by other aspects of wellbeing such as the ability to find paid work to obtain money, to buy clothes and to pay for health treatment and school expenses. A poor man in Thompson Pen in Jamaica says, "Work makes all the difference in the world. I feel bad, miserable, sick, and can't take doing nothing. My wife, at 78, is still working. My dream is a little work to make ends meet."

In rural areas work takes many forms; it is usually agricultural and linked with land. In urban areas it means a steady job, which is stressed again and again by those who are without work or who are striving to make a livelihood through casual labor or informal and illegal activities. Whether it is Malawi, where one idea of wellbeing is both husband and wife working, or Russia, where participants stress the importance of wages that are regularly paid, the desire is for productive work to provide an adequate and secure livelihood.

Bodily Wellbeing: Being and Appearing Well

Material wellbeing is rarely mentioned without other critical aspects of a good life. These include the bodily wellbeing of health and appearance, as well as a good physical environment.

Almost everywhere, health and access to health services—whether informal or formal—are important. A healthy and strong body is seen as crucial to wellbeing—not just for a sense of physical wellbeing in itself, but as a precondition for being able to work. A person who is sick and weak cannot work or cannot work well.

For some, especially for girls and young women, the importance of appearance—of both body and clothing—comes through forcefully. Quality of skin is often referred to. In Muchinka in rural Zambia the bodies of the better off are said to "look well." For urban poor people in Jamaica criteria for wellbeing include "skin tone looks balanced" and "looking well fed." In Gowainghat, Bangladesh clothes, oil for the hair and soap are important to young women. Across cultures and contexts being able to dress well and appear well is repeatedly stated as part of a good quality of life.

The third dimension of physical wellbeing is physical environment, with wellbeing in Accompong, Jamaica associated with, for example, "the fresh air in the hills of Cockpit County." The aspect of physical environment, however, is more often used in a negative context and is described, for example, as the bad experiences of living in "the places of the poor."

Social Wellbeing

Social wellbeing includes care and wellbeing of children; self-respect and dignity; and peace and good relations within the family, community and country.

Being Able to Care for, Bring up, Marry and Settle Children. In Nigeria, of the 48 aspects of wellbeing identified, no fewer than eight of them refer to children. Having happy and healthy children, feeding them, clothing them, being able to take them for treatment when sick, and being able to send them to school and pay school bills are common concerns strongly expressed. In Bangladesh households that are financially well off are those that can afford clothes and education for their children.

To be able to marry and settle children is a frequent aspiration. In Malawi and Uzbekistan wedding ceremonies conducted in good style are important. In Ampenan Utara, Indonesia one of the criteria for differentiating wellbeing groups is the ability to meet the costs of children's weddings: the top group has no problem; the second group can meet the cost; the third has to become indebted to meet the costs; and the issue for the bottom group is simply not mentioned. Landless women in Dorapalli in India identify a major impact of poverty as "difficulty in marrying girl children." In Eil-bil-ille, Somaliland the well off are those who can afford marriage-related costs and who always marry at an early age.

Self-Respect and Dignity. Self-respect and dignity, as described by poor people, means being able to live without being a burden to others; living without extending one's hand; living without being subservient to anybody; and being able to bury dead family members decently. In Nigeria this includes being listened to, being popular, and being able to fulfill social obligations and to help others.

Peace, Harmony and Good Relations in the Family and the Community. Many poor people consider the absence of conflicts essential for family and social wellbeing. In Ghana this is expressed as unity in the household or community. In Uzbekistan it means peace and calm in the family, in the country and in one's own community.

Good relations extend to social cohesion and support, and to helping one another. In Vietnam near Ha Tinh poor people state their priorities as being able to "encourage people to visit, support and give presents (show feelings in general) to households dealing with crises and during the holidays."

Security

Security includes predictability and safety in life and confidence in the future.

Civil Peace. A group of elderly residents of Ak Kiya in the Kyrgyz Republic comment, "Among all wellbeing criteria, peace is the most important one. Now there is war in Yugoslavia and in other countries. God willing, it would not happen here. As they say, 'be hungry but live in peace.'" Even in contexts without recent experience of civil conflict or war, such as this one in the Kyrgyz Republic, civil peace was often ranked high. Peace—the absence of war, violence and disorder—is the most important component of wellbeing for those living in the context of recent war or disorder.

A Physically Safe and Secure Environment. Wellbeing means not being vulnerable to physical disasters, threats and discomforts that are so typical of the places of poor people. These included floods in urban Argentina and rural Bangladesh, wild animals in Sri Lanka and India, water pollution from industry in Bulgaria, the disaster from the Aral Sea in Uzbekistan, and air pollution from industry in Olmalyq, Uzbekistan. These are named among many other physical, often seasonal, threats.

Personal Physical Security. "Here we live with our door open," report participants in rural Argentina. A man in Jamaica says that "this is a ghetto community, but you don't have any violence; you can walk (around) here any hour of the night and no one is going to harm you." Again in Jamaica, the relaxed atmosphere and the high level of personal safety in the countryside are valued.

Lawfulness and Access to Justice. Refugees in a Russian city who survived the horror of a civil war and genocide and who were objects of constant abuses describe "peace" and "the absence of constant fear" as the main prerequisites of a good life. Lawfulness and access to justice are widely seen as aspects of wellbeing, particularly in Nigeria. Security from persecution by the police and other powers that be is a priority for many, especially for urban vendors.

Security in Old Age. Particularly for older people, security and support in old age are a primary concern. An old woman in Khaliajuri, Bangladesh says that, for a good quality of life, a son must not sever the family bond after marriage and he must provide food to his mother.

Confidence in the Future. The good life is also frequently defined as being able to look forward to the future. Especially in countries like Bosnia and Herzegovina and Russia that have experienced recent national traumas participants value being able to have confidence in a stable and predictable future. They say that they once had this, but that it is now only experienced by a few rich people.

Freedom of Choice and Action

The research team from Brazil puts it like this:

> *People tended to equate poverty with powerlessness and impotence, and to relate wellbeing to security and a sense of control of their lives. A woman from the community of Borborema established a connection between power and control, and wellbeing. She argued, "The rich one is someone who says, 'I am going to do it,' and does it." The poor, in contrast, do not fulfill their wishes or develop their capacities.*

Freedom of choice and action extends to having the means to help others. Being able to be a good person is a feature of the good life that poor people often highlight. A young man in Isla Trinitaria, Ecuador wants to be able to buy clothes for his sisters. In Malawi a good characteristic of one high category of wellbeing was to love everyone and help others when they have problems. Wellbeing is quite frequently linked with moral responsibility, with having the wherewithal to help others, and with having enough money to be able to give to charity or a religious organization.

What people say they wish to be able to do covers a huge range: to gain education and skills; to have mobility and the means to travel; and to have time for rest, recreation and being with people—among others. Underlying all of these—and the material, physical, social and security dimensions—

is a fundamental aspiration. Participants in many contexts say that they want to be able to make choices, to decide to do basic things without constraint, to live in a predictable environment and have some control over what happens.

Diversity by Context and Person

For all of these commonalities, there are differences of aspiration and of concepts of wellbeing. They vary by continental region, by rural and urban areas, by livelihood, by age and by gender.

The contrasts are perhaps not surprising, but listing a few of those that are more striking can make and illustrate the point without any attempt to be comprehensive:

> ▸ In Eastern Europe, Central Asia, Bulgaria, the Kyrgyz Republic, Russia and Uzbekistan, wellbeing is frequently defined nostalgically as the "normal" condition, meaning before the end of communism. In Russia wellbeing criteria are taken from the past and not the present.
> ▸ Among pastoralists, whether Somalis in Somaliland or Kalmyks in Russia, wellbeing is often intimately linked with animals.
> ▸ Poor rural people emphasize land and livestock, farming capital and inputs for livelihood activities, and being able to farm on one's own.
> ▸ Poor urban people repeatedly emphasize employment, a job, infrastructure, housing, security of tenure, and physical security. They sometimes have higher material aspirations for consumption goods than rural people. In one urban site in Malawi participants say that wellbeing entails leading a European (Western) life (*moyo wachizungu*), having houses to rent out to others, having decent and well-paying jobs, and having very good houses with electricity.
> ▸ Women tend more often than men to mention peace in the family; good social relations in the community; adequate and nutritious food; good drinking water; being able to bring up children in good conditions, keep them healthy, and send them to school; and not being maltreated in the family.
> ▸ Men tend more often to mention material productive goods, and time to relax. There are exceptions to these generalizations, and there is a danger of overstereotyping gendered priorities and values, especially at a time when change in gender roles in many places is rapid.
> ▸ The views of some poor children were asked. In Chittagong, Bangladesh, according to children, wellbeing means having neat and clean surroundings, with facilities for education, being able to play freely, living in a building, having good food

(fish, meat, vegetables, etc.), going every morning to *madrasa* (traditional Muslim school), and everybody living in harmony. Peace and harmony in the family and in society are important to children.

Wealth and Wellbeing Are Different

In discussions on criteria for a good life, the researchers report:

> ▸ "The group of young people underscored the need to have a family, to feel supported and understood."—According to a youth group in Barrio Universitarios, Bolivia
> ▸ In Bulgaria, "wealth and wellbeing are not identical, for the rich have money but don't have security, nor are they respected by the community. Illbeing is, however, identical with poverty: this is 'our situation.'"
> ▸ In Russia, "the life of the well-to-do people was never called a 'good life.' Ultimately, when both the younger and older participants talked about the well-to-do people, they would never call their life a 'good' one."

Good living or wellbeing in Zambia, "can mean being liked, but also can make others jealous and bring hatred and death." Participants repeatedly distinguish between wealth and wellbeing. Those who are wealthy are by no means always in the top category for wellbeing. For example, a widow who is rich might not be put in the top wellbeing category because widowhood is a bad condition.

The wealthy can be generous and good, but often they are seen in a bad light. A 54-year-old man from Kok Yangak in the Kyrgyz Republic says:

> One can make a fortune, but if it has negative effects for
> the rest of the community, such wealth gives just an illusion
> of wellbeing, because it does not do any good for people.
> If somebody's wellbeing is based on the illbeing of others,
> it is not a true wellbeing. There are rich people in the village.
> They made their fortune by selling alcohol and vodka. The
> community does not like these people, because their prosperi-
> ty is only possible due to the growing problem of alcoholism
> in the village.

In contrast, poverty and nonmaterial wellbeing can sometimes be found together. In rural Accompong in Jamaica the researchers write that "the lives of all citizens are impacted by this peace within the neighborhood. Despite hard times and obvious poverty among most of the households an open welcome and hospitality to visitors and strangers to the community gives a distinct feeling of wellbeing and a good quality of life."

Part II. Illbeing: The Bad Life

*The family was housed in a thatched hut and there was no
way that they could have two square meals a day. The lunch
would be finished by munching some sugarcane. Once in a
while they would taste "sattu" (made of flour), pulses, and
potatoes, etc., but for special occasions only. During the rains
the water used to pour down the thatched roof and the family
would go to seek cover in the corners to avoid getting wet.
Their clothing would be of coarse material and they would
content themselves with one or two pairs of clothes for a
year. The wages then used to be paid as 1 kg of grain per day.
After three years of marriage, unable to bear the harassment
of the mother-in-law, both Nagina Devi and her husband
separated from her.*

—A poor mother, Manjhar, India

Illbeing and the bad life bring with them different sorts of bad experience.
These are many and interwoven. Some correspond to the opposites of the
clusters of wellbeing: lack and want are material; hunger, pain, discomfort,
exhaustion and poverty of time are physical; bad personal relations, exclusion, rejection, abuse, isolation and loneliness are social; vulnerability and
fear relate to insecurity; and helplessness, frustration and anger reflect powerlessness. It is also striking, though, how much of the bad life they miss, for
there are others that flow from and feed them: loss, anguish, grief, humiliation, shame, and persistent anxiety, worry and mental distress. Box 2.2 features selections from poor people's definitions and criteria of illbeing.

The Multidimensionality of Illbeing

As with wellbeing, participants describe illbeing as multidimensional.
The most frequently mentioned dimensions of illbeing correspond
closely to dimensions of wellbeing. The bad life is marked by many bad
conditions, experiences and feelings. Box 2.3 illustrates the range of
expressions that poor men and women from Ethiopia used to describe the
bad life.

Material Lack and Want

Food. The most frequently mentioned want or lack is food. In every country poor families report that they miss meals. They often only eat once a
day and sometimes have nothing for days on end. A saying in Ethiopia is,
"If one eats breakfast, there is no supper." Hunger is highly seasonal in
rural areas. In urban Russia it peaks towards the end of the month, before

Box 2.2 Expressions of Illbeing

The words and expressions used for the bad life are naturally different in different language groups, countries and continents. A selection gives a sense of the range.

Illbeing and wellbeing have close equivalents in Spanish-speaking Latin America—*malestar* and *bienestar*. *Malestar* is a common word in Spanish, meaning a sense of unease or discomfort, which can be physical, social or psychological. It is not a synonym for poverty (*pobreza*). In urban Argentina, the words *situación crítica* (critical condition), *vida complicada* (a complicated life), and *malaria* (situation where everything has gone wrong, total scarcity) are also used.

In Bolivia, *tristeza* (sadness), the opposite of *felicidad* (happiness), is used for illbeing, based on pictures of a sad face and a happy face, to which participants were invited to react.

In Malawi, *ukavu* means a state of constant deprivation. It is explained that households described in this group lack peace of mind because they are always worried about how to make ends meet. In most *ukavu* households, couples quarrel and fight a lot because they desire good lifestyles (*umoyo uwemi*), but they lack the means. "It is not surprising that most men from these households are drunkards because they drink to forget home problems."

Women from Mbwadzulu village in Malawi say that they consider it illbeing when "people sit on the floor...people going to their gardens without taking any food...they have no latrines; they cook under the sun [have no kitchen], have no pit latrines, no change house [bathing place outside the house, constructed from grass] and no plate drying rack."

In Buroa, Somaliland, extreme illbeing is defined as the experience of war and famine.

In India, the word *dukhi* (and in Bangladesh *asukhi*), the opposite of *sukhi*, is close to illbeing, unhappiness, a bad condition of life in terms of experience, whether material, social or psychological.

In Chittagong, Bangladesh, illbeing is *asukhi* (unhappy) or *kharap abstha* (bad condition), the opposite of *bhalo abstha* (good condition).

In Bulgaria, one aspect of illbeing is a pervasive sense of loss, of moving backward in time to an earlier century—from cultivation by tractors to having to cultivate by hand, from buying soap and bread to having to make and bake your own. This is described as going wild (*podivyavane*), being obliged to work in a manner considered humiliating, uncivilized and inefficient.

pay when there can be days with an absolute lack of food. In many rural areas the poorest people rely on wild foods. Provision of food for children is a constant worry for parents, who themselves stint and starve. A mother in Nuevas Brisas del Mar, Ecuador says, "In the last two years our children leave for the school without having coffee. Sometimes I have some money but if I fix them some breakfast there is not enough for lunch." Urban starvation is less dramatic or obvious than that in rural areas, but poor people in Jamaica say it is more prevalent. In urban areas in countries that have

---

Box 2.3 The Bad Life in Ethiopia

The following are literal translations of phrases used by poor men and women in Ethiopia to express their state of illbeing.

"We are left tied like straw"

"Our life is empty; we are empty-handed"

"Living by scratching like a chicken"

"What is life when there is no friend or food"

"Life has made us ill"

"We are skinny"

"We are deprived and pale"

"We are above the dead and below the living"

"Hunger is a hyena"

"The poor is falling, the rich is growing"

"A life that cannot go beyond food"

"We simply watch those who eat"

"Difficulties have made us crazy"

"We sold everything we had and have become shelter-seekers"

"It is [like] sitting and dying alive"

"My relatives despise me and I cannot find them"

"Life is like sweeping ash"

"From hand to mouth"

"A life that is like being flogged"

"A life that makes you look older than your age"

"Just a sip and no more drop is left"

"If one is full, the other will not be full"

"Always calf, never to be bull"

"We have become empty like a hive"

---

undergone severe restructuring crises, study teams were shocked to learn of a quiet, hidden urban starvation. Some who starve are too proud and decent to beg or steal. In Ivanovo, Russia, "a woman told us that sometimes she did not have food for several days and was only drinking hot water and lying in bed so as not to spend energy." In Ethiopia a 30-year-old married man in Kebele 10 says, "We eat when we have, and we go to bed hungry when we don't."

Livelihood, Assets and Money. Uncertainty of livelihood sources and employment is virtually universal. Returns to work are low. Casual labor is both uncertain and badly paid. Insecurity from lack of assets and money is often mentioned, but more often implied. Money is needed for access to many services, especially health, education and transport; for bribes and fines; for daily necessities and often subsistence; for social occasions; and for clothing. Poor, ragged, secondhand and worn clothing is repeatedly given as a mark of being badly off. High-interest debt is common. Many needs and wants trace back to the lack of money.

Housing and Shelter. Virtually everywhere, shelter and housing are a source of discomfort and distress. Shacks, huts, houses or tenements are small. Many people crowd into small spaces. Possessions are insecure. Huts and shanties leak and flood, fall down, blow down, burn down or are knocked down. People have to stand when the ground gets wet. Dirt, filth and refuse are always there. Urban sanitation is often nonexistent or disgustingly bad. Sewers—where they exist—sometimes overflow and flood into huts, and health suffers as a result.

Physical Illbeing

Hunger, Pain and Discomfort. The physical illbeing of hunger and sickness, and the pain, stress and suffering they bring, are a common theme. Women in a group in Nigeria do not have sufficient breast milk to feed their babies. In Bedsa, Egypt an older man says, "Lack of work worries me. My children are hungry and I tell them the rice is cooking, until they fall asleep from hunger." In Ethiopia there is "burning hunger" and "fire of hunger." Poor people are more often sick and injured, and are often sick for longer, and treated, if at all, later than the nonpoor. The reasons are many. Sickness itself is a frequent cause of suffering and impoverishment, leading to physical weakness, dependence and disability. Finally, poor people live in discomfort, in unhygienic, dangerous, dirty, badly serviced, and often polluted environments where they are vulnerable to many physical shocks, stresses and afflictions.

Exhaustion and Poverty of Time. The sheer exhaustion and lack of energy many poor people experience is easily overlooked. For many, their body is their main or only asset. It is uninsured. Shortage of food and sickness not only causes pain, but also weakens and devalues the asset. Those short of food are badly stressed by hard work. There are "lazy" poor people, but inactivity is often conservation of energy. Poor people are often described as tired, exhausted and worn out.

The increasing burdens of their expanded roles are driving many women deeper and deeper into physical exhaustion. These burdens also expose them to "time poverty," meaning that they have little or no time to rest, reflect, enjoy social life, take part in community activities, or spend time in spiritual activities. Whereas men are often increasingly out of work, women are under more pressure.

Bad Social Relations: Exclusion, Rejection, Isolation and Loneliness

Exclusion takes many forms. Ignorance of or lack of fluency in a dominant majority language can be excluding. Minority groups around the world share the linguistic exclusion of women in Guadalupe, Bolivia who do not participate in public community activities because they feel embarrassed to speak their native language, Quechua. Denial of education can be excluding. The parents of Um Mohamed, a girl in El Gawaber, Egypt, forced her to leave school: "They sentenced me to death when they did that." In Brazil there is exclusion when parents try to enroll their children in public schools and are unable to find places for them.

Rejection is associated with poverty in many ways. The extremely poor are often rejected, even by those who are also poor. Two other forms of rejection are the abandonment of children and of old people. The feelings of rejection, isolation and loneliness are most often cruelly inflicted on those who suffer most in other ways.

Loneliness and lack of social support are no longer an uncommon experience of poor people generally, particularly the elderly. Those with little social support are described as being "poor in people." In rural Bulgaria, an old woman says, "Young people have nothing to do here. You can't imagine how I feel, as lonely as the dawn, but I was the first to prompt them to move to the city. I would have felt even worse watching them waste their lives here." Old men in Mbamoi, Nigeria say, "We poor men have no friends. Our friend is the ground." This isolation is most acute for those who are very poor indeed and for those who are too weak to be able or to wish to assert themselves, especially the old. In Nuevas Brisas del Mar in urban Ecuador, where the team shared a meal with participants, an old man who had been present for three days and had hardly taken part at all was identified as "the voice of those without voice, the voice of hunger."

Self-exclusion occurs when inclusion is seen as dangerous or bad, and is a cost of a violent or abusive environment. Says a woman in Dock Sud, Argentina, "Now I am with my grandson. He is seven and the teachers in kindergarten tell me I have to let him be with other boys, but what for? To be a drug addict when he grows up? Here there are kids that are eight years old who do drugs, and after that they start to rob. No, I'd rather see him alone, isolated, like they say in school, but I'd rather have him at home with me; I take care of him."

Self-exclusion also occurs for reasons of shame. A poor person may not be invited to a wedding. If invited, a poor person may decide not to go because of being unable to appear and behave appropriately. Many of the self-excluded are the "invisible poor," especially the "new poor" who will not confess that they are poor. In a city in Bulgaria a poor man comments, "There was a man in our apartment building. A silent, shy fellow, always very neatly dressed. They found him dead in his apartment. The doctor said that he had become so feeble that he died of a common cold; they found just a piece of stale bread in his flat. It's a pity we never spoke with him. He had dignity, that fellow."

Insecurity, Vulnerability, Worry and Fear

There's great insecurity now. You can't make any plans. For all I know, tomorrow I might be told that we'll be laid off for a couple of months or that the factory is to shut down. We work three days a week even now, and you're in for a surprise every day.
> —Participant, discussion group of men and women, Kalofer, Bulgaria

I am going to be poor and even hungry if I cannot labor in the coming years due to old age.
> —A resident, Ha Tinh, Vietnam

Insecurity and vulnerability are deeply embedded in the bad life. Insecurity comes through exposure to mishaps, stresses, and risks—to dangers in the physical environment, in society, in the economy, and in the administration and legal systems. Vulnerability comes because poor people are defenseless against damaging loss. Together these generate worry and fear: of natural disaster, of violence and theft, of loss of livelihood, of dispossession from land or shelter, of persecution by the police and powers that be, of debt, of sickness, of social ostracism, of the suffering and death of loved ones, of hunger and of destitution in old age.

Lack of confidence is frequently mentioned as a result of poverty. In Bosnia and Herzegovina, the inability to find a job makes people feel worthless to themselves and their families.

Powerlessness, Helplessness, Frustration and Anger

Again and again, powerlessness seems to be at the core of the bad life. In Russia it is articulated as a complete sense of political impotence. More generally, powerlessness is described as the inability to control what happens, the inability to plan for the future, and the imperative of focusing on the present. In Zawyet Sultan, Egypt the condition known as *el-ghalban* and *ma'doom el hal*, words used for the poorest, mean helplessness and having no control over sources of one's living and therefore no control over one's destiny.

Time horizons are then short. Young people in Kalofer, Bulgaria say, "Each day is unpredictable—you can't make any plans, don't know what you're in for tomorrow." The sense of impotence is compounded when the future is seen as getting worse. Urban youth in Esmeraldas, Ecuador are reported as saying, "You can't think of the future because you can only see how to survive in the present." The report continues to say that everybody in the group agrees that in the future there is only going to be more poverty. At this stage the facilitators had to stop the meeting because the youth got fed up.

Poor people want to be able to take the long view, but they cannot. Having to live "hand to mouth" is not a choice, but an immensely frustrating necessity. The experience is daily anxiety, and having to eat the moment they receive food or money.

Worry about the future, especially the future of children, coexists with concerns for the immediate present. According to the report of an interview with a woman in Pedda Kothapalli, India, "She is worried about the future of her children and the struggles they have to face once they grow up. Her immediate concern is to which house she should go for a loan of some food grains for their food that day."

Part III. Psychological Experience of Wellbeing and Illbeing

The experience of wellbeing and illbeing is inextricably psychological. The dimensions of good and bad quality of life contribute to and are part of good and bad states of mind and being.

The Experience of Wellbeing: Peace of Mind, Happiness and Harmony

Being well means not to worry about your children, to know that they have settled down; to have a house and livestock and not to wake up at night when the dog starts barking; to know that you can sell your output; to sit and chat with friends and neighbors. That's what a man wants.

—A poor man, Bulgaria

Interwoven with other dimensions of wellbeing—material, bodily, social, security, and freedom to choose and act—is psychological wellbeing. This is variously expressed as happiness, harmony, peace, freedom from anxiety, and peace of mind. From Novi Gorodok, Russia comes, "Wellbeing is a life free from daily worries about lack of money"; from Gowainghat, Bangladesh, "to have a life free from anxiety"; from Nova Califórnia, Brazil, that quality of life is "not having to go through so many rough spots" and "when there is cohesion, no quarrels, no hard feelings, happiness, in peace with life"; from Nigeria, "wellbeing is found in those that have peace of mind, living peacefully. It is to be filled with joy and happiness. It is found in peace and harmony in the mind and in the community."

For many, too, a spiritual life and religious observance are woven in with other aspects of wellbeing. Poverty itself could get in the way. An old woman in Bower Bank, Jamaica says, "I got up this morning and all I want to do is read my Bible, but I share a room with my son and my grandchildren and all they do is make noise, I can't even get a little peace and quiet." In Padamukti, Indonesia, being able to make the pilgrimage to Mecca means much, as does having *sholeh* (dutiful and respectful) children who will look after their parents in old age and pray for them after they are dead. In Chittagong, Bangladesh, part of wellbeing is "always [being] able to perform religious activities properly." For older women in Cassava Piece, Jamaica, their church gives them a spiritual uplift and physical support. The importance to poor people of their sacred place—holy tree, stone, lake, ground, church, mosque, temple or pagoda—is repeatedly evident from their comparisons of institutions in which these frequently ranked high, if not highest.

The Experience of Illbeing: Humiliation, Shame, Anguish and Grief

Experiences of illbeing can be seen to combine and to compound each other in bad states of mind and being. Some connections stand out strongly. It is striking how often participants raise aspects of mental distress when describing the effects of poverty. Women in Tabe Ere, Ghana, for example, connect poverty, anxiety, begging, shame, isolation and frustration. They explain that poverty creates "too much pressure on individuals and often renders a person mad with worry and anxiety." Begging is seen as a degrading activity, which brings about insult and disgrace to the family. This results in shyness within the community that in turn leads to frustration in life. Participants in different countries speak of mental stress and breakdown, depression, madness and suicide, together the antithesis of the wellbeing of peace of mind.

Humiliation, Shame and Stigma

The stigma of poverty is a recurring theme. As a consequence, poor people often try to conceal their poverty to avoid humiliation and shame.

One deeply felt deprivation is not being able to do what is customary in the society. Frequently cited, for example, is not being able to entertain visitors or enjoy social life. In Malawi, there is shame from not having toilets for visitors, or money to buy a coffin for burying a relative. In Beisheke in the Kyrgyz Republic, an elderly village man says, "In the Soviet times we had no idea what poverty was about, we were equally wealthy, and now we feel humiliated because we cannot afford to receive guests in our houses, or visit friends and relatives. It was for that reason that we could not invite you [the study team] to our house when we first met."

Poor people sometimes feel shame and anger in accepting or having to accept alms or special treatment. In India this does not appear to apply to programs that give poor people well-recognized rights, like the government ration shops. Similarly in Viyalagoda, Sri Lanka, those who are poorer say it is a great help that their children are getting school books and uniforms: earlier their uniforms had been yellowish in color after several washings and they were ashamed. Now their children can sit together with others without any shame. By giving books and uniforms instead of money, the government has done a great thing.

By contrast, in Novy Gorodok, Russia even the most needy are humiliated to take poor quality goods provided for them by the welfare office. One participant commented, "[The food] is spoiled, and at prices higher than in the shops. I took a sack of flour once, and there were worms." Sexual abuse, with its physical violence as well as humiliation, is a greater threat for those in poverty, especially for women, given the places in which they live. In Dock Sud, Argentina most rapes are not reported because of shame. The same applies with sexual abuse, harassment and exploitation. In Bulgaria, a participant in a discussion group of women says, "Only young girls aged under 20 or 22 can find a job. If they are 25 or older, nobody wants them. I can do the job of a waitress perfectly well, but the boss wanted somebody who'd do another job for him just as well."

Poor people often experience humiliation in their encounters with officials and those delivering services. In Chittagong, Bangladesh discussion groups report that "*thana* [administrative unit between the village and district level] officials are corrupt, unaccountable 'to anyone' for their dishonest acts and only show 'special respect' to the rich." Color prejudice is mentioned in Brazil and Ecuador.

Appearances and clothes, as well as being an important part of physical wellbeing, are mentioned as important for self-respect and, conversely, they can be a source of shame. In Etropole, Bulgaria "people who cannot afford warm clothes for the winter go to work. Then they come back and stay at home under a pile of blankets, shivering with cold. They don't go out. They are ashamed to meet other people. If they run into a friend and are invited for a drink they must refuse. So they would rather not go out at all." In the Kyrgyz Republic a middle-aged woman says, "My daughter came from school crying. Somebody at school called her a beggar, because she was wearing the jacket that we received as humanitarian aid. She refused to go to school."

Anguish, Loss and Grief

Anguish, loss and grief are implicit in so many life histories of poor people, and these speak through the pages of the case studies. Sickness and death are very frequent. Anguish, when loved ones are sick and treatment is known but cannot be afforded, is found in all societies, and not only among poor people. For many participants, though, this experience is common, acute and agonizing, and for many it comes more and more often. Especially in Africa, the rising incidence of HIV/AIDS and malaria has combined with shrinking access to affordable treatment.

Psychological illbeing is marked where there has been a sharp decline in the levels of living and wellbeing, and where people from former middle classes have become impoverished. This is most notable among the former middle classes in Bosnia and Herzegovina, Bulgaria, the Kyrgyz Republic, Russia and Uzbekistan who are now the "new poor." The Bosnia and Herzegovina National Report speaks of "psychological ill health" in all the communities. In one, the psychological effects of economic misery are listed as "one's psychological health, distancing oneself or withdrawing from others, tensions between people, irritability, insecurity, apathy, nervousness, monotony, and dissatisfaction."

The burden of war and civil disturbance for those caught up in them is expressed in Bosnia and Herzegovina, for example, in Bijeljina, especially by anguished women whose husbands and sons were fighting. The trauma of refugees and others who have suffered from violence is an extreme form of mental distress. Instant impoverishment often combines with fear and the anguish of loss, especially when family members are at risk or have been killed. Just how terrible the effects can be is expressed by one older woman in Bijeljina: "I had to send a husband and two sons to the front lines and wait for them to return—or not. I did not think about eating, sleeping, dressing or anything. I would lie down and awake in tears. What have we lived to experience?" For her, spiritual poverty is more devastating than her material poverty: "You can never recover from spiritual impoverishment."

In the former Soviet region, participants express a profound sense of loss regarding their earlier level of living, when they had guaranteed jobs, free education and health care, social safety nets and recreation. Nostalgia is too weak a word to describe what they feel. At the same time, as with other loss and bereavement, they know it has gone forever. "Those who don't feel sorry about the collapse of the Soviet Union have no heart, but those who think that it may be restored have no brain," says an elderly man in the Kyrgyz Republic.

Bald figures of life expectancy do not show what they mean in human terms. The horrors, separations and losses in war and civil disorder have become the commonplaces of journalism and television. The avoidable loss of loved ones in the quiet crisis of poverty is on a much larger scale, but unseen. The experience is worse when the bereaved are denied the last rites, grieving and consolation, which are customary and due in their society, because of the simple fact of their own poverty.

Table 2.1 Dislikes and Fears of Children in Ho Chi Minh City, Vietnam

Girls	Boys
▶ Having to drop out of school, special classes closing down	▶ Sickness of teacher, causing class to close down
▶ My forthcoming school exams	▶ Failing to move up a grade; having to repeat a class
▶ Fighting in the community	▶ Sniffing heroin, drug addiction, young drug addicts stealing and robbing
▶ Homeless people being cold during storms	▶ Gambling
▶ Drug addiction in the neighborhood	▶ Fighting and quarreling in the community
▶ Gambling	▶ Robbery, especially of dogs
▶ Loan sharks	▶ Street accidents happening to children
▶ Leaking roofs in the neighborhood	▶ Neighborhood fires
▶ Flooding of the neighborhood and houses	▶ A dirty and polluted neighborhood
▶ A dirty and polluted neighborhood	▶ Prostitution among young people in the community
▶ That our house might collapse	▶ Spread of AIDS
▶ Friends being too poor to afford new clothes	▶ Sickness of my family members or mother
▶ Neighborhood children dropping out of school and working hard	▶ Fights and conflict between my mother and father
▶ Drunken men beating up their wives and children	▶ Divorce of my parents; family splitting up
▶ Quarreling between my mother and father	▶ My mother running off with another man
▶ That my mother works too hard	▶ Sale of our house to repay a debt
▶ That my family might break up	▶ Having our house demolished and cleared away
▶ Having no money to buy rice	▶ Having a roof that leaks
▶ Having no money to pay for rent or medical treatment	▶ Having no house of our own; having to share a room with other families
▶ Having nobody to look after me if my parents are sick	▶ Having no money
▶ Being robbed, break-ins and theft	▶ Being unable to get a job
▶ Having our house and neighborhood cleared away	▶ Rich people scolding the poor people they hire
▶ The rich looking down on the poor people	▶ Richer families not allowing us to watch their TV
	▶ Rich people living in luxury, not helping poor people
	▶ Richer people looking down at us

The Illbeing of Children

Parents are again and again preoccupied with securing a good life for their children. So the children's own experience and view of the bad life have a double importance: for themselves as children and for adults as their parents and guardians.

In Ho Chi Minh City, Vietnamese children summarize their feelings about the consequences of being poor as deprivation and resentment (see table 2.1). They resent that they cannot go to school or to the school they want, and that their parents have neither the time nor the money to take them on outings. Boys and girls over 10 resent being scolded because of indebtedness and the failure to repay loans. The boys say that everyone in the family is working, but there is still not enough to eat; that they have to accept beatings from others and can do nothing in return; and that they are always blamed when something is stolen. Boys under 10 cannot have a birthday party like other children. Girls under 10 are teased by richer children because they are poor. And girls over 10 resent having to agree with richer people and act as their inferiors, even if what they [the rich people] say is wrong.

The vivid directness of what girls and boys see and experience as the bad life is revealing. The Ho Chi Minh City report concludes that "what the young emphasize more than any other group...is the effect of poverty on the family itself. They see poor families as tense, conflictual and subject to breakdown." It is perhaps no surprise that family harmony matters much to children, but worthy of note that they see a link between poverty and bad relations in the family. Also, both girls and boys mention the behavior of the rich, and being looked on badly and being treated badly by them—something that adults, perhaps through prudence, mention only occasionally.

For their part, the parents' pain when they cannot provide for and look after their children is shown to be a big part of adult illbeing.

In Muynak, Uzbekistan in the extreme of distress, there is an ultimate way out: "There are families who do not eat and drink in three days. People die of hunger. For example, Ayagan was a good guy. He could not provide his family with food, his children cried and then he shot himself."

Reflections

In understanding what a good experience of life is, there is perhaps no end, no final answer. But if development is to enhance the wellbeing of poor people in their own terms, there is much to reflect on in what they say.

The discussions in Ethiopia generated the list of dire statements in box 2.3. Yet one of the team leaders in Ethiopia, on approaching a very poor, remote community, heard singing and dancing. This can jolt us into recognizing that there are many good things, each in its own culture, which contribute to wellbeing: not only singing, dancing and music, but also festivals, ceremonies and celebrations; good things in their seasons; love, kindness and sacrifice; and religious and spiritual practices and experiences. But to many of those who are most deprived, these fulfillments are diminished or denied.

The overarching questions are then whether, where and why human wellbeing is being enhanced or eroded; whether for many millions the singing and dancing are dying or renewing; whether the conditions for material, bodily, social, mental and spiritual wellbeing are improving or getting worse; and above all how to enable poor people to gain for themselves more of the good life to which they aspire.

Chapter 3

The Struggle for Livelihoods

Summary

Adequate and secure livelihoods emerge as a central concern to poor people's well-being. In rural areas much hardship is linked to reduced access to land, bad soils, adverse weather, lack of fertilizer and other inputs, deficiencies of transport and marketing, and overexploitation of common resources such as fish, pastureland and forests. In both countryside and cities, people speak of lack of permanent employment and reliance on badly paid and unreliable casual labor and petty trades. Participants also frequently mention harassment and corruption from officials as well as mistreatment from employers and having no recourse to redress grievances.

To cope with such precarious livelihood conditions, poor people often struggle to diversify their sources of income and food: they work on the land and in quarries and mines; they hunt down temporary jobs and sell an endless variety of goods on the streets; they do piecework in factories and from homes; they patch together remittances; and they cultivate home gardens. Many poor people count on local moneylenders and shopkeepers for credit in emergencies and during lean times; few have access to formal credit and savings services. With opportunities so limited, many are driven and drawn into livelihood activities that are to various degrees dangerous, illegal, and antisocial, including theft, drug dealing, sex work, trade in women and children, and child labor.

A large majority of men and women in the study view better livelihood opportunities as distant from them and economic conditions as worsening. In parts of Asia and a few communities elsewhere, however, people see poverty as declining. In Vietnam poor people link this improvement to market and land reforms, and successful diversification of income.

Case studies of those who have managed to improve their wellbeing indicate that entrepreneurship is the most frequent path out of poverty. Having multiple sources of income is also characteristic of many people who move out of poverty. In addition to entrepreneurship, these income streams include wages and salaries, benefits from family, agricultural earnings, and access to land.

Poor People's Priority

First, I would like to have work of any kind.
—An 18-year-old man, Isla Trinitaria, Ecuador

*If we knew that there would be an end to this crisis, we would
endure it somehow. Be it for one year, or even for 10 years.
But now all we can do is sit and wait for the end to come.*
—A woman, Etropole, Bulgaria

*I teach others now. Work is now my capital; work adds value
to my life. Before I used to work, my life was empty.*
—A woman, Foua, Egypt

The men and women who participated in this study worked in small
groups to identify and rank into a list their communities' most pressing
problems and concerns.[1] In a very large number of groups across the countries material wellbeing and livelihood difficulties emerge as critical.[2] And
when asked in a separate exercise to develop a diagram of the causes and
impacts of poverty, livelihood concerns again arise prominently as a cause
in all the regions. Although livelihood issues are not a specific focus of
attention in the study, they still emerge as central to poor men's and
women's perceptions of wellbeing, security, risk and opportunity, priorities
for action and gender relations.

The chapter opens with a look at conditions in rural areas and then
shifts to urban and casual work. With livelihood opportunities so limited,
the chapter goes on to explore the widespread use of informal credit channels, difficulties with accessing formal credit, and the various livelihoods
outside the law that are important coping mechanisms for some poor
people. A final section explores views on opportunities and the findings
from profiles of men and women who have managed to escape poverty.

Rural Livelihoods: Producing amid Scarcity

*There are no fertilizers, and soil is getting more and more bar-
ren. There are no chemicals against weeds, so we have lots of
weeds and lose much of our crops this way. There are no medicines for the animals, so lots of them die, and some of them
have infectious diseases that can affect humans, too.*
—Participant, discussion group of elderly,
Uchkun Village, the Kyrgyz Republic

*Ten years ago lack of food was not such an issue. We had
enough fertilizer to do what we wanted with. Now we are
depending on things like mushrooms and caterpillars.*
—Participant, discussion group of men and women,
Muchinka, Zambia

In rural communities around the world, the poor report a host of agricultural difficulties. The nature and intensity of these problems vary from one village to the next, but broad patterns do emerge. Farmers and herders often mention problems with gaining access to land, land shortages and fragmentation, costly inputs and declining profits, and problems with accessing credit and extension services and with transporting goods to markets. People also report that problems of soil infertility, declining fish stocks, degradation of grazing lands and forests and other environmental problems pose very serious threats to rural livelihoods for many.

While agriculture predominates, rural livelihoods are in fact quite heterogeneous. The discussion below explores sedentary farming and herding, followed by an overview of livelihoods that depend on the common property resources of fishing, forests, and pastureland. Concerns related to casual labor and petty trades cut across urban and rural communities and are raised in sections on migration and remittances and on urban and casual livelihoods.

Access to Land

It is necessary to use every inch of the land.
—An elderly man, Dangara, Uzbekistan

All our problems derive from lack of land. If we have enough land we will be able to produce enough to feed our households, build houses, and train our children.
—A man, Elieke Rumuokoro, Nigeria

There is no hope of someone to help us. I wanted a loan, but they are requiring the land title, but I can't provide it.
—A man, Isla Trinitaria, Ecuador

Many engaged in farming report that their livelihoods are becoming less and less viable. Lack of access to farmland stands out as a particularly acute and widespread problem, with discussions about the causes of land shortages often yielding a quite complex and dynamic mix of factors. These include rising land costs, unfavorable agricultural and land tenure policies, population growth, fragmentation of holdings, and overuse and degradation of cultivable lands. Many groups discussed the problems associated with landlessness or land shortage, which included intense competition for off-farm work, migration, and rising rural crime.

In Africa difficulties with accessing land are most frequently associated with interlocking demographic and environmental pressures and with agricultural and land policies. In Malawi rural participants say they now have less land due to rapid population increases and high land prices. "There are so many of us...we don't have enough land to cultivate and no longer harvest enough food," remarks a youth in Mtamba, Malawi. In Elieke Rumuokoro, Nigeria lack of access to land emerges as the top problem on the lists among both men and women. As one man observes, "We used to be good farmers. Now, only those who can afford the money travel to Igritta to rent land to farm." In the village of Bedsa, Egypt people tell researchers that steep climbs in land rents and payment terms are leading to dramatic increases in landlessness. Farmers there say they are only left with wage labor, or what they call *agir*, a derogatory term that implies exploitation by landowners.

In Bangladesh, India and Vietnam lack of access to land is identified as a particularly important cause of poverty in several of the rural communities. Across many of these villages, people indicate that households without access to land are especially vulnerable to deepening cycles of indebtedness from which it is very difficult to escape.

In Latin America land titling insecurities emerge as an important hardship for several communities. Farmers feel trapped by land insecurity, ambiguous relationships with land owners, and vicious cycles of subsistence production, loans, repayments, and more loans. In Bolivia, for instance, a farmer explains,

> *Ten years ago land titles weren't a problem. Now the owners have consolidated the lands telling us to work tranquilly and that they would take responsibility for getting us the titles. Since these promises were not kept, the farmers who rent distrust the owners who want to take possession of all the land and throw them out, and for this reason land titles are an important worry.*

Diminishing Inputs and Returns

> *Cotton and cattle used to be worth more, and there used to be credit.*
> —Participant, discussion group of men and women,
> Argentina

> *Price of fertilizer incompatible with price of rice.*
> —A group of older men, Galih Pakuwon, Indonesia

Discussion groups in quite varying contexts report that farming is less profitable than in the past. A frequent concern is the high cost of inputs, which in some countries is traced to reduced government subsidies for seeds, fertilizers, pesticides, and sometimes other needs such as tools, machinery, and medicines for animals. Men and women also frequently mention problems with getting fair prices for their goods and with accessing markets and transport.

High input costs are most striking in the rural reports from Africa and Eastern Europe and Central Asia, but can also be found in the reports from Asia. Discussion groups from a number of rural communities in Africa, and particularly Malawi and Zambia, link increased hunger and food insecurity to the higher costs of inputs in recent years, especially of fertilizer. In Zambia, where problems of fertilizer are mentioned more often than hunger among discussion groups, a man from Nchimishi explains that "the major cause of hunger here is the lack of fertilizer."

Among rural villages in Eastern Europe and Central Asia, steep production declines are especially associated with the collapse of collective farms and the system of centrally managed markets for agricultural inputs and irrigation and for distribution of produce. In Weerapandiyana in Sri Lanka farmers say that the high cost of inputs and equipment is driving them to abandon agriculture and sell their lands, or to shift to other often less lucrative crops that require fewer inputs. In Indonesia poor people describe input problems in terms of "lack of capital," or not having the cash, tools and inputs needed for agriculture. Farmers in many of the rural communities of Latin America link production problems to lack of credit and indicate that it used to be more widely available.

In many countries, poor people also report difficulties with accessing markets and getting fair prices for their goods. In four of the rural communities visited in Sri Lanka, for instance, farmers mention a shortage of markets and getting squeezed by middlemen as important problems. In Thailand farm workers complain that the economic recession has sharply reduced the prices of rice and rubber, greatly cutting demand for agricultural labor. In the Kyrgyz Republic during the Soviet era, consumption cooperatives (*Potrebsoyuz*) purchased farm produce, but now individual farmers have to find buyers and "often end up selling their products to wholesale traders at very low prices." Reaching markets and getting fair prices are also problems for several villages visited in Argentina, Bolivia, Ecuador and Jamaica. The rural poor in Argentina indicate that the price of crops such as cotton has fallen, as have earnings from cattle and animal skins, and they point to these price trends as a major reason why "we are worse today."

Few Institutional Supports

> *We wish...we had the mandate to caution him.*
> —A villager referring to the poor performance of the local
> agricultural extension agent, Khwalala, Malawi

Although the study was not designed to evaluate particular services, it is notable that few villages mention agricultural extension services as institutions of local importance. Where they exist, these services are often viewed as unresponsive.

Residents in some communes of Ha Tinh Province in Vietnam complain that extension services have to be paid in advance rather than on credit and that the new seeds and pesticides being promoted do not perform as well as traditional crops and husbandry. All the same, they would value better guidance on pest control and training on new agricultural techniques. In

Nchimishi, Zambia people say the local extension officer sells very expensive but ineffective drugs to fight tick-borne diseases in their cattle, but "the cattle continued to die."

Although there may be difficulties getting external help, poor people frequently value their own local organizations highly. In Somaliland poor people sometimes consider their local pastoral and farming groups among the most important local institutions. Members are involved collectively in livestock rearing, managing irrigation, and transporting and marketing produce.

Common Property Resources under Stress

We know that cutting down trees will cause water shortages and that making charcoal can cause forest fires, but we have no choice. Because we lack food, we have to exploit the forest....

—A resident of Ha Tinh, Vietnam

Earlier we worked from morning till evening, and now young people do not work...if they start to earn something for the family—for example, catching fish—the militia will not leave them in peace.

—A poor youth, Muynak, Uzbekistan

Many poor rural women and men rely for all or part of their livelihoods on common property or publicly owned resources, such as forests, woodlands, lakes, rivers and common grazing lands. Some of the very poor in Malawi fetch and sell river sand, and in Kalofer, Bulgaria a participant in a discussion group of men and women commented that "old people survive by grazing animals in the woods." In most cases, however, availability of these resources is in crisis because of restricted access, overexploitation or both.

In Somaliland access to grazing land and the need for alternative fodder appear as important priorities for the poor. Researchers note that grazing lands are becoming increasingly eroded, which in turn has compelled some landowners to use common lands in the dry season for grazing rather than their own lands. Poor people think privatization of common lands has intensified pressures on the remaining common areas.

Fishing communities in countries and conditions as varied as Bangladesh, Ecuador, Egypt, Malawi and Uzbekistan report serious problems with declining fish stocks, increased competition, new regulations and diminishing wage labor opportunities on boats.

The reasons for declining stocks vary. In Thailand they are tied to pesticide runoff (Nakorn Patom) and wastewater from processing plants (Kaoseng). In some African communities people blame the shortage on overfishing and point to growing populations and more commercial fishing. A youth from Mangochi, Malawi informed the researchers that dwindling stocks there are due to greater population pressures and the introduction of large shipping vessels that use nets to "catch even the smallest fish. The fish are not given enough time to breed.... In the past we only caught fish with bait and hook."

To preserve fish stocks and allow for their recovery, many local authorities are requiring fishing permits and placing temporary moratoria on fishing near the coasts, which are popular breeding grounds. Poor fishing communities seem especially hard hit by these regulations as well as by increased competition from large commercial shippers. In the fishing village of Borg Meghezel, Egypt a two-month fishing prohibition in the early summer interrupts livelihoods not only for the fishermen but also for those involved as merchants, boat owners, and drivers. In Bangladesh fishing opportunities for the poorest are heavily restricted by government leasing requirements affecting fishing rights on all water bodies; in many cases, the only opportunities left for the poor are to work as day laborers in fishing boats. From Bangladesh and Egypt come reports of poor fishermen going out in the dark and risking physical assault from permit owners and the hazards of working at night.

In all regions communities are experiencing the effects of deforestation, and poor people see the loss of forest areas and its impacts as threatening their livelihoods and food security. In most places where the problem is identified, the poor attribute deforestation to human pressures and lack of alternative livelihoods, fuel and food. In Adaboya, Ghana the researchers indicate that economic hardships and the lack of jobs push many into charcoal burning and cutting wood to sell. Similarly poor people rely heavily on firewood and rattan collecting, charcoal burning, and hunting to generate income in the highland forest communities of Ha Tinh, Vietnam.

Women and men acknowledge the pressures that their activities place on the local environment, but they see few alternatives. They also describe a host of indirect effects from the loss of tree cover, such as damage to local water supplies, more intense flooding, and in a few cases, adverse changes in weather. In Gowainghat, Bangladesh, for example, deforestation contributes greatly to erosion of cropland and of earthen roads and embankments.

Migration and Remittances

> *Most men now abandon their homes. Women now work the fields ... Women have taken charge of everything. They pay heavily and endure this life.*
> —Discussion group participants,
> Caguanapamba, Ecuador

In struggling farm, pastoral and fishing communities across the study countries, people make numerous references to seasonal and permanent migration of both men and women who travel to areas with greater opportunities for work as wage laborers and in petty trades and domestic services. Paradoxically, although poor people often acknowledge that the remittances from such work are crucial, they largely hold negative views of migration as a livelihood strategy.

The rural poor view migration both as a cause and an effect of poverty, and discussion groups by and large focus on migration's harmful aspects. Men and women in Argentina and Ecuador speak of the hardships of leaving children behind to be raised by women alone or increasingly by grandparents. In Kehelpannala, Sri Lanka researchers reported a widespread perception that overseas employment is devastating for families, especially children. A discussion group of men in Tabe Ere, Ghana feel that security has declined in the village because adult children have migrated to urban areas in search of jobs rather than staying to help parents in their old age.

Poor people widely mention and greatly value remittances from family members who have migrated. Most families in the villages of La Calera and Juncal, Ecuador, for instance, are said to have male wage earners in the cities who provide their primary source of subsistence. People report that remittances from overseas are very important to communities in Bangladesh, Jamaica and Uzbekistan.

Although rarer, the rural poor sometimes consider migration a stepping-stone to opportunities and a better life, but even in these cases many hardships are often acknowledged. A 30-year-old builder from the village of Oitamgaly, Uzbekistan—where women make up 70 percent of the population—says he migrates for two or three months at a time and that a "person who learned some trade will survive." However, he also indicates that some risks are involved because "now the police are checking the residence stamp everywhere." Migrants often find themselves doing the hardest work: in Uzbekistan this includes difficult jobs on construction projects and hauling carts inside markets.

Understandably the men and women who have managed to move out of poverty who were interviewed for this study often share quite positive experiences with migration, such as the story in box 3.1.

**Box 3.1 From Rickshaw Puller to Landlord:
A Tale of Entrepreneurship from Bangladesh**

Mahood Rab was destitute when he arrived in the slum of Chittagong City with his wife at the age of 18. He left his village after his father died, and his family had become impoverished covering medical expenses. When Mahood arrived in the city, he worked as a rickshaw puller, and his wife took jobs as a maidservant in several homes. Through hard work, and with his own and his wife's savings, he was finally able to buy a rickshaw. Within a year, he owned four. Today, at age 50, Mahood owns eight rickshaws, but does not rely just on this business. He took out a loan from *Proshika* (a national NGO) and rents five houses he built in another slum area. Mahood shared with the researchers that due to his wealth everyone knows him, and he is among those who are respected and take part in the major decisions of the neighborhood.

Diversified Livelihoods in Cities and Countryside

*I got the capital for my fritter [fried dough] business from
my husband.... In times of shocks like famine, I use the
business money to buy foods and so shocks are not such
a blow on our family.*

—A woman, Chitambi, Malawi

With so few prospects for sufficient and reliable incomes, researchers heard countless reports of men and women working harder and diversifying livelihood activities to make ends meet. With a decline in opportunities for men in agriculture and for permanent employment, women across the world report taking on work outside the home to bring food to the table. "We [women] are getting out of the house, learning to knit, to sew...to make a vegetable garden.... We can contribute a few pesos to the house, just like my husband," explains a woman from Isla Talavera, Argentina. (See also chapter 6, "Gender Relations in Troubled Transition.")

In places where formal sector jobs used to be available and provided adequate earnings, many people don't consider their patching together of temporary jobs to be real employment. Bundles of livelihood activities can sometimes be a way forward—as shown in a section below on individual breakthroughs. For many, however, the push to diversify income and assets is but a coping strategy that involves constant juggling and struggle. In Geruwa, India discussion groups had a term—*hujuk*, or caprice—to describe their unstable work and the practice of jumping from one occupation to another.

Diversification strategies are part and parcel of rural as well urban livelihoods. In remote villages of Lao Cai, Vietnam families report:

▸ Collecting and selling minor forest products such as medicinal herbs and bamboo shoots.
▸ Hunting and selling birds, mammals and reptiles.
▸ Specializing in growing particular medicinal herbs that few other people grow.
▸ Making tools, equipment and household domestic items.
▸ Making food products to market, such as maize and buckwheat cakes, bean curd and wine.
▸ Making cloth and clothes.

The push to diversify even touches those in the study with permanent employment—teachers, civil servants, mechanics and shop attendants. They often indicate that their wages are much too low to move their families out of poverty, so they take on extra work. This is particularly frequently noted in Eastern Europe and Central Asia, and in Latin America. While mining is the main enterprise in Etropole, Bulgaria, for instance, most also engage in subsistence agriculture on weekends and holidays, and some hold second jobs as security guards (men), shop attendants (women) and waitresses (young women).

Getting Hired—Connections Needed

> *You can't do anything unless you have friends in high places. Connections. You're not judged on your own personal authority but on the authority of someone else who might not even be an authority.*
>
> —A young man, Krasna Poliana, Bulgaria

In quite varied contexts, participants talk about the need to have connections, especially to find work. In Dahshour, Egypt people say there is "much bitterness" because any opportunities that may come along for a better or more permanent job from a *wasta* (or middleman) are always taken by the rich. Similarly, villagers in Phwetekere, Malawi indicate that better-off people do not face difficulties in finding jobs because they are "often well educated and well networked." A woman from Phwetekere observes that they "change jobs as if they are pairs of trousers."

Discrimination adds another obstacle to finding work for ethnic and caste groups. "There are vacancies at the labor office, but once they see you're dark they turn you down," exclaims a Roma man from Bulgaria. The researchers note that in all of the sites where there is a large Roma population, 80 percent of the males and 100 percent of the females are unemployed, most for as long as three years. In Manjhar, India people identify caste-based discrimination as a problem when seeking jobs, and blacks in Brazil and Ecuador mention similar obstacles.

Lawlessness on the Job

> *I worked six years in a company that did not pay me correctly. So I sued them and they threatened to kill me. I had to hide.*
>
> —A poor man, Sacadura Cabral, Brazil

> *To be able to open this coffee place I had a very big problem with the sanitary authorities.... They tormented me and tormented me until in the end we settled it for 300DM. Whenever they see us they want bribes.*
>
> —A 49-year-old woman, urban Bulgaria

All too often poor people report experiencing law and law enforcement not as a means to a better life, but as obstacles. They say a key challenge is staying ahead of public authorities and well-organized criminals bent on shutting them down, intimidating them, or demanding bribes.

Municipal regulations and licensing make many creative economic activities illegal. In Ho Chi Minh City, Vietnam those without permanent resident status are denied access to permanent jobs. Street vendors and bicycle rickshaw drivers mention that they are finding it increasingly difficult to earn a living because of increased competition and new laws limiting the streets where they can work.

Because poor women most commonly run petty trades, they are often most exposed to harassment. In Olmalq, Uzbekistan a vendor named Nigora tells researchers of a policeman who threw away her goods because she was trading in an unauthorized area. She tried to move the officer to pity by crying and shouting curses and explaining that her husband had not worked for three months. She then teamed up with five or six other women to pool a large bribe. In exchange, the policeman now looks the other way and has made sure that the tax collector does not disturb them.

In fact, the need to pay bribes to stay in business came up quite often in the research. A tea shop owner from Patna, India complains that he paid a succession of "taxes" after opening his shop at the railway station. The researchers report that "he started earning more in his new occupation, making a profit of Rs 150–200 per day, but had to pay 'rangdaari tax' [money extorted by force] of Rs 25–50 to the contractor or to the constables of the Railway Police Force. Besides, the officials and contractors used to have tea at his shop, but never bothered to pay."

The particular problem of delays in the payment of wages and payments-in-kind cut across rural and urban sites in Eastern Europe and Central Asia: "We don't work there because they don't pay people for their work," says a participant from a group of unemployed young men in Ulughnor, Uzbekistan. People say that plenty of jobs are available in the local *sovkhoz* (collective farm), but wages are never paid on time and they feel discouraged from taking the jobs. "Why should I get all that vodka and mayonnaise when I need to buy a medicine for my daughter?" complains a father from Ivanovo, Russia about how he is being paid.

Seasonal Fluctuations

> *Nothing to do during three to four months of rainy/stormy season.*
> —A group of young women, Ampenan Utara, Indonesia

> *It is much easier after spring—there are jobs offered if you are not lazy. Well, they are not real jobs, with regular wages and social security, but you won't die from hunger.*
> —A 43-year-old man from Plovdiv, Bulgaria

> *The few jobs that are created in the area [are] seasonal—only when the tourist season is at its peak.*
> —A poor youth, Little Bay, Jamaica

Rural and also urban opportunities and rewards for work can be sharply seasonal. During the rains in Somaliland, livestock sales plummet and prices for food rise sharply, putting at a disadvantage those poorer people who need to sell animals to buy food. The Bangladesh study finds a widely varying seasonal range of wages, at one site going from Taka 100–140 per day at the time of harvest to Taka 40–60 per day in the slack season, and elsewhere as low as Taka 15–20 per day.

Fishing is reported to be highly seasonal in Bangladesh and Egypt. Women in Madaripur, Bangladesh report that during the rainy season they cannot work in the brick field or chip bricks or sell dried fish. Seasonal rural migration of men and families in Ghana, India, Nigeria, and elsewhere is a widespread strategy with its own stresses of travel and uncertainty, and of leaving behind children, the sick, the disabled, and the very old to manage on their own.

The timing of school expenditures is also an issue, coming as it sometimes does at bad times of the year for some poor people. As reported in Vietnam, at times of seasonally heavy labor demand there is an incentive to withdraw children from school to help.

Shortages of food and having to stint and starve are often mentioned. When debts are assumed as a means to survive the bad times, they carry over: their repayment in Bangladesh is reported to take up much of poor families' income in the better seasons. In the bad months many of the poor in Bangladesh and in other countries mortgage and later lose their land to feed themselves and survive. In the bad months poor people become poorer.

Money in Short Supply

> *A man is ashamed to go to the neighborhood. You can't ask for loans from everyone. Times are hard for everybody.*
> —A discussion group participant, Sarajevo, Bosnia and Herzegovina

> *Now we don't even have one cent in our pocket.*
> —Participant, discussion group of men and women, Moreno, Argentina

With some exceptions, people in the study report that they have no or only limited access to banks and credit schemes. Men and women say they need credit not only to improve their livelihoods and for emergencies but also sometimes for daily expenditures during difficult periods. When networks of relatives and friends are not sufficient, poor people say that, to survive, they frequently turn to moneylenders, shopkeepers and pawnbrokers.

Informal Credit

> *When we want a small loan, we do not have to go after people, and we do not have to waste our time at the bank.*
> —A woman from Wewala, Sri Lanka speaking of the local credit group run by women

There are six of us in the family—one pension and two in-comes—but all irregular. We live from the first of the month to the first of the month. Sometimes we borrow from friends, but only from those we trust and who trust us.
—A poor resident of Sarajevo, Bosnia and Herzegovina

Local moneylenders appear with surprising frequency on poor people's lists of institutions of local importance, but views on whether they play a positive or negative role vary widely. In Kebele 11, Ethiopia, a group of young males say the local moneylender is their only hope for starting a small trading business some day. Researchers in Pegambiran, Indonesia note in the report that "when members of the community required a significantly large amount of cash (such as for business capital, school fees, hospitalization expenses), the *linkah darat* (literally 'bloodsucker') or loan sharks were the available alternative."

Some say that they appreciate and count on the speedy service and flexibility that moneylenders provide: they often extend loans on the spot without collateral requirements and allow payments to be made in kind, with cash, or through the provision of labor. Others, however, are very critical of moneylenders for charging high interest rates, and they fear the consequences for not making payments. In Khaliajuri, Bangladesh elderly men say they have full trust in the local *mohazan* (moneylender), but others express bitterness because he forcefully evicts people from their homes if payments are delayed.

Informal rotating credit groups play valued roles in several communities visited in Africa and Eastern Europe and across Asia. There appear to be endless varieties of these groups. Credit group members usually know one another well—either as friends, neighbors, colleagues, or relatives—and they decide collectively the amount they will contribute monthly. One arrangement is that the group leader gives the collection to a different member of the group each month, who may use the funds in any way he or she wants. The credit groups in Egypt are most popular with women, who might join a group to buy clothes, prepare a daughter's trousseau, save for a washing machine, and so forth. Poor women of Bedsa rank the credit group among the most important local institutions, along with the health unit and the schools. In Ethiopia, the local rotating credit group is called the *idir* and is also identified as a very important community institution that focuses on covering funeral expenses.

Worldwide, local shop owners are also highly valued for lending food and other items and, quite often, cash on credit. In Pegambiran, Indonesia, local shops and kiosks are viewed as the most effective institution in reaching poor people and extending timely support at a "meaningful level." In Russia and elsewhere in Eastern Europe and Central Asia, credit from shopkeepers can be very important because of problems of wage arrears and being paid in kind.

Study participants widely report that they secure emergency cash by selling off personal property. A young man from a discussion group in Dahshour Village, Egypt explains that "my wife was ill and I had no money to take her to the doctor and get medicines, and it was impossible to wait, so I just sold a couple of pots to solve this problem." A 47-year-old miner from Kok Yangak, Kyrgyz Republic confides that "I've been working in this mine for 27 years and I had some property, but sold it all when they stopped paying us. All we have in our house now are two beds with mattresses, and my wife and son are hungry all the time."

Formal Credit and Banks

While the rich get loans, the poor get consideration for loans.
—A poor resident in Ha Tinh, Vietnam

Everything I have is at home. I have no money in the bank,
no savings—you should be crazy to keep money in the bank
with that inflation—so if somebody steals my animals, I will
be izgorja [burned out].
—An older poor woman, Etropole, Bulgaria

I do not have a chair. I cannot be given a loan. What will they
confiscate from me?
—A villager from Mbwadzulu, Malawi

Many people report they have no access to banks or to savings and credit schemes, and where these services are available, their quality can be quite mixed. More favorable reports on credit schemes can be found in Thailand and in Vietnam. Many poor people view credit as a strategy for improving their livelihoods, but say they will require much better access to savings and credit services and more favorable terms than are currently available.

Even where opportunities to borrow are growing, it can be difficult for poor people to access credit programs because of unrealistic collateral requirements and excessive interest rates as well as corruption among lending officials. In the four communities visited in Jal Abad, Kyrgyz Republic, for instance, discussion group participants argued that long-term loans could be a way out of their difficulties, but that loans were now only available for those with money, and lending officials expected bribes.

Moreover, concerns about falling into debt run deep. The act of borrowing itself can set people on a downward slide rather than providing them a bridge to a better life. Difficulties related to indebtedness are mentioned most often in Asia. In Thailand the poor report that overborrowing from rural banks is common, which can then trigger a vicious cycle of further borrowing at higher rates from local moneylenders. Women in a discussion group in

Tanjungrejo in Malang, Indonesia say they are stuck in their livelihood of scavenging because they have fallen deep into debt and lack money to start a business. Moreover, their school-age children have been forced to drop out of school to work as scavengers as well. As the local researchers indicate, "That was the only way possible for them to survive."

In Ho Chi Minh City, Vietnam people speak highly of the increased availability of low-interest loans in recent years and of the official credit program (HEPR). Nevertheless, people still have concerns about uneven coverage, collateral requirements, and exclusive focus on income-generating projects. Loan funds also are badly needed for health care, hospital fees, children's education, and house repairs. In addition, permanent resident requirements further hinder poor people's access to credit and, in some cases, might disqualify entirely some of the neediest families. The researchers note that more than 100,000 loans were made under the official program, but that this amounted to just 16 percent in the district with the greatest coverage.

People in the Baan Kang Sadao, Thailand discussion groups generally regard with favor the Bank for Agriculture and Agricultural Cooperatives (BAC). They praise the agency for giving loans during the recent economic crisis and for allowing payments on the principal to be deferred. In Baan Chai Pru all groups but one ranked the BAC high and informed the researchers that its officers "pay attention to their work, understand the villagers' livelihood and are flexible...and that they can negotiate with the BAC about every issue except the issue of interest."

Livelihoods That Steal the Future

All we need is funds—employment first of all, then we can go on with a thing. No work causes other problems and makes you think evil things.
> —A man, Thompson Pen, Jamaica

Because of unemployment, young people drink to excess, commit crime, rape, steal livestock.
> —Participant, discussion group of men and women,
> Ak Kiya village, Kyrgyz Republic

I've worked for 23 years, and I've never touched somebody else's property. But just look at my leg now—it was broken when I was stealing manganese from the railway station; the train pulled off just as I was trying to climb on board. Do you think that I would risk my life for nothing if I had a job? Do you know what it's like to have your children crying because they are hungry?
> —A Roma, Bulgaria

*Criminality is a result of poverty. When you're hungry, you
have to find a way. Hunger doesn't ask.*

—Discussion group participant, Sarajevo,
Bosnia and Herzegovina

Participants confide that sometimes desperation and hunger lead to anti-social and illegal activities. "A man loses his head with unemployment. He risks everything and gets the guts to do things he never thought he would," says a man from Sacadura Cabral, Brazil. For some, the conditions of their lives drive them to steal, drink, take drugs, sell sex, abandon their children, commit suicide, or trade in women and children. And then the household and often the wider community must face the fear and anxiety that these means of coping bring in their wake.

In many communities the poor mention rising crime and sometimes relate this to deepening poverty and hunger. Poor men and women also report that they are frequently targets of violence and theft, including of organized crime. In Nchimishi, Zambia people make a direct link between food insecurity and increased theft. Hungry people are said to steal crops from fields and granaries in Zambia. At one community in Indonesia all groups report that crime has risen, and the older women's group says that because of poverty, many people's minds become cloudy, and this makes them look for an opportunity to solve their problems by stealing or cheating.

Illegal activities can also be stepping stones in the struggle to escape from poverty. Vo, a young man from Ho Chi Minh City, Vietnam came from such a poor family that for his wedding there was no party or celebration. Later, one of his economic activities was a small but illegal business trading in government coupons. Through this he saved enough to launch a successful and legal small business making paper money that people burn for their ancestors.

For some, the main sources of livelihood are drug-related. Although marijuana cultivation is known to be illegal in Jamaica, many rely on the income it brings. In Brazil and elsewhere in the region, people single out drug trafficking as a major source of violence. A women's group observes, "There is almost no violence when there are no drugs in the middle." In Thailand some discussion groups identify drugs as important problems, leading to "petty larceny" and harming the image of their communities.

Poor people frequently report that sex work is an outcome of poverty, especially in Africa and Asia. References to prostitution and the spread of HIV/AIDS are most common in Africa, although also mentioned in Asia and Latin America. In Adaboya, Ghana some participants report receiving remittances from daughters engaged in commercial sex work in other parts of the country, and they point out that some of their daughters have contracted AIDS and returned to spread it to other "innocent people in the community." In Khwalala, Malawi discussion group participants describe how prostitution has led to family breakdowns, the spread of HIV/AIDS, and having to cope with the devastating phenomenon of large numbers of orphans.

People in other regions as well report male, female and child prostitution. In Sri Lanka participants from the tourist area of Wewala indicate that some poor families receive income by supplying male prostitutes to tourists and by allowing some of their children to be adopted by French and German families. One man says that his son is with a man in France, and they send money when they visit the country every year; other villagers share similar stories. In the three communities visited in Ho Chi Minh City, Vietnam the researchers were told of a growing phenomenon of girls being "sold" to Taiwanese men either in marriage or for temporary relationships (see box 3.2). Often these girls are under 18 years old, and brokers mediate deals between the families. Foreign couples seeking to adopt also look to brokers, with payments of $50 to $500 per baby reported.

In every region people mention child labor. Discussion groups in two sites in Egypt report sending children to work as one way of coping with declines in household wellbeing. In Dahshour, for example, children work in a storehouse packing vegetables for sale. During periods of disaster in Ethiopia children are taken out of school and sent to towns to be employed as servants, with their earnings sent back to the family. Similarly, in the lean seasons in Ulipur, Bangladesh children go to other houses or villages to work on farms, tend cattle, or carry out household tasks in exchange for food. The researchers note that the parents are aggrieved by the undue physical labor of their children and worry especially about the vulnerability of girls to beatings and sexual assaults.

Box 3.2 Selling Women in Ho Chi Minh City, Vietnam

Trinh has seven daughters. Her husband is dead. A few years ago her eldest daughter, Phuoc, got a job in a restaurant, and from there went on to prostitution to support her mother and sisters. Two years ago, through the services of a broker, Phuoc was married to a Taiwanese man for around $4,500. One year later, another of Trinh's daughters divorced her husband and married a Taiwanese man. Trinh's house has now been repaired. It is in good condition and well furnished.

Limited Opportunities

*Every day there are more unemployed. Every day one sees
more men around the neighborhood all day long.*
— Participant, discussion group of men and women,
Moreno, Argentina

There are no opportunities. In the past, there were more.
— Participant, discussion group of men and women,
Bedsa, Egypt

*The majority in our neighborhood live in poverty. That's be-
cause they don't have luck and skills. Those who were well off
before are well off now too. Those who were poor before are
just as poor now.*
— A 21-year-old from Varna, Bulgaria

The large majority of men and women in the study view new opportunities as unattainable and economic conditions as worsening. However,
in some places that research teams visited, people feel otherwise. News of
forward momentum comes mostly from Asia, but sporadic reports from
other regions show that some people perceive that they are moving ahead.
In addition, the researchers in every community specifically sought out
women and men who had climbed out of poverty and interviewed them.
Their stories suggest the sorts of opportunities that can provide pathways
out of poverty.

The researchers asked discussion groups to reflect on how their list of
pressing problems had changed over the course of the past 10 years or so. In
their responses, people especially mention far greater insecurity of livelihood
than in the past. Although the impact of declining fish stock is context specific, this explanation of a list of problems and priorities from participants in
a Mbwadzulu, Malawi discussion group is typical of views elsewhere that
earning a living has become increasingly difficult:

*We are ranking lack of fish and hunger on position 1 [as the
worst problem] because lack of fish is making us suffer from
hunger. The lake is our granary. Lack of money is now on position 2, but in the past it was on position 8 because, as we have
said, the lake is our granary. In the past we had more fish than
now; in that case money was not a problem.*

Or this from a group of young men in Kajima, Ethiopia:

*Ten years ago we didn't have unemployment. We were never
given land. There were no schools to teach us skills, but there
was a literacy program. Today we still can't find jobs to do or*

*land to plow. Even those of us who went to schools can't find
jobs. What is the use of going to schools? Most of our problems are the same as 10 years ago.*

And in a workshop in Juncal, Ecuador, a discussion group of adult
women say "it was better before" because:

*There is nowhere to work. We get sick and we don't have the
money to get cured. We don't have medicines because they are
expensive. The government makes everything expensive. There
is no land. There is no money. We don't have livestock to
work. We have to get loans. We are poor. We are forsaken. We
cry. We only have sorrow. We don't have money to buy fertilizers, seeds. Everything is in dollars. We don't have anything to
eat.... Everything is so expensive.*

The lists of problems had changed greatly over time in Eastern Europe
and Central Asia, but here again the central message relates to the hardships
of livelihoods. Poor people report that unemployment was not a problem 10
years ago. A group of youths from Sofia, Bulgaria share, "Still, back then
there was a safety net associated mainly with the availability of jobs and social security, and even though people were underpaid back then too, they nevertheless had a sense of security."

Where Life Is Better

*Economic conditions are improved if we compare our lives
with how they were in the past. But after thinking about it
a little more, we find that we are still going down because
while we have come up one step the rest of society has gone
up 10 steps.*

—A poor resident, Ha Tinh, Vietnam

*Fifteen years ago, getting cooked lentils, rice, curry, and
vegetables was a dream!*

—A poor woman, Manjhar, India

Vietnam stands out starkly as a very positive exception among the 23 study
countries. Groups at all sites in this country say economic opportunities have
increased, and poverty has declined substantially in the last 10 years, thanks
to changes in government economic and social policy. The implementation
of the Renovation and Open Door policies in the late 1980s led to
development of markets, land allocation to households and freedom to
travel—changes that people perceived as laying the foundation for increased
opportunities. An emphasis on building assets and development of secondary
sources of income such as raising livestock, gardening, tree cultivation and

trading, as well as an extensive network of credit provision, has helped people generate incomes. However, those who still are poor, such as migrants to Ho Chi Minh City, feel left out of the opportunities and discriminated against by official government programs. They feel constrained in particular by lack of credit: "I know how to generate an income but cannot do anything because I have no money."

In several communities in Bangladesh, India and Sri Lanka groups speak of greater economic opportunities, but they consider access to such openings as sometimes limited to those who are better off. In some communities in Bangladesh the poor say that opportunities are slightly greater because of the work of NGOs and new opportunities in garment factories. Participants in Dhaka and Chittagong, Bangladesh explain that their main problem is not the lack of jobs but the low wages offered. In almost every community visited for the India study, the poor perceive that interventions by NGOs and the advent of self-help groups and village development committees have improved the social status, livelihood security and availability of livelihood alternatives, but they do not think these gains are shared among some of the poorer groups.[3]

In some communities that perceive opportunities to be growing, people often associate the advances with the provision of new infrastructure. In Nakorn Patom, Thailand people report that recent investment in "water, electricity, and transportation has vastly improved, making work easier." Poor people make similar observations on better living and work conditions in some of the *favelas* (slums or squatted land) of Brazil. The chapter that follows examines the importance of infrastructure in the lives of the poor more closely.

Individual Breakthroughs

In both difficult and supportive contexts, many poor women and men obviously can and do manage to get ahead. To learn more about how poor

Box 3.4 Resilient and Resourceful: Bouncing Back from Destitution in Ghana

Neema (43) is from Twabidi, Ghana and has six children. Like many others in the community, she migrated to Twabidi in 1984 with her husband to do cacao farming with the hope that they would be able to get out of poverty. A "good Samaritan" gave them land to farm under the condition that their produce would be shared in equal part with him. This they did for two years, and life began to get better. Just around that time, however, her husband fell ill for almost two months, and she had to sell everything they owned to pay his medical bills. The situation was so difficult that even obtaining food was a problem. They had to depend on the generosity of others.

"Even though life was tough for me, I never gave up hope. I started helping people on their farms in exchange for food. This enabled me to feed my family and even sell some at times. Soon, somebody gave me his cacao farm to look after, and I decided to intercrop the cacao with oil palm trees. This went very well, and when I harvested, I had enough money to start my own farm. With hard work and determination, we have about four different oil palm plantations now. I have been able to put up a house here in Twabidi and another at Asotwe, in the Ashanti region where I migrated from."

people pull themselves up and out of the web of poverty, the researchers were asked to identify, interview and write a short life history of a man and a woman in each community "who were poor earlier and are better off now." The analysis here was informed by a review of factors that people said helped them to escape poverty in a collection of 147 case studies gathered during the fieldwork. The interviews were free flowing.

The mini case studies suggest that many factors contribute to movement out of poverty. As illustrated in figures 3.1 and 3.2, self-employment or entrepreneurship is the most frequent path out of poverty.[4] As illustrated in the story of Ameena from Ghana in box 3.3, men and women also often report multiple sources of income, including from wages and salaries, benefits from family, and income from agriculture and access to land. Approximately one-third of these upwardly mobile manage income flows from all these sources. Many of their stories tell of interruptions and setbacks along the way to a better life (see box 3.4).

Several in this "better off" group mention that they or a spouse managed to save enough from wage labor to then strike out on their own and improve their earnings. Hasina, a 52-year-old married woman with three children in Buq, Somaliland explains that she used her earnings as a midwifery trainer to launch a vegetable business. Today she takes truckloads of potatoes and other vegetables to neighboring areas, and her husband runs a small shop. Salim from Dahshour Village, Egypt began learning the export business while

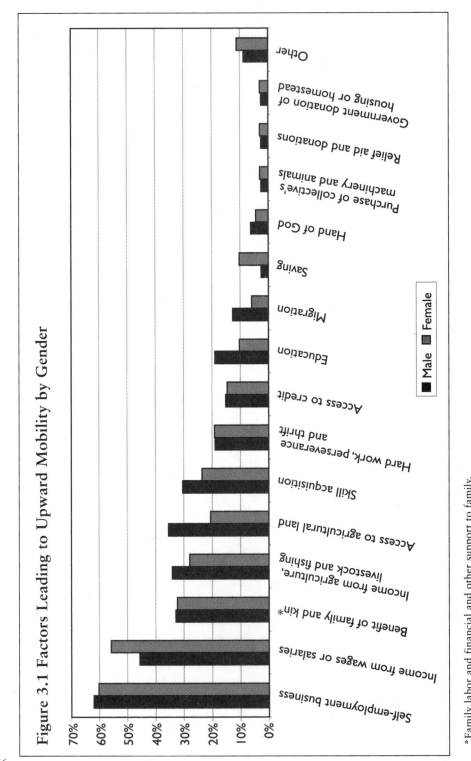

Figure 3.1 Factors Leading to Upward Mobility by Gender

*Family labor and financial and other support to family.

Figure 3.2 Factors Leading to Upward Mobility by Region

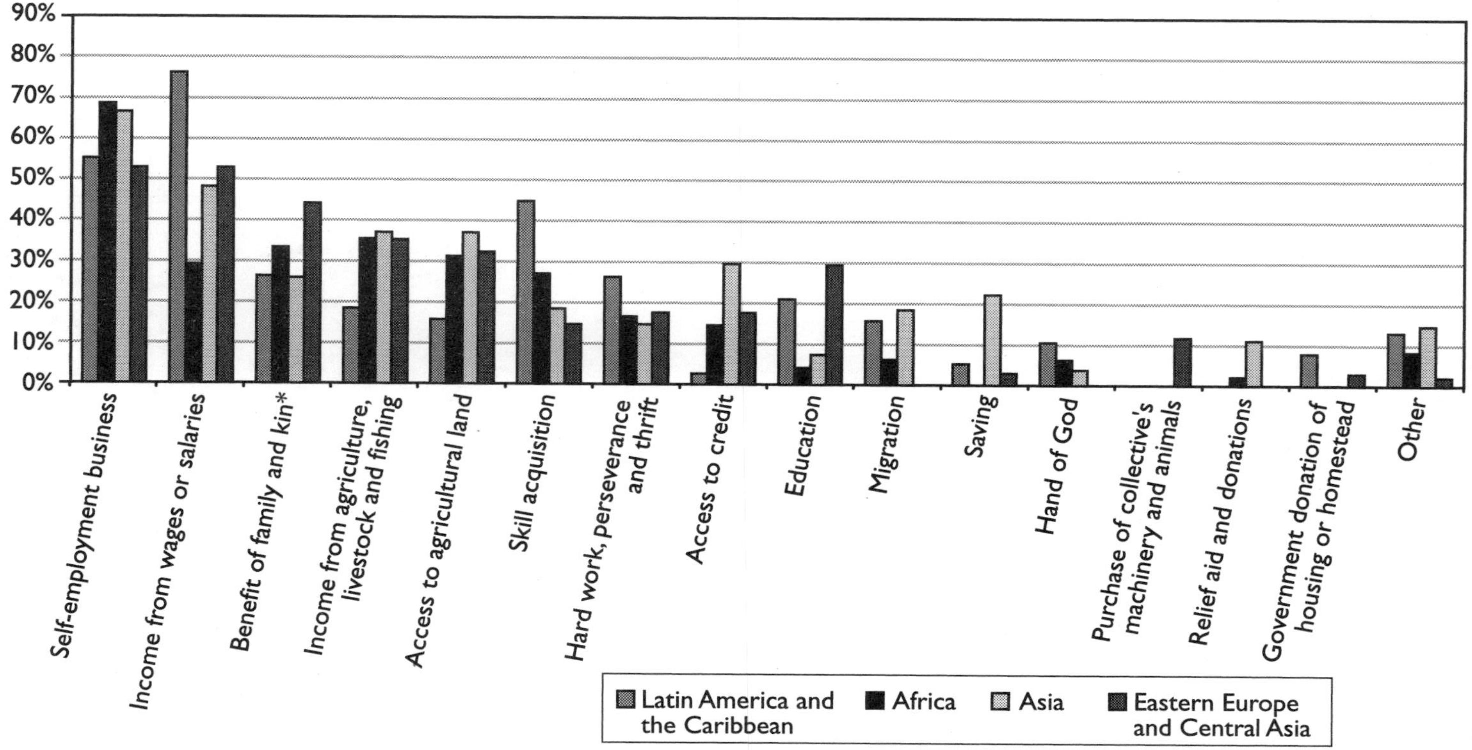
90%
80%
70%
60%
50%
40%
30%
20%
10%
0%
Self-employment business
Income from wages or salaries
Benefit of family and kin*
Income from agriculture, livestock and fishing
Access to agricultural land
Skill acquisition
Hard work, perseverance and thrift
Access to credit
Education
Migration
Saving
Hand of God
Purchase of collective's machinery and animals
Relief aid and donations
Government donation of housing or homestead
Other
Latin America and the Caribbean
Africa
Asia
Eastern Europe and Central Asia

*Family labor and financial and other support to family.

working as a driver. His first venture with the exporting of watermelons failed, but a few years later he found a new partner and began exporting onions with much greater success.

Men and woman refer frequently to the value of acquiring skills and a willingness to learn on the job. Aldin from Varna, Bulgaria says he earns a good living by working constructions sites, and he learned skills such as plastering and bricklaying while serving in the Army Construction Corps. Kofi from Twabidi, Ghana spent four years in an apprenticeship to become a qualified gin distiller and started his own distillery soon after. Nong from Ha Tinh Province, Vietnam raises chickens, ducks and pigs, and he tells the researchers that "farmers need to know how to choose breeds." He learned this by reading books and participating in agricultural extension programs.

In fact, a quarter of those interviewed mention skills acquisition, learning to run a business, or acquiring particular skills, while they mention education less frequently but with strong regional differences. The case studies from Latin America and the former Soviet Union speak more about education than those from Africa and Asia.

This group also includes some elderly people who acknowledge receiving critical support from their adult children. Sixty-four-year-old Eliana from Vila Junqueira, Brazil says she moved to her neighborhood long ago to put her children in school. Eliana's husband is recovering from a stroke, and she explains that they are coping reasonably well because "we have, with the help of our sons, a good medical plan. They help in everything."

Many in this better off group also speak of weathering setbacks, periods of recovery, and then continuing to move forward. Family illness and death, particularly of the leading breadwinner, commonly disrupted gains, as was the case with Neema in box 3.4. Other interruptions include divorce or desertion, economic and political crises, and natural disasters.

The Challenge of Livelihoods

If you earn a minimal wage or so, and pay 110 reais for rent, what will you live on? You'll live on odd jobs in order to eat...you can't study, put your kids in school...under-employment crushes all of this...when you are underemployed, you can't study, go to the doctor and take care of other basic necessities.
—A discussion group participant, Morro da Conceição, Brazil

Although caught in the struggle to survive, poor people want opportunity, not handouts: "We do not want money; we just want you to employ us. We need factories that would draw all these unemployed people from the streets" (El Gawaber, Egypt). Indeed, people often offer specific recommendations that would create opportunities for better livelihoods. Here are some:

- ▶ "To improve the future living standards of the village," suggest residents of Jaffna, Sri Lanka, "they expect the two lending institutions, the United Currency Society and the Social Development Center...to extend a helping hand by encouraging savings, and giving loans when necessary."
- ▶ From Dibdibe Wajtu in Ethiopia came the idea that "if the widowed and landless women are given some sort of vocational training, they can make it a means of living."
- ▶ In Beni Amer Village, Egypt it is suggested that the government should "build a factory of onion drying or small-scale projects of manufacturing palm wood "grid" or...provide people with money to start an artisan work such as clay manufacturing or local carpet kilim."
- ▶ Conditions could improve in Muynak, Uzbekistan if "somebody will redistribute...the rights of accessibility" to the lakes.
- ▶ Day care is requested in Novo Horizonte, Brazil: "It is very important, especially for those mothers who have to work."
- ▶ "If we had fertilizer some of the problems like medical fees, education fees...could be solved" is a suggestion from Ilondolac Chinsale, Zambia.

Achieving a better livelihood emerges as an urgent priority across the study countries. It came from those in villages who depend on farms, pastures, lakes and forests; and from those in cities and the countryside who are forced into temporary and very poorly paid but high-risk, degrading or humiliating work.

The priority and urgency of better livelihoods for poor women and men raise many challenges:

- ▶ What kind of actions would make the most direct and meaningful difference in poor people's lives?
- ▶ How might their exposure be reduced to the vagaries of climate? To the exploitation of employers and traders? Or to the unpredictable "taxes" set by those who are wealthier and more powerful?
- ▶ How might this policy agenda become much more a focus of local, national and global attention?

Notes

[1]In small group discussions, participants identify and rank their community's most pressing problems and priorities. Groups then assess whether the problems have changed over the past 10 years and discuss hopes for the future. Participants reflect on which problems the community could solve itself and which require outside support, and in a separate exercise they identify, rank and evaluate the most important institutions in their daily lives and during a crisis. Groups also analyze the causes and impacts of poverty. In addition, individual interviews provide brief life histories of men and women who have escaped poverty as well as of those who have always been poor or have slid into poverty.

[2]Food and money problems were often at the top of lists as well lack of work, and these were often associated directly with livelihood hardships in the discussions about the lists. Groups focused more on communitywide problems, rather than on personal or household-level concerns. While family problems may be extremely acute for some (e.g., domestic violence), they figure only sporadically in the work of the groups on problems and priorities. This activity was not carried out in Sri Lanka.

[3]The studies in Bangladesh and India were conducted in areas where NGOs are active. The researchers used these contacts to gain speedy entry into the communities and to facilitate follow up action.

[4]The data in figures 3.1 and 3.2 are based on 147 mini-case studies or life histories of people who were identified as moving out of poverty. The sample is not statistically representative, however, and results should be viewed as illustrative. Case studies were selected where upward triggers could be readily identified from the reports on the open-ended interviews. The categories were established through an inductive process of data analyses of the factors underlying upward mobility.

Chapter 4

Places of the Poor

Summary

Many poor people are disadvantaged and endangered by the places and physical conditions where they live and work. They often experience: problems with water that is scarce, inaccessible and unsafe; isolation with bad roads and inadequate transport; precarious shelter; scarcities of energy for cooking and heating; and poor sanitation. Poor communities are typically neglected, lacking the infrastructure and services provided for the better off. Access to services often costs poor people more. Poor people from many communities emphasize how the politics that underpin the provision of infrastructure and public services often reinforce inequities. Those in communities with improved amenities acknowledge the gains to their quality of life.

Many places where poor people live present multiple disadvantages that include not only missing and inadequate infrastructure and services, but also unfavorable geography, vulnerability to environmental shocks and seasonal exposure. Quite often these disadvantages combine in ways that endanger or impoverish those who live there. Poor people's places in congested urban areas are especially risk-ridden from pollution, sewage and crime. Variously steep, low-lying, too close to waterways, or drought-prone, many urban and rural places are vulnerable to the vagaries of weather. Many of the worst deprivations that come with living in these places are seasonal in nature, including property damage by rain, wind, floods and landslides, and unsanitary conditions from flood waters mixed with sewage. Those who live in "places of the poor" are frequently insecure in person and property. Most poor people can find only "places of the poor" in which to live. These places then keep them poor.

Introduction

Every country has a wide range of groups of poor people. The researchers sought out some of the diverse places where they live. In most countries both urban and rural communities were visited.[1]

Poor people are often born into marginal places and conditions. Then, if they move, they find the better sites already taken. Often the places they do find are bad in many ways, variously isolated, infertile, insecure, vulnerable and dangerous. They include areas that are hilly; remote; drought-prone; exposed to landslides, floods or pollution; distant from or too close to water; and open to extremes of weather.

This chapter explores how these places of the poor impose multiple disadvantages and discomforts on those who live and seek their livelihoods in them. It opens with highlights of poor people's discussions about the hardships of missing or inadequate infrastructure and basic services. The chapter then examines what emerged in the discussion groups about the politics of infrastructure. A final section highlights how the disadvantages of living in the "places of the poor" interlock to keep people poor or drive them further into poverty.

While the types and combinations of hardships vary widely among places, on balance the urban poor seem to struggle more. Their places are often distinguished by persistent crime and the many forms of pollution that can accompany crowded living without adequate infrastructure and services. A defining hardship of rural places seems to be isolation and lack of communication. But such divides are not clean. Crime and pollution touch many villages, and limited transport and access to information effectively isolate several urban neighborhoods visited for the study.

Infrastructure and services are more readily available in some of the communities, most notably in Brazil, Indonesia, Sri Lanka and Thailand. The people who live in such places widely acknowledge the importance of these improvements to better quality of life.

The Missing Basics

When discussion groups identify and rank their communities' most pressing problems and priorities, what frequently emerges are serious gaps in access to basic services and infrastructure. Although priorities vary with local contexts, a great many lists indicate difficulties with access to water, roads and transport, housing, fuel and sanitation.

Water—Inadequate and Unsafe

> I repeat that we need water as badly as we need air.
> —A woman, Tash-Bulak, Kyrgyz Republic

> We need boreholes because we rely on unsafe water from streams and unprotected wells. It is a critical problem because

most of these streams and wells dry out during the dry season.
We have to travel long distances searching for water.
—A participant in a discussion group of poor men
and women, Madana village, Malawi

How can we sow anything without water? What will my cow
drink? Drought is so often here. Water is our life.
—A resident of Orgakin, Russia

People in many communities speak forcefully of the lack of adequate and safe water as an acute deprivation. Water shortages and difficulties accessing safe drinking water appear most serious and widespread in the African countries. However, poor women and men from all the regions describe daily struggles to obtain water for human use. There are problems of distance, quantity, seasonality, quality and safety of supply; environmental issues like flooding, siltation and pollution; questions of maintenance; and often combinations of these. Water is also critical for animals and crops.

For many, water scarcity means daily hardships. "We have to spend more than an hour to fetch and bring a pot of water," say villagers of Dibdibe Wajtu, Ethiopia. In Netarhat, India women trek 2 kilometers to fetch water and face many risks along the way: "danger of boulders slipping out of the rock joints...of wild animals, many wolves, and hyenas." As noted in box 4.1, women find themselves fighting in Ayekale, Nigeria to get at the village's only well.

For many rural people, water availability and quality vary with the seasons. As rivers and streams dry out or water sources deteriorate, people suffer shortages. An illustration comes from Malawi. Villagers from Madana gratefully acknowledge the two new wells in the community, but growing demand and shortages in the dry season leave people still traveling "long distances searching for water." A general observation from Malawi is that water scarcity is linked to deforestation and the resulting siltation, which, as one of the researchers observed, "has covered most of the springs."

Many people in the study share concerns about water quality and pollution, particularly in urban communities. In both El Mataria and Borg Meghezel (which sits just on the outskirts of a city), Egypt discussion groups fear the effects of water pollution and say, "We hope for our kids not to suffer as we did." In Etropole, Bulgaria a middle-aged man exclaims:

Look at our river! The cows stop milking when they drink
this water. When I was a boy we used to go fishing there, and
there were good fish. Now even the frogs have disappeared.
We have no choice but to use it for the gardens—so all the
metals are soaking in the soil and we eat them. They can take
more copper from my lungs and bones than from one meter
of cable.

Box 4.1 A Case Study of Priority Needs in Ayekale Odoogur, Nigeria

The village of Ayekale Odogun lies in Kwara State of southwest Nigeria and is inhabited by 1,200 people across 100 households. About 85 percent are of Islamic faith, and Yoruba is the main ethnic group. It is important to note that Ayekale is better off than many other villages in the study—it has electricity and access to a nearby town and its market, but there is no local health service and the school is 3 kilometers away.

The table below shows how two of the six discussion groups identify and rank the most pressing problems in the community. Lack of drinking water stands out as the most urgent priority. Women and children spend a large part of their day trying to get water from a single hand-dug well, and it is indicated that "women commonly fight over access...." After water, concerns about the long distances to a health center and schools follow. It is interesting to note that with the exception of the female elders group all the discussion groups ranked access to water, health care, and schools above problems related to more material or livelihood needs. This suggests that farming in Ayekale, which has a tarred road and is close to a market, may be more successful than is the case for many poor rural communities elsewhere in the study.

There are some gender differences in priorities for action that relate to men's and women's different livelihoods. About 90 percent of the men farm and some 70 percent of the woman engage in informal trading, mainly of processed garri (from cassava). Women single out problems with the distance to the market and equipment for palm oil and cassava processing, as they now have to travel to other villages for processing as well as for trading. Men highlight the lack of industries. Both men and women agree on the need for a local market and better-functioning cooperatives.

Prioritized List of Problems from Ayekale Odoogun, Nigeria

Problems	Ranks given to problems by different groups	
	Elders (male)	Elders (female)
Lack of potable water	1	1
Lack of a health center	2	3
Lack of primary school	3	4
Lack of industries	4	
Lack of a periodic market		2
Lack of oil palm or cassava processing equipment		5
Poor sales	5	6
Poor performance of cooperative societies	6	7
Poverty		8

In speaking about water contamination in Plovdiv, Bulgaria a poor man declares, "I am tired of going to the municipality and insisting that they do something. Of course we are ill." In the urban site of Florencio Varela, Argentina unsafe drinking water is mentioned by a group of young women in these terms: "If two out of three children become ill and begin to vomit...it is due to the water; even though you can add chlorine, you're never sure what you are drinking." Water quality appears in most problem listings for nine communities in Ecuador and is ranked as more pressing in urban than rural sites. Polluted water is also found in rural areas: in Millbank, Jamaica poor people suggest that the use of insecticides and other inputs in banana farming contaminate local water supplies.

For many, water problems arise from inadequate infrastructure and lack of maintenance. People in Urmaral in the Kyrgyz Republic say they rely on a single hydrant and badly need a pipeline. Elsewhere, broken pumps are common: of the six available hand pumps in Dorapalli, India only three are in working condition and just two provide potable water. Even piped water systems, mainly mentioned in Latin America and Eastern Europe and Central Asia, are said to be unreliable, with sometimes broken pipes and often sporadic water delivery. In Nova Califórnia, Brazil participants complain that "the piped water comes every 8 days, at times every 15 days...there is a lot of water shortage." In Ulugbek, Uzbekistan discussion groups say that when there is no water pressure in their pipes, people have to go to slippery and polluted drainage ditches, which is a "terrible hardship in the cold of winter."

People attribute the lack of maintenance to various causes. The researchers in Malawi point out that "many water points have been disconnected because the committees misappropriated the fees collected...meant for routine maintenance checks and settlement of bills." In Accompong, Jamaica it is said to be difficult to get the water agency to come and fix broken pipes.

In many rural communities, shortage of water for crops and animals threatens livelihoods and household food security. Lack of irrigation water is identified as a major problem in four out of the six rural sites visited in India. In Eastern Europe and Central and East Asia, poor people mention problems with poorly functioning or damaged irrigation systems repeatedly and farmers express concerns about making the difficult transition of having to pay for irrigation water. And there were communities across Africa and Asia where discussion groups consider new or improved irrigation systems vital to helping them combat drought.

Isolation and Poor Access

A community without roads does not have a way out.
—A poor man, Juncal, Ecuador

If we get the road we would get everything else, community center, employment, post office, water, telephone.
—A young woman, Little Bay, Jamaica

Many of the poor communities in the study are isolated by distance, bad road conditions, lack of or broken bridges, and inadequate transport. In both rural and urban areas, these conditions make it difficult for people to get their goods to market and themselves to places of work, to handle health emergencies, to send children to schools, to obtain public services and to keep in touch with events and influence decisions.

In rural areas people repeatedly mention roads and often bridges when discussing community problems. In isolated tropical communities, an all-weather road passable in the rains tends to be seen as the key to much else. In all but 1 of the 10 communities visited in Malawi, participants identify better roads as an urgent need. In the three rural communities visited in Argentina, people report that there is no transportation into the nearest town and during heavy rains households become cut off by flooding and lack of radios or telephones. People in Chota, Ecuador lack a bridge and have to navigate a river to reach the nearby Pan American highway. A group of poor women mentioned how when the river is low, it takes 10 minutes to cross by boat, "but when the river is high, it's very dangerous and people have died crossing the river."

Difficulty getting crops to market is a recurrent concern. In Twabidi, Ghana truck drivers are said to charge very high fees because of the bad road. As a consequence, much of the food crop is locked up on farms, leading to postharvest losses. The researchers note that the condition of the road is thus a disincentive to production and productivity. Villagers in Millbank, Jamaica talk about the poor condition of the road and distance to a market: "Often times our food rots in the fields, and people are starving here in Jamaica and round the world." A man from Asociación 10 de Agosto in Ecuador complains, "There are no good roads. To get the products out of the farm you have to use horses, but those who don't have a horse cannot do it." In Vietnam, poor villagers indicate that they need to be self-sufficient in food because of costs and the distance of markets, which limits their opportunities to diversify crops.

Travel to clinics or hospitals for treatment, especially in emergencies, is another common concern. A woman from Little Bay, Jamaica might be speaking for many in other countries when she says, "If anybody takes sick in the community it costs a lot to go all the way around; and if you are not careful the people can die before they reach the hospital." Attracting staff to remote villages lacking infrastructure is equally a problem: participants from Okpuje, Nigeria say health personnel avoid their remote village like "a plague because of absence of basic infrastructure."

Across Eastern Europe and Central Asia, participants speak bitterly about how things have become worse, with a largely collapsed transportation system and harsh traveling conditions. A 42-year-old woman in Kalaidzhi, Bulgaria complains of having to walk 20-plus kilometers a day to work and back: "And after work we have to take care of the animals, cook.... By 9 p.m. I can barely stand on my feet." In Sredno Selo, Bulgaria as well as Kalaidzhi, participants indicate that bus lines have closed down, road conditions have deteriorated and private cars have become too expensive to run and maintain.

Urban isolation of the places of the poor is less obvious but serious. Bad roads, lack of roads and lack of transportation are reported as problems. Researchers, for example, describe the isolation and other infrastructural gaps that exist where a Roma community lives in Dimitrovgrad, Bulgaria. (See box 4.2.) In Malawi the researchers note that the roads into the three urban settlements are full of large potholes and both public and private transport operators have withdrawn service. Women indicate that this has made their lives unbearable because they now either have to walk to work or stay home and earn nothing.

In differing contexts, people illustrate how the lack of roads and other means of communication can limit them, making it more difficult to find jobs, negotiate better prices for their produce, access services such as credit or social assistance, or shape events that affect them. A poor man in Tash-Bulak in the Kyrgyz Republic explains that he did not know how to get loans: "There is no telephone communication in the village, no post office. Newspapers and magazines are expensive, and we cannot afford to buy them." Members of a poor household in a district of Tra Vinh Province Vietnam talk of feeling isolated and helpless without a television or radio. With travel so difficult, participants in many poor places express regrets about their lack of access to elected representatives and other officials.

Box 4.2 A Gypsy (Roma) Ghetto in Bulgaria

Let us take the places the Roma live in, for instance, in Dimitrovgrad. There is a drastic difference in the image of Dimitrovgrad as presented by official sources and the Roma's perception of the town. According to the records, Dimitrovgrad has a more or less excellent infrastructure—which, however, does not apply to the poor quarters and, in particular, the Gypsy ghetto. The latter has nothing to do with "official" Dimitrovgrad—there are neither roads nor telephones, the plumbing is disastrous, many houses have no electricity and there's a bus every three hours. The situation is the same in Sofia—the Roma quarters are entirely different from other Sofia quarters; there is no sewage; the shafts are clogged; drinking water is dirty and stinks; there is no garbage collection or other communal services. The thus-segregated Roma feel truly stigmatized, totally forgotten by one and all, victims of discrimination: "Treated like dogs."

Bad Housing and Shelter

> *It's drafty, humid, leaking. Just try living here in winter. Our children have fallen ill. And the adults too. There are bugs, cockroaches, what have you. It's cold.*
>
> —A group of young Roma men and women,
> Krasna Polania, Bulgaria

> *A dwelling leaked so much that it woke people up: it was like a court when the judge is arriving and people say "khoti liime!"—or "all rise!"*
>
> —A woman, Malawi

Poor people almost always have bad housing and shelter. Exceptions can be found: where there have been sharp economic declines, as in the Eastern European and Central Asian countries, some who are now very poor still live in relatively good housing; and sometimes where a series of disasters has hit a once better-off family, they may still reside in the same relatively good house.

Most, though, live in huts or hovels of temporary and unstable materials, such as adobe (Egypt); "mud, thatch, bamboo" (Ha Tinh, Vietnam); "reeds...ruined zinc" (Barrio Nuevas Brisas del Mar, Ecuador); or mud walls and roofs thatched with grass (Malawi).

With such precarious shelters, the poor are more exposed to the elements. In rural Ghana participants explain that those with reed roofs are more vulnerable to bush fires and storms than those with aluminum. Similarly, in La Matanza, Argentina a group of middle-aged men describe how a lodging needs to be secure from the weather; otherwise, "if a storm comes, the roof flies away and what little there is inside washes away." In Malawi, during the previous two years, the collapsing of houses had become more of a problem because of heavy rains.

Poor people report that fire is frequently a hazard. The danger is acute in slums built of combustible materials. Dwellings crammed together make them especially exposed to the spread of fire, like the one that swept part of a slum in Dhaka. Even with more permanent housing, in Ozerny in Russia, people point out that electric wiring, having not been updated for 50 years, is a fire hazard.

For participants, better shelter and housing are sometimes a pressing priority. The many reasons include physical security and health. In Novo Horizonte, Brazil, for example, a group of poor women express the desire to live in *barracos*, little block houses that would offer greater security from thieves and from "contact with rats, cockroaches, scorpions...that cause some deaths."

Energy Scarcity

> *Finding firewood for cooking is the problem. Very soon we may have to go to the town to buy firewood.*
>
> —A woman, Viyalagoda, Sri Lanka

*Gas heating is a great joy for us—it was very difficult to
stoke with wood that you first need to gather and fetch from
far away.*

—A poor elderly man, Takhtakupyr, Uzbekistan

The places of the poor typically lack energy sources and supplies. In the warmer countries, people mention energy scarcity and cost mainly in relation to fuel for cooking. In the colder climates, notably the Eastern European and Central Asian countries, it is mainly in relation to heating and electricity.

In the warmer countries, most poor households appear to rely on firewood for cooking. But there is evidence of growing scarcities. In some places, forest areas are disappearing. In the villages of Wewala, Viyalagoda and Elhena in Sri Lanka, for example, women report deforestation as a major problem. Elsewhere firewood is already being purchased. In the rural community of Kajima, Ethiopia a group of men indicate that women make and sell local drinks to raise money for purchasing household needs such as firewood. With the increased migration of men, women in rural Ecuador complain that they must now collect firewood and tend the farm and they are finding it difficult to feed their children and accomplish other household tasks.

Electricity features less in people's priorities from warmer climates. For some, especially in rural areas, it is not perceived as a realistic issue. A women's discussion group in Twabidi, Ghana explains why they had not identified electricity as a priority. They point out that even the closest large community in the area has no electricity, and even if they had it, they would not be able to pay for it. High charges can be a problem, as in Sri Lanka.

Some discussion groups, mainly in towns and cities, do, however, list electricity as a priority for both their homes and street lighting to reduce neighborhood crime. In Kebele 30, Ethiopia a women's discussion group values receiving electricity to reduce their household work burdens and suggests that "lighting may contribute to decreasing birth rates." Although not given a high priority, several discussion groups in different parts of the world mention street lighting for socializing at night and as a deterrent to crime. As a middle-aged woman from Razgrad, Bulgaria explains

> *There is no street lighting since 1991. Eight years they did not
> put a lamp. There should be one at least on the crossroads. The
> people have to walk with electric torches and sticks [for the
> dogs]. And the lonely women? They close their doors at 6 p.m.*

Energy scarcity emerges as especially acute for poor people in the urban areas of the cold-weather climates of Eastern Europe and Central Asia. The cost of heating fuel is a frequent problem. In Orgakin, Russia all the discussion groups mention struggling with gas shortages over the previous winter: "We have to pay for it—or else the gas supply will be cut off. We won't survive." In rural areas of Eastern Europe and Central Asia, as in the other regions of the study, people report gathering firewood from nearby forests for use in their homes and for selling.

> ### Box 4.3 Old, Cold and Alone
>
> The problem of fuel shortages in Eastern European and Central Asian countries is severe for the elderly. Many poor elderly participants identify winter as a painful time because they are alone without wood for heating and they have no children nearby to help out. In Etropole, Bulgaria the researchers were told, "There are grandmothers staying alone all the day, trembling under their blankets all the winter. They do not go outside because they are cold; they do not even walk in the room." Similarly, a man in Razgrad, Bulgaria explains: "They tell me that they try to drink almost no water, because it is too cold to go to the loo and come back to the bed. Do you imagine how they live? They are too old to read, because of the eyesight; they conserve on electricity, so they do not watch TV; they do not go outside to see somebody else—they disappear in November, and we see them again in April."

In Eastern Europe and Central Asia, the cold of winter and the lack of warm clothing and heating touches many aspects of life. A young woman from Dimitrovgrad, Bulgaria explains:

> *Winters are worst. Summers we can work in the field. Winters are also worse because there's nothing to keep us warm. There aren't any allowances from Town Hall...no firewood. Clothes and shoes are a problem in winter, and so is school for the kids. There's no money for snacks and textbooks.*

Elsewhere in Eastern Europe and Central Asia, people talk of cold classrooms and the inability of schools to afford fuel. Cold and lack of clothing are a problem: students often wear coats in the classrooms and many children rotate attending school, sharing shoes and coats with their siblings. "My neighbors' children have one pair of shoes and take turns wearing them. It's a good thing they go to school in two different shifts," reports a participant from Bashi in the Kyrgyz Republic. A woman in Bratunac, Bosnia and Herzegovina with a child in primary school reports that parents must supply funds for heating wood or their children will not receive their completion certificates. The woman is upset that "the people who run the school do not ask themselves whether the parents can afford all of this." Box 4.3 illustrates the suffering endured by the elderly as they struggle through winters. As in so many domains, so with energy scarcity: the poor and vulnerable suffer, and finally the children.

No Sanitation—Filth and Stench

> *Where I live has two toilets in it, and they broke. I have to eat and sleep on it [the sewage], and it is a mess.*
>
> —A poor woman, Cassava Piece, Jamaica

Dirty roads that are full of rubbish.
                    —A pressing problem listed by a discussion group,
                                                      El Mataria, Egypt

Sanitation problems are acute in many communities, especially urban ones. In Bangladesh, however, poor people note a scarcity of latrines in rural as well as in urban areas. They also mention difficulties with paying for building materials and, in urban settlements, with finding space. In the settlement of Kebele 30 in Ethiopia people say that most households have no latrines and public ones are not available. Sewage there "runs openly on the roads," endangering children playing in the streets. Pressing concerns about health risks, particularly to children, and smells of open sewage canals are particularly striking in the reports from the Latin American settlements.

Rain adds to the dangers of lack of sanitation. In Nova Califórnia, Brazil a discussion group participant complains that "the sewage runs in your front door, and when it rains, the water floods into the house and you need to lift the things...." At Barrio Las Pascuas in Bolivia a woman says, "Just look how the kids are playing in the street with so much dirt. The water in the streets brings infections, and it is because of a lack of a sewage system...."

The hazards of garbage-filled alleys and unreliable waste collection are mentioned most frequently in urban places in Latin America. At Isla Trinitaria in Ecuador a group of adult women describe how the houses are made of cane and stand on top of the water at the pier or embankment at the far end, where there is garbage contamination, "a plague of flies" and "illnesses are caused by pollution." In the settlements of Sacadura Cabral, Morro da Conceição, Borborema and Nova Califórnia in Brazil the residents complain of foul-smelling garbage building up at the doors of their homes and "causing all types of diseases affecting all the community and especially children." In a discussion group of women in Nova Califórnia, they say, "Waste brings some bugs. Here we have rats, cockroaches, spiders and even snakes and scorpions." On their list of pressing community problems, a women's group in Sacadura Cabral emphasize "rats and cockroaches" along with "sewage on the streets."

The Politics of Infrastructure and Place

*Last summer before the election of the mayor...a first-class
road was built here. But after the election, the researchers were
told, all the work stopped.*
                    —Researcher team, Dzerzhinsk, Russia

Discussion groups in widely differing contexts emphasize the disparities that exist between areas that are poor and those that are better off. Poor people not only note that their communities are worse off, but that the politics surrounding the provision of infrastructure and public services frequently reinforce these inequities. They often express a sense of having been abandoned or forsaken by their governments.

Discussion group participants quite often point out how their wealthier neighbors enjoy better access than they do to services such as water, electricity, latrines, sewerage, transport and telephones. Typical of this is the observation in villages in Bihar, India that the approach roads go to the upper-caste localities and then end. Likewise, in Genengsari, Indonesia the researchers write that the "road stopped near the better-off homes, leaving the part going to poorer homes uncompacted." And in Galih Pakuwon, also in Indonesia, public toilets and washing-bathing facilities are built close to better-off households, although many of them already have their own toilets. In Oq Oltyn, Uzbekistan participants indicate that while they have no water in their pipes, the neighborhood across the road with the "employees of district organizations" has water.

Though many places of the poor are the most environmentally threatened and in need of infrastructure, they are the least likely to get it: "The conditions of life get better as you get farther from the river bank," and the rich with cars live the farthest away, noted a researcher in La Matanza, Argentina. Also, distance and isolation can mean that others do not perceive the lack of amenities, as in the case of the Gypsy ghetto in Dimitrovgrad in Bulgaria (see box 4.2).

To make things worse, people in poor areas sometimes have to pay more for what they do get or have to provide services for themselves, as shown in box 4.4 on one part of Ho Chi Minh City in Vietnam.

A number of study participants blame politicians and governments for arbitrary decisions and actions. In Isla Trinitaria, Ecuador a discussion group of men declare that "water is a political tool. The tubing is already installed and the work is done. The politician who wants support will give the drinking water." In the Asociación 10 de Agosto neighborhood, also in Ecuador, a women observes, "The works for drinking water have stopped. Now they say we have to do the paperwork all over again. Nobody gives us anything. They say there are no funds." In Florencio Varela, Argentina a woman shares her frustration with not being able to get additional water taps installed: "For two years we knocked on all of the doors...we went to the municipality and here we are with the plans for water taps...and without the water." Were it not for corruption and inefficiency, a man from Entra a Pulso, Brazil stresses that the water shortages in his community would not occur: "The money is stolen and consequently there are no investments. There is a lot of water in this country's underground. I say this because I have worked for 30 years digging wells in this country."

Where basic infrastructure and services have been provided, participants express deep appreciation for the difference these have made in the quality of their lives. This is marked in some of the communities in Brazil, Indonesia, Sri Lanka and Thailand.

With water, electricity, telephones and garbage collection services now available in his *favela* a man in Nova Califórnia, Brazil gratefully acknowledges that "10 years ago...life was much, much worse.... Today, in comparison with the past, we live 'in heaven.'" EMASA, the local water agency for Novo Horizonte, Brazil is well regarded by the residents there despite problems with erratic supplies. The researchers mention that EMASA staff have helped the community by "giving containers to people to collect water...it means that they are helping those who cannot pay for the service."

The community of Accompong, Jamaica recently acquired electricity from the Jamaica Public Service Company and "some returning residents regard this as the greatest achievement of the community as it has made it possible for them to decide to return home and live in the community." Discussion groups in Pegambiran, Indonesia note that several important improvements have been made in recent years to their community: clean water service has been provided since 1990, several latrines have been built and garbage collection has increased to once a week. In Baan Pak Wan, Thailand the NGO Population and Community Development Association is credited with helping the community to build a water system by lending money and providing technicians for building water tanks and household water jars.

These are exceptions, though. Most study participants convey that their needs for basic infrastructure are as urgent as ever and much too little has been done. In some cases, they link growing pressures for basic services to rising populations in their communities. They also repeatedly express the sense that adequate services should have been provided to them and that their governments have let them down.

Trapped in Poor Places

Many participants from diverse communities provide illustrations of how their safety is endangered and their lives greatly limited because of the difficult and risky conditions where they live. Very frequently these disadvantages can be found in combinations; and sometimes they interlock in ways that present serious hazards to local people. Missing infrastructure makes many communities in the study more vulnerable to environmental shocks and seasonal weather hazards. Unfavorable geography adds to the risks. Further insecurities, particularly for the urban poor, relate to heightened levels of crime, uncertainties over property tenure and a stigma attached to their slum. Poor children in many communities face a multitude of risks to their safety.

Environmental Risks

> The water in the estuary is completely contaminated with solid waste (trash, dead decomposing animals, etc.) and liquid waste (sewage) and toxic waste from the industries in the port of Guayaquil.
> —A researcher reporting on problems common to all groups in Isla Trinitaria, Ecuador

> Unfortunately for me, the land on which I made my farm was a swampy area and when it rained the whole farm submerged with water. That also destroyed my farm.
> —An elderly man, Atonsu Bokro, Ghana

The study illustrates repeatedly how many poor villages and urban settlements are sited in environmentally vulnerable places, largely because the better places have long been taken over. Many of the communities the researchers visited sit on flood planes and in swamps, beside and over waterways, next to industrial sites, along steep hillsides and in drought-prone areas sometimes quite distant from water sources.

Among rural areas, Bangladesh and Ethiopia stand out. For Bangladesh major dangers include flooding, erosion of riverbanks and rivers changing course. Those who settled the Khaliajuri site had been displaced earlier by a river, but Khaliajuri itself, where they resettled, is similarly vulnerable, perhaps relatively unoccupied for precisely that reason. During the 1998 floods, half the village at the Khaliajuri site was swept away. In rural Ethiopia, people say it is lack of rains and drought that combine with the increasing fragmentation of landholdings to create devastating and recurring famines. A villager from rocky and mountainous Mitti Kolo, Ethiopia says the "hope" for crops "is squeezed to emptiness" by drought.

Urban environments are described as, if anything, more vulnerable and dangerous than rural ones. Combinations of high population density, missing or inadequate infrastructure and physical vulnerability make these places susceptible to multiple and sometimes quite severe environmental threats. The barrio of Isla Piedad in Ecuador illustrates the point. It is on top of a sand landfill that joins a river, with many houses hanging suspended over canals. When the tide rises some 2 meters or more, many of the houses get flooded. A canal of sewage runs through the barrio, causing a "nauseating stench." During El Niño in 1997–98, the barrio suffered serious floods and whatever infrastructure existed was destroyed. During the same period, an oil spill from the Trans-Ecuadoran oil pipeline, which runs from the Amazon to the Esmeraldas refinery, resulted in a fiery, exploding river, affecting all those who lived along the banks.

Those lodged next to industrial sites face particular hazards to health and livelihood. The town of El Mataria in Egypt is located alongside a lake where many poor people's livelihoods are tied to fishing. The continuing pollution of the lake from city waste threatens both the health and incomes of the poor. This has become worse as the lake has been dried out to increase building space. In Dzerzhinsk in Russia people say the strong summertime winds blow hazardous dust from nearby chemical plants across their town. Rates of cancer and other illnesses are especially high among the workers at the plants. The shifts at the plants are only four hours long and workers usually retire by 45. Voluntad de Dios, Ecuador, a community of mostly indigenous people, is surrounded by two oil-drilling refineries. Oil has seeped into the soil and water. One of the participants from the community comments, "Everything is contaminated: land, water, plants, and people."

Seasonal Stress: Worst at Bad Times

Participants frequently mention the seasonality of poverty and illbeing. The problems they face often reflect the time of year. While the bad times differ in warmer and colder climates, adverse factors tend to coincide and reinforce each other.[2] Everywhere, bad places are worst during the bad times. Deprivations include greatly reduced work opportunities, damage to shelter by rain and wind, unsanitary conditions from flooding and sewage, ill health, physical isolation and environmental vulnerability. These last two deserve elaboration.

Seasonal weather often compounds difficulties of transport and travel. During the rainy seasons in Bangladesh, India and Indonesia, people repeatedly mention how flooded and rain-damaged roads make it impossible to seek work or get to hospitals for care. Poor people from Twabidi, Ghana identify as their second most pressing problem, after a health clinic, a better road linking Twabidi to Tepa. The current road is impassable during the rainy season.

Seasonal access to school is a recurring physical difficulty taking different forms. Padamukti in Indonesia and Khaliajuri in Bangladesh are among the sites where seasonal floods make it difficult to get children to school. At Urmaral in the Kyrgyz Republic, residents say that especially in winter it is difficult for children going to school, since there is no bus service between villages.

Environmental vulnerability is also markedly seasonal. Its most stark form is perhaps the havoc wreaked by seasonal floods. In Khwalala, Malawi participants report that serious problems arise if all of the boreholes break down during the rainy season: it is often risky to take water from the lake because it is filled with wastes from the highlands. In Indonesia several of the urban sites are located in low-lying areas with poor drainage that are prone to frequent floods. The river that runs along Pegambiran, for instance, brings in silt and garbage from the city and overflows during heavy rains. In Padamukti people consider floods the most pressing problem because they cause skin and eye diseases, harvest failures and damage to homes. In Tanjungrejo the rainwater seeps into the homes and sits in "stinking puddles."

Seasonal floods, landslides and mudslides are feared "calamities" for people in the hilly villages of Bashi and Achy in the Kyrgyz Republic. Residents of Bashi say that in the Soviet times there was some government help to rebuild homes destroyed by mudslides but now such funds are not available. The landslides in Achy have driven some people to move into the valley, where unemployment and the cost of living are reported to be higher.

In varied ways adverse seasonality interacts with disadvantages of place. And many of the sorts of infrastructure and services that would improve the places of the poor and make them more livable would also reduce those seasonal hardships.

Insecurity and Stigma

> After 11, when it's dark, it's better not to go out, especially in winter. A neighbor of mine went to the liquor store, and when he was coming back, he was stripped of everything in the doorway of the entrance, the money, the bottle, everything.
> —A resident of Ekaterinburg, Russia

Rural places of the poor vary in security. In urban places of the poor high levels of crime and violence cause more consistent and often severe insecurity of both person and property, as chapter 8 reports. Poor people also report being shunned by would-be employers because of where they live.

Legal insecurity is also widespread. Again and again, poor people are residing and working on land to which they have no rights or rights that are uncertain and insecure. In rural areas this can be the land of a big landlord. In rural Ethiopia insecurity of land tenure is national in scale. In urban areas, such as Vietnam's Ho Chi Minh City, this can be land scheduled for clearance or land that has been appropriated by a boss or landlord, or public land. Shelter and housing are often also legally insecure.

People in Isla Trinitaria, Ecuador spoke of the constant threat of being thrown out after they had "invaded" an area and grabbed land. After filling in the land in the area, the municipality carried out a census, and a participant confided that "in that moment we didn't sleep for fear that [we might] be evicted or the neighborhood burned down, but they didn't throw us out, thanks to God. After, the census came and then we knew the *solares* [small plots of land] were ours." In the early period of the land invasion, the squatters had to stand guard all the time, because if they did not their plot would be sold to someone else by a land trafficker. Sometimes the same piece of land was sold over and over again.

In Latin America and the Caribbean generally and perhaps more widely, those who live in the places of the poor suffer area or ghetto stigma. In Brazil and Jamaica residents find it difficult to get jobs if would-be employers know they come from places with bad reputations: "You can't give a downtown address if you want to get and keep a job," says a poor person in Bower Bank, Jamaica.

Catastrophic for Children

The children keep playing in the sewage.
—A woman, Sacadura Cabral, Brazil

Many places of the poor are especially dangerous to the health of children. In some communities they play amid the filth, rubbish and open waters, and among gangs and drug dealers. Bad infrastructure also brings dangers. A person in Vila Junqueira, Brazil says about an electricity connection,

---

Box 4.5 Five Small Children Drowned or Dead in Mud: Battala, Bangladesh

In part of Battala slum, Dhaka City, Bangladesh shanties of bamboo have been constructed on raised platforms over a big ditch, which is used for all sorts of waste. Below the shanties is thick and greasy mud or water covered in water hyacinth. Rani worked as a maidservant in two houses. Her husband left her and married again. She lives in a bamboo shanty with her two children, since she earns very little. She has no alternative but to leave her children in that house. One day when she went to work, her two-year-old daughter dropped into the ditch and could not get out.

In the last two years five children have been lost in Battala this way. If a baby drops in, he or she drops with force and sinks deep into the greasy mud or goes into water under water hyacinths. Any rescue operation under the raised platforms is difficult. So there is no hope of getting back alive the babies that fall in.

"The cable goes through my kitchen and if a child touches it he will die...there are five to six families using the same connection." Parents—especially single parents—who must leave children to go for work are particularly worried. Leaving a child home risks injury, abduction or death (see box 4.5). Not going to work can mean penury and starvation.

The Challenge of Poor Places

Many places of the poor snare poor people in a web of disadvantages, including isolation, problems of water and energy, sewage, garbage, pollution, filth, environmental hazards, ill health, seasonal exposure to the worst conditions, insecurity of person and property, and stigma of place. These disadvantages are not universal, but many apply in many places much of the time. And they interlock as a trap.

In the struggle for livelihood and a better life, the places of the poor deepen deprivation. Poor places make it difficult for poor people to escape. Poor places keep people poor. And poor places also kill.

Notes

[1] This chapter draws on small group discussions of wellbeing and illbeing and the characteristics and proportion of different social groups in the community. Discussion groups also identify and rank their community's most pressing problems and priorities, assess whether the problems have changed over the past 10 years and discuss hopes for the future. Participants reflect on which problems the community could solve itself and which require outside support, and in a separate exercise they identify and evaluate the most important institutions in their daily lives and during a crisis.

[2] In weighing evidence, the seasonality of the fieldwork needs to be borne in mind. Researchers visited communities for this study mainly in February, March and April of 1999. On the one hand, in the countries in warmer climates north of the equator, these are generally better times of the year: in rural areas following harvest, when poor people tend to be relatively healthy and less poor. On the other hand, these months have a lot of rain for warmer countries south of the Equator, and farther north, it is still winter.

Chapter 5

The Body

Summary

Poor people repeatedly cite bodily illbeing as a part of the bad life. They often speak of being hungry, weak, sick, exhausted, in pain or mentally distressed. Recurring themes involve the body: importance of appearance; how a strong and healthy body is needed to work and earn a livelihood; how those who are hungry and weak cannot work well and consequently are paid less and less reliably; and how, in sum, health and strength matter most to those who have them least and who are most likely to lose them.

Participants identify ill health as both a cause and a consequence of poverty. Discussion groups in Africa and Latin America and the Caribbean list poor physical health more frequently than any other single condition as an impact of poverty. Especially in Malawi and Zambia, HIV/AIDS is seen as an acute problem. In discussing the cause and impacts of poverty, participants also point to the close relationship between poor mental and physical health and other aspects of the bad life, such as food insecurity. In case studies analyzed, multiple factors—loss of income coupled with cost of treatment and the transformation of a wage-earner into a dependent—make injury and illness common triggers of impoverishment.

In most countries, and especially in Africa and Eastern Europe and Central Asia, participants think health services have become more expensive and difficult to obtain. Combinations of factors deter and exclude poor people from receiving medical care: physical inaccessibility and the high cost of transportation; lack of medicines; legal and extralegal charges for treatment and medicines; time taken traveling and waiting; poor treatment; callous, rude, discriminatory and humiliating behavior by health staff; and their own, often deepening poverty and inability to pay.

On the positive side participants appreciate public food and income support, such as ration books and the public distribution system in India, samurdhi (a subsidy program) in Sri Lanka and free meals in Argentina. Poor people, especially in Brazil, praise committed and compassionate health workers. Even when traditional and private practitioners are more expensive, poor people often prefer them because they are more accessible, treat people more quickly, and allow payment by installments or in kind. Sri Lanka stands out as a country with a largely free, uncorrupt, and considerate medical service, contrasting with countries and conditions where poor people who are sick and injured cannot afford treatment and "just sleep and groan."

Introduction

For me, a good life is to be healthy.
—An old man, Dibdibe Wajtu Peasant Association,
Ethiopia

*Let hunger be ranked first because if you are hungry you
cannot work! No, health is number one because if you are
ill you cannot work.*
—Discussion group of women and men,
Musanya Village, Zambia

To be well and strong in the body and without hunger, discomfort or
worry feature repeatedly in participants' descriptions of the good life.
In describing illbeing, in contrast, they reveal how often and deeply they
suffer pain and distress from being hungry, weak, exhausted and sick.[1]

In discussion groups, physical health is by quite a margin the most frequently identified impact of poverty, exceeding even food. In Africa physical
health holds a striking lead over other effects of poverty, with crime in second place. Indeed, groups in Africa mention ill health more frequently as a
consequence of poverty than any other factor in any region. In Latin America
and the Caribbean it comes in first, with food second. In Eastern Europe and
Central Asia it places second after crime. In Asia, it is one of many impacts
of poverty.

The chapter opens with findings about the hardships of poor appearance,
hunger, exhaustion and illness. It then explores how poor people's bodies are
crucial but vulnerable assets, and the deeply impoverishing effects of illness
and injury. The next section highlights the series of obstacles faced by poor
people when seeking medical care, including corruption in fees, preferential
treatment for those with influence and money, difficulties getting to clinics
and hospitals, shortages of medicines, being asked to wait a long time for service, and being treated with rudeness and indifference by medical staff. The
chapter closes with some examples of positive experiences with public health
care and social assistance programs, and with traditional and private sources
of treatment.

How the Body Looks and Feels

Again and again, people describe the very poor as those with poor appearances, and those who cannot feed themselves adequately or afford
treatment when sick. More than appearances, participants stress the physical and mental experience of hunger, weakness, exhaustion and sickness.
Among these, hunger and sickness stand out most.

Physical Appearance

One part of physical wellbeing is to appear well and strong. Appearances matter especially for girls and young women. Female adolescents in Gowainghat, Bangladesh probably speak for many girls and young women in South Asia when they describe good quality of life as being able to eat to their heart's content and having a father who will provide them with clothes, oil for their hair and soap. In Malawi the poorest are known as "the stunted poor." In Ethiopia people say, "We are skinny" and "We are deprived and pale."

Hunger

> *They [the children] sometimes just get sick for no reason. Sometimes it's because of lack of food. We are poor. We have no money to buy or to feed ourselves. Now, everything is so expensive that we can only buy pasta, salt, and oil. Some days we have nothing to eat but* chichita *[a drink] because there is no money.*
>
> —A woman, Voluntad de Dios, Ecuador

Not surprisingly, participants often call food their highest priority. In wellbeing rankings, especially in rural areas, wellbeing groups are distinguished by the number of months of food security in a year and the number of meals a household usually has in a day. In numerous areas in different countries wellbeing is linked with being able to have three meals a day.

Pressing problems of hunger appear most frequently in the reports from Africa. Food insecurity is a pervasive preoccupation in the rural and some urban areas in Ethiopia, Ghana, Malawi, Nigeria and Zambia, and especially for refugees in Somaliland. Across all groups in Zambia, access to food is perceived as the main determining characteristic of wellbeing and wealth. It is perhaps indicative that a group of youth in Zambia analyzing causes and impacts of poverty make it "poverty/hunger." Especially in Africa the poorer groups in communities often report that they can have only one meal a day, usually lunch, and that they are hungry at night. Some occasionally go without food for days.

Though most widespread in African communities, such deprivation is also found elsewhere (see box 5.1). Poor people in Bangladesh, Ecuador, India and Indonesia frequently mention hunger to the researchers. Food insecurity and hunger is the second most frequently mentioned impact of poverty in Latin America and the Caribbean. Despite Sri Lanka's relatively effective support for poor people, they report hunger there too.

Researchers uncovered surprising degrees of food shortage and even quiet individual starvation in the Eastern European and Central Asian countries. In one community in rural Kyrgyz Republic six out of eight groups

Box 5.1 Hunger Even in Sri Lanka

Many poor families have to be satisfied with one full meal a day. A housewife from a poor family in Elhena/Ganegoda, Sri Lanka relates how they manage to spend the day forgoing meals. Her husband who goes out to work as a wood cutter has to be satisfied with a cup of tea for lunch while the children who attend after-school classes have only a light meal for lunch. The dinner is the only meal prepared for the day. It consists of rice and one curry.

discussing changes in wellbeing identify "malnutrition and hunger" as replacing "enough for everyone" and "a nutritious diet." In Dimitrovgrad, Bulgaria a group of men and women comment, "We're so hungry that we can barely stand on our feet."

Poor people have diverse responses to food shortages and hunger. The hungry sometimes resort to theft. Those who steal tend to explain their actions as necessary to feed their children. People also turn to God. In Dobile Yirkpong, Ghana a men's discussion group says that, to cope with declines in wellbeing and periods of hunger, they "pray to God for help and for peace of mind."

Exhaustion: Poverty of Energy and Time

> *A normal person has to have some self-esteem, to take a*
> *holiday, read a book. While now—you work here or there*
> *all day in order to have something to eat, and at night you*
> *can't even exchange a couple of words like normal persons,*
> *you drop off asleep as if you were dead. It's as if you were*
> *dead while you were still alive.*
>
> —A middle-aged woman, Bulgaria

Again and again, participants speak of the stress of hard work when underfed. Older men in rural Bangladesh say that they have to work very hard on very little food. Participants in a discussion group from Paján, Ecuador report, "People look desperate. There is nothing to eat...there are people in the fields who only drink a little water with herbs in it and a roasted banana, that's why they are malnourished, but imagine if we didn't get a harvest, they couldn't even eat the banana."

"Time poverty" compounds these difficulties for many, especially women. As the burden of work to earn incomes shifts to more and more poor women, they have more and more to do. Many women lack time for anything but work and tending others. A Vietnam report says of a 29-year-old woman supporting a chronically sick husband, a mother-in-law aged 70, and five children, "[Her] life is about managing time." The increasing burdens of women's expanded roles mean they have little or no time to rest, reflect, enjoy social life, or take part in community or religious activities.

In poor people's analyses of the causes of poverty, laziness and apathy are quite commonly cited. This seems to conflict with the perception that many poor people are hardworking and resilient. The apparent contradiction, however, might be resolved this way: workers short of food become exhausted. "Apathy" and "laziness" minimize effort. Such attitudes and behavior can be seen as a strategy for conserving energy. A man in Kajima, Ethiopia says: "We eat when we have. We sleep when we don't." "Laziness," apathy and sleep save energy and food.

Some poor people, some or much of the time, are underoccupied. But many are stressed by too much to do. Many activities are harder and take longer for poorer people than for the less poor. Fetching and queuing for water is an example, demanding both time and energy. Going to the toilet can be time-consuming: in Chittagong, Bangladesh a serious shortage of toilets means that every day a long queue forms outside them. Accessing governmental and other services also often takes much time and physical energy, with many communities distant, isolated and with inadequate roads and transportation. In addition to the service fees, the time and travel costs of getting medical attention deter many.

Sickness of Body and Mind

During the study, poor people mentioned quite a broad range of injuries and illnesses: broken limbs, burns, poisoning from chemicals and pollution, diabetes, pneumonia, bronchitis, tuberculosis, HIV/AIDS, asthma, diarrhea, typhoid, malaria, parasites from contaminated water, skin infections and other debilitating diseases. Mental health problems are often raised jointly with concerns about sickness and injury. Poor people also frequently discuss hardships associated with drug and alcohol abuse.

Mental health problems—stress, anxiety, depression, lack of self-esteem and suicide—are among the more commonly identified effects of poverty and illbeing by discussion groups. They are most frequently mentioned in Latin America and the Caribbean and least frequently in Asia. A middle-aged participant in Bijeljina, Bosnia and Herzegovina notes connections: "The rise in the number of people with heart complaints, high blood pressure, depression has become normal for us. There is not a person in Tombak that does not suffer from at least one of [these]. All of this has been brought on by poverty and war." In some African communities, people often describe a mental condition associated with poverty as "madness." The researchers' report from Barrio Sol y Verde, an urban site in Argentina, describes depression and a sense of impotence. Death is very present in different ways: sickness, accidents, physical aggression related to crime, or family mishap and suicide. A common theme is the stress of not being able to provide for one's family. In the words of an older woman in Isla

Trinitaria, Ecuador with 18 children: "I want to commit suicide, I want to run out...because to see the kids crying and I do not have one sucre to give them some bread...life is so sad."

People associate all forms of sickness and abuse with stress, anguish and illbeing, but participants pick out three for special mention: HIV/AIDS, alcoholism and drugs.

Those who took part in the discussions in Argentina, Ghana, Jamaica, Thailand, Vietnam, and several other countries mention HIV/AIDS as a problem. Its impact is by far the most marked in Malawi and Zambia, where poor people frequently raise and discuss the subject. In Zambia a group of youth made a causal diagram that links poverty to prostitution to AIDS and finally to death. Many people there are dying of AIDS and related diseases, which affect livelihoods and strain the extended family.

Poor people foresee a bleak future. The problem of orphans is serious and becoming worse. In Mwadzulu, Malawi a group of village women say, "These children lack many things in their lives, and we cannot manage to provide them with everything." Discussion groups in another village predict that AIDS will force a lot more people into poverty in the near future: "We do not think that life will become any better for our children and even for generations to come."

Groups in many places mention a syndrome of poverty—money spent on alcohol or other drugs, male drunkenness and domestic violence. In Latin America and the Caribbean, ill health is the most frequently mentioned impact of poverty. People link it with disease, alcoholism and drug abuse. Poor people regard drug use and alcoholism as causes of violence, insecurity and thefts.

Alcoholism is especially prevalent among men. In both urban and rural Africa poor people mention it more frequently than drugs. A cause-and-

---

Box 5.2 Drug Abuse and Misery

When I give money for bread, my heart aches, but when it is for—heroin—I feel so nice, my soul feels so pleasant, I feel great. But then I wake up in poverty, and it is horrible.

—Kamen, a 30-year-old heroin user, Bulgaria

This heroin has ruined my life. Look at my arms [shows his arms, all in beads from inoculations]. And it hurts a lot. I have very bad pains; I am dying. Can you arrange for me to get into a hospital?

—Aldin, an 18-year-old heroin user, Bulgaria

Now there are nine-year-olds taking drugs. Their parents see them so drugged up that they cannot do anything, so they just protect the other children.

—A woman, La Matanza, Argentina

impact diagram, resulting from several group discussions in Kuphera, Malawi shows that beer-drinking leads to promiscuity and diseases and then to death. In Eastern Europe and Central Asia poor people see alcoholism as a significant consequence of poverty and as linked with other aspects of the bad life. In Ak Kiya village in the Kyrgyz Republic a woman says, "There are a lot of people in this village who drink vodka in the morning, and then go and do something bad, commit crime." Many discussion groups from all regions in the study report problems of physical abuse of women when husbands come home drunk.

Drug abuse is mentioned frequently, especially in urban areas, including urban Latin America, Bangkok and Ho Chi Minh City. It also comes up in parts of Bulgaria, Kyrgyz Republic, Russia and Uzbekistan. Those addicted are miserable, as are those who are worried about their addicted children (see box 5.2).

The Body as an Asset

> *We have nothing but our hands.*
> —A resident, Ha Tinh, Vietnam

> *I have been overstrained with the number of deliveries I have made, which has made me too weak to work.*
> —A mother of seven, Dorapalli, Andhra Pradesh, India

For many poor people, the body is their main asset. For some, it is the only asset they have. The poorer people are, and the less educated or skilled, the more their livelihood is likely to involve physical work, whether in farming or other physical urban or rural activities. Shortage of food and sickness then not only cause pain and anguish but also weaken and devalue the asset and reduce returns to work. Risk and vulnerability are high: the body is both indivisible and uninsured. Where accident or sickness makes work by a breadwinner impossible, food and income supplies cease. And paying for treatment further impoverishes a family. At a stroke, the body can flip from being the main asset to being a costly liability. As the researchers from Bedsa, Egypt write, "The poor always say that their strength or health is their main capital."

Poor people are therefore vulnerable to situations in which they overexert or maltreat their bodies, as they may do to gain a livelihood. Excessively hard or unhealthy work can lead to sickness. The Malawi National Report observes that "some people from households that are desperate resort to casual labor that they said is hazardous to their health because they said in most cases, they tend to overwork themselves with the aim of making more money. Their wages are miserable." A man in Olmalyq, Uzbekistan, whose work in bad conditions in a zinc factory made him ill, lost his job. As economic conditions deteriorate, people can work harder with greater ill effects: in Thailand all the groups at Kaoseng spoke of the problems of unemployment, debts and the rising costs of living. The research team reports, "They unanimously agreed to work harder, regardless of the workload and time. Some worked until they were sick."

For poor women, girls, and some boys, their bodies are potentially income-earning assets in sex work. In the words of a group of women in Malawi, "There is no reason for them to suffer when they have money in their bodies..." But this has its well-known hazards. In Malawi researchers report, "Many women have over the years become prostitutes, and this has led to family breakdowns...some have contracted HIV/AIDS."

The hungry and weak are also vulnerable in another way: they are liable to be paid less. Occasionally this is charitable: some people may be employed at a minimal rate to give them some income, food and self-respect, like an old widow in Ghana (see box 5.3). More often, employers are exploiting the workers. In a fishing community in Malawi participants complain that employers usually take advantage of people's desperate situations to make them work more for low wages. A group of men say,

> ...we get some K 5.00, buy some maize for one day's consumption; when it is finished we go again.... The problem is that these boat owners know that we are starving. As such we would accept any little wages they would offer to us because they know we are very desperate...we want to save our children from dying....

Food and health are thus fundamental not just to physical and mental wellbeing but also to sustain adequate livelihoods. Whether vicious or benign, the causality is circular (see figure 5.1).

A seasonal dimension further aggravates problems of inadequate work, health risks and other disadvantages that poor people face. In winters of cold weather climates, these include enduring isolation and cold. When asked how her family survived the winter, a poor woman from Ak Kiya, Kyrgyz Republic replied, "It was difficult. Children didn't have food for five to six days."

Box 5.3 Sick, Weak and Cannot Work Well

In rural Ghana a poor and old widow borrowed money to pay for the coffin and funeral when her husband died. She lives now as a day worker. She manages to buy soap, but not clothes. The amount paid to her for a day's weeding is small, but "she admitted that because she is old, she cannot weed much so that people who employ her do so just for kindness."

In the words of a report from Egypt, "the poorer group in the community cannot afford to treat themselves. This causes them to feel tired, or illness eventually disables them. At the end, illness and inability to afford medical treatment decreases the ability to work in poorer households."

In the rainy seasons of tropical climates many disadvantages afflict poor rural people at the same time, including shortages of food, indebtedness, sickness, and hard work. Researchers in Khaliajuri, Bangladesh note that "due to minimum food intake in crisis period, men and women cannot do labor-intensive work. Consequently, they do not get proper wages from the employer on time." The hungry and weak may then not only be paid less, they may be paid less reliably. There and elsewhere in the study, rainy seasons can be times of exhaustion; sickness (such as malaria, Guinea Worm disease, dengue fever, diarrheas, skin diseases, eye infections and snakebite—reportedly rampant in one Ghanaian site); discomfort in cold, wet, dirty and unsanitary conditions; flooding and landslides; leaks and collapse of housing; isolation from markets, supplies and services; malnourishment; and neglect of children. It is a time when children most waste and die. The rains are also a time of agonizing choices, when adults are tired, sick, and hungry: a time of having to trade off one illbeing against another and of choosing who in the family will suffer.

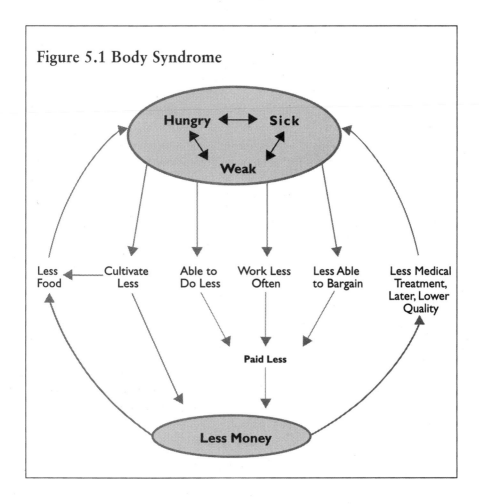

Figure 5.1 Body Syndrome

Body Blows: How Injury, Illness and Their Costs Impoverish

We face a calamity when my husband gets ill. Our life comes to a halt until he recovers and goes back to work.
— A poor woman, Zawyet Sultan, Egypt

Poor people cannot improve their status because they live day by day, and if they get sick then they are in trouble because they have to borrow money and pay interest.
— A woman, Tra Vinh, Vietnam

Poor people from very different contexts remark on the incidence and impact of injury and illness. These effects are perhaps less conspicuous as a general phenomenon at the group and community level than at the personal and household level where they can be dramatic and disastrous. Their devastating effects are borne out in selected case studies of individuals and households where illness, injury and death are common triggers that make poor people poorer (see also chapter 11).

Participants in India and Vietnam emphasize how impoverishing injury and illness can be. The India National Report concludes that "expenditure on health appeared to be by far the strongest impediment for a poor household to remain afloat. Households with sick and elderly people were invariably on the brink, on account of heavy expenditure on treatment of the patients."

Similarly in Vietnam long-term illness or death is one of the most frequently mentioned reasons for family difficulties. In Ho Chi Minh City a research team reports:

> *Any serious illness in a poor family will inevitably aggravate their poverty, since there is seldom enough money in hand to cover the cost of treatment hospitalization. Some families sell their house, if they have one to sell, in order to pay such costs, or borrow money from loan sharks for this purpose, which leads to a further loan being taken to repay the first.*

Case studies (see box 5.4) also illustrate how disabling, costly, sudden and devastating illness and injury can be for poor households, especially when a breadwinner or other active adult is struck down. A common scenario starts with an immediate loss of income from work. The sick or injured person needs care. Either the afflicted person goes without treatment, or the costs impoverish the family: assets are sold and debts taken on. A downward spiral begins from which there is no recovery. Food becomes scarce and children malnourished. Children are withdrawn from school to save money and to work. The poor household becomes permanently poorer. Where an active

Box 5.4 How Accidents and Sickness Make People Poor

Accident and permanent disability

A man from El Afweyne, Somaliland is 50 years old. His livestock died from disease. He then worked as a porter loading and unloading trucks. A pile of food grains fell on him when he was carrying a 50-kilogram sack, breaking his left hand and right leg. He was bedridden for about a month. The children were very young, and the family had nothing to survive on. One child died of malnutrition. Since then he has been handicapped, and the family depends on gifts from neighbors and relatives. He has no aspirations because, he says, "We have no wealth, nor am I strong enough to improve the situation."

Costly but ineffective treatment

A man in Lao Cai, Vietnam is 26 years old. His family has 12 members. They used to be one of the richest families in the village, but now they are one of the poorest. In recent years they have suffered two shocks. First, his father died two years ago. That left only two main laborers in the family—him and his mother, aged 40. He has two young children. Two years ago, his daughter also had a serious illness and needed an operation. His family had to sell four buffaloes, one horse, and two pigs to cover the expenses of getting treatment. The operation cost several million VND, but she is still not cured. All the people in his community helped, but no one can contribute more than 20,000 VND. His younger brother—who was studying in grade 6, had to leave school to help his family. The man says that if his daughter had not been ill, his family would still have many buffaloes, he could have a house for his younger brother, and his younger brother could study further.

Disability and costs of treatment combined

A woman in Geruwa, India is 30 years old and the mother of four daughters, the eldest of whom is seven and the youngest still in her lap. Her husband used to work in a dairy, cleaning buffaloes. For over a year now he has been suffering from diabetes and can no longer do labor-intensive work. To raise money for her husband's treatment she sold her house and her land to another resident of the village for Rs 1,300, although the actual current value was over Rs 20,000. She knows she was underpaid but feels indebted to the buyer because he has allowed her to retain a small room in the house to keep her ailing husband and children. She has taken over supporting the family by carrying on her head wood for fuel a distance of about 10 kilometers every other day. She has little hope for the future. She lives hand to mouth, for her daily earning hardly suffices for 2 kilograms of rice a day. Her daughters do not go to school, and she is hardly keen that they should do so. She laments the closure of the government ration shop, due to corruption, where her red card let her purchase subsidized rice and oil.

adult dies, the ratio of dependents to adults jumps up. Where an active adult is permanently disabled and dependent, it is even worse, with a person who cannot earn but must be fed.

Health expenditures wipe out savings. The more a poor household has saved and accumulated, the more it has to lose. But often the poorer cannot obtain or afford health treatment. So those who are most exposed to health risks, whose work entails most risk of accident or debilitation, and who are most dependent on the strength of their bodies—in short, those who need health care most—are those who can afford and obtain it least. And when they do obtain it, they are the most impoverished by the cost, having to sell assets and take on debt.

Troubles with Treatment

We do not go to the hospital because it is necessary to bring our bed linen, dishes, sometimes even a bed.
—A young women Muynak, Uzbekistan

You go to the hospital, you have to get a number, you go to the guard, the nurses are chatting. You have to wait until they fancy giving you a number...“Is the doctor here?” “No, the doctor isn't here.” They lie.
—A 25-year-old woman in Los Juríes, Argentina

The importance to poor people of access to good affordable health care is difficult to exaggerate.

This is not just for reasons of love and compassion for close relatives and others who are sick, or concern for personal bodily wellbeing. Again and again it is also for livelihood and survival. Good treatment relieves pain and suffering; it is also an investment in restoring the body as means of gaining a livelihood.

It is not surprising that poor people so often simply do not go for treatment. As explored below, poor people face problems of distance, transportation, time required for travel, suffering or danger of death while traveling, shortages or lack of medicines, costs (for transportation, treatment, bribes, and medicine), discrimination that humiliates and delays in treatment, staff absenteeism, callousness, and ineffective treatment—all or some of which can combine as disincentives in any one situation, amplified by uncertainties at every step.

Very many poor people in the study thus regard accessible, effective and affordable health treatment as a priority when ranking institutions of local importance. The patterns vary, however. In Malawi especially, all groups give clinics and hospitals high ratings (first to fourth place) for importance, for reasons including medical care, early childhood clinics, prenatal clinics, and reducing mortality of both adults and children. Elsewhere, the priorities that men, women, youth and the elderly attach to health facilities varied. In Khaliajuri in Bangladesh middle-aged women and old men cared the most. In Egypt women rate them higher than men, except for men who are manual laborers and men with chronic illnesses.

Women generally focus more on health problems of the family than on their own health problems.

Participants in Africa and in Eastern Europe and Central Asia feel that health care is becoming less accessible, less affordable and worse. The picture is more mixed in Latin America and the Caribbean and in Asia.

Lacking Physical Access and Medicines

> *While you are healthy it is OK, but if you get a snakebite that is not simple, you have to go to Los Juríes and hope to God it's not a stormy day with much rain. How would you get a sick person out of here? Walking it is impossible, a vehicle would not get out, you could not go by horse— how long does it take to go by horse?! The ill person would die!*
>
> —A young woman, Los Juríes, Argentina

Distance to health-care facilities, problems and costs of reaching them, and lack of medicines often make obtaining treatment difficult.

In Africa and elsewhere, people report a sheer lack of health posts, clinics and hospitals—and discouraging distances to the ones that exist. Rural areas suffer the most marked lack of services. In discussing problems in obtaining medical care, participants in parts of Ethiopia, Ghana, Malawi, Somaliland and Zambia mention the long distances that have to be traversed more often than problems of cost or quality. The same is true at least in parts of Bangladesh, Brazil, Bulgaria, and Jamaica. The study teams heard of people dying or babies being born ("under the tree") on the way to hospital. In Malawi an increase in disease, especially HIV/AIDS, has made the lack of accessible facilities a more pressing problem.

In a number of countries, the lack of drugs at treatment centers compounds the problems of distance and transportation. In Malawi, researchers report men's and women's groups as saying they used to have drugs at a health center 10 kilometers away, "but these days when we go there we are told there are no drugs and we travel all the 30 kilometers to Mangochi to get treatment"; "...there is no medicine to treat people with. We just trouble ourselves traveling to the hospital just to get two aspirin tablets." "In the past we also used to have an ambulance which transported serious patients to Mangochi, but these days we are told to hire cars, so where do they expect us go get cash?" As they put it, "Diseases are not ending due to lack of medicine."

Time Spent

The time taken to travel, get treated, buy medicines and return is a widespread complaint and a disincentive to going for treatment at all (see box 5.5); it is aggravated by discrimination in favor of those of higher status and those who could pay bribes. A 25-year-old mother in Los Juríes, Argentina, describes what can happen:

> *The people in town...can go in the afternoon. We in the country get up at 6 a.m. to take the collective bus. We arrive. We go to the doctor at the hospital. You arrive at 8 a.m. or sometimes not until 1 p.m. You are stuck there until the afternoon, without eating, without being able to drink a* mate *(traditional drink) first, so as not to lose time...you spend hours and hours hungry. You have to go back before the doctor has seen you. You miss the bus. You have to go however you can...so you can get home, even walking.*

Financial Costs

> *We are not allowed to get sick anymore because we have to pay for medication...what with?*
> —An older man, Zenica, Bosnia and Herzegovina

> *Poverty makes them helpless in the face of diseases as the health services are too expensive for them.*
> —A man, Nchimishi, Zambia

> *Before medical treatment was free, now one has to pay for everything.*
> —An unemployed man, Ivanovo, Russia

I have a daughter who came from Esmeraldas with pains in her legs...I have no means to take her to the doctor...that's why I say that life is sad, because I don't have any way to pay for a doctor, an injection or anything.

—A woman, Isla Trinitaria, Ecuador

The high costs of treatment and drugs are problems in countries as diverse as Bosnia and Herzegovina, India, Kyrgyz Republic, Malawi, Russia, Uzbekistan and Zambia. Costs have risen for different reasons: official policy in some cases, corruption in others, and frequently both. In consequence, poor people tend to be excluded or to exclude themselves. As a researcher in Belasovka, Russia notes, "In cases of sickness, the patient has to buy his own medicines, which, considering average income rates, is practically impossible if the illness is really serious." The costs compound the stress of sickness. In Los Juríes, Argentina the president of the Neighborhood Commission says "...it is not enough that a doctor gives you a prescription if you can't afford to buy it...if you don't even have enough to eat, then the doctor gives you a prescription of $30, that does not cure a thing, on the contrary, it is worse, what with the worry that it causes."

In Bower Bank, Jamaica a daughter of a mother of eight was badly burned with boiling water. She took her daughter to hospital. She had no money, but managed to beg the money to register her. However, she could not pay for the treatment her daughter received. Later her daughter needed to return because she could not use her hand properly. But the hospital would not see her until the earlier bill for treatment was paid.

Even when there are propoor reforms that make health care more accessible, the poorest can still experience problems. In one Indonesian community, medical facilities have improved, but the documentation requirements remain a problem for the poorest. Although entitled to free treatment, they have to have a health card, which they have difficulty obtaining. Those without the card have to borrow money or postpone going to a hospital until their illness becomes severe. In Ethiopia, during several recent epidemics of diarrhea and typhoid, many poor people were reported to have died before they could complete the long process to receive the certification they needed for free hospital care.

The Behavior of Medical and Health Staff

The hospital is like a prison.

—Participant, discussion group of men and women, Magadan, Russia

Poor people complain about the lack of medical staff. Understaffing is noted in Brazil and Nigeria, and absenteeism in Bangladesh and Egypt. When staff are present, say poor people in Bangladesh, they give rushed and ineffective consultations. In Borg Meghezel, Egypt people receive what is meant to be free medical care, but villagers report, "There isn't a single tablet in the clinic and the doctor has turned it into his private clinic." Elsewhere, poor people say that the absence of physicians is critical in emergencies and that people are given the same pills for everything. In other countries, poor people report wide discrimination against them, rudeness, and corruption.

Preferential treatment goes to those who are well dressed, or have influence or money, while those without money are penalized. In El Mataria, Egypt a woman says, "At the hospital they do nothing to people unless they are staff relatives, or rich people that have power or authority." Another participant in El Mataria says, "One time my leg was broken and I went to the hospital for treatment. I was shocked when the doctor told me that 'you are all right and you do not have a broken leg'! I went to a private doctor as I had no other choice." In Belaskova, Russia remarks made by discussion group participants include "You have to pay the dentist; otherwise, they just stuff your tooth with sand and it all falls out." In Takhtakupyr, Uzbekistan two men were taken to the hospital and diagnosed to have life-threatening poisoning from having drunk bad vodka. The man with relatives who could put up the money for treatment survived. The second man, with no family to pay for him, died.

In Sofia, Bulgaria a special discussion group was held with nurses and a participant there might have been speaking for many other nurses in saying:

> There are elderly people who spend half the week in the
> hospital. They just refuse to understand that there are also
> other people who are ill, that the times are different now.
> They accuse us. Or there are others who start explaining
> that they are old, that they have no money for medicines.
> Then they start insulting us. Or they complain: "So when we
> grow old, you do not need us any more and want us to die
> (kutcheta ni jali—let the dogs eat us)." As if we can change
> something. There is no money for free drugs. I cannot feel
> [good] when there are people abandoned by everybody like
> them, and me not being able to do anything.

When whole health systems are stressed, it is hard for good staff as well as for patients.

Poor Quality

Whoever goes to the health clinic healthy comes out sick.
—Participant, discussion group of men and women,
Borg Meghezel, Egypt

Poor people are sensitive to quality. Talking of the hospital in Los Juríes, Argentina a group of men call it an important institution, but "you go and they don't attend to you, there are no medicines, it's a disaster." In La Calera,

Ecuador a young man says, "In the hospitals they don't provide good care to the indigenous people like they ought to; because of their illiteracy they treat them badly...they give us other medicines that are not for the health problem you have." In one village in Vietnam nearly all the families interviewed say that they took, or will take, family members to the border security guards who have some medical training and supplies to treat more serious illnesses. The health station and the border post are the same distance, and treatment and medication at both are free. But as a man explains, "People don't go to the medical station because the professional skills of the health workers are low."

Positive Experiences

> Whenever we get sick, we go to the government hospital and
> get cured.
>   —A 38-year-old poor woman, Vellur, Sri Lanka

Against the depressing backdrop of ineffective government services, a few positive experiences are also reported.

Poor people widely appreciate food and income support programs. Programs like Samurdhi (a subsidy program) in Sri Lanka, ration shops supplying cheap or free food to the poorest in India, food stamps in Jamaica, soup kitchens in Argentina and Ecuador, and the food supplied to a refugee camp in Bosnia and Herzegovina provide a partial floor under the poorest, mitigating their destitution and providing at least part of their basic needs for food. In Barrio Sol y Verde in Argentina women rate the local health post highly: "We go there more than anywhere for medicines...and there are boxes of groceries for old people, and they give you milk every day." In Dock Sud, Argentina a group of women rate the health post top of all institutions, saying, "it is important because they are the only ones who provide care for us." The Brazil National Report notes that the most striking aspect of participants' assessment of institutions is that, despite the ubiquitous criticisms of government and politicians, the people very positively evaluate governmental community health programs and food distribution schemes.

In health services, contrasting with the frequently grim picture of lack of access, discrimination, corruption, and inadequate treatment, some good examples do stand out.

Participants generally appreciate local workers more than those who work in distant clinics and hospitals. Village doctors in Bangladesh are an example. In Brazil poor people highly praise the programs that provide health care to people in their places of residence and unanimously regard them as very efficient. This high regard extends to the health community officers and staff of Saúde em Casa of whom it is said in Itabuna, despite some queuing and rationing: "If the problem cannot be solved there...they take us to hospital ... they give preference to senior citizens...they have a general practitioner, a dentist...it is very good for the community." As often in other contexts, poor people trust and value local workers and institutions.

Elsewhere, in the midst of bad practice, poor people point to outstanding, selfless and committed individuals who provide good service. For example:

▶ In Bangladesh men at Gowainghat identify the government family planning worker as one of the most important institutions because, they say, he stands by them in their moments of crisis. He takes information and prescribes medicines for sick people. He even collects medicine for them when he does not have it himself. Above all he gives them good advice.

▶ In Malawi a group of poor men and women say that in 1997 the Ministry of Health and Population sent a staff member from Zomba Central Hospital to help a village health committee. "He is a hardworking man because he can come any time when called or even at night. He does not favor anybody; he treats us equally."

▶ In Nigeria a clinic is seen as "the toast and savior of the community" in Elieke Rumuokoro. It was founded because of restricted access to the hospitals and clinics in Port Harcourt. It is available to poor people and ready to help with their health problems. The clinic allows patients to pay their bills in installments and even dispenses drugs free to those who cannot pay. The proprietor readily refers cases he cannot handle to hospitals that can do so, in contrast with the practice of some unscrupulous clinic owners who will keep the patient to die and then charge a high bill.

▶ In Los Juríes, Argentina a young woman says of a private doctor, "You go at any time and he sees to you. You go day or night; whatever the time is he gets up and sees to you.... We go and we say to him, look doctor today we haven't got enough for the consultation...he sees us. Now he has a pharmacy...take all the medicines you need and pay me when you have it...all our family give thanks to this doctor...."

Even where corruption is believed to be rampant, there can be surprises. In Ivanovo, Russia one man in a discussion group of unemployed had been treated recently in a hospital and his arm was still bandaged. He felt rather awkward in telling the others he had been given medicine and injections, all free: "I was surprised myself."

Though it is rare for mainline government health systems to be well regarded, two exceptions stand out: newly created federal health schemes are highly rated at five areas in Brazil, and in Sri Lanka poor people appreciate and usually hold in high regard the government health service as a whole. There is, to be sure, one hospital that is not visited because the doctor is said to be callous with patients, and one case where a man reports that he had paid money to get a doctor's care, but these were exceptions. Elsewhere in Sri Lanka, and more typically, there are remarks like "The village people believe that doctors and the facilities available at this hospital are excellent" and "The two new doctors are very kind to patients." There is also a sense of service getting better, as was articulated by a discussion group participant in Ihalagama, Sri Lanka:

> *About two years ago, as medicine was not available at the hospital, we had to get it from private pharmacies. Now it is not so. The hospital has undergone a cleanup, and now more doctors are present and the hospital pharmacy has enough medicines. We do not have to go to private pharmacies any more.*

Private Treatment

Participants often value traditional and private treatment, finding it more accessible, easier to pay for and faster.

Traditional and private treatment is usually closer to hand than formal health services, requiring less travel. In Lao Cai villages in Vietnam, taking a sick child to the commune health center, which might be 2 to 6 kilometers away, means that the family could lose a day's labor. Along the same lines, a woman in Samalamkulan, Sri Lanka, who had asthma, went for private treatment because she could not wait for hours in the government hospital. Local practitioners might also make home visits.

Arrangements for payment are usually flexible: even if traditional and private treatment are more expensive, payment can typically be deferred, or given in kind or through labor. Exceptionally, poor people could have the best of both worlds: the Chitambo Mission Hospital in Muchinka, Zambia is reported to be "very helpful to the community by allowing them to pay for medical services in kind—beans, chickens, and maize."

The Challenge

There is perhaps no better way to sum up the development challenge on health than to note the starkly contrasting experiences reported during the study.

Poor people in Sri Lanka, for instance, have basic food support in the Samurdhi program and access to good state-provided medical services. From Ihalagama, Sri Lanka researchers note, "Villagers say they are lucky to have hospitals which provide free medical services. Otherwise they would have died long ago."

Elsewhere, poor people are denied treatment by poverty and lack of services. For example, in Ethiopia an old man says:

> *Poverty snatched away my wife from me. When she got sick, I tried my best to cure her with tebel [holy water] and woukabi [spirits], for these were the only things a poor person could*

afford. However, God took her away. My son too was killed
by malaria. Now I am alone.

In Malawi, of those who cannot afford transport to hospital, and who cannot pay for private treatment, it is said, "they just sleep and groan."

Notes

[1]This chapter draws much of its evidence from poor people's descriptions and analyses of wellbeing and illbeing, of problems and priorities, of causes and impacts of poverty, their experiences with institutions, and also from case studies. While health concerns frequently emerge from these topics, the discussions generally did not focus on specific health issues and their impacts on particular social groups, such as poor women, men, elderly and children.

Chapter 6

Gender Relations in Troubled Transition

Summary

Women's and men's roles are going through major changes, creating turmoil at the household level. In many cases male unemployment and deepening economic stress have placed greater responsibilities on women to seek paid work. Some women are finding that their increased earnings help to increase their decisionmaking authority in the household, but the extent of changes reported vary widely across countries and communities. Women report heavy work burdens as they add livelihood responsibilities to their household duties.

Men express humiliation and anger over being unable to maintain their role as the household's main or sole breadwinner. Discussion groups indicate rising alcohol and drug abuse among men and increased domestic conflicts. Physical violence against women is widespread and has increased in some communities. However, in others levels of domestic physical violence are declining. This is associated with women's increased economic role and with increased awareness, participation in women's groups, and supportive actions by NGOs, churches, the media and in some cases, the police.

Introduction

If you have a job at all now, you're overworked and under-
paid.

—A young woman, Dimitrovgrad, Bulgaria

My husband who is not working has taken to hard drinking...
I have to feed and clothe him in addition to my children. All
the above has made life very hard for me now since my income
is not much.

—A woman, Tabe Ere, Ghana

The insufficiency of income is what affects the man-woman
relationship. Sometimes she wakes me up in the morning ask-
ing for five pounds, and if I don't have it I get depressed and
I leave the house. And when I come back, we start to fight.

—A man, Borg Meghezel, Egypt

Poor people across a majority of communities state that women's roles are undergoing tremendous change.[1] As men's and women's sense of well-being is often linked to their gender identities, the shifts in these identities are a source of deep anxiety for both sexes. With increased economic hardship and rising male unemployment, poor women are working outside the home in larger numbers than ever to supplement, sometimes very substantially, household budgets. Women's rising economic responsibilities, however, do not automatically give them greater power and security in their households.

The chapter opens with findings on women's greatly increased economic activities, and then reviews highlights on changes in gender roles, responsibilities and decisionmaking in the household. Many women report feeling overburdened with having to add or increase livelihood responsibilities on top of their household chores; however, they do acknowledge greater influence over household decisions, but with strong differences across countries and communities. Men often share feelings of humiliation and anger over being unable to maintain their status as the sole or main breadwinner in the home.

The next section focuses on poor people's definitions and causes of domestic abuse. Discussion groups of both sexes acknowledge the presence of more intense quarreling between husbands and wives as well as alcohol and drug abuse among men, and often link these trends to increasing economic hardship. As a woman from El Gawaber, Egypt confides, "Problems have affected our relationship. The day my husband brings in money we are all right together. The day he stays at home [out of work] we are fighting constantly." The chapter then moves into findings on trends in physical violence against women in the household. A very large number of communities report that domestic violence exists where they live; however, trends in the level of violence are mixed, with strong regional differences.

Changing Gender Roles and Responsibilities

Both men's and women's roles and responsibilities are in flux and are a source of turmoil within households in many parts of the world.

Diversification of Women's Work

We women will work for what no man would work for. Women will come down to get better or to keep the home going, but the man stands on his pride.

—A woman, Jamaica

Before, day cares were not needed, but now they have the young ones all day and they feed them because before the women did not have to work with what the men were able to earn.

—A woman, Moreno, Argentina

Across the study countries, women are stepping outside of their household responsibilities to earn a living and help bring food to the table. Typically, women's livelihood activities include petty trade, vending, casual labor (including agricultural labor), factory employment, piecework and service sector jobs (mainly menial and poorly paid work). As the team from Malawi writes in their report, "Many men have been retrenched, are jobless, and do not have any steady sources of income. As a result, women have assumed the role of the breadwinner in many households."

In several places people stress that the poorer the household, the more likely it is that the woman will be involved in some form of work outside the household. In the village of Borg Meghezel, Egypt a married woman reports, "The good woman doesn't work. Her husband is the one who travels and has boats as well as money in the bank." The researchers from India report that more women of disadvantaged castes and tribes are taking jobs outside the home than women in other castes.

While it is not new for women to be involved in some economic activities, participants indicate that pressure on women to secure a livelihood is far stronger today, and reports from nearly all communities narrate the trend of increasing numbers of women entering into temporary wage employment and informal commerce.[2] Poor people most frequently mention male unemployment as the principal factor driving women to work, but other important factors include improvements in women's education status, greater awareness about rights, and increased access to information (media), credit, property and NGO-supported activities. In Eastern Europe and Central Asia women are benefiting from reduced barriers to trade. There and in Latin America and the Caribbean a growing service sector has also opened up opportunities for women. In many communities around the world men and women mention that women are more willing than men to take up menial and very low-paying work.

Participants in discussion groups from Kowerani Masasa, Malawi explain that "times have changed" and women "need not rely on their husbands" but rather "have to complement" them by working because men "do not have well-defined [substantive] means of livelihood." In Doryumu, Ghana, researchers observe similarly, "women have taken over some of the functions of their husbands like providing for all the needs of the children and making decisions because the men are not gainfully employed." A discussion group of men and women from Umuoba Road, Nigeria explains that women assume the responsibilities for paying school fees, purchasing clothing, and providing food when the husband is jobless or deceased; even when husbands do bring in income, women also supplement household expenses. In the village of El Gawaber, Egypt women are working less on family farms and engaging increasingly in wage labor. In the village of Dahshour, Egypt women purchase a basket of vegetables on credit or bake bread to sell in the market, "however little they may gain." The researchers in El Gawaber observe, however, that men are reluctant to admit this change as it is a sign of their own inability to provide for the household.

In India women in rural and periurban households are also taking on increased responsibility for bringing income into the household. They often engage in petty trades like selling wood for fuel and are making a "significant contribution toward meeting household expenditure." In Bangladesh increasing numbers of poor women are taking part in NGO-supported activities, which has boosted their incomes as well as their workloads. With the availability of credit, women are also engaged in self-employment activities like cattle and poultry raising and petty trade.

In Villa Atamisqui, Argentina a discussion group of 21 women rate unemployment among women as a pressing problem. They explain that men spend three or four months at a time out of the house and while some women find work providing domestic services in the cities, they have to leave the children with grandparents. Many times both parents never return. The increase in both male and female migration has been propelled by farming and herding difficulties in the wake of a dramatic drop in the water levels in a local river. In Atucucho, Ecuador a 23-year-old poor mother says that the situation of women is difficult because of extremely low wages: "Some mothers work as domestic employees for 250,000 sucres per month. You know how much bus fare costs these days; they have little money left for anything else."

Gender differences in educational status and expansion of the service industry also contribute to women's increased economic roles in the region. In both Brazil and Jamaica discussion groups indicate that women often have more education and job opportunities than do men. In Jamaica, for instance, there is discrimination against men for several types of urban jobs, and women feel they have better chances of getting hired. Women are even working in construction, traditionally considered a male preserve. The report for Florencio Varela, Argentina notes, "For men, if they are more than 35 years old, not a single place will take them." In Brazil, meanwhile, many factories have left the São Paulo area, and men have been the most affected. The researchers there say that "sectors that typically employ men, e.g., construction industry and manufacturing, are in decline whereas the service industry is expanding apace."

In Eastern Europe and Central Asia a very different set of forces has led to the double bind of female and male unemployment. With the collapse of the communist system, women who were primarily employed in the service industry and as civil servants have lost their previous livelihoods and are increasingly involved in trading and the informal sector. Many women are becoming their family's main breadwinner in the transition. Women from the village of Achy in the Kyrgyz Republic, for instance, report that they make crafts and beautiful bedclothes to sell. A 41-year-old mother of five from Oitamgaly, Uzbekistan says, "To be able to feed my children I have been selling sunflower seeds in Urada [a district in Tashkent] for four years. I go there 3–4 days since 1995....When my brother heard about it, he reproached me and said it was shameful. I stopped going...."

Women in Eastern Europe and Central Asia are also increasingly involved in trading activities that take them across the country borders, away from home for days and sometimes months. Researchers in Kyrgyz Republic observed in the village of Achy that "most of the rural men found themselves unemployed, while rural women who used to stay at home and obey their husbands began trading." Since 1993, they note, women have been involved in shuttle trade (also known as "bazaar economy") and *chelnochny* business (that of traveling to other towns and even countries to purchase goods and products for resale). Liberalization of the economy underway in the country has created better opportunities for trade, especially for women. Urban and, to some extent, rural women travel to Kazakhstan, Russia, Uzbekistan, and even more remote countries such as the Arab Emirates, India, Iran, Italy, Pakistan, Syria, Thailand and Turkey, where they go on buying tours, and resell goods in the Kyrgyz Republic. Discussion group participants explain that it is easier for the women to undertake this kind of trade, as they are better at handling the authorities at the borders (police, customs officials and taxation authorities). Women are better at "gritting their teeth and getting on with the work" and in resisting the harassment meted out to them at the border. Women also feel that women traders are more likely to bring home their earnings, unlike most male traders who "spend their money on vodka with friends."

It also seems that a growing number of women are taking over as heads of households. In Ivanovo, Russia where woman are said to have greater opportunities as street peddlers and in selling food in the market, discussion groups mention a growing trend of women driving "the husband out of the house because he doesn't earn money." Apart from male unemployment, female-headed households can be triggered by civil strife, divorce and desertion, a husband's migrating away from home for long periods, a husband's ill health or death, or women simply deciding to live without a male partner. In Kowerani Masasa, Malawi discussion group participants report women take over because they are divorced, widowed or have "irresponsible" husbands. The researchers in Jamaica note that growing numbers of women have entered the work force at the same time as men have faced rising unemployment, resulting in a new phenomenon of women becoming their families' chief breadwinners. In Little Bay, Jamaica for instance, women are increasingly involved in the fishing industry as well as farming.

In Buroa, Somaliland the women's discussion groups estimate that women are the breadwinners in almost 70 percent of the households. And, as the researchers from Buroa note:

> *The participants agreed that opportunities have improved for women, which is probably the only positive thing that came out of the conflict. Because women could move across the territorial borders of warring clans and could culturally belong to any clan they marry into, they had taken over almost all small- to middle-sized trade and business. This provided women with a lot of economic clout in the family and at the community levels.*

Increased Work Burden of Women

> *These men now have realized that we women are overworking and the work itself is tiresome.*
> —A woman, Mbwadzulu, Malawi

While women may be working outside the home in larger numbers than ever before, the demanding responsibilities of running a household remain largely with them. In Ethiopia participants generally feel that "the more the men become jobless, the heavier the burden on the women." As a woman from Bode, Brazil puts it very clearly, "Women have really managed to improve their lives, to be more independent, but there is no doubt that they are overloaded." Similarly the research team in Oq Oltyn, Uzbekistan reports, "[Women] are taking more responsibility for providing for their families, but they also do the same amount of housework as before. On the whole, this means that they have to work more than they used to."

In Indonesia both men and women participants agreed that stereotypical gender roles in the household have not changed much in the last 10 years even as women have taken up more work outside the household. "It is both our destiny and old tradition that women should be playing a bigger role than men in the household," a woman from Ampenan Utara explains. Researchers in Vietnam stress that women are "quite clearly overworked," with consequences that include increased health problems. Women there say they have little time for outside activities such as evening literacy classes, community events or even informal socializing.

In Eastern Europe and Central Asia, the collapse of all forms of state support have added to women's burdens. Working women before (typically in state enterprises or as civil servants) enjoyed access to childcare, health care and schools for children. Not surprisingly, discussion groups of women from Latin America as well as Eastern Europe and Central Asia frequently mention a pressing need for day care.

Household Gender Roles: A Blurred Divide

> *Women are working at the market while men are cooking.*
> —A man, Kok Yangak, Kyrgyz Republic

> *Before? Before they [men] were like the master and señor....*
> *Not lifting a finger in the house.... Things are changing slowly,*
> *but they are changing.*
> —A woman, Florencio Varela, Argentina

> *It is Allah who has differentiated women's and men's responsibilities. It will culturally be out of the way and shameful if a man does any of women's responsibilities.*
> —A man, Mitti Kolo, Ethiopia

Both women's and men's traditional gender roles are changing, sometimes marginally, sometimes more dramatically. Increasingly, household budgets depend on women's earning capacities. The increase in women's relative economic power shatters the generally accepted image of the man as the breadwinner. According to researchers in Russia, "Unlike the unemployment of a woman, unemployment of a man is seen as a huge violation of the norm, which dramatically affects his role also of a husband and father." The report adds that the division of gender roles started blurring a long time ago. With the notion of "man as the provider for the family and the woman taking care of the home" so deeply rooted in people's minds, it is only after years of widespread unemployment that the violation of these traditional roles has become more explicit.

Examples of men stepping in to assume household responsibilities are few and scattered. Isolated incidents of men sharing some of the "female" responsibilities include when the wife is unwell, away visiting relatives, attending to other social obligations, or when work keeps her away from the home for long periods (Bangladesh, Brazil, Indonesia, Malawi and Zambia). In Indonesia the researchers find that only men who are 35 or younger are helping out more with housework and childcare, and then only when their wives obtain a factory job or go overseas to work. The researchers add that casual work by women doesn't seem to merit additional help from husbands with household chores.

There are also cases of almost complete role reversals, with the men assuming the bulk of the cooking, cleaning and looking after children. Typically, this occurs where men are unemployed and at home, while women bring home the wages (Argentina, Bulgaria, Ecuador, Jamaica and the Kyrgyz Republic). As a woman in Dock Sud, Argentina puts it, "Now there are more men who help at home. The men are gaining awareness.... They are only a few, but they are changing. If the woman works and earns more, the men take care of the children and even take them to school sometimes."

Reports from Argentina, Ecuador and Jamaica and, to some extent, from Bulgaria and Russia, suggest that some women prefer to be independent of men once they have access to some economic resources. A Russian woman, for instance, shares that "it is easier now to survive alone with a child than with a husband in the family." In some communities in Jamaica female-headed households are perceived to be the best off in the community. The presence of domestic violence, in addition to economic independence, is sometimes mentioned as a factor pushing women to manage households on their own. Women from Latin America and the Caribbean especially speak of having gotten the confidence to move out of abusive relationships, and this, reports a study participant from Jamaica, is "because the women can now afford to have separate homes."

Decisionmaking at the Household Level

> When I was working I used to decide. When she is working, she owns her money and does anything she wishes.
> —A man, Vila Junqueira, Brazil

> They exercise some rights. They decide on how much salt or pepper is needed for the household. This is because they know these things.
> —A man, Kajima, Ethiopia

Most women report that they participate more in household decisions compared with 10 years ago, but the extent of change varies quite widely from country to country and community to community. A small positive change for women in a traditionally conservative culture can be experienced as a big change, while still falling far short of equity. Where women are actively seeking equity and significant changes in gender roles and identities, this is strongly linked to their rising economic power, and generally associated with changes in male attitudes and growing awareness about gender inequities because of church activities, NGO programs, education and the media.

The diversity of cultures and contexts across the study countries makes comparisons of shifts in power relations at the household level very difficult. In some communities the changes reported can be quite small. As a man from a discussion group in Nchimischi, Zambia explains, "Generally it is the men who make major decisions about the use of finances. The wife is only consulted, and her advice may not be taken." In many communities men and women report that men continue to be responsible for major decisions (e.g., the purchase or sale of assets). With some frequency, however, women acknowledge having gained more decisionmaking power over household budgets, food purchase and consumption patterns, and children's education, health care and marriage. In some places they also can influence decisions on types of crops to be planted, their own travel and employment, the use of family planning methods and, in very rare cases, divorce.

An interesting illustration of the different meaning of change can be found in comparing women's views in Bangladesh and Jamaica. In general, most women from both these countries feel that they can take more part in decisionmaking processes at home and feel more "free" and confident. However, the two groups are referring to very different types of freedom. In Bangladesh women feel they have more freedom because their husbands now permit them to move outside the house to buy groceries and attend women's group meetings. The women thus feel they have more contact with the outside world and have some control over the household budgets. At the urban sites in Jamaica women talk about their freedom to choose family planning methods, as well as the confidence to walk out of an abusive relationship. Importantly, similar trends could not be found in rural Jamaica.

While exceptions are found everywhere, some communities in Asia, Egypt and Ethiopia seem to be at one end of the spectrum, where local customs and tradition continue to dictate the roles men and women are expected to play within a household and community, whereas some urban communities in Argentina, Brazil, Ecuador and Jamaica seem to lie at the other end, with women there expressing a need for, and gaining, more freedom and independence.

Inequitable gender roles are reported in Indonesia in the eastern islands of Nusa Tenggara Timor (NTT), where local customs and tradition define the lower status of women. "A woman is 'a second-class creature' and *belis* [bought] by her husband, by paying the agreed price to her parents in cash, cattle, and other assets. A 'bought woman' is not expected to have opinions; her sole contractual obligation is to obey and serve her husband."

In South Asia (Bangladesh and India) in the communities studied women say they are now more involved in handling household budgets as well as in decisions related to their children's education and marriage.

Some slow but positive changes come from Africa. In Somaliland women see the increase in their decisionmaking power as a result of the war, when men were either away from home for a long period or were restricted in their movements. In Ghana, Malawi, Nigeria and Zambia a positive link is found between women's earning capacity and their role in household decisions. A discussion group from Adaboya, Ghana laughed loudly when asked whether the women have more or less power in the household. The researchers note that the men believe "women have virtually become the landlords [household heads]!"

In some *favelas* of Brazil, many women identify a strong relationship between their income and their decisionmaking authority in the household. In one community, the women list "the decision to separate from the husband" and "to lodge complaints about aggressive behavior of men" as the top two decisions they can take. They add that they would not have had the courage to take these decisions in the past. A woman from Entra a Pulso relates her income-earning role to freedom and to the power to make decisions: "Today we go out, knocking at every door, looking for a job...this is what making decisions in life is about...it is to feel free."

In Argentina and Ecuador as well, a number of women seem to have gained far more decisionmaking power at the household level in recent years, especially in urban areas. Again, they link this to their income-earning power, as "decisionmaking is related to who earns the money." In Florencio Varela, Argentina researchers are told, "Now that the woman goes to work outside the home and takes care of the household expenses with what she earns, she decides many more things."

In addition to economic factors, reports from some countries indicate that a woman's age affects her relative power in the household and the wider community. In Bangladesh, India, the Kyrgyz Republic and Somaliland, older women have more influence in household decisions than younger ones. In Somaliland older women settle minor disputes among women. They also acted as goodwill ambassadors or couriers during peace-making efforts among the clans.

Male Frustration, Anxiety and Sense of Inferiority

> ...if you lose your job outside, you lose the job inside.
> —A man, Bower Bank, Jamaica

> The unemployed men are frustrated, because they no longer can play the part of family providers and protectors. They live on the money made by their wives and feel humiliated because of that. Suicides among young men have become more frequent.
> —An elderly woman, Uchkun village, the Kyrgyz Republic

Unemployment and loss of economic power accompanied by a relative increase in women's economic power is perceived, especially by many men in the study, as a serious violation of the accepted gender norm. Several men report feelings of humiliation and the sense that they have lost control within the household. According to an elderly man in Kenesh, Kyrgyz Republic,

> Before it was clear that the woman is to keep the house and take care of the family, while the man was earning the daily bread. Now the woman buys and sells stuff irrespective of the weather and earns the income for the family, while the man is sitting at home and takes care of the children, fulfills the traditional women's work. This is not right; this is not good.

This emerging male frustration and anxiety is most visible in the reports from Eastern Europe and Central Asia (and to some extent in Latin America and Jamaica) where communities are witnessing rapid changes. Men at several sites talk about the psychological illbeing they feel. Says one man from Ozerny, Russia, "I cannot feed my children normally any more. I feel ashamed to come home." In Kyrgyz Republic, the researchers note that many men fear and oppose their wives' financial independence and ability to develop a career. Some men, especially when they are unemployed, view the success of their wives as their own failure.

In Doryumu, Ghana men who cannot provide a home for their families and rely on their wives are nicknamed "Salomey," or "almost a nonperson in the man's world." Or this from a woman in a discussion group in Entra a Pulso, Brazil: "Today when a woman earns more than her husband, he has to obey her...he cannot complain about the kind of work, because it is with this wage that the family is maintained."

In Bower Bank, Jamaica researchers write:

> The men stated that their status and position are worsening.
> They expressed feelings of helplessness at the erosion of their
> "power" resulting from having less access to work. Both adult
> men and the younger men seem to be more accommodating of
> women turning to more than one man to help support the
> household. One man went as far to say, "If I come home and
> find a man in my bed, and the woman says to me, 'That man is
> the one providing the food,' I have to say to her, 'Cover him up
> better because he is providing the food.'"

The study reveals clearly that male frustration weighs heavily on other members of the household as well, often leading to increasing levels of tension, violence and even family breakdown.

Domestic Abuse and Violence

> In my home I am abused in ways that I can't even tell...let's
> not get into it.
> —A woman, Vila União, Brazil

> Brutes have always beaten and will go on beating their wives.
> —A youth, Krasna Poliana, Bulgaria

As part of the discussions on gender relations, participants were asked to define domestic violence and share their perceptions of why domestic violence occurs, and whether they perceive changes in the levels and types of violence in the household. Although the focus was on violence faced by women, the issue was left open to allow people to articulate whether men face some forms of abuse and violence as well. For this analysis, "violence" refers to physical assaults and "abuse" to verbal and psychological forms of aggression.

Definitions of Domestic Abuse and Violence

There are times when a man hits for the wrong reasons. I think it's fine when he hits me if he's right.

—A woman, Esmeraldas, Ecuador

In defining domestic violence, participants provide a very wide spectrum of responses across communities—ranging from rape, beating and insults faced by women at one end, to husbands not getting their meals on time or their wives not giving them a massage at night at the other end. Domestic violence also is interpreted in a variety of ways across different gender and age groups within the same communities (see box 6.1). In most cases both women and men also view the violation of social norms and the failure of their partners to play their expected gender roles as domestic abuse and violence.

The reports from a large number of the communities indicate that both women and men are victims of violence and abuse, and both perceive that these behaviors exist in many forms. With some exceptions, discussion groups of men and of women conclude that women endure both more varied and more severe forms of abuse than do men. As one example, the Malawi researchers note that both men and women are identified as victims of beatings, catching sexually transmitted diseases, "being left alone overnight" or locked out of the house, "obscenity," and "selfishness." Women alone, however, also experience rape, being beaten for refusing a proposal, and not having "enough money for the household."

Following in table 6.1 are some of the main types of domestic abuse and violence women and men mention that cut across most of the study sites in the 23 countries.

Box 6.1 Men's Perspectives of Violence: Views from Tabe Ere, Ghana

Men see the usurpation of control over sheanut and dawadawa (the West African locust bean, used in fermented food and seasoning) proceeds from them by the women as a form of violence against men. In the past it was the sole preserve of the man to instruct his wife to pick sheanut and dawadawa from the farm, and the man determined the way proceeds from these should be used.

Some of the men, however, admit that there is some violence against the women, too, because some husbands beat up their wives when they refuse to obey what the man says. Some also beat up their wives when they do not readily give in to sex. Consequently, rape is another form of violence committed against women. Some of the men, however, argue that by virtue of the fact that it is the men who pay the bride a price they must have unrestrained access to sex.

Verbal and psychological abuse is the most frequently mentioned form of domestic conflict. While it is directed at both women and men, women appear to be victims of more severe and frequent abuse than do men. This description by a woman from Kawangu, Indonesia is typical: "My husband never beats me. We are sometimes engaged in little family disputes but at the most he just chased me and shouted at me." In Vila Junqueira, Brazil women say that men practice "silence aggression" more than in the past, and they consider this one of the worst forms of mistreatment because they are isolated in their own homes.

Depriving the man or woman of food, shelter or sex is the next most frequently mentioned form of abuse. In Tabe Ere, Ghana a group of women indicate that refusing sex is the most common cause of women being beaten, and often the husband is drunk. They add that this problem is growing worse for women there. Women in Doryumu, also in Ghana, say that wife beating is on the decline and mention other forms of abuse, such as divorce, separation, no "chop money" (for housekeeping), having to endure the husband's infidelity, men's refusal to eat what the women cook, and denial of sex. Where women are dependent on their husbands for social and

Table 6.1 Typology of Domestic Abuse and Violence

Type of abuse and violence	Victims
Verbal abuse (nagging, arguments, shouting, harsh comments, questioning, etc.)	Women and men
Deprivation (denying food, sex, shelter [locking the husband or wife outside], water for bathing, the right to visit friends and relatives, and permission to work outside the home, and restricting freedom, etc.)	Women and men
Physical abuse (beating, raping, pulling by the hair, throwing out, dragging, "flying dishes," giving drugs and "potions," etc.)*	Usually women, sometimes men
Drinking and gambling by men	Women
Polygamy (affecting women), promiscuous behavior and casual sex	Women and men
Property grabbing (Malawi, Zambia)	Women
Dowry (India, Bangladesh) and bride price (Ghana, Indonesia, Uzbekistan)	Women (also both parents of the bride)
Divorce and desertion	Women, sometimes men
Teenage pregnancy (Jamaica, Malawi, Zambia, etc.)	Women
Abusive in-laws (Bangladesh, India, Uzbekistan)	Women

Abduction and rape were also mentioned in Ethiopia, although it is usually men from outside the family who are involved in these. Similarly, throwing acid at women is one form of physical violence that women face at the community level in Bangladesh. "Ritual murder" was mentioned in one case in Umuoba Road, Nigeria.

economic support, many view promiscuity, divorce or desertion by a husband as forms of abuse.

In many households across the study communities, physical violence against women appears to be widespread and considered part of everyday life. "A married woman gets beat just as a woman with cattle gets meat" goes a proverb shared by a middle-aged woman from the village of Urmaral in the Kyrgyz Republic. In a number of the villages and slums visited by research teams, the women themselves do not consider domestic violence to be a serious form of mistreatment if it does not occur with great frequency. This, for instance, is the view expressed by a group of women in Umuoba Road, Nigeria. Similarly, according to an old woman from Mitti Kolo Peasant Association in Ethiopia, "It is sometimes necessary for husbands to beat their wives when they commit mistakes to correct them...it also improves love to be beaten and reconcile...it is also a sign of strong manhood...." In some communities, women are also reported to be vulnerable to violence from in-laws.

Selected cases of physical violence against men were reported in Brazil, Ghana, Jamaica, the Kyrgyz Republic and Malawi. In Tabe Ere, Ghana men point out that women who are physically stronger than their husbands do sometimes beat them. More typically, however, women do not respond to hardships by externalizing their frustrations with physical aggression. When a discussion group of women in Dock Sud, Argentina was asked whether they hit men when they don't have work, a woman responds negatively, adding, "Women get depressed...we're very different from them."

Men and women also view any deviation from the accepted traditional gender norms and roles as acts of abuse. Women feel that unemployment whereby men cannot provide for the household is a form of abuse. In Kok Yangak, the Kyrgyz Republic people say there have been instances in their community of husbands who cannot provide financial support being beaten by their wives and forced out of the house. There are also many cases of men who feel abused if women do not perform expected duties around the home or when their wives go out to work and control decisions at home. In Bangladesh women mention that they find it difficult to take care of their domestic responsibilities when they return home tired after working for wages all day long. When the meals are not prepared well, or when the woman is too tired to massage the husband's legs at night, the husband flares up and shouts at his wife and sometimes beats her up or denies her food. In such cases both the man and the woman feel abused.

Causes of Domestic Abuse and Violence

Sometimes women are hit because lunch is not ready when he gets home.

—A woman, Entra a Pulso, Brazil

It's because of unemployment and poverty that most men in this community beat their wives. We have no money to look after them.

—A man, Teshie, Ghana

In many societal contexts, domestic violence is supported by social norms. Both men and women talk about economic pressures and changing gender roles and relations as leading factors in domestic violence, but they also frequently mention alcohol and drug addiction, gambling, polygamy and promiscuity. Again, both men and women in many communities refer to violence against women as an accepted behavioral norm, especially when a women fails to meet expectations of the man or his relatives.

Both men and women in many areas mention that, under economic stress, they have more arguments and there is verbal abuse directed at both men and women. From a discussion group of women in Dock Sud, Argentina flow these comments: "Men are less patient; they tell you to shut up when they don't like something or when you want to give your opinion; they are easily angered all the time; if they are without work, they become nervous and take it out on you." A discussion group of men from Chitambi, Malawi agree that while women may be better off today with their increased earnings, "we men are not happy because these women are taking advantage of us and they are being rude to us."

Alcohol and drug abuse is also frequently mentioned. Indeed, as a participant from Bijeljina, Bosnia and Herzegovina describes, much of the physical violence against women occurs when husbands come home drunk: "Under the influence of alcohol a man...spends the money, and sometimes he beats his wife or abuses the children, which creates enormous insecurity and fear in a woman." In addition to alcohol, people in Argentina and Brazil associate violence with increased drug use. A young woman from Nova Califórnia, Brazil remarks, "I think that it is the drugs that make them more aggressive."

Women's dependence on their husbands for social and economic support also makes them insecure; thus, many view promiscuity, divorce or desertion by a husband as forms of abuse. According to a group of young men from Freeman's Hall, Jamaica, the occasions where quarreling among husbands and wives might lead to violence usually involve infidelity: "...only if the woman is not behaving herself ['giving him bun'], then he would have to beat her."

In some countries the tradition of the dowry (in India and Bangladesh) or a bride price (Ghana, Indonesia, Uzbekistan) can lead to continued abuse of women because of issues around how much dowry was promised or paid or the sense of owning a woman after "buying" her through bride price (see also box 6.2). A group of women from Ghana report that a girl child may be "tied with a string or rope and given into marriage" as payment for borrowed food or cattle from another family. In Ethiopia, *telefa* (abduction of women), which can result in rape and desertion or in some cases marriage by

Box 6.2 A Father's Story

A poor father in Gowainghat, Bangladesh, while explaining how he got his eldest daughter married to a 50-year-old man, explained, "I had no financial capacity. If I had, I would not give my daughter to marriage with that old man. It was difficult for me to wait to give her to a good marriage as she was young. Bad Muslim boys teased her, and I got afraid. Villagers also blamed me at that time for not getting my daughter married on time."

He got his second daughter married when she was seven years old. He sold one of his cows, and villagers also helped him by providing some money to give dowry for this marriage. At that age she was not able to satisfy her husband sexually and do any household work, so her husband and mother-in-law physically tortured her. Sometimes, her husband and mother-in-law stopped giving her food and other daily necessities. To avoid this torture, she returned to her father's house. After two years of separation, her father got her married again, this time with a 45-year-old widower.

force, is another form of traditional abuse, one that has long-term consequences for women.

In a number of the communities where women's awareness of their rights is growing and they gain a measure of independence as they secure a livelihood, they are often becoming less tolerant of irresponsible behavior by men. When women argue, ask questions, or answer back, men feel threatened and insecure. In Russia, for instance, people report that it is typical that "the woman starts the quarrel, and the man gives back." Many men describe the changing traditional roles and values as abuse against them. Men and women (especially older men and women) from several sites felt that women are now more disrespectful toward men—yet another change that has led to domestic conflicts and breakups. In Ekaterinburg, Russia women explain that "relations have become tougher, because there are more problems. There can be conflicts in the family because the woman makes more money than the man." In Duckensfield, Jamaica a group of young women say that as women become more independent they become more intolerant of men's weaknesses. This same group also indicates that some women are now demanding more from men sexually and become violent if the men fail to perform.

Changes in Levels of Domestic Violence

Physical violence against women exists in about 90 percent of the study communities where gender violence was discussed. The picture of trends in physical violence in homes over the last 10 years is mixed with strong regional differences (see figure 6.1).[3] In 21 percent of communities, groups

Figure 6.1 Global and Regional Trends in Domestic Violence against Women

Global

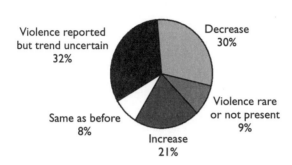

Violence reported but trend uncertain
32%

Decrease
30%

Violence rare or not present
9%

Increase
21%

Same as before
8%

Latin America and the Caribbean

Violence reported but trend uncertain
17%

Decrease
44%

Same as before
15%

Increase
17%

Violence rare or not present
7%

Asia

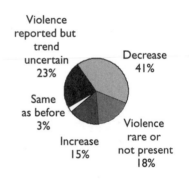

Violence reported but trend uncertain
23%

Decrease
41%

Same as before
3%

Increase
15%

Violence rare or not present
18%

Eastern Europe and Central Asia

Decrease
0%

Violence reported but trend uncertain
65%

Violence rare or not present
0%

Increase
32%

Same as before
3%

Africa

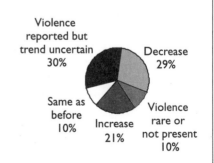

Violence reported but trend uncertain
30%

Decrease
29%

Same as before
10%

Increase
21%

Violence rare or not present
10%

report that physical violence has increased while another 8 percent report that physical violence is at the same levels as before. In another roughly 30 percent of the communities, people speak about the presence of violence, and often mention very high levels, but the discussion groups either disagree on trends or do not identify a trend. However, in 30 percent of the communities visited, discussion groups conclude that physical violence has declined over the last decade.

The extent of violence reported by both men's and women's groups is remarkable both because of the sensitivity of topic and because of the brevity of the researchers' visits with the communities. In many communities the world over, there is still a strong code of silence surrounding violence, with women deeply ashamed and sometimes blaming themselves for their husbands' wrath. In Ethiopia the researchers state that rural women "are not willing to provide information" on "husband-wife relations, violence against women, and conflict in the family" because the topics are too sensitive.

Similarly, the local researchers in the Kyrgyz Republic could not manage to raise the subject of gender violence in four of the smaller communities where everyone knew one another. Instead, they asked discussion groups to consider trends in the "abuse of women's rights on a household level." Although each of these communities reported the abuse of rights to be increasing, whether this encompasses physical violence cannot be determined and so these reports have been set aside with the others that lack information on the topic and are not part of this analysis. Kyrgyz researchers did discuss violence directly in Urmaral, where there are 164 households and the village is "quite transparent, and 'can be seen like on a palm of your hand.'" Discussion groups there reported violence to be absent or very rare, with the exception of one old woman who confided to the researchers that the women in her discussion group "don't want to talk about it because many of them are beaten by their husbands." Overall discussions about gender violence were often easier when people reported declines in violence than otherwise.

Where Physical Violence Has Decreased

> Men know that we can survive without them, so they will treat us better, men are no longer "lord and savior."
> —A young woman from Bower Bank, Jamaica

> The beatings are now less compared to the problem years... this is because a spouse can be taken to court and people [men] are afraid.
> —A man from Nchimishi, Zambia

The biggest declines in physical violence against women are found in Latin America and the Caribbean, with 44 percent of the communities reporting decreases where violence was discussed. This is followed by Asia, 41 percent, and Africa, 29 percent, with no declines in Eastern Europe and Central Asia (see figure 6.1). As mentioned before, in Asia the sample was strongly biased to include only those communities with active NGO presence.

Dramatic declines in physical violence in cultures where traditional gender relations have been inequitable points to the importance of a mix of interventions to reduce physical violence against women in the homes. These findings establish that norms and values about what is tolerable behavior can change in relatively short periods, although deeper change may take longer. It is important to note that even in households where physical abuse of women may be declining, it is not accompanied by a similar decrease in other forms of abuse that women face within the household. Indeed, a large number of discussion groups across the study countries indicate that verbal and psychological abuse may actually be increasing. In addition, even while communities report overall declines from previous levels, violence may remain widespread. For example, in Ecuador, wife battering is mentioned in almost every discussion group by both women and men.

Group discussions in Latin America and the Caribbean identified a complex mix of reasons for declining physical violence in the homes. As unemployed men realize that they are dependent on women's incomes, the relationship often becomes less physically abusive. Discussion groups also frequently mention women's greater awareness of their rights through participation in women's groups organized by churches and NGOs and women's decreased tolerance of their husband's abusive behavior.

Women in this region mention a number of options for taking action against abuse, including fleeing to safe houses, filing complaints with women's police stations, seeking training and counseling, or even leaving abusive marriages. Fears of public humiliation and of being put behind bars appear to act as useful deterrents to male violence against women in some communities.

In Bangladesh women speak of their growing empowerment as well as the contributions of NGOs. Groups of youth and the elderly in Madaripur, Bangladesh, for instance, attribute the decrease in violence against women to increases in literacy and enlightenment as well as livelihood activities. In the words of one young woman, "Women are more powerful than 10 years ago because of self-sufficiency coming from educational and economic empowerment." In Gowainghat women mention that with NGO support they have seen a reduction in the practice of dowry.[4] In Khaliajuri, another community in Bangladesh, women explain that NGOs and the media have raised women's awareness of their social and legal rights. However, the women also point out that the local village institutions as well as the police and legal systems do not support them when they protest against polygamy and divorce in their village.

In Indonesia 8 out of the 12 communities visited report declining levels of violence against women. The reports from discussion groups in Waikanabu are typical. Both men's and women's groups agree that violence is coming down, with a comment from a women's group attributing the declines both to women's changing roles and to increased awareness "because women have begun learning, been educated and had courage to oppose." The men's groups also credit frequent house visits by church elders, and women's growing role in bringing in extra income.

Scattered news about declining violence can also be found in Africa. In Doryumu, Ghana some men mention that they used to beat their wives, but not anymore as they realized that beating wives is not a good practice. A man from Mbwadzulu Village of Malawi indicates that violence against women has decreased because "in the past when you quarreled with a woman and if she reported to the political party, you were beaten.... We were not in freedom, I tell you." In three communities in Nigeria, discussion groups generally perceive that violence against women is declining, and the trend is linked directly to women's gains in economic power, education and awareness. However, women in the southeast say female genital mutilation, rape and ritual murder do occur as before, but violence at the household level has decreased. While four communities in Zambia report increased violence, the researchers summarize in their National Report a few factors that study participants think are helping to slow down and reverse the trend (see box 6.3).

While declines in violence were not reported by discussion groups in Eastern Europe and Central Asia, box 6.4 illustrates the case of a mother of five from Uzbekistan who reports that household conflict has "quieted down" after she took a job to help with economic difficulties.

There are a few observations from discussion groups that violence sometimes declines over time within marriages, and some of the reporting may reflect this tendency. From a men's group in Nchimishi, Zambia, "Women are often beaten by their husbands, especially the newlyweds. The husband is at this point trying to establish standards, i.e., showing the wife what he likes and what he does not like." Similarly, in Oq Oltyn, Uzbekistan the researchers report that violence is said to be higher among young families.

Box 6.3 Reasons for Declines in Physical Violence against Women in Zambia

▸ Men have been so weakened by hunger that they do not have the strength anymore to beat their wives.
▸ Husbands do not want to beat and antagonize the breadwinner because they will go hungry.
▸ The Victim Support Unit of the Zambia Police is very active in defending women's rights, especially those that have been beaten by their husbands and those whose property has been grabbed by the relatives of their deceased husbands.
▸ People have been sensitized to the problem by churches and NGOs.

Where Physical Violence Has Increased

> *Women must take care of everything and, to top it all off, get beaten up every night if he comes home drunk.*
> —A woman from Dimitrovgrad, Bulgaria

Eastern Europe and Central Asia stands out as the region with the largest increase in violence against women, 32 percent, and not a single case of declines in or absence of gender violence was reported. Sharp economic decline and accompanying stress, breakdown of state institutions and lack of support to women have led to dramatic increases in violence in homes. Discussion groups from the region speak of greater conflict in the household, with verbal abuse not only of women but also of men. The heightened conflict sometimes compounds men's frustrations and violence. In Plovdiv, Bulgaria where discussion groups reported increased violence, one participant observed that people used to step in and break up fights when they heard "some noise" from their neighbors' homes, but "now nobody wants to interfere and there always are noise and quarrels anyway. It is quite normal now."

Much of the research details specific accounts of wife-batterings. In a discussion group of men in Beisheke, the Kyrgyz Republic one admitted that he beat his wife every now and then, but says it is her own fault. What's more, women from the group agreed with him: "We women start quarrels when there isn't enough food or clothes, and our husbands are very well aware of these problems themselves. They don't need our lecturing, so, when they ask us to stop and we don't, they may hit us a couple of times."

People also say that with the deterioration of the legal system in recent years, women's rights have eroded and women have less protection than they had in a communist society. According to a woman from a discussion group

---

Box 6.4 Changing Fortunes and Role Reversals: Uzbekistan

At the beginning our life was good, but someone put the evil eye on us and everything started to go wrong. My father-in-law even threatened me with an axe, saying that my husband was a weakling, and my husband beat me after that. Just like that, with no reason. Times were hard for me then. In the morning I was supposed to bring my father-in-law warm water for his washbowl— neither too hot, nor too cold, and exactly at the right time. But I also had five children. So, I adjusted their feeding times so that it wouldn't interfere with my father-in-law's schedule. The poor kids cried, waiting for me to feed them. But at five in the morning I was expected to bring the warm water to my father-in-law. The chairman of the *aulsovet* [rural citizen assembly] failed to understand my problem and did not support me. Now everything has quieted down because of the financial problems at home. It's me who is making money, and my husband cannot order me around.

in Kenesh, the Kyrgyz Republic where violence against women is reported to be increasing, "The state does not think about the women. The woman has to resolve her problems herself and it is very difficult to do now." A Bulgarian female attorney with a local practice in Varna told the researchers:

> There is no law which defends the wife, child, or husband in cases of domestic violence. From the prosecutor's office they say, "This is not a problem of ours," while the police find an excuse in saying that they cannot interfere in family affairs. Being afraid, the women refuse to sue the man who terrorizes them, while with Roma women this [filing complaints] is absolutely out of the question.

In Brazil women say that although they are becoming more proactive on violence, discussion groups in 6 of the 10 *favelas* visited report that violence against women continues to rise. There and elsewhere in the region women link this increase to alcohol and drug abuse stemming from greater male unemployment

Where Violence Remains Widespread, but Trends Unclear

> I cannot say that whether men beat their wives more in the war than now, but I personally know individuals who beat their wives when they come home drunk, and sometimes they beat the children. That is something that has always existed and always will.
> —A young woman from Sekovici, Bosnia and Herzegovina

Violence remains widespread with unclear trends in 40 percent of the communities with regional variations. The distribution is as follows: 68 percent of these are in Eastern Europe and Central Asia, 49 percent in Latin America and the Caribbean, 42 percent in Africa, and 40 percent in Asia. These figures include communities which report that violence is the same as before or that it exists, but they do not identify a trend. Some of the most extensive reports of violence against women come from Vietnam, but discussion groups there did not conduct a trend analysis. In a highland village of Lao Cai Province, a women's group estimates that 70 percent of husbands subjected their wives to regular physical violence, and a great deal of violence is also alluded to, especially by children, in other communities visited in the country. A woman in one community confides, "Lots of women in this neighborhood are beaten by their husbands. Lucky for me my brother lives nearby, so if my husband starts coming after me I run to my brother's house."

Parents, particularly in Latin America, also frequently mention the abusive behaviors and attitudes of children. In some cases, concerns are expressed about undue physical punishment of children as well as violence among siblings and children hitting their mothers and grandmothers. In Villa

Atamisqui, Argentina a discussion group of young women explains that "the role of the father in the house is to punish the children." "The women also hit...." "The sons hit the mothers." "The father teaches the children to hit their wives." In Moreno, Argentina discussion groups spoke of terrible fighting in the home involving children, and they blame increased economic hardship and the harmful influences of alcohol and television.

The Opportunity and Challenge

To be able to pour your heart out to someone.... To know you have someone you can rely on.

—Participant, discussion group of men and women
from Krasna Poliana, Bulgaria commenting on
gender roles and responsibilities

In very many communities, traditional gender roles of men as providers and women as homemakers are changing, but the transition is proving difficult and highly uneven. With their roles uncertain, men and women express confusion and experience difficulty in establishing new interdependent partnerships. In Renggarasi, Indonesia women say they still turn to men to make decisions even though they have their own women's groups for support: "We are still in doubt to make decisions, afraid of making mistakes or wrong decisions."

The findings about the linkages between decreased violence, women's increased economic roles and the benefits of supportive actions to reduce violence give hope. Activities that are specifically aimed at building awareness about gender inequities and improving gender relations have made a difference where they are available. In communities with NGOs that run gender awareness training and counseling programs, where safe houses and police protection exist, or where church members reach out to curb the violence, women speak of improvements in their lives. Without access to comparable support, men sometimes express resentment about so many resources targeted to women.

A particularly inspiring story comes from Leticia of Isla Trinitaria, Ecuador. During an interview with the researchers, Leticia credits a training program run by Habitat for changing her life. She shares that the gains are

> *...not only material...but also in knowing how to show love to my son and husband. This is happiness...now I am not a person who shouts and hits...now I talk and communicate...the best is when the father sits down with his son to have a conversation. Before, he [her husband] treated me badly, not physically but verbal abuse...now he respects me. He changed with me. Together we are changing. This is the result of the training...only because of the training.*

When subsequently asked about what opportunities she sees, Leticia adds, "my opportunity is that I have free space, to decide for myself, no longer dependent on others. For me, this is a source of pride, my husband asking me [my advice]...now there isn't this machismo...there is mutual respect...together we decide."

To help reduce gender inequality and domestic conflict, there needs to be far greater attention to helping women and men in groups to work separately and together to come to terms with changing gender roles and identities.

Notes

[1]This chapter draws mainly on the findings from small group discussions of women and of men on changes in women's and men's responsibilities and decision-making in the household, as well as on changes in domestic violence against women. In some cases, the researchers reported very tense discussions. In one community in Ecuador, discussion groups of men and women were reduced to shouting at each other after findings were shared.

[2]We found only one exception to this phenomenon in the Muslim community of Jimowa, Nigeria. It was reported that Jimowa women traditionally used to go out to sell their milk products. However, about 12 years ago a man from the village attended a religious meeting outside the village and came back with the message that the women should remain indoors, in purdah. Since then women have not gone out to sell. While the elderly women can step out, even the girls in the village are encouraged to stay at home.

[3]The analysis on trends in gender violence is based on 163 community and provincial (in the case of Vietnam) reports. The topic was not addressed at all or was only discussed in vague terms in an additional 61 reports (19 of which are from Sri Lanka, where the topic of gender relations was not addressed). The category "violence reported but trend uncertain" refers to reports that mention the presence of physical violence such as beating, kicking, biting, battering, slapping, hitting, etc., against women in the household, but do not provide information on perceptions of trends. In many reports discussion groups identify violence in the household in terms of fighting, quarrels, conflict, being ordered around, promiscuity, etc.; however, these activities were not considered indications of physical violence for purposes of this analysis. Some communities reported that there was no domestic violence. In addition, a very small number of reports conclude that domestic violence in that community is "rare," "almost unheard of," or "not common," and these were added to the "violence rare or not present" category.

[4]However, this was not the case at the other sites in Bangladesh.

Chapter 7

Social Illbeing:
Left Out and Pushed Down

Summary

Social illbeing is the experience and feeling of being isolated, left out, looked down upon, alienated, pushed aside and ignored by the mainstream socio-cultural and political processes. Social illbeing is one of the multiple dimensions of deprivation and disadvantages poor people face at the community and household levels. Social illbeing can be experienced both collectively and individually. This alienation seems to manifest itself as lack of access to resources, information, opportunities, power and mobility. It usually overlaps with economic deprivation and is sometimes determined by sociocultural factors (e.g., traditional social hierarchy, religion, ethnicity, color, and individual attributes and behavior that the community considers "deviant"). Often gender is an additional factor. Outside of Argentina and Brazil, many women feel they play a minimal role at the community level. Even where women are more active, they often feel that men retain positions of power and decisionmaking.

Social cohesion, another aspect of social wellbeing, is determined by unity within a community—exhibited by shared understanding, mutual support and reciprocity in relationships. Participants, in general, feel that social cohesion has declined in the past decade. However, economic stress and hardship seem to affect communities in two nearly opposite ways. As individuals and households struggle to make ends meet, they have little time for friends and neighbors, or for community activities and concerns, and many discussion groups report declining cohesion. At the same time, poor people come together to help one another overcome survival, safety and social problems.

Introduction

You grow in an environment full of diseases, violence, and drugs....You don't have the right to education, work, or leisure, and you are forced to "eat in the hands of the government"...so you are an easy prey for the rulers. You have to accept whatever they give you.
—A young woman, Padre Jordano, Brazil

Whether we are present in any of the occasions or not present, no one will take notice. When a poor man dies no one even cares to pay him condolences.
—A group of poor men, Foua, Egypt

A researcher in Uzbekistan writes, "The socially excluded could be conceived of as encompassing all those strata deprived of opportunity." They are individuals, groups within communities, or entire communities. Ask them, and they will tell you they are shunned by mainstream culture and society. Participants in discussion groups voice three main dimensions of social illbeing:[1]

> ‣ the process of alienation and isolation (social exclusion);
> ‣ strained social relations and diminishing social cohesion; and
> ‣ unequal gender relations at the community level.

Poor people understand their exclusion on a number of levels, cited as alienation from community events, from decisionmaking, from opportunity and from access to resources or to information. Certain forms of exclusion are based on social hierarchy and differentiation—the case of the lower-caste groups in India, Somaliland and Nigeria, or of indigenous populations and ethnic groups out of the mainstream sociopolitical domain, such as black people in Brazil and the Roma Gypsies in Bulgaria.

Poor people associate the word *exclusion* with groups that are despised, forgotten, ignored, feared, hated or discriminated against, and they can frequently identify elements of society more excluded than they.

The chapter begins by identifying the types of individuals who are excluded and reviews the various factors that are reported to trigger social exclusion. It then presents participants' reports of both diminishing and increasing social cohesion and the causes for these changes.

Who Is Excluded?

If his Bulgarian name is Angel or Ivan or Stoyan or Dragan, he'll get all the application forms and be asked to come in. As soon as he does and they realize he's Gypsy, Roma, he's turned down, they drop their voices and tell him to come some other

*time.... If you decide to lodge a complaint they tell you, "Who
do you think you are, what are you fighting for?" You might
be slapped in the face so hard that they'll send you flying
through the door.... What about those rights we're supposed
to have?*

—Participant, discussion group of Roma men and
women, Dimitrovgrad, Bulgaria

The types of people whom participants identify as excluded from opportunities, resources, decisionmaking and other social processes vary from context to context. The list in table 7.1 below includes a wide range of people and categories. Where these overlap the sense of isolation is intensified. There are variations to the list across communities within regions, and even within countries. For example, in urban areas in Jamaica people mention lack of tolerance for homosexuals, the elderly, those who are HIV-positive, political opponents and others. Yet those in rural communities feel responsible for members who cannot help themselves because of "madness and poverty." However, they look down on "bad habits," such as those of "coke heads" and "rum heads."

The Bottom Poor

In Egypt they are called *madfoun*—the buried or buried alive; in Ghana, *ohiabrubro*—the miserably poor, with no work, sick with no one to care for them; in Brazil, *miseraveis*—the deprived; in Russia, *bomzhi*—the homeless; in Bangladesh, *ghrino gorib*—the despised or hated poor.

Table 7.1 The Types of People Excluded

Region	Types and categories of people excluded
South Asia	Ragpickers, the hated poor, landless people, low castes, women
East Asia	Ethnic minorities, migrant communities, drug addicts, poor, women, migrants
Africa	The very poor, physically disabled (blind, epileptics, people with leprosy), demon possessed, mentally ill, adulterers, thieves, prostitutes, elderly, women, witches, lower-caste clans, internally displaced people, unmarried and childless men
Eastern Europe and Central Asia	Very poor people, beggars, state pensioners, state enterprise workers, homeless, ethnic minorities, women, migrant communities
Latin America and the Caribbean	HIV sufferers, thieves, homosexuals, elderly, black communities, unemployed, people living in a particular locality or area known for high rates of crime and violence

In Zambia participants describe the *balandana sana* or *bapina* in these terms: "lack food, eat once or twice, poor hygiene, flies all over them, cannot afford school and health costs, lead miserable lives, poor dirty clothing, poor sanitation, no access to water, look like mad people, live on vegetables and sweet potatoes." In Malawi the worst off are called *osaukitsitsa*: "They eat maize bran that is meant for pigs, mainly households headed by the aged, the sick, disabled, orphans, and widows." Some are described as *onyentchera*, the stunted poor, with thin bodies, short stature and thin hair, bodies that do not shine even after bathing, and who experience frequent illnesses and a severe lack of food. In all countries in Africa, participants estimate that these bottom poor have increased in the past decade.

Poor people can often identify others who are even worse off, even more left out, even more pushed down. These are likely to include those listed in the table above, as well as those who are disabled, orphaned, widowed, chronically sick, mentally unwell, stunted by deprivation, homeless or simply destitute. These poorest of the poor were only occasionally participants in the study, in the case of the ragpickers in Hyderabad, India, for example. The bottom poor, then, are seen by most participants as separate and different, and regarded with mixtures of pity, fear, disgust and even hatred.

The Basis of Social Exclusion

Participants identify a range of sometimes overlapping factors that contribute to social exclusion.

The Stigma of Poverty

> I am far from the people who have money. The rich man closes his door in my face.
> —A woman, Foua, Egypt

The stigma of poverty, and the perception of deviant behavior associated with it, are recurring themes in discussions with poor people. In Brazil groups of poor people speak from bitter experience of being looked down upon or viewed with suspicion by the rest of the society simply because they are poor. Says a participant in a discussion group in Padre Jordano, Brazil, "When we go to hospitals we know we will have to wait beyond the expected time.... There comes somebody who is "higher" than us and jumps the queue without much fuss."

In Russia "some participants noted that the old pensioners, the unemployed, and other poorest categories steadily approached the border that used to divide the homeless people from the rest of the community and society, and whose behavior was considered...antisocial (begging, stealing, eating from the trash)." In Dangara, Uzbekistan researchers find that "many people feel excluded from the community not because of their religious or ethnic background, but because of their poverty."

Children of poor households feel exclusion most poignantly. In Vietnam, the youth explain that "the poor children are looked down upon by others and have few friends. Children of rich families have many friends." A 42-year-old unemployed and disabled woman from Uzbekistan laments that "the rich students are laughing at our children's clothes." In Kaoseng, Thailand a participant in a women's discussion group commented that the rich "never look at the poor, never allow their children to associate with those of the poor."

Poor people often also feel the stigma of poverty in their inability to exchange gifts and presents, thereby compelling them to avoid celebrations, festivities and other forms of social interaction. "I do not visit my friends anymore. If you go to visit them, you have to buy some presents, at least a packet of biscuits—and how could I afford them? And after that I have to invite them on my turn—how could I afford that?" asks a participant in Plovdiv, Bulgaria. Another man from Plovdiv explains,

> Well, we are old and all of us started to claim that we do not drink alcohol anymore. Of course I do drink alcohol, but a bottle of vodka [costs] 2,000 leva. So we do not serve alcohol. We started to meet together with our women over a can of homemade jam. The women always gather to try their new homemade jam, so we also started to integrate ourselves. We didn't do that before.

In Foua, Egypt researchers note,

> [Poverty] drives the poor to exclude themselves from the surrounding social networks. Indeed people stay interconnected if they maintain their neighbor and kinship relations. The maintenance of relations requires money. One of the metaphors used to illustrate this social exclusion is "There are houses that never open. People who are deprived or excluded do not have the material means to live with the rest of the population."

Indebtedness means humiliation in Vietnam where people feel they cannot hold their heads up as they walk in the neighborhood. Moneylenders further exploit this humiliation, using it to extract payment from defaulting households. In one case, a woman was stripped naked and photographed, and her picture posted around the neighborhood. In Ghana the researchers write:

> When one is socially excluded because of...poverty, reintegration is only possible when one regains wealth. Such is the lot of the poor! Whereas a criminal, like a rapist and others, can be reintegrated into society, the poor, whose situation is no

choice of his has no chance of ever being reintegrated into the community.

Lack of Money and Power

Social and economic factors reinforce each other in a cycle of alienation and powerlessness. Poverty deprives people of access to resources, to opportunities and to contact with those more influential. Without resources, opportunities and connections, economic mobility becomes exceedingly difficult.

In Kaoseng, Thailand a discussion group of poor youth say, "The poor are excluded from the community because they do not have the rights to borrow from the savings fund, no collateral," and "When there are loans, the rich are given, while the poor have no rights." Youth in Khwalala, Malawi point out that poor people are denied access to credit facilities:

> *Most lending institutions, including informal moneylenders demand collateral which they cannot simply manage. The poor do not [therefore] have any prospects for social and economic mobility. Most of the loans are extended to... well-to-do women who, to one degree or another, have political connections.*

Young men in Dahshour, Egypt say employers place difficult conditions on employment eligibility such as requiring a university degree or living close to the workplace, which is difficult for them to meet.

Rural poor in the Kyrgyz Republic express concern that their children will not be able to seek higher education because of their inability to bear the expenses of the newly introduced paid education system. Discussion group participants in Borborema, Brazil ask, "How can the student study if the school requires a uniform that is too expensive...how can this student get better off in the society if he/she needs the school and he/she cannot get into it because he/she does not have a shoe?...If he/she buys the uniform, he/she cannot eat."

Many children in Ho Chi Minh City, Vietnam do not have their birth certificates because mothers abscond from the hospitals after delivery to avoid paying for the services. Without birth certificates, it is difficult to register children in school.

Lack of contacts and connections with influential people in high offices and positions of power also furthers the feeling of alienation and lack of opportunity among poor people. In Zawyet Sultan, Egypt a young man reports that "job opportunities are a lot but not for us. I applied for 10 jobs. The one who relies on nepotism is the one who works; the one who doesn't they tell him to go home." Another man from the same community says, "One applies for a job, and if he doesn't have a 6,000-pound bribe, he doesn't get the job."

In Russia "power" is believed to rest with top officials, rich businessmen (with big money) or top policemen and mafiosi (who have armed support). The rest of the population feels distanced from power. Women there must struggle hard to get to the office with requests for help for their children or themselves, only to be badly insulted by male officials. In India many consider influence in government establishments and other high places within and outside the respective communities an important indicator of one's status. In the opinion of a fisherwoman from Konada, India, "If you don't know anyone, you will be thrown to the corner of a hospital!"

Participants in Malawi say that one needs to be "lucky" to have access to resources and services. What does lucky mean? "Being related to the people administering the activities or being very close to them, being a relative of the chief, being a patriot of the ruling party and being rich, such that it is easy to bribe the organizers."

Lack of representation perpetuates social exclusion. A discussion group participant in Foua, Egypt says, "Nobody is able to communicate our problems.... Who represents us? Nobody."

Ethnic, Linguistic, Racial and Cultural Isolation

Many times people despise you because of your color and
many of them deny you a job when you tell them that you live
here, and this is wrong.
—A young woman, Nova Califórnia, Brazil

Worldwide, discrimination on the basis of race, ethnicity, language and religion persists, compounding the isolation of whole communities of poor people. This is true for black people in Brazil, for Roma and Pomaks in Bulgaria, migrant Tajiks in Uzbekistan, indigenous people in Ecuador and minority communities in the northern uplands and the Mekong delta of Vietnam. Religious discrimination is described in the study affecting Hindus in Bangladesh and Protestants in Ethiopia's Dibdibe Wajtu Peasant Association. Traditional social hierarchies exist, affecting lower castes in India, and lower-caste clans in Somaliland and southeast Nigeria. And even language can marginalize groups of people, such as the Khmer communities in Tra Vinh, Vietnam.

Hindus far outnumber their Muslim neighbors in parts of Gowainghat, Bangladesh but because they are a minority in the country, problems of discrimination touch them in myriad ways. The Hindu participants describe being alienated and discriminated against in development activities and flood relief provided by the government. When Muslims from other parts of the village encroach on Hindu property, Hindus cannot protest out of fear. Muslim boys tease Hindu girls, and Muslims pick quarrels with Hindus. In Dibdibe Wajtu, Ethiopia the predominantly Orthodox Christian community does not mix with the Protestants in the village.

Tajik refugees in the Kyrgyz Republic do not have passports and so cannot access health care services, employment or loans, and cannot vote in elections. In addition, they face hostility from the local people who say that "we had enough problems ourselves, and now you're here to add to them."

Problems of discrimination also extend to the classroom. A group of elderly Roma men report that teachers refuse to enroll Roma children in their classes so they don't attend school.

In Ecuador an indigenous man complains that "teachers would also discriminate. They would say, 'You are an ass; this is why you can't.' 'You are an animal.' Treating us badly in school is a form of discrimination." In addition, parents in every region view non-native language education as a problem because they feel it affects their children's education as well as their prospects. The indigenous people in Ecuador consider education and training (broadly defined) as high priorities for two reasons: first, "men and women without education cannot get good jobs," and second, "men and women without education are an easy target for fraud by businesses."

Physical, Mental and Health Disabilities

Those with disabilities become isolated because they often cannot attend and participate in community gatherings and activities. In Khwalala, Malawi all the participants mention that some people in the community are either marginalized or left out altogether, including those who are disabled or blind. They are considered "incapable of anything" and have nothing to offer. In Krasna Poliana, Bulgaria the research team finds that

> ...the disabled are invisible, confined to their homes, hidden
> from public view, left to cope alone with their problems; they
> are excluded from society because it demonstrates its alienation
> virtually everywhere—the high steps in public places, the ab-
> sence of elevators, inconvenient transport, rutted roads, even
> polyclinics that have no conveniences for wheelchairs. For
> them the world is inaccessible.

Ill health also acts as a barrier to integration within the community in another way. People tend to keep away from those who have contagious diseases (or diseases perceived as contagious). People mention in particular HIV/AIDS, tuberculosis, fits and epilepsy, and leprosy. In Tabe Ere, Ghana a group of men say, "The first people to be excluded are those with fits or convulsions. The belief is that this disease is highly contagious and that a person with such a disease is necessarily a witch or wizard." In urban areas of Jamaica the larger community keeps its distance from those infected with HIV.

Behaviors outside Community Norms

> *Who will deal with those who dig in the trash and eat right*
> *from the waste bins? They are ill with tuberculosis. They are*
> *full of insects. They never wash themselves.*
> —A discussion group participant, Magadan, Russia

Certain behaviors—drug and alcohol addiction, homosexuality, criminal activities, immoral activities and just bad behavior—identify people as different from the rest of the community. Each society has its own behavioral norms, some explicit and others not so clear, and behavior elicits varying responses depending on the context. For instance, people in rural communities of Jamaica seem more tolerant of different behaviors than those in urban areas. Similarly, men and women in the same community may view alcoholics differently. What is typical across communities is that deviants from that community are excluded from the mainstream.

In Thompson Pen, Jamaica researchers report that those most left out of the decisionmaking process are beggars, thieves and those with HIV/AIDS:

> *This group of persons is believed to be a danger to themselves*
> *and others because of the stigma associated with their sexual*
> *orientation or bad fortune. It is firmly believed by all groups*
> *of women that if the beggars and thieves change their life-*
> *styles, it is possible that they can be re-integrated into the*
> *community.*

In Ho Chi Minh City, Vietnam households with drug addicts are often avoided by other households and stigmatized as being involved in "social evils."

Area Stigma

> *One day I was called to work for a company...when they saw*
> *that I lived in Bode, they didn't call me because they thought I*
> *was one of those* marginais *[vagrants or street thugs]...they*
> *didn't trust me.*
> —A resident of Bode, Brazil

Not only are people in remote areas isolated from services and opportunities, but they are often shunned as well by virtue of their addresses. In some areas, especially in Latin America and the Caribbean, entire communities of poor people are stigmatized by society's general perception of their neighborhood as a ghetto or one where violence and crime prevail. "Employers refuse to hire residents of *favelas*, particularly of the poorest ones that have a record of violence," say participants in Brazil. Residents of *favelas* give false addresses and show borrowed electricity and water bills from friends with better addresses to their prospective employers. A woman from Sacadura Cabral says that her husband never gives his address to his colleagues "because of sheer shame."

The Roma in Bulgaria, who are physically isolated and dwell in segregated spaces within the communities in which they live, exclaim, "We're excluded as if we were lepers; we've been left here to die."

Self-Exclusion

> We are social outcasts...we are like refuse, like animals. Like a rubbish bin.
>
> —Homeless people in Sofia, Bulgaria

In Vietnam researchers report that when village leaders cannot speak or write Vietnamese well, it constrains the flow of information down to households. Similarly, the community's ability to represent itself at a higher level with decisionmakers is also constrained: "The effect is to make the whole community more introspective and introverted so they partly self-exclude themselves from wider society. The Khmer communities in Tra Vinh...reported feeling vulnerable when trading or going to market because of their linguistic disadvantages and lower literacy skills. They felt they had no way of knowing if they were being cheated."

Humiliated because of their poverty—which often is exacerbated by neglect from other community members—poor people feel inferior and ashamed of their situation. Even when the rest of the community does not actively exclude them, they may choose to cease mixing with other people. Poor people often perceive a distance between themselves and the better off.

In Tra Vinh, Vietnam poorer households feel looked down on by wealthier households, as exemplified by the case of one poor farmer who "went to buy some *la* [a kind of leaf] and the owner asked me how I could have the money to buy this. I felt very ashamed and didn't go back again."

Young women in Kenesh, Kyrgyz Republic also exhibit low levels of self-esteem when they ask, "Who needs our opinion? Who is going to listen to us?"

The Exclusion of Women

> When a woman gives her opinion, they [men] make fun of her and don't pay attention.... If women go to a meeting, they don't give their opinion.
>
> —A woman, Las Pascuas, Bolivia

> A poor woman is...doubly voiceless due to her gender and social status.... Community decisions are the rights and responsibilities of menfolk. Women's role is only to accept and implement them.
>
> —Research team, Indonesia

The spectrum of changes in gender roles witnessed at the household level (see chapter 6) is not repeated to the same extent at the community level. Women in many of the study communities are less seen and heard in public spaces than are men. Women do take part in some community activities, but often as an extension of their traditional "female" roles (i.e., they cook, clean, decorate, fetch water). Especially disturbing are reports from the former Soviet bloc countries that women feel more invisible now than they did a decade ago. In Asia and Latin America, however, there are signs of women playing a more active role in community affairs.

Even in communities where women are now far more involved in their household decisionmaking processes, they are marginalized or themselves keep away from community-level decisions. Some women and men feel that community decisions are male territory and, thus, out of bounds for the women. Other women express a sheer lack of time and energy to be involved in community issues.

The Indonesian researchers indicate that while formal decisionmaking processes are an established part of community life, the "'Community' normally means just the men":

> *Women's groups everywhere confirm that women are neither invited nor expected to attend village meetings, which are often conducted at male-only events and places such as the Friday post-prayer meeting at the mosque or Balai Desa [village forum]. In Java women have their own community gatherings and activities in PKK [Family Welfare Movement for women] meetings, Posyandu [primary health care], and saving and credit groups [Arisan]. These are, however, for implementing development programs or self-help initiatives, with little community decisionmaking elements. While some of them may attend the general village meetings, women's expected role is generally that of silent observers or servers of tea and refreshments.*

There are some variations within communities where better-off groups of women may feel less alienated than other groups of women in the same community. On the Nusa Tenggara islands in Indonesia, for instance, some better-off women may have some voice, but poorer women have "no right to speak" at community gatherings: "If poor women protest, their voice will not be heard, or even worse, they would be chastised for speaking in public."

In communities with high levels of male migration, women sometimes step in and assume leadership roles by default. Such behavior was mentioned in some of the rural sites from Ecuador and Thailand, for instance.

In South Asia women who were traditionally homebound and not visible in the community are now more active among women's groups supported by NGOs. As a result, there is evidence of increased awareness and confidence among the women. However, as in Indonesia, their participation at the community level appears to be limited to attending meetings and activities organized by the women's groups.

There are some countries, such as Bangladesh, Jamaica and Malawi, where women in a number of communities perceive a marginal improvement in their role at the community level and where they sometimes are included in decisions regarding development activities. According to researchers in Malawi,

> Most of the groups agreed that women now make inputs into community-level decisions. Ten years ago, they did not have any voice.... For example, women today can decide on where to locate a clean water point. They can even have a say on where to build a new health facility. The changes have come about because of the change in the political system and...[because] a good number of women are enlightened and empowered.

The leadership of women in community affairs is perhaps most pronounced in Latin American and the Caribbean countries (except in Bolivia, where the situation seems to have changed little). There many women enjoy access to women's organizations and other NGOs and have organized a myriad of collective activities and campaigns for better community services and infrastructure. According to a participant in a discussion group of married women in Florencio Varela, Argentina, "I go to school meetings and I see women, I go to church meetings and I see women, I go to Plan Vida meetings and I see women.... Anyone know where the men are?" At the final question women began laughing. In fact, and as is indicated in box 7.1,

---

Box 7.1 Gender and Power in Novo Horizonte, Brazil

In Novo Horizonte, a man argues that the women have more power than men do and related this empowerment to education: "Woman has more power than man. Today we go to offices, and there are only women. In the bank, in the post office, in the police station we only see the women [in authority].... Women had access to education, had the options that they did not have in the past. Today they are aldermen, mayors...the women have more power and rights than men. All the men have today, they have to share with them."

The women in the group disagree with this perception of the men and argue that "the woman has more power today than in the past but no more than men...

At the time of the struggle for the community causes, women were very united...They wanted to fight for their ideals....They went to the streets with pans, glasses, wooden spoons to confront the policemen and the local government officials when the houses were built and knocked down...women have a new vision of the world now, more power."

in several communities in the region it is felt that women participate more than the men at the community level. In a number of cases, however, discussion groups indicate that men often continue to exercise power over major community decisions.

Women in Eastern European and Central Asian countries seem to be at the other end of the spectrum, as they have seen a decline in their involvement in community activities and decisionmaking over the last decade with the collapse of the Soviet Union and the economic crisis that followed. In explaining their growing alienation, women speak of shouldering increasing work burdens and also mention declining public support for women's participation in community affairs. In Kenesh, Kyrgyz Republic an elderly woman reports, "Before the collective farm meetings without us would not be valid. We had the right to express our views and participate in taking a decision concerning the village life. And now no one even listens to us." The women in Kenesh express concern over distancing themselves from community affairs while some men say that it was never any of the women's business anyway.

Changes in Social Cohesion

> *There was a fire on our street one month ago. Somebody put my neighbor's barn on fire....The neighbors started to shout "fire, fire." I ran with a bucket and saw just five or six people hurrying. At the end there were no more than a dozen of us. The rest of the neighbors stayed at their homes and did not intervene....Ten years ago the whole street would have been there in five minutes.*
> —A middle-aged woman, Razgrad, Bulgaria

Poor people describe social cohesion as unity within a community where there is shared understanding, mutual support and reciprocity in relationships (see box 7.2). In Brazil the researchers note,

> *The poor define social cohesion in complex ways. Sometimes it is articulated as solidarity and patterns of reciprocity in social interaction. In many instances, it is associated with a sense of belonging to the community. This sense is not the result of social cohesion but, rather, the recognition of equality in poverty conditions and their past or current situation as squatters.*

Social cohesion is also often described in terms of coming together in informal and formal groups, often to solve community problems. Typically, these institutions are strictly local, either rooted in tradition or involving relatively small groups in face-to-face relationships. Where social relations are under stress, local organizations often suffer. Many discussion groups in the study indicate that levels of community bonds and action are declining, and they associate this trend with rising economic hardship. At the other end of the spectrum, however, and sometimes even within the same communities, a seemingly contradictory pattern of change is reported: hardship also catalyzes social ties and drives people and their communities closer together in their struggle for survival.

Box 7.2 Poor People's Definitions of Social Cohesion

In the Kyrgyz Republic researchers note, "Social cohesion is understood...as a possibility to resolve problems of the community by a joint effort of all community members, and as unity and friendship between people of different ethnic backgrounds." In Jamaica the definition of social cohesion includes "unity, togetherness, no political war, understand each other, share experiences and show respect."

In Togdheer, Somaliland participants define social cohesion as "supporting each other during hard times, having common community leadership, extending a helping hand to most unfortunate members of the community and solving problems together in a cooperative and peaceful manner." Older people there think social cohesion exists both during conflict as well as peaceful times, since pastoral groups need to act together in their kinship or clan systems to face the harsh nomadic pastoral environment.

Social cohesion for the residents of Kurkura Dembi, Ethiopia means "sharing ideas, helping each other, praying together, sharing the good and the bad together, sing together at marriages and cry together at funerals."

In Duckensfield, Jamaica social cohesion is defined in terms of "togetherness" or "unity within the community." Clubs and small groups that get together according to age and gender are mentioned as examples. They include "old man parks," "middle class club" and places where the youth meet—"round the corner" and the "long wall."

Men in Tabe Ere, Ghana describe social cohesion in terms of how well different groups in the community come together to build a classroom for the local school or to weed along the roads, as well as contributing money to buy or brew beer and to prepare meals at funerals. The local word they use is wontaa, which means unity and togetherness.

Strained Social Relations and Reduced Collective Action

No one helps anyone, the hungry lives for himself, and the satiated lives for himself.

—A resident, Zawyet Sultan, Egypt

When food was in abundance, relatives used to share it. In these days of hunger not even relatives would help you by giving you some food.

—A young man, Nchimishi, Zambia

In discussions about changes in social cohesion in their communities, many participants mention that economic stress and poverty frequently make people more self-centered and individualistic as they try to cope with their survival. "Now everyone is boiling in their own broth [they have their own problems], there is no time to think about the society," suggests a young man from Kenesh, Kyrgyz Republic. In explaining the lack of community activism in Padre Jordano, Brazil a man shares, "Life for us is so difficult that there is no time left to think about these things...sometimes there comes someone who says, 'Folks, we need to unite ourselves,' and later he disappears." People in Khwalala, Malawi describe disintegrating kinship ties. With declines in food production, relatives hide food and pretend to have run short of supplies so that they don't have to share their food with the more needy relatives. This creates resentment and tension.

In Africa the scourge of HIV/AIDS is breaking up not just communities but families as well, as the disease drains limited resources and the stigma tears them apart. In discussing the impact of HIV/AIDS, discussion groups in Malawi and Zambia highlight the strain of caring for the orphaned. A group of women reflecting on HIV/AIDS from Llonda, Zambia mention that the elderly are also greatly affected, because they are the ones left with the orphans while the "able-bodied women and men are dying."

The difficult political and economic transitions in Eastern Europe and Central Asia, say many participants there, have resulted in significant declines in social cohesion. According to a middle-aged woman from Ak Kiya, Kyrgyz Republic, "There is no unity in our community. We don't visit each other. In the past, we used to help, pool money if somebody had a death in the family. We no longer do. How can people help others if they don't have enough for themselves?" Says a participant in Plovdiv, Bulgaria, "One of the main consequences of poverty is becoming like strangers to each other."

In Bosnia and Herzegovina the devastation of the war and slow recovery have greatly strained local support systems, "No one helps, not anyone," says an older woman of Vares, "I would gladly help someone, but how, when I am in need of help myself. This is misery. Our souls, our psyches are dead. We do not experience any help from our neighbors. If you seek help from your neighbor, he can't help in any case, and they won't because everyone is just fending or grabbing for themselves." Or this from a resident of Sarajevo, "People don't organize themselves. They don't care about other people. If someone gets a donation, they keep their mouths [closed].... Before the war, people cared. There were the trade unions and firms, and now there is no one to help."

Poverty of time, political indifference and lack of unity present further obstacles to organizing at the local level. Rewards are uncertain, and risks many. When probed by researchers on possibilities of organizing, a group of weavers in Foua, Egypt say, "We as handicraftsmen cannot agree with one another. We cannot find food, and we look for work." Similarly, a woman in a discussion group in Esmeraldas, Ecuador commented that unity within the community is needed before they can approach the municipality to get support. The rest of the discussion group looked on with very long faces, as if the woman had said the worst possible thing, or something that was impossible.

What Brings People Together?

Paradoxically, discussion groups in quite varying contexts highlight that hardship can also galvanize people and draw them closer together. This seems to be the case especially among family and kin. "Even if you are on bad terms with your relatives, you always know that if you are in real need, they will help you," says a participant of Kalaidzhi, Bulgaria. People in most every context view the family as a dependable source of support on which they could always rely during a crisis. Poor people turn to extended families for loans, food and sometimes contacts for jobs or funds for health emergencies. In Malawi people cite grandparents for providing moral and social values and advice, especially among the youth.

Beyond the immediate and extended family poor people also turn to friends, neighbors and a diverse range of local groups. Through these networks, poor people highlight countless examples of helping each other to overcome survival, safety and social problems: a neighborhood watch in the Zambian farming village of Kabamba works to deter theft; a library provides after-school care for children in Duckensfield, Jamaica; women members of an NGO in Madaripur, Bangladesh raised Tk 50,000 from local villagers to help a couple with their daughter's marriage, which was being postponed because of the demands for dowry.

Death, devastation and other stresses perhaps most frequently trigger community action. In Mbwadzulu, Malawi a discussion group of men and women explain,

> Whenever there is a funeral, we work together...women draw
> water, collect firewood, and collect maize flour from well-wish-
> ers...while the men dig the grave and bury the dead.... We
> work together on community projects like molding bricks for a
> school project.... Women also work together when cleaning
> around the boreholes.

In Borg Meghezel, Egypt a poor man describes how an accident brought out community cohesion in sharing the grief:

> Some time ago we had a major accident when one of the boats
> disappeared with all its crew; none of them returned. For a
> whole year we refused to have any wedding, to turn on any
> television or radio, or to have any kind of celebration, so as to
> express our mourning to those who disappeared.

In the village of Pegambiran, Indonesia neighbors regularly share corn, peanuts and cassava among needier families. In Foua, Egypt the researchers found few groups where poor people could turn in times of crisis. Some mention taking their case to the imam of the mosque. They go to him on Fridays, the day of the week set aside for congregational prayer, and a handkerchief for donations is placed at the mosque's entrance.

Social cohesion sometimes exists among people performing the same type of work. For example, in El Mataria, Egypt discussion group participants report, "Whenever there is a crisis, the fishermen help each other by collecting money for the person needing help." Similarly in Mbwadzulu, Malawi villagers say, "At times when a person is in trouble in the middle of the lake, for example, his lamp has run out of kerosene or he has lost his paddle...when he shouts for help, we always go to assist."

The Opportunity and Challenge

We live together, and when there is something we need to discuss together, we gather here as we have done now.
—Discussion group participants, Mbwadzulu, Malawi

Participants in Kajima, Ethiopia indicate several organizations that bring them together for religious, social and financial needs. The researchers note, "These are all informal local institutions that, this way or another, bring the people together. They have contributed a great deal to bring about social cohesion among the people in the community." Any potential conflict, including among individuals, is resolved by the elderly of the community.

So often poor people's support systems go unrecognized. Their informality and diversity makes them both easy and tempting for public officials and NGOs to disregard. Although local actors and groups provide vital resources in the daily lives of poor people, on their own these networks are unlikely to propel people out of poverty. As a poor woman from Achy, Kyrgyz Republic acknowledges, "If I borrow 5 kilograms of flour from a neighbor, I will have bread for two days. On the third or fourth day I'll have to return the flour." When stressed, these vital bonds can break down, leaving poor women and men even more vulnerable and isolated.

Poor people's networks are fragile. The biggest challenge for development is to build on these. In the case of support for poor women and other excluded groups, NGOs appear to have an important role. Although few, there are some success stories of NGOs working with particular excluded groups—ragpickers, the disabled, and, in India, scheduled castes (the lowest of the four castes) and tribes, sex workers and orphans—helping them assert their rights and gain status and acceptance in society, and self-respect.

Notes

[1]Small groups discussed issues related to social cohesion and social exclusion, usually after the participants had analyzed wellbeing and illbeing. Researchers first asked participants to provide their own criteria for analyzing wellbeing. If these included social exclusion and cohesion, participants were asked to elaborate and give examples. However, in cases where the group did not mention these, the facilitators introduced these issues by asking specific questions, such as: Are some people or groups left out of society, or looked down upon or excluded from active participation in community life or decisionmaking? Who gets left out and on what basis? What is the impact of such exclusion? Is it possible for those excluded ever to become included? How do people define social cohesion? Is there more or less social unity and sense of belonging than before? Why? Is there more or less crime and conflict than in the past, or has it stayed at the same level? Why? Are there tensions or conflicts among groups in the community? Which groups? Why? Have intergroup conflicts increased or decreased? Why? How? Researchers also asked participants to analyze whether they have seen any changes in gender roles and relations at the community level.

Chapter 8

Anxiety, Fear and Insecurities

Summary

Poor people repeatedly stress the anxiety and fear they experience because they feel insecure and vulnerable. Most say they feel less secure and more vulnerable today than in previous times. They describe security as stability and continuity of livelihood, predictability of relationships, feeling safe and belonging to a social group. Forms and degrees of security and insecurity vary by region and differ by gender. Women are vulnerable to abuse and violence in the home, when widowed, and in the workplace. Men, particularly young men, are more likely to be picked up by the police.

The origins and nature of insecurities are related to types of threat, shock and stress. People most frequently mention the following:

> ▸ *Insecurities of work and livelihood.*
> ▸ *Natural and human-made disasters.*
> ▸ *Crime and violence.*
> ▸ *Persecution by the police and lack of justice.*
> ▸ *Civil conflict and war.*
> ▸ *Macropolicy shocks and stresses.*
> ▸ *Social vulnerability.*
> ▸ *Health, illness and death.*

Insecurities and mishaps are an integral and pervasive part of the illbeing of the poor, threatening them and making them anxious, fearful and miserable. Preventing and mitigating shocks benefit the poor. The practical question is: To achieve security for the poor as a base for material improvement, social wellbeing, and peace of mind, what and who has to change?

Introduction

Everyday I am afraid of the next.
—A youth, Ekaterinburg, Russia

Where there is no security, there is no life.
—A man, Dagaar, Somaliland

With only a few exceptions, notably in some isolated communities, poor people report feeling less secure and more fearful than they did 10 years earlier.

The chapter begins with poor people's definitions of security. Regional trends and some gender differences are then highlighted. This leads into a typology of shocks and stresses. The chapter concludes with some reflections.[1]

What Does Security Mean to Poor People?

Security is peace of mind and the possibility to sleep relaxed.
—A woman, El Gawaber, Egypt

To be well is to know what will happen with me tomorrow.
—Middle-aged man, Razgrad, Bulgaria

The term *security* seems to describe one of poor people's major concerns. In general, security implies stability and continuity. Vulnerability implies the inability to cope with shock or misfortune. Increases in insecurity and vulnerability result in pervasive anxiety and fear. For poor people, security has many local meanings. Based on the views of a range of groups in Krasna Poliana, Bulgaria, security has four dimensions: stability of income, predictability of one's daily life, protection from crime and psychological security.

Financial security means a stable and steady income. Pensioners say, "There is security, stability when you have a job and stable pay...before 10 November 1989 life was better: there was greater security because the prices of foods and medicines were low and stable." Or in the words of a young person from Sofia, "Jobs provide security; if there are jobs there'll also be support for the elderly and large families." Young people in Bulgaria say, "There was greater security before, higher incomes, more work. People are now afraid, especially older people. Ultimately security is measured in terms of money; it all boils down to money."

The second type of security—predictability of daily life—is prominent in descriptions by the Roma people. They worry more about unpredictability than income security. A community report from Bulgaria says that Roma men describe security as knowing "what to expect."

The third type of security—protection from crime—is linked to feeling safe. Insecurity arises from lack of law and order and increased crime. A group of men and women in Krasna Poliana say,

People are afraid in general. Of crime, of going home alone late at night. Large-scale drug addiction and prostitution have also become a threat. To feel safer, people now have iron bars installed on their windows and doors; there should be tougher laws and coordination among authorities.

The fourth meaning of security—psychological security—focuses on the emotional, psychological sense of belonging to a social group. A group of men and women explain, "You have a sense of security when you are free and loved by your close ones." The youth raise both practical anxieties and more existential ones: "How could you feel secure when you are a mere mortal and could die suddenly? I am insecure, but I don't think I will be surprised by anything."

The complexity and multiple dimensions of security can also be seen in rural Ghana. In Adaboya men define security to mean protection against all forms of harm from both physical and spiritual forces. Security includes having property that can be sold in times of need, but it also includes having a "soul guardian," to protect a person. It entails making sacrifices to shrines and ancestors, possessing bangles and rings that have magical powers, owning livestock, having NGOs or governments construct irrigation dams, having direct roads to markets, forming youth action groups, having children who support aging parents, having many wives or children, having a stable job and having enough to eat.

Although poor people see the conventional understanding of insecurity and vulnerability as important, in the study a strong psychological dimension emerges. Not knowing, a lack of control, and inability to take defensive action emerge as important factors in various ways. A participant in a discussion group in El Mataria, Egypt says, "Vulnerability is something that we do not know and we cannot face or anticipate. It is also the thing that we know is going to happen but at the same time we are unable to face." In the same community in Egypt people describe weakness and vulnerability as the inability to face others due to the difference in physical power and material wealth: "Even if I am not harming anyone, people will still harm me because I am weak." In northern Ghana women define insecurity as a series of risks, including sickness, death, hunger, fear, theft and possible destruction of crops by monkeys. Throughout these and other discussions across regions, anxiety emerges as the defining characteristic of insecurity, and the anxiety is based not on one but on many risks and fears: anxiety about jobs, anxiety about not getting paid, anxiety about needing to migrate, anxiety about lack of protection and safety, anxiety about floods and drought, anxiety about shelter, anxiety about falling ill, and anxiety about the future of children and settling them well in marriage.

People are also anxious about declining family, community and charitable support. A poor person in Dahshour, Egypt notes that "the poor person who gets help is even more vulnerable, because the day may come when the charitable person may stop helping. Then what would become of him? He expects this to happen and worries about it."

Trends and Patterns

> *Before, thieves wouldn't rob in their own neighborhood.*
> *Before, your neighbor wouldn't rob you. Now the rules have*
> *changed.*
> —Participant, discussion group of men and women,
> La Matanza, Argentina

Poor people across countries report a decline in security, but there are some regional and gender differences. Although reasons vary, increases in insecurity come from multiple causes that feed into one another, making it difficult for the poor to escape spiraling insecurity.

Regional Trends in Security

Poor people report a decrease in security over the last 10 years in every region, though the reasons vary. In Africa they are closely related to basic agriculture and survival that depend on the vagaries of nature, rains, droughts, etc. In Eastern Europe and Central Asia, people see the collapse of the state and the switch to market economies as the central reason for increased insecurity. In South Asia, both in India and Bangladesh, lack of land, land-related issues, and natural disasters—both floods and droughts—dominate in rural areas. In urban areas, people feel insecure because they may be evicted. In East Asia, people cite the economic crisis, loss of jobs, and tight markets for those who are self-employed. In the Latin American and Caribbean countries, people point to lack of safety, crime and lack of economic opportunities as key reasons for increased insecurity. In urban areas poor people also mention greater environmental vulnerability.

Gender Differences

Women in many countries feel their security is linked to the fate of their husbands. Men are more likely to associate insecurity with events outside the household that affect income, such as unemployment, natural disasters, increasing crime and lack of social and external support.

In Bangladesh in the study communities, security for women means having a male earner in the household, a son to every mother, and a monogamous husband. Older women say it means sons should not sever ties with their mothers after the sons get married. Women's definitions of security in some places include being financially well off, being able to provide for children, being able to provide meals for the family and having a house. In many areas women also mention respect as well as freedom from fear of robbery. Men describe security in terms of access to cultivable land, health, and employment.

In Kajima, Ethiopia women in rural areas say that because their physical mobility is more limited than that of men, they are more dependent on agriculture for their livelihoods and hence are more insecure. In the Kyrgyz Republic a 21-year-old woman says that a single woman living in a dormitory "may be humiliated, insulted, and sexually harassed by local men who know that the woman has no husband to protect her." This woman had left her husband because he drank to excess and beat her.

Although both poor men and women are forced to look for jobs, credit and assistance, women and men both report that women face special vulnerability. In many contexts, women must face the humiliation of sexual abuses. In Brazil and Jamaica, women report feeling vulnerable to sexual assault and rape. In Bangladesh, insecurity for women includes abduction and being forced to spend the night with the abductor and being returned the next day, being "teased" on the road by men, and being victims of acid-throwing incidents. For their part, men feel more insecure because of their greater likelihood of being picked up by the police. In Brazil, Jamaica and Russia young men feel vulnerable to police harassment and brutality. A poor youth in Dzerzhinsk, Russia said he had been detained on false accusations by the police and was kept in a cold cell to the end of the month so the police could fulfill their quota. Young people feel that, instead of catching real criminals, the police target youth because they are easy to apprehend.

In Uzbekistan, people say it is common practice for the police and customs officials to insert drugs in the belongings of migrants trying to take part in cross-border trade in consumer goods with neighboring Kyrgyz Republic. To avoid prosecution, the Uzbek men then have to leave behind a large portion of their goods. It is precisely because of men's higher risk of conflict with Kyrgyz police that women are now more active in this trade.

Types of Insecurity

On the basis of poor people's descriptions, types of insecurity can be broadly linked to the following factors:

- ▶ Survival and livelihoods.
- ▶ Natural disasters.
- ▶ Crime and violence.
- ▶ Persecution by police and lack of justice.
- ▶ Civil conflict and war.
- ▶ Macropolicy shocks and stresses.
- ▶ Social vulnerability.
- ▶ Health, illness and death.

Survival and Livelihoods

> *As if land shortage is not bad enough we live a life of tension worrying about the rain: will it rain or not? There is nothing about which we say, "this is for tomorrow." We live hour to hour.*
>
> —A woman, Kajima, Ethiopia

> *You can't be sure that when you do a job, you'll get paid for it.*
> —An older woman, Dimitrovgrad, Bulgaria

> *Today, we're fine; tomorrow they will throw us out.*
> —A poor woman from a squatter settlement in
> Isla Trinitaria, Ecuador

Poor people speak of anxieties about sheer survival, hunger and the search for food and shelter. They express many concerns about insecurities of work and sources of livelihood. In rural areas the focus is on agriculture, natural resources and limited options. In urban areas the main focus is on employment and illegality.

Rural: Uncertain Returns to Farming

> *Rainfall is erratic and unreliable. Sometimes it is too much, and sometimes it is just not there. There are also many pests. To make things worse, our farmland is continuously decreasing as a result of concessions given to poultry farms by private investors.*
> —A group of poor men and women, Kajima, Ethiopia

In rural areas, poor people worry about the climatic and other insecurities of agriculture. Ethiopia provides many examples of climatic stress with uncertain rains combining with other factors, including destruction of houses.

In Kajima, Ethiopia women characterize poverty as the state of "dying while seated" or when "water becomes a big thing." The main factor for this state of affairs in their community, women say, is their dependency on the rains: "Sometimes it doesn't rain when it should and there is no harvest, or the pests eat up the crops and there isn't much we can do. All people here suffer equally since this is God's will and there is no poor or rich, all are equally exposed." These poor Ethiopian women see no escape from their precarious existence, or from having to fall back on other means of livelihood: "As long as our soul has not parted from our body, we will make a living selling cow dung."

In Bolivia poor farmers in Horenco talk about their fears of environmental vulnerability. They speak of changes in climate and weather patterns that make farming that is dependent on rainfall insecure and highly risky. "Before it rained in its season; now there are changes in time and climate; it doesn't rain when it has the chance. Some have production and some don't." "Diseases in crops and livestock cause losses and worry." People speak about notable deterioration in the land because of unpredictable weather and about increases in crop and livestock diseases for which new technical knowledge is required. To cope, they have attempted to diversify and combine rural activities with work in the city.

Urban: Insecure Work, No Bargaining Power

> Risk is the acceptance of endangering one's honor, or safety
> or future, in order to earn an income or to cover immediate
> expenses.
>
> —Poor man, Bedsa, Egypt

Insecure casual labor is widespread in urban and rural areas. Salaried employment even at low wages is prized for its security above irregular higher-paying jobs. In Dimitrovgrad, Bulgaria youth say, "Security means to know that you have a regular job and regular pay, to live more or less decently."

Those searching for jobs suffer the frustrations of powerlessness. Being denied information adds to their humiliation. A poor man in Plovdiv, Bulgaria describes his job hunting:

> The first thing I do everyday is to buy the Maritza [local news-
> paper] and look at the announcements. Then I go from one
> employer to another looking for a job. And usually they say
> no, without any explanation. The employer can keep you up to
> three months on a temporary contract without signing a per-
> manent contract. At the end of the third month he just says
> "Go away," without explaining how and why. Just "Go
> away." He could send you away even earlier if he did not like
> you. If you say anything, if you cross him, he says, "Go away,
> there are thousands like you waiting for your position."

Employment in the private sector, even when obtained, is insecure. Poor participants speak about their vulnerability and lack of recourse against the injustices of employers. In Mohammadpur, Bangladesh garment workers can lose their jobs because of any irregularity. Men also report that a garment factory owner refused to pay overtime compensation to workers for losses incurred during strikes, when owners closed factories to keep them safe from terrorist attacks. In Russia people feel the working class is no longer protected because there are no trade unions: "They force you to quit your job, but they wouldn't lay you off themselves, because then they would have to pay you severance [benefits]. It makes no sense to go to court. Workers are a class not protected anymore." They contrast their predicament with the past: "We didn't have to worry before; everybody had some savings. At work we had special money pools...." But now their insecurity and worry are heightened because they have no savings to fall back on.

In the urban casual labor market, poor people find themselves in a weak bargaining position. In Bangladesh poor men in Mohammadpur say they cannot protest when they receive lower wages than agreed upon because plenty of others are waiting for the few jobs there are. Rickshaw pullers lose their rickshaws when they are late in payment. In fishing communities in Borg Meghezel, Egypt, those who are most dependent on whether the boat owner needs extra cheap labor on their boats feel the most insecure: "Everyday we do not know whether we are going to eat or not."

In Bolivia the urban poor say they constantly search for jobs and that, in the end, there is always the chance they will not be paid. An elderly man in Esmeraldas, Ecuador says, "There is no work there [in the countryside], nothing, and if you go to work they don't pay you. I went to get paid up there...nothing...not even half—in any case the life you lead is bad, because you work and don't get paid. That's how life is."

The poor often take dangerous jobs. In the village of Borg Meghezel fishermen tell of the risks of being out in the seas. Everyday they say, "We are working while carrying our lives between our hands." In La Matanza, Argentina a discussion group of men spoke of their community giving up hope. They observed that young people drop out of school saying, "If the adults are unemployed, why should I live?" One of the men in the group went on to comment that "before, in my father's time you were without work for one week, a week without work; today years go by when you don't have work; the only alternative is to die."

Natural and Human-Made Disasters

The biggest shock we ever had was Hurricane Gilbert: the shock was because all that we found after Gilbert was one wooden chair.

—A woman, Millbank, Jamaica

The atmosphere is not rewarding us; lately the climate has been adverse.

—A poor male farmer, Río La Sal, Bolivia

Many poor people link insecurity to natural disasters and dangers and to degraded and polluted environments. Poor people often live and work precisely where these hazards prevail and combine. And in Jamaica, a country subject to hurricanes, the community report summarizes security for fishermen in Little Bay as "the ability of persons to cope with disasters."

People mention many natural disasters and dangers, including landslides, floods, high winds and hurricanes, riverbank erosion, fires, and wild animals. Some disasters can be quite localized, such as one or a few houses burning down. In Achy, Kyrgyz Republic people speak of a landslide in 1994 that buried several houses and a big barn in the soil and killed some villagers.

Hippopotamuses destroyed crops in Mbwadzulu in Malawi. In Bangladesh and Ecuador poor people speak about the devastation from floods.

The dangers of storms and winds stand out. In the village of Borg Meghezel in Egypt, the risk of typhoons prevents fishing in the winter. More dramatically, very high winds leave lasting damage. In Little Bay, Jamaica villagers talk about houses destroyed 11 years earlier by Hurricane Gilbert that have never been repaired or replaced. Fishermen there have also been unable to replace the fish pots they lost in Hurricane Mitch.

In urban shanties, fire is a special danger. Fire can consume everything, leaving people destitute. A Vietnamese couple in Lao Cai, Vietnam say, "Everything was in the fire, even the chopsticks." In Battala slum in Mohammadpur, Bangladesh a fire lasting for two days in February 1998 left almost all houses and shops burned except for a few brick ones; the fire was followed by outbreaks of diarrhea, fever and pneumonia. For Ali Akbar, "all belongings were burnt to ashes" in that fire. NGOs and local authorities provided satisfactory levels of relief, but people are still afraid as a result of the fire.

Natural and human-made disasters affect all households, but poor people report limited ability to recover. In rural areas in Vietnam the poor spoke about the difficulties in recovering from natural disaster, floods, drought, storms, pests, or animal death due to disease. They said that those with capital have a buffer and are better able to survive and recover, whereas poorer households without capital reserves go under with even the smallest shock.

Crime and Violence

> *I do not know who to trust, the police or the criminals. Our public safety is ourselves. We work and hide indoors...and of dangers at school...I am afraid that they might kill my son for something as irrelevant as a snack.*
> —From a women's group, Sacadura Cabral, Brazil

> *Violence is a chain: the man beats the woman, the woman takes it out on the children, and the children are violent even with the animals.*
> —A youth, Barrio Universitarios, Bolivia

To one degree or another, poor people speak of declining public safety as an element of increasing insecurity in almost every country, in both rural and urban areas. People mention it least in India and most often in Brazil and Russia. Increasing crime is linked to breakdown in social cohesion, difficulties in finding employment, hunger, increased migration, drugs and drug trafficking, actions and inactions of the police, and the building of roads that allow strangers to enter communities easily. Poor people connect crime with decline in social community, with competitiveness and people looking out only for themselves. While the well off have more to lose from theft, Jamaicans say that "crime and violence are experienced by poorer more than richer households."

Rural communities in different countries especially fear theft of livestock, crops and vegetables. In some communities in Ethiopia women identify increasing livestock theft as the greatest risk to their security. They feel that if such theft is not curtailed, it will be increasingly difficult to deal with urgent needs in the usual way through the sale of livestock. For many poor families, theft of livestock is like having their savings account stolen. Crime and violence emerged as issues, particularly in Latin America and the Caribbean, Eastern Europe and Central Asia, and Africa.

Latin America and the Caribbean

> *One of the neighbors died and his wake was held not at his house but at a funeral home. When the family came back they returned to an empty house. The thieves took full advantage of the fact they weren't home and stole everything.*
> —Participant, discussion group of men and women,
> La Matanza, Argentina

> *You have no control over anything, at any hour there could be a [gun] shot, especially at night.*
> —A young poor woman, Brazil

Poor people in the slums of Brazil have a pervasive sense of being exposed: "To live in a *barraco* is the same as living in the streets." In Bode, poor people in slums link crime with the presence of the *marginais* (vagrants or street thugs) who are defined as "those who without thinking smoke crack and go out killing us...." People say, "The *marginais* are present in the everyday reality of the community...the life of the people is bothered by these underdogs, who are involved with drugs, gang fights, vandalism, and organized crime."

In Brazilian urban slums, people express fear for their children and themselves. Drug use among children and teenagers and the absence of police control add to the problems. To change the situation, people want government action and police presence, as well as the development of solidarity and integration between people. Young men and women say that "people are like a dog...only protect their house...if outside the house someone is robbed or dead...nobody cares."

In slums in Ecuador, although environmental insecurity and illegality are primary concerns, people also speak about runaway criminality in some areas. A group of adult men in Isla Trinitaria say, "There are gangs and delinquency and lack of protection by the police" and "there is absolutely no safety; there is no law and no police."

Jamaicans define risk as being afraid or prone to harm. In Duckensfield people think the greatest risk is having the business stores robbed. People feel that thieves operate from within the community and that houses that are not fenced are regularly robbed, and thefts, rapes and killings have increased. The situation in Duckensfield contrasts sharply with Accompong, however, where people in fact "feel safe and secure in the surroundings, walking freely at night and even leaving doors unlocked." Despite obvious poverty, "in times of trouble, people help each other, although both genders openly express disgust with the level of dependency and support required by the other gender. When crimes are committed, people say they can always identify the perpetrator. Disputes are settled quickly when they arise, with very little hard feelings on both parts. There is a record of only one murder since the community was established."

Europe and Central Asia

> *In spring they stole the onions from my vegetable garden. I had just planted them; they hadn't even grown.*
> —A poor woman, Belasovka, Russia

In Russia people report that as a result of lawlessness, organized crime, unemployment and extortion, poor people have to deal with theft and crime in their lives (see box 8.1).

In Novy Gorodok settlement in Western Siberia participants speak about increases in theft and criminality linked to increased drug trade. Roma men in Krasna Poliana, Bulgaria say, "Anything might be in store for you. What sort of security are you supposed to have when you never know if they'll cut off your power supply, if the skinheads will attack you, if you'll have supper for the children tonight?"

In the Kyrgyz Republic participants attribute the increase in crime to poverty. In the village of Bashi, they most frequently mention the theft of cattle and sheep, as meat commands high prices in town. People also report an increase in murders, which had once been rare. In Bashi, a group of poor men and women put it thus: "People are no longer surprised when someone kills his brother."

Box 8.1 Theft of Vegetables in Belasovka, Russia

"They steal everything from our vegetable gardens; they dig up potatoes, garlic, tomatoes, carrots, marrow."

"They steal plastic sheets from hothouses and from garden beds."

"They steal piglets and chickens."

"We watched over our potatoes with a gun. People from other towns pretend to come to pick mushrooms. They sprinkle a few mushrooms and some grass over the top of the basket, and underneath they have potatoes."

In countries of Eastern Europe and Central Asia those who have done well economically are often identified as criminals. This was true of "new Russians," whom poor people see as mafiosi. In Sarajevo in Bosnia and Herzegovina the only people who are perceived as doing well are the "mafiosi" and the "war profiteers." Older women mention "war plundering" of factories and industrial machines as an example of criminal activity.

Africa

> *People can now rob you in broad daylight.*
> —A discussion group participant in Kowerani
> Masasa, Malawi

Although more acute in urban areas, even in rural areas of Africa, poor people report an increase in levels of theft. In rural Kowerani Masasa, Malawi all discussion groups emphasize that crime has worsened in the last two years. People say that the rise in crime is forcing people into poverty, "but we are very cooperative when one is attacked." They define security as "*chitetzo*, a household protecting itself from theft. The rich were better able to do this because they have the money to recruit security guards and build fences around their homes." Crime includes acts of theft, robbery, burglary, murders and other acts that pose physical threats to people's lives. All communities, except one rural village, report such acts.

In the Adaboya region in Ghana, men define crime as any act that makes another feel bad or hurt. They also define theft, adultery, incest and rape as crimes and think these crimes are increasing because "everybody is trying to get rich by foul or fair means." Thefts focus on livestock, cattle, sheep, goats, pigs, fowl, and sometimes money. Women say increasing theft of livestock has threatened their livestock rearing.

Persecution by Police and Lack of Justice

> *Now even the police will rob you; you go in to report a crime and you come out feeling violated.*
> —A 44-year-old woman, Dock Sud, Argentina

> *When the police come here, it is to rob us…to humiliate everybody.*
> —A discussion group participant,
> Entra a Pulso, Brazil

> *Imagine when we send these thieves to the police. We end up being disappointed to see them back the same day.*
> —Participant, discussion group of poor men
> and women, Chitambi, Malawi

The police are an unfortunate necessity; they are transitory vigilantes; if you call them, they don't come; they sleep and when you need them you have to pay a bribe.
— Participant, discussion group of men and women,
Isla Trinitaria, Ecuador

Perhaps one of the most striking revelations of the study is the extent to which the police and official justice systems side with the rich, persecute poor people and make poor people more insecure, fearful, and poorer. Particularly in urban areas, poor people perceive the police not as upholding justice, peace and fairness, but as threats and sources of insecurity. Women report feeling vulnerable to sexual assault by police, and young men say they have been beaten up by the police without cause.

This negative experience is not universal. In some cases, the police support and help the poor. Poor people in parts of Africa give more examples of good performance and favorable evaluation than in other regions. In Ethiopia, participants (female students) say the presence of the police station protects the poor from thieves and helps maintain peace and order in the community. In Zambia groups often cite the police as an important institution, and the police are seen as providing protection from theft. The Victim Support Unit of the Zambia Police also receives positive remarks. In Munamalgasvewa in Sri Lanka poor people feel the police get along with the villagers, and preschool classes are held inside the police post.

Communities also report cases in which the relationship has changed from negative to positive. One such community is in Malawi. During the Mozambican war, the Police Mobile Forces Officers were stationed in the community to maintain peace and order as Mozambican refugees came in. According to the local people, many police came in and were accused of "victimizing innocent people, especially men, and raping women." The community changed this by insisting that the policemen be replaced every month. Consequently, the police now are "helping catch thieves [and] thugs, guard market places, and help in loan recovery." People say the police are doing a very good job.

Regional Patterns

The criminals have public safety; we do not.
— A woman, Sacadura Cabral, Brazil

Officers do not even care to talk...if they are not given money. If a poor man is beaten by a rich man and goes to file a case against the rich man, the officer concerned does not even register the case.
— A discussion group participant, Gowainghat,
Bangladesh

Overall, participants report extraordinarily widespread evidence of corrupt, criminal, and sometimes brutal activities by the police, especially in Latin America and the Caribbean, Asia and Eastern Europe. The range of reported bad behavior by the police includes being

> ▶ *Unresponsive:* Absent where needed, not coming when called or coming very late; only coming when someone has been killed.
> ▶ *Corrupt:* False arrest, accusation, and imprisonment, with release only on heavy payment; theft, including stealing money from children; bribes for documents or to register cases; lying; threats, blackmail, and extortion; demanding protection money; using drugs; and conniving with criminals and releasing them when arrested.
> ▶ *Brutal:* Harassing street vendors and other poor people; confiscating identity documents; raping women who go to police stations; beating up innocent people; torture; and murder, including killing street boys.

In Brazil poor people rate the police as the worst institution in 7 of the 10 urban communities. However, in the other three communities as well, experiences with the police have been negative. In Vila Junqueira a man says, "We do not have safety in the suburbs; the police show up only by chance." Others say the police refuse to come unless someone has been killed. In Entra a Pulso, when people in 6 of 10 discussion groups were asked which of the institutions needed to change, they picked the police.

Despite these low ratings, people say they desperately need police to provide a modicum of safety in neighborhoods. In response to mounting violence in one community, Bode, Brazil, people organized, collected money, built a police station on their own and invited the police to come and work from it. In November 1992 after great pressure, the police agreed to come, but they left in February 1993 because some *marginais* destroyed the police station.

In the slums of Brazil poor people cite the lack of protection from violence and crime as the most important reason for their vulnerability. An observation from Bode is typical: "The police don't do anything because they don't want to." Violence affects every aspect of life—schools, streets and the home. Numerous incidents are cited, coming from every community except one. A group of women in Sacadura Cabral say, "You see a lot of drugs around here. They kidnap and kill boys, 11–12 year olds." and "Once I was kept tied up for an hour. They stole a watch and a blouse to sell and buy drugs."

Poor people in Argentina consider police presence a blight, particularly in urban areas. In Dock Sud, a group of young males equate insecurity with police presence: "The police? If you think about it, the police are like the rubbish: it's everywhere. They come and pick you up for no reason. There have been several cases of police killing. The police kill; they are loose and we're locked up." While in Barrio Sol y Verde, a discussion group of men and women comment, "The police ask for money when you go to get a certificate. They demand that you give them what you have. The other day some children had to give them their travel money, and they had to walk all the way home."

In Ecuador, based on discussions, the researchers concluded that the "military is more reliable than the police."

In Jamaica, while poor people consider the police important, the police receive mixed reviews. In urban areas, they are rated negatively because of their inability to protect the innocent from criminals, and for violence, illicit fees, and beating of young men, who the police assume are "looking for trouble" when they are "looking for work." Overall, poor people's experiences can be summarized as "the police lie and steal from the poor."

In Bangladesh, poor people distrust the police because the police are said to harass the poor and would never register a case without taking large bribes. In the slums of Dhaka they say, "The police always catch the innocent people instead of the guilty ones. They never come on time when incidents happen in the slum." Chittagong slum-dwellers define vulnerability as "the failure to protect their young daughters from hooligans as well as protect themselves both from the harassment of outsider hoodlums and police."

In the state of Bihar in India poor people see the police as a constant threat to their livelihoods of foraging in forests or on railroad tracks or vending on the street. They also feel that the "menace" of the police has increased many times over. Rethvi Devi of Patna has to pay a bribe to the railway police to collect coal dust on railroad tracks. Every sack of coal dust she brings home fetches Rs 40 after she kneads the coal dust into lumps of coal and takes the coal to the local factory. Her monthly income from this laborious effort is Rs 500 to Rs 800, from which she pays out money in bribes to the railway police. Box 8.2 summarizes conclusions based on the India study.

In Dangara, Uzbekistan poor people's experiences with the police are summarized as "the police have become the rich people's stick used against common people."

Workers in Tashkent, Uzbekistan speak extensively about the humiliation and extortion they experience in their contacts with the police. Following the bomb explosions in February 1999, everyone now needs either temporary or permanent resident permits to work in Tashkent. This has become another opportunity for extortion. Migrants who come to work say the police take their passports to examine and then charge them with lack of papers, demand substantial sums of money to return the passports, or make them work for nothing in their bosses' homes and treat them brutally.

With the Roma in Bulgaria the relationship with the police can go either way. In Fillipovtsi, Sofia, Roma groups feel the main problem is lack of protection by the police. The Roma say that when they are attacked by skinheads, the police often beat up the Gypsies and let the skinheads go free. Police brutality against both Roma men and women is reported to be common. In Dimitrovgrad, however, the police and the Roma seem to have arrived at a peaceful coexistence, at least from the men's point of view. Of all institutions, the men rate the police the highest precisely because they are not playing out their punitive role: "The only respect Gypsies get is at the police station, [because] they know that people have no other chance and steal as a last resort. Only the police show some respect, no one else. If they decide to lock us away, there won't be a single one of us left." A young man says, "They know what we are [criminals] and understand us— we have nothing against them, and they don't have anything against us." Only women say, "They [police] are all in the game. If an innocent person becomes a victim, they won't come and help because they're guarding those other guys...."

In Russia reports of harassment by the police and of the police and criminals working together are widespread. Older people complain that they do not feel protected by the police. Young boys in several places report cases where the police persecuted them: "They take us into the cell on any pretext or without, to show their bosses they are active in arresting hooligans."

Insecurity in the face of police is often heightened by legal status. The informal livelihoods of poor people often make them vulnerable, being either illegal or on the fringes of the law. Lack of tenure rights to the land where they live is perhaps an even more acute and very common insecurity. Let a woman in Brazil have the last word:

> When a government official comes here and says that we have
> to leave the area, I freak out. I gather my things...but don't
> know where to go.... I don't know if I should take my sons
> out of school...if I should pack food so that we don't run out
> of food on the road.... I feel insecure, lost. At this moment, it
> is just God and me.

Civil Conflict and War

When we fled our homes, we left everything that was of value,
all the things that we had worked all our lives to have, to build
a home.

      —A woman, Bijeljina, Bosnia and Herzegovina

I fled to Ethiopian refugee camps with my family...where we
experienced incredible problems—we faced bad health, malnu-
trition, and lack of income. Something we will never forget for
the rest of our lives. We returned to Yo'ub-Yabooh with empty
hands.

            —An old man, Somaliland

Due to the war situations people left for Chavakacheri and
Vanni areas in 1995. Due to the war about 20 percent of the
houses were totally destroyed and damaged.
        —Research team, Jaffna, Sri Lanka

While almost everyone pays the price for war, it wreaks havoc and further adds to the insecurity poor people face. Four of the countries in which the study took place—Bosnia and Herzegovina, Ethiopia, Somaliland and Sri Lanka—have experienced recent civil conflict and war. In all these countries discussion groups state that civil conflict destroys the basis for livelihoods and makes it harder to rebuild lives.

In Somaliland most groups speak about how conflicts cause insecurity. People define security as "when an individual, family or community has no fear for their lives, property or their dignity." Old men in Dagaar, Somaliland say security is the key to prosperity: "If there is security, there is no fear; people can go wherever there is a market for their produce; transport trucks can cross all boundaries, and there is no fear of land mines." Poor people attribute many of the current problems of poor markets for produce and animals, bad roads, and the poor production to past instability. In the post-conflict situation, though, they say social and political conditions have improved. In Qoyta village people say neighboring clans have settled conflicts, and bonds between families in the village have strengthened. The immense destruction of infrastructure, including water supplies, however, continues to make sheer survival difficult.

In Sarajevo, Bosnia and Herzegovina people note that in the past, almost everyone was comfortable and middle class. On returning to their homes after the war, person after person faced destitution: "I knew that we wouldn't find our furniture, but I didn't expect that there wouldn't be a bathtub, tiles, or light switches."

In Bosnia and Herzegovina, the most vulnerable groups emerging from the war are widows and children who lack networks and protection. In Vares, Bosnia and Herzegovina a young Croat woman speaks for many when she cries, "I am a displaced person in my own city. I don't have anyone left here. I never married, so I am completely alone. Anyway, I don't care about me. What upsets me is the way I see young people having to live. I was born here and I will die here. I am just counting the days."

Similarly, in the civil conflict in Sri Lanka the Tamil minority faces great insecurity. In one community people say, "Tamils were restricted. They were not in a position to take their fish to Colombo and sell them, due to the fact that vehicles they travel in were subjected to inspection frequently. Moreover, there were times when the newly formed fishermen's group requested the army to detain such fish lorries purposely so that the fish would get spoilt. In view of the above situation they mostly sell their catch of fish in the local market itself." Many Tamil families have slid into poverty from interrelated processes triggered by the ethnic conflict, particularly harassment by gangs, injury and fear of land mines, increase in transportation costs because of loss of bicycles and carts, the breakdown of the smallholder agricultural economy, and government restrictions on economic activity.

The fear of war, the memory of loss, and the difficulties in recovery emerge in Ethiopia as well, which at the time of the study was not engaged in any war. In Kebele 11, Ethiopia participants say that during war, "we will be asked to contribute money, our children go the war front and die rather than helping us." Another women in Somaliland says, "Peace is the mother of the good life."

Macropolicy Stresses and Shocks

> Before I had secure work and money was worth more. Now
> I cannot afford anything.
>> —A participant, discussion group of poor men,
>> La Matanza, Argentina

Poor people experience macropolicy-induced shocks as sources of insecurity and material poverty, including loss of employment and sources of livelihood; increased prices of food, other basic necessities and agricultural inputs; and decreases in prices paid for agricultural and other produce. Poor people are usually hit not just by one of these trends, but by combinations of them; and the combinations vary by region, country and community. Poor people discuss the effects of debt and exchange rate adjustment, market liberalization and privatization.

Debt, Exchange Rate Adjustment, and Factory Closures

> Our currency has lost power; it was strong in the past.
>> —Participant, discussion group of men and women,
>> Madana Village, Malawi

Participants in Argentina and Ecuador talk about insecurities created by external national debt, economic instability and hyperinflation. A group of young women in Chota, Ecuador agree: "Poverty affects us all because of the government debt to foreigners...then the rise in fuel prices makes fares and product prices rise...we sell cheap, but it's only enough to pay for the transport." In addition to pointing to income inequality and absence of social policies, poor people in Morro da Conceição, Brazil say, "the government is ruining everything to pay *agiotas* [loan sharks]."

In Russia the impact of currency devaluation is so sharp that people use the date "August 17, 1998," as the marker in talking about life. In various parts of Russia, referring to August 17, people speak about the "uncontrollable surge of prices," the low salaries, unpaid and delayed salaries, and they say, "We were fooled again." An older woman pensioner in Ekaterinburg, Russia reports that after the August 17 devaluation, she could no longer survive on her pension. She survived by picking berries and mushrooms in the summer.

Another woman from Ekaterinburg describes her hardships as follows:

According to Tania, after the 17 August crisis, her husband
has been making less money, and his earnings continue
to go down. Although he is paid his salary every week,
sometimes they don't have any money at all. Tania's family
also give them some financial support. Her parents own
a house and have a plot of land where they grow some fruit
and vegetables. They help Tania with food and her grand-
parents help with money. Tania also gets some money from
"sponsors."

Indonesia and Thailand shared the regional financial crisis of 1997, which took place after 10 years of improving economic conditions. The crisis dragged many back down into poverty. In speaking about communitywide shocks, for example, discussion groups from Harapan Jaya, Indonesia mention large-scale layoffs by industrial and construction companies and sharp rises in prices of basic goods stemming from the prolonged economic crisis (box 8.3).

Market Liberalization

Market liberalization hits poor people in countries with diverse conditions and economies. Lack of protection from cheaper imports undermines local production. In Jamaica, a woman in Freeman's Hall remarks that she has difficulty selling her chickens because "people now would rather buy chicken from foreign lands," and if she lowers her prices to match the imports she will sustain a loss.

In Bulgaria pensioners blame the West, which they see as "forcing on Bulgaria closure of enterprises, the ruin of agriculture, and absence of protectionist policies." Several middle-aged and elderly participants interpret competition from cheap European and Turkish imports as a grand Western conspiracy against Bulgaria: "They forced us to liquidate our cooperative farms in order to sell their produce cheap; now they are closing down the enterprises in order to force us to buy their goods." "All the markets are glutted with cheap Turkish goods," says a mixed group in Bulgaria.

At a personal level, people in countries of the former Soviet Union feel that they cannot easily reorient and adapt to the mentality and requirements of a market-dominated economy. People feel that it is very difficult to adapt to wildly fluctuating prices of agricultural produce and no guarantee of either prices or buyers.

Restrictions on international trade can affect poor people's livelihoods very directly. In Somaliland numerous study participants mention the widespread hardships created by the disease-related ban on Somaliland's major export goods—sheep and goats—to the Gulf States, Saudi Arabia and Yemen.

Two other important macropolicy stresses have been the removal of subsidies, particularly on agricultural inputs, and the dismantling of government-run cooperatives. A typical example comes from the life history of Thomas, an ex-miner and farmer living in Muchinka in Zambia. After leaving the mines he returned to farming maize; with money saved he could afford to buy fertilizer and seed. Things began to get difficult in 1994, though, when agricultural policies were reformed. "Because we cannot afford fertilizer we are now concentrating on growing millet, sorghum, and cassava," he says.

Privatization

In many parts of the world poor people speak about the negative impacts of massive privatization. In Eastern Europe and Central Asia privatization without accountable institutions is seen as leading to mass fraud. "The politicians are either incompetent or corrupt or both," says a youth from Sofia, Bulgaria. Many poor people express concerns with the lack of investment in national industry and technology, lack of industrial machinery and equipment, lack of inputs for agriculture and erratic payment of wages. In the face of broader economic hardships, participants across the region also speak bitterly about the loss of social programs and "a state that does not take care of its citizens."

An older woman from Sofia, Bulgaria who took part in the first wave of voucher divestment says,

> Privatization comes in two forms: vouchers and cash. The
> prices are set by those who have money. That is, by the
> mafiosi. This is how money's laundered. We have been paid
> ridiculous dividends by the privatization funds in which we are
> shareholders. That's why we're not taking part in the present
> wave of mass privatization. In general, privatization is a gold
> mine for a handful of people.

Poor people often identify a combination of factors as contributing to poverty. Both in Ethiopia and Nigeria they speak about the ripple effect through local economies of reducing government employees, demobilizing soldiers and dismantling cooperatives: high inflation combined with loss of civil service jobs means that many people no longer have the capacity to purchase local goods and, to survive, they start growing vegetables and other crops themselves. According to discussion groups in Ayekale Odoogun, Nigeria,

> The local people produce a lot of farm products such as gaari
> [processed cassava], but there is very little market for these
> farm products. As governmental workers' salaries became inad-
> equate, many of the workers have become part-time farmers.
> The effect of this is that those who used to buy farm produce
> locally in the past have become emergency farmers.

Social Vulnerability

> To feel all right—well, you need to eat three times a day; not to
> overeat, but just not to be hungry. To have decent shoes and
> trousers, so as not to be ashamed when you go to the street. To
> have a tape recorder. To have a drink with some friends and to

feel easy. To have good children who could find a decent job,
who could marry and have their own children.
　　　　　　　　　　　　—Participants, discussion group of middle-aged
　　　　　　　　　　　　　　　　　　　　Roma men, Etropole, Bulgaria

Social vulnerability stems from insecurities related to social status resulting in exclusion, discrimination and lack of protection. Examples include the sudden destitution and stigma of widowhood for women, the hardships created by divorce and dowry, vulnerability of the elderly, the discrimination and harassment experienced by minority groups, and the exclusion resulting from the breakdown of social ties.

In some African and Asian cultures, widowhood can be a devastating shock: its adverse social and economic consequences are irreversible, and they affect not only the widow, but also her children. Relatives are known to come and seize the family's possessions, leaving the widow and her children with almost nothing (box 8.4). In Ecuador discussion groups report that widows and single mothers are victims of the most disrespect and violence.

Box 8.4 Widowhood Leads to Destitution: Bangladesh and Zambia

In Bangladesh, Mumtaz came from a relatively well-off family. She was given in marriage at the age of 12 to a man aged 50. After nine years of the marriage he died. At that time she was pregnant and already had a 2-year old child. After the birth of the second child, the elder brother of her husband grabbed all her property and turned her out of her house. She took shelter with a neighbor and worked in the neighbor's house for food. She migrated with other landless people to obtain land but could not because she did not have an adult male in her family. Now she is 65, her elder son dead from small pox and her younger son mentally disabled. She says, "I have already forgotten the feelings of happiness."

In Zambia, Mary is a widow with five children. When her husband died in 1998, his relatives grabbed the family's possessions, including the furniture, her husband's sewing machines (he used to be a tailor) and his bank book. Mary was left with nothing but her children—not even pocket money. She was told by her father-in-law to leave the house with her children, and only come back when she had bought white material and three white chickens so that they could cleanse her according to tradition. Luckily, her husband's friend drove her to her village with her children. And now she has too many things to worry about: her parents are very old and poor; her two children were sent back from school because she could not pay. According to Mary they had not eaten the previous day because she did not sell her dress. There was no sign that they were going to have anything for lunch. Her children were feeding on unripe mangoes.

Women are also vulnerable to discrimination through divorce and dowry. In Malawi divorce was identified by women's discussion groups from three sites as a shock specific to women. In Bangladesh and India dowry makes unmarried females a liability. In Bangladesh "if a daughter is not married in time, the parents run a risk of being stigmatized and the girls a risk of being violated." A father in Bangladesh with three daughters (and no sons who might have brought in dowry), explained that to start marrying off his daughters he sold his cow and goats, the only valuable assets of his household. He was left very poor and acutely anxious:

> *If I die there is no one to marry off my youngest daughter. I do*
> *not know whether I will be able to get food tomorrow. I do*
> *not see any light of hope. If anybody provides me with a piece*
> *of land and my wife with a job then we will be able to survive.*
> *I have no son and no land. Those who have sons and land feel*
> *secure and happy in the society. If they fall in any sudden diffi-*
> *culties they can overcome the situation quickly.*

Insecurity and anxiety come from knowing that the high expenditures of marriage will have to be met or children and their families face a bleak future. While in Bangladesh and India this is dowry for daughters, for Karalpak people in Uzbekistan it is bridewealth or *qualym* for sons. The size of the *qualym* "is always at the very limit of the maximum financial ability of the groom's family." A father in Uzbekistan confides, "As you may see, I have helped all my children to get married, and now I live without anything, sitting on the floor. I gave up everything and gave it all to their families."

Socially, old age is increasingly a painful and lonely crisis for many poor people. Economic pressures are fraying the traditional family care of the elderly in many parts of the world. In Bangladesh security for old women was linked to a son's not severing his family bonds after marriage and still providing food for his mother. In Vietnam, Mr. D, 57 years old, is slowly but surely sliding into poverty as his strength to work his small bit of land declines and illness takes over. In Bedsa, Egypt isolation and the three miles to the post office, where meager pensions must be collected, results often in a "death trek" toward the end of every month. A group of men remark, "Come on the 20th or 24th of the month, and you see the problems of the elderly. When they go to get their pensions, you see them walking on their hands and feet. The way is long and painful...people walk a little, sit a little, and there are three death cases on this road annually among the elderly." Similarly, in Cassava Piece in Jamaica, a woman states, "there are many elderly persons in the community who are unable to help themselves. Once per month the government's poor relief officer could visit them." In Todgheer, Somaliland, older men say that they have to walk longer distances and do more work because their teenage children "abandoned rural life and left them behind in the range lands."

Social discrimination not only decreases opportunities, but increases insecurities through threats, abuse and violence. Indigenous peasants in the rural highlands of Cañar, Ecuador fear attacks when they travel into towns. In La Calera, until recently, Indians, especially the elderly, were not allowed on buses because "they said they carried diseases." In the Amazon settlements of Voluntad de Dios and 10 de Agosto, Quijos Indians report both physical attacks and attempts to usurp their lands. Racism against blacks is summarized as "when you see a black man running, you are looking at a thief."

Economic stress places a heavy burden on family and community relations. Security means participating in community affairs, voicing opinions and being respected in society. Inability to follow community norms and participate in community affairs leads to exclusion. These effects are particularly striking in reports from the Eastern Europe and Central Asia region. In the town of Etropole, Bulgaria the combined effect of poverty and crime has led to "estrangement," or people "behaving like savages." "Going backwards in time," the return to subsistence agriculture as a means of survival for people who have lived in towns, has taken a devastating toll on the human psyche. "All day among animals—you become like them, you cannot speak normally anymore," states a middle-aged man from Etropole, Bulgaria.

Tensions created by money difficulties are reflected in relationships. People speak about quarrels within families, brothers and sisters quarreling and cutting each other off as everyone scrambles to stay alive. A youth in Plovdiv, Bulgaria says, "My parents died, and I left my share of the family lands to my sister to look after them. Once or twice I go to my native village to see her and to take some victuals. She is giving me less and less: lard instead of meat, some potatoes, some cabbage—cheap and heavy things, difficult to carry. She has started to look at me as if I am a drone."

The breakdown of social relationships extends to friends and colleagues as well. Says a man in a discussion group of unemployed men from Plovdiv, "I meet sometimes with my friends. We all have our problems, everybody is facing difficulties. How could I ask them for anything? We share our problems, we exchange news on the family, and everybody goes in different directions. Sometimes I meet an old friend who I know is doing well, but he starts from the beginning explaining how serious are the difficulties he is facing just now. And later I stop seeing him—he is visiting different places, he is talking to different people. Well, we are still friends but I know I can ask him for only one thing—so I would prefer to bother him with something that is really important."

In the village of Belasovka, Russia people describe the dominant emotional tone as "everyone is on their own now; the poor envy the rich and the rich scorn the poor; we don't visit friends as often as we used to; people are hostile and alone."

Health, Illness and Death

You can get good treatment but only with money.
—A resident of Ivanovo, Russia

Poor health, illness and death can impoverish people and they are a major source of insecurity and anxiety (chapter 5). At a blow, the body can flip from asset to liability, incurring heavy costs for treatment and having to be cared for and fed. Deaths can impoverish decisively, both from losing the labor of the deceased and, where custom requires, from costly funeral rites (see box 8.5). In the Naryn region of the Kyrgyz Republic, at least one horse must be butchered at a funeral ceremony. A 56-year old woman explains that failure to do this is viewed as a disgrace, so poor people will borrow heavily to buy a horse, and then have difficulty repaying. In a Bangladesh case, when a husband died, his two widows sold a third of the land he had left in order to perform his last rites. Across the 10 sites in Malawi, deaths and funerals were, after hunger, the most commonly named shocks; and the poor suffer more because they have to think how to borrow money for the coffin and then how to repay.

Box 8.5 The Cost of a Funeral, Kyrgyz Republic

A 53-year-old woman in Kenesh, Kyrgyz Republic says, "Tomorrow's the funeral of my eldest daughter's mother-in-law. We have to contribute at least 500 som and a good carpet to be hung on a wall. I have neither, so I borrowed 300 som from a neighbor. My daughter-in-law borrowed a carpet for the floor, but relatives told me that it won't do, so I had to take another, better carpet, which costs 500 som—so that my contribution is like everybody else's. I'll have to repay these debts, eventually, but I don't know how. Many people don't lend us anymore, because they know we have nothing to repay the debt with. See, it's difficult for the poor to maintain the links with the relatives."

In Search of Security

The wealthy can recover losses in one year, but the poor, who have no money, will never recover.
—A resident of Ha Tinh, Vietnam

Misfortune and disasters can strike at the rich, but the rich are less vulnerable. In the words of a participant in Egypt, "The one who is untroubled is the rich and his mood is serene." Poor people are vulnerable in many ways: their work and livelihoods are more at risk; they live in the most insecure areas, their assets are the most insecure, their housing is the most liable to damage, they have the least with which to protect themselves, they suffer most from crime, they are most at the mercy of the police, their rights are the least secure, and they struggle most to meet their social obligations. To make things worse, diminishing social cohesion and strained social relations are tending to reduce mutual social supports. Overall, the evidence indicates, poor people are becoming more insecure.

For those with little, small shocks have big effects on wellbeing. Setbacks are also harder or impossible to reverse. Reducing poverty requires searching for ways to avoid or mitigate the effects of loss of work and livelihood, natural and human-made disaster, civil disorder, crime and violence, persecution by police and justice, macroeconomic shocks, social vulnerability and illness and death. Insecurity has many causes and interventions need to take them into account. Confronting these in antipoverty terms may be highly cost-effective. It may be cheaper and easier to prevent poor people becoming poorer through shocks and insecurity than it is, once they are poorer, to enable them to claw their way back up again.

As we have seen, though, security as a characteristic of wellbeing is more than material. It is also peace of mind, social harmony, good relations with others, and mutual support. A remark from a group of women in Egypt touches on these reciprocities. They say, "Security is to have someone to care about and someone to take care of." In Bosnia and Herzegovina a young man says, "I would like for people of all ethnicities to accept Bosnia and Herzegovina as their homeland, their state, and for all to live in peace. For all to look for ways to prosper and live better, and not to live to spite each other because someone is a Croat or a Bosniac or a Serb."

We are left with questions:

How can the anxiety and fear of poor women and men be diminished and their peace of mind enhanced?

How can justice and police protection be provided for poor men and women?

How can the shocks that strike at them be prevented, removed or reduced?

How can poor people be helped to become more resilient and better able to cope?

How can macropolicy changes be informed by poor people's realities?

What has to happen so that poor children, women and men can feel secure, be physically safe and be socially included?

Notes

[1]Discussions on security, vulnerability and risk were held in small groups with men and women. These issues were raised following discussions on wellbeing and illbeing and after sketching out linkages between the causes and impacts of poverty. Invariably these issues emerged as part of overall discussions of wellbeing and illbeing. In addition researchers were encouraged to explore the following issues: How do people define security? How do people differentiate between secure and insecure households? What makes households insecure and why? Has security increased or decreased? Are some people better able to cope with sudden shocks to sources of livelihoods?

Chapter 9

The Character of Institutions

Summary

What does character mean in terms of institutions? What qualities define the essence of an institution? What meaning do these qualities have in different contexts for different people? Since values are embedded in cultural contexts, what people value the most varies. The qualities many poor people value in institutional character are trust, participation, unity, ability to resolve conflicts, caring, compassion, respect, listening, honesty, fairness, understanding, hardworking behavior, timeliness, responsive support, access, and contact with the institution.

By these criteria, most state institutions score poorly. NGOs and religious organizations are more trusted than state institutions, but they do not rate well in accountability or in engaging poor people in decisionmaking. Religious organizations receive high praise for being caring and supportive, but they are faulted for sowing seeds of disunity in communities. Shops and moneylenders are trusted, but not loved. Most institutions, except poor people's own informal networks of family and kin, are not rated positively for participation in decisionmaking or accountability.

Since institutional character determines whether poor people will become engaged with an institution, design and redesign of institutions for effective partnerships with poor people must reflect the values and behaviors most cherished by poor people.

Introduction

The village office turns a deaf ear to our opinions.
    —A woman, Harapan Jaya, Indonesia

*We consider trustworthiness the most important criterion be-
cause even though an institution has all the criteria,...if it is not
trustworthy, it cannot perform as we expect it to.*
    —A discussion group participant, Nampeya, Malawi

*An institution should not discriminate against people because
they are not well dressed or because they are black. If you
wear a suit you are treated as sir; if you are wearing sandals
they send you away.*
    —A woman, Vila Junqueira, Brazil

*When we were rich, they came very often. Now they forget
about us. They have left us.*
    —A resident of Orgakin, Russia

Poor women and men interact daily with a range of formal and informal institutions. This chapter explores the qualities of relationship, behavior and effectiveness that poor people consider important in the character of institutions with which they interact in their daily lives and during crises.

Poor men and women articulate a range of criteria they consider important. The debates in small group discussions about institutions were often passionate and long and they reflect the complexity of the issues involved. Poor people do not distinguish between the terms *organization* and *institution;* therefore, this book uses them interchangeably.[1]

While the most important criteria people use to evaluate the character of institutions vary, they can be divided into three broad categories: quality of relationships, valued behaviors and effectiveness. By far, poor people put greater emphasis on a wide range of relationship criteria than on any other aspect. These include trust, participation, accountability, unity and the ability to resolve conflicts. Behavioral criteria include extent of respect, honesty, fairness, listening, loving, caring and hardworking behavior. Effectiveness includes timely support and access and contact with the institution. The essential character of institutions affect their functioning, effectiveness and use.

This chapter is organized in four sections: quality of relationships, valued behaviors, institutional effectiveness and a final note on "in search of character."

Quality of Relationships

The criteria that poor people speak extensively about are trust, participation, accountability, unity and conflict-resolution ability. Poor people consider these characteristics important to achieve responsiveness, honesty and fairness, as well as other good behaviors.

Trust

> *Trust is believing in someone or something.*
> —A discussion group participant, Teshie, Ghana

Trust is variously viewed as confidence, reliability, dependability or promise keeping. Trustworthiness in addition is associated with someone who keeps secrets.

Participants in Indonesia define trust as the "feeling of assuredness that our problem will be solved when we approach the institution." Along with effectiveness, two women's groups in Ampenan Utara, Indonesia identify "highly trusted/trustable" as a leading criterion and indicate that they cannot even listen to what an institution has to say unless trust is first established. They also say institutions are trustworthy if they exhibit behaviors such as honesty, promise keeping and transparency.

Issues of trust are key elements for the high ratings given to Yayasan Danda Sosial Ibu Hindun, a group that provides microcredit and training in Indonesia. Fisherwomen report that the Ibu Hindun trusts them not to default and thus they make an extra effort to repay the loan. For the Lombok fisherwomen, reciprocity is the most important element of trust: "We trust Yayasan Ibu Hindun because it trusts us."

Women in Mtamba, Malawi call dependability an important criterion: "One needs to be sure about each and every institution; we have to know if it's worth it for us to depend on it or not." They rank the village headman the highest (with a score of 50 out of 50) because "everybody depends on the headman. We know that whenever we have a problem he is going to assist us in one way or the other so we all rely on him." However, based on the same criterion, they score the government, religious groups, and neighbors much lower. The women say, "We have given them 20 points each because sometimes they let us down so we don't really feel safe to depend on them." Others fare even less well. The agricultural field assistant got a score of 10 because "we don't trust the agricultural field assistant fully. As we have said earlier, he only visits the gardens of those people he knows so our trust in him is not that much." The farmers club scored zero on trust because "members in the farmers club are not united; hence, it is difficult to trust them. Others fail to repay loans; as a result they run away leaving the ones remaining behind to pay."

In Novo Horizonte, Brazil based on group discussions researchers note that "the groups put trust in some of the institutions, especially in those that are closer to the community, such as the president of the community...and they trust less in institutions like the police." Similarly in Baan Ta Pak Chee, Thailand a researcher writes that villagers "trust the institutions with which they have a direct relationship." In deciding whom to trust, people "will consider whether the help from that institution is sincere and they do not want anything in return."

Participants in Olmalyq, Uzbekistan choose trust as their most important criterion and, in ranking institutions, give the maximum score of 100 points to both relatives and friends. Then come neighbors, although at a somewhat lower level. Confidence in employers and in official institutions is much lower. The researchers note that the "police, local authorities, office of public prosecutor, court...did not enjoy any trust."

Similarly, in India a group of Muslim men and youth in Andhra Pradesh rate the relative importance of different criteria: "Trust of the institution emerged as the most important criterion followed by benefits to women, help provided in times of crisis, effectiveness, impact, and finally control of the people over the institution."

Participation

Only God listens to us.
—A participant in a discussion group, Zawyet Sultan, Egypt

Participation is "the ability to have a say in what happens."
—Discussion group participant, Thompson Pen, Jamaica

...when people have access to participate and express their opinion in any decisionmaking process without any fear.
—A discussion group participant, Dewangonj, Bangladesh

Nobody asks the people anything.
—Sekovici, Bosnia and Herzegovina

People define participation as engaging in decisionmaking, getting together to participate in discussions and meetings, expressing opinions and being heard, and having control or influence over the decisions made. For every activity, "to be discussed/negotiated with the community" is the most important criterion among several discussion groups in Kawangu, Indonesia.

Poor people in Mtamba, Malawi say participation means involving people in decisionmaking. Women's groups say, "Whenever one wants to join a certain institution, he/she should first of all have the right of making decisions in the institution." Similarly, in Nampeya, Malawi "the group said that people's participation in decisionmaking was more important than providing advice.... They cannot benefit from being advised if they do not take part in decisionmaking." The same group rates trust as more important than participation. They argue that "only those who are trustworthy are able to provide help, and it is this trustworthiness that allows people to participate in decisionmaking...it takes one's trust in order to be free to participate in the institution."

Institutions rating high in participation in Mtamba are the chief, the village funeral party, church and the school (scores of 50); the police score the lowest of all institutions (with a score of 10). In explaining their decisions poor people say,

▸ "We feel we have power and influence over church and the village funeral party. These institutions are formed by local community members."
▸ "We do not have influence over police because we don't normally sit together to discuss certain issues."
▸ "We don't have influence over the police because we fear the police."
▸ "We don't have influence over the hospital because they don't take our advice."

In the same village the women base their rankings on a bundle of criteria, including "trust," "provides help when needed," "effectiveness," and "people play a role in decisionmaking." They rank the Catholic Church as the most effective institution, followed by the Ministry of Health. Although the church is number one on their list overall, the women give the church a score of zero on participation.

Participants from Kok Yangak in the Kyrgyz Republic rate most government institutions quite low and say they are inefficient and that "their officials do not listen to people, dictate their own conditions, and cannot be...influenced by anybody."

In Thailand poor people describe participation in decisionmaking as problematic, consisting of "discussion, meeting, and news announcement," a process from which they are excluded. Poor women in Kaoseng, Thailand knew nothing about the child-care center under construction: "The group of poor females know that 'there is a construction without any further details' and 'see there is construction' but do not know much else...the group of poor fishermen expressed that 'we are very tiny, they [the savings groups] wouldn't consult us. They consult with the powerful individuals and our community has only acknowledged their decision.' The group of poor women found that 'NGOs hold informal meetings' from which they were excluded."

Residents of the province of Ha Tinh, Vietnam say, "Local people should be entitled to discuss important issues such as the amount of loans they get, the building of infrastructure, and the division and use of land." Members of a discussion group in Tra Vinh, also in Vietnam, say, "They don't invite me to meetings, but they invite me to public works," and "they talk a lot, so I cannot remember what they said in the meeting."

With some exceptions, poor people's own informal organizations score high on participation in decisionmaking while government institutions—

Table 9.1 How Institutions Fare on a Range of Evaluation Criteria

Institution	Responsiveness	Trust	Participation	Accountability	Unity/conflict resolution	Respect	Honesty and fairness	Caring, loving, listening
1 Municipalities and local government	—	—	—	—	—	—	—	—
2 Schools	—	—	—	—	—	—	—	—
3 Health services	—	—	—	—	—	—	—	—
4 Police	—	—	—	—	—	—	—	—
5 Politicians	—	—	—	—	—	—	—	—
6 Banks	—	—	—	—	—	—	—	—
7 Private enterprise and traders	—	—	—	—	—	—	—	—
8 Shops and moneylenders	+	+	—	—			—	—
9 Service delivery NGOs	—	+	—	—				
10 Emergency NGOs	+	+		—		+		+
11 Religious organizations	+	+	—	—	—	+	+	+
12 Community-based organizations	+	+	+	+	+	+	+	+
13 Local leaders	+	+		+	+	+		+
14 Kin and family	+	+		+				+

A positive rating (+) implies that the majority of responses were positive, and a negative rating (—) means that the majority of responses were negative. Blanks imply either that the criterion was not applicable or that there were insufficient data.

particularly health centers, hospitals, police and government ministries—rank low. Municipalities, local government, schools and courts occasionally receive high rankings; politicians, with a few exceptions in Ghana, receive low rankings. Private enterprises also score low in participation (see table 9.1).

In civil society groups, NGOs often receive low rankings on participation, but people's own organizations, such as burial societies, informal credit groups and kinship networks, receive high rankings. Religious groups are usually rated low, although local leaders (primarily informal) and other traditional councils often score well on participation.

Not all groups value participation equally, however. In Varna, Bulgaria the Romas dismiss the issue of people's involvement in decisionmaking as irrelevant. What matters to them is respect. A discussion group of older women in Indonesia considers participation "not important" and instead places "fairness/justice and equitability" at the top of their list.

Participation has costs in time; it can mean income will be forgone. Participants in Baan Ta Pak Chee, Thailand feel that if the institution has engaged in surveys and "thorough consideration" of the help they are providing, then they would have few concerns over the extent of participation.

Similarly, in Baan Kang Sado, another Thai community, poor people are satisfied with the systematic consultation an NGO conducted to ensure that the program responded to poor people's needs:

> *The NGO ranked in the second place because the NGO has helped the villagers for a long time and has the projects that suit the villagers' needs, for example, the establishment of the buffalo and rice bank, promotion of the revolving capital in the village. In addition, the implementation of the NGO is systematic. Study on the needs of the villagers has been conducted, training of the village headman is arranged, projects have been arranged for evaluation. These make the villagers feel that the NGO helps them seriously. Another reason that make the villagers favor the NGO is that the NGO helps them without complicated financial conditions, unlike other organizations.*

Accountability

> *We would wish to have more control over the government and NGOs.*
>
> —A man, Adaboya, Ghana

> *They [the City Council members] are corrupt and visibly favor the rich because they offer a little something. All the good land is allocated to them.... This creates a gulf of disunity within the community.*
>
> —A discussion group participant, urban Malawi

> *[They] want to have influence over the activities of chairman, members, thana and the NGO.... Members of the* union *parishad [local councils] work in isolation from the poor people. They are not responsible to anyone for nonfulfillment of their commitment. ...Thana officials are not responsible for their dishonest acts.*
> —Discussion group summary by research team,
> rural Bangladesh

Poor people desire to have influence and control over institutions that affect their lives. The reality, however, is one of exclusion and alienation. What emerges is corruption and domination of public institutions by the powerful and rich, with little apparent accountability to anyone. In Ecuador, with some exceptions, poor people also say they have little control or influence over government services. A poor man in Paján reports,

> *Sometimes they attend to your needs, sometimes not. First they see your face, and they decide if they will attend to you.... If they like you...or if you don't go with money to [bribe them], then they don't attend to you.... This has been going on forever.... This is why poor people cannot get help.*

Most poor people in Egypt define themselves as being excluded from the decisionmaking process, seeing it as a privilege that they do not enjoy. Jamaican poor people say, "We want to have more influence over government."

In a city in Bulgaria the participants declared that they had no control over the institutions. "We the Bulgarians are serfs. We all know that if you are down...we are afraid of those on the top. The people cannot gather together to put them in their place. There are some young ones who wanted to make a debate with the mayor on the local TV; they announced that everybody could ask him questions and what happened? He asked them not to interrupt him when he was speaking, they cut the telephone lines, he delivered a speech, and he went home."

Very occasionally participants feel they have some control. In Adaboya, Ghana a group of men say they can sometimes influence the chief and the assemblyman (elected member of the local council). The men also express a desire to have greater control over government services and the international NGO World Vision in order to solve the problems of their town better. Poor men say that because "all other institutions ride on the back of the government, if they are involved with the government they would have many institutions coming to their community to help them." Many poor people also characterize NGOs as not being accountable. The sentiment can be summarized as "they may be doing good work, but we know nothing about them."

Unity and Conflict Resolution

*Social cohesion means working together the way we normally
do at funerals and the community projects.*
—A poor man, Musanya, Zambia

*[An institution that is] uniting means one that brings people
together in a peaceful manner.*
—A discussion group participant,
Madana village, Malawi

The theme of unity or unifying and the ability to resolve conflicts emerges
particularly strongly as a criterion in Africa. People say that when institutions
sow disharmony among people, they do more harm than good even though
they may provide important services.

In Mtamba, Malawi people choose unity as the most important criterion.
Discussion groups say that "unity is important because without unity all
other criteria cannot work. All the criteria depend on the unity of the institution." This group ranks "faithfulness as 2, dependability as 3, providing
help as 4 and people's participation as 5 because they don't mind not being
involved in decisionmaking as long as everything is O.K." In Ethiopia the
sacred tree emerges as one of the most important institutions because it
brings about unity among people in addition to promoting a sense of wellbeing and togetherness.

Poor people give a low score for two reasons to a commercial mill in
Adaboya, Ghana even though it provides services. Youth say that "preferential treatment was given to community members who were in the Salvation
Army Church. This attitude does not promote unity.... Apart from that
nobody in the community was consulted before deciding to provide them
with the mill."

The ability of local councils, particularly traditional councils, to unify
groups, avoid sowing dissension, and actively resolve conflicts emerges as
a valued attribute in several places. In the village of Borg Meghezel, Egypt
the tribal dispute council is rated as "one of the most important institutions
since it resolves disputes between families, and thus is supported by most
of the community." Participants in Daanweyne, Somaliland rate the
Council of Elders *(Guurti)* as the most important institution for the community in every level:

> *The Elders solve disputes between individuals and groups in
> the community; ensure proper sharing of water during scarcity;
> negotiate with people outside the community over blood com-
> pensation for murder cases and injuries; organize meetings and
> congregations for festivals; and ask help for needy in the com-
> munity. Elders play the role of the local administration and se-
> curity agencies. The* Guurti *can spend nights and days to solve*

*a case without eating sometimes. They can stay away from
their family needs for months to finalize a community need.*

In Kok Yangak, Kyrgyz Republic the Aksakal court, or the court of the
elderly, scores100 out of 100 in trust, efficiency and participation in decisionmaking. It scores 90 out of 100 on timely support.

The Kebele office, the lowest-level government office, emerges as the
most important institution in Kebele 11, Ethiopia, particularly among adults.
The second most important institution is the church. The Kebele office is
rated the highest because "it resolves conflicts.... Peace is so highly valued
that all institutions that contributed to maintaining peace rated high.... The
police station is important for them because it protects them from thieves and
maintains peace and order in the community. The courts are useful because
they resolve civil cases and contribute to justice. Also important are the
church and the *idir* [burial society]." The *idir* is also valued because it "brings
people together to talk about current issues in the community."

In Waikanabu Village, Indonesia women say that "an institution with
benefit will surely be one that creates peace and security." In Manjhar, Bihar,
India women give great importance to security or the "we" feeling.

Valued Behaviors

*It is important to go there and be well treated independent of
race, religion, money.*
                                    —From a group discussion of poor men and women,
                                                        Morro da Conceição, Brazil

Over and over again, poor people speak about a range of behavioral criteria important to them. These include the following: respect, not
being rude, honesty, fairness, not being corrupt, truthful, not lying, not
cheating, listening, and being caring, loving, kind, compassionate, hardworking, helpful and professional. The terms poor people in Novo
Horizonte, Brazil use, for example, highlight the importance of behavioral
criteria:

> *...be there; treat with good manners; have patience; listen to
> people; try to understand the needs of people; give attention;
> don't always say come back later; say honestly if you can or
> cannot solve the problem; work with love; do not treat us
> with ignorance, respect the community's problems; be there
> on time; give equal treatment, do not discriminate; solve the
> problem.*

In Bulgaria the researchers conclude that the study participants base
their rankings "on the extent to which people trust an institution or, more

precisely, on the respect and compassion it shows its 'clients': In other words, on the human attitude of the respective officials."

Respect

We feel the institution should not underrate anybody, because if we underrate people, we will not feel comfortable to seek help from them.
>   —A discussion group participant, Nampeya, Malawi

Poor people, like all people, value their dignity, value courtesy, and prefer being treated with respect. This treatment, however, seems to be in short supply. In Egypt a group of poor people say, "Capital is even involved in being respected; if a rich man sits in the local café you find 30 people gathered around him serving him, but the poor man is neglected." Similarly, in the village of El Gawaber in Egypt, poor men and women report that the rural hospital is the worst service provider: "They have their noses up in the air and they neglect us"; but the local clergyman "is sensitive to our needs" and rates very highly.

In Thompson Pen, Jamaica poor people speak about the importance of being "courteous, being nice, understanding, and helpful." In Little Bay, Jamaica poor people also consider important the extent to which interactions with the institution "help to build pride in the community."

Residents of the former Soviet Union complain about the behavior of officials and humiliation at the hands of government. As noted in one urban community in the Kyrgyz Republic,

Such social institutions as school, clinic, library, post office, and the local branch of Social Fund are assessed as important but inefficient. The informants said that officials and employees of these institutions often abuse their power, humiliate clients, refuse to help clients who are critical of their activities and cannot be influenced by the community. This is particularly true in the case of the social service officials who do not care about people's needs, engage in the unlawful practice of paying pensions and social benefits in-kind by overpriced goods and products, and pocket the cash meant for pensions and benefits.

Honesty and Fairness

To tell the truth. If they cannot solve the problem, they can give us hints, so we can find a solution. Because they lie, you carry on with the lies without knowing it.
>   —Participant, a group of women, Vila Junqueira, Brazil

*Another criterion we have considered important is that of
not favoring. An institution is not supposed to favor anyone
because it does not give a good example, but if it does not
favor, people tend to like it because they know that they will be
helped whenever they have problems.*
> —A discussion group participant, Nampeya, Malawi

*He's lying to people. There's no roads, no money, no food, yet
he'll build a huge villa. When was the last time any improvements were made here? Which year?*
> —Participant, a group of middle-aged Roma
> women, Bulgaria

*[The rich] can do everything through the thana by giving money
to the officials. They can take loans from the banks easily.*
> —Participant, discussion group of men and
> women, Bangladesh

Honesty, lies, deceit and corruption go hand in hand. Poor people discuss the criterion of honesty as part of other attributes or by itself. While corruption and lack of honesty are spoken about most frequently with reference to state institutions, their importance cuts across institutions.

In Mtamba, Malawi women express greatest trust in the village headman of Mtamba not only because of his willingness to always help, but because "he doesn't favor anybody since we are all one community." In Kuphera, Malawi one men's group identifies "not favoring" as a key criterion, ex-plaining that institutions should not discriminate on the basis of who they are and the wellbeing category to which they belong.

Listening, Caring, Love and Compassion

*After trustworthy, we consider loving because if an institution
does not have any love, there is no way it can help us.*
> —A discussion group participant, Nampeya, Malawi

He is sensitive about our needs.
> —Participants, discussion group of women about
> a clergyman, El Gawaber, Egypt

*To listen more to the people. Sometimes they do not even
let you talk. They say that they already know the problem
and that they will solve it.*
> —Discussion group participants, Vila Junqueira, Brazil

The need to be heard, loved and treated with compassion is one of the reasons leaders of religious organizations receive high ratings even when they may be unable to help in material terms. In Umuoba Road, Nigeria participants value the local churches for both their spiritual and "welfarist" roles, such as "feeding of and caring for the very poor, provision of funds for personal expenses, conducting befitting funerals for dead members and offering compassion in addition to serving as a medium of communication with God."

In Vila Junqueira, Brazil the first criterion of importance to men is sincerity and the second is listening. For women, the first criterion is to have efficient and polite professionals and the second is to solve problems. Both men and women speak about the importance of being listened to and women in addition specify "being open to criticism." In group discussions, while people agree that solving problems of those who seek help is important, poor people also emphasize that how they are treated is extremely important.

Hardworking Problem-Solvers

> *If an institution has interest in its work, that means it will*
> *also be interested to hear our problems and find ways of*
> *solving them.*
>
> —A discussion group participant, Nampeya, Malawi

Poor people in Nampeya, Malawi say, "An institution is supposed to be hardworking. We feel the institution is hardworking if it will try its best to help us whenever we need its help. Another criterion we considered is interest in its work." Clearly poor people want people who have the mind-set of problem solvers and not people who use rules to justify doing nothing. In another village, over and over again the agricultural field assistant received low ratings, sometimes 2 points out of 50, because he was described as "lazy and selfish," and as someone "who does not help when people need him."

Institutional Effectiveness

> *The ability of an institution to offer people what they ask for*
> *and acting as expected.*
>
> —Discussion group of men and women,
> Kowerani Masasa, Malawi

Poor people have clear definitions of effectiveness. According to a man in Nampeya, Malawi effective institutions "have goals and meet their goals." In Varna, Bulgaria people define effectiveness as "when things move; when things happen; when you are not like one lost." A woman in Teshie, Ghana says effectiveness is when what has been planned comes to fruition. She explains for example, "if you go the hospital and you tell the doctor what is exactly wrong with you and the doctor will understand you and apply his knowledge of medicine to you, then I'd rate him 20 [out of 20] for effectiveness."

In Thompson Pen, Jamaica poor people define effectiveness as "help given" and providing "what is needed." For most groups, effectiveness depends on the "accessibility and affordability of the service, the benefits of the service, and being able to negotiate arrangements for the repayment of services." People cite both the school and hospital as examples:

> *You can talk to the teacher and you tell her that you will bring the fee by next Monday, and in the hospital you can talk to them and pay the fee later or pay half now and the rest when you have it. The health center, on the other hand, offers no negotiation in terms of payment of services. If you do not pay the "registration fee," you can't be seen today.*

In Khaliajuri, Bangladesh poor people consider an effective institution to be one that influences the life of the people positively. They describe an effective institution as one from which cooperation can be expected from all and not only with familiar faces; good counseling is received; benefit is accrued; there is no trouble; assistance is received in time of adversity; no distinction is made between males and females; importance of poor people's opinion is respected.

The two sets of qualities that seem to characterize poor people's notions of effectiveness are timely, responsive, and caring support as well proximity, access and contact with institutions or their representatives.

Timely, Responsive and Caring Support

> *Support is when you get help when it is needed.*
> —A discussion group participant, Varna, Bulgaria

Provision of support and help when needed emerges as an important criterion of effectiveness in many communities across the world. In Ampenan Utara, Indonesia people define support as assistance, aid, or donation, which could be physical or nonphysical. Similarly, men's groups in Waikanabu, Indonesia feel that the most important indicator of effectiveness is the "form of aid" and whether it is "efficient, and in conformity with the community's desire."

Poor people in Teshie, Ghana define support as receiving both emotional and material acknowledgment from someone. In Cassava Piece, Jamaica support to young men under 20 means "help, not handouts; give skill to build; self-teach a man to fish; to be independent, not dependent." For young women, support means "encouragement and a place of refuge in times of crisis." In Musanya village, Zambia groups of men and women identify support received as the most important criterion. Poor people evaluate support in terms of "the help they give, e.g., medicine, material, and moral support."

Villagers from India gave "usefulness or fulfillment of needs" as their first response when asked what were the most important attributes associated with a good institution. The list of evaluation criteria generated by a discussion group of very poor in Jaggaram, India includes "promptness in coming to people's help in times of distress." In Kaoseng, Thailand people rate efficiency as the most important criteria. Researchers note, "They assessed efficiency in terms of 'fruitful operations' and contributions to the community."

Gowainghat, Bangladesh participants say an institution is effective when it delivers the "necessary service within the least time possible and trouble at the time of their need and get benefited after the service." In Nampeya, Malawi people emphasize "fastness" as the first criteria because:

> *...an institution that is important is the one that reacts fast.*
> *They gave an example saying that in times of funeral, relatives*
> *are the first to provide help; that is, they react fast.... They also*
> *gave the example of an epileptic person, saying if someone was*
> *epileptic and falls, the relatives are fast to react and help.*

In a village in Malawi researchers note, "On 'understanding,' the group said the village headman, religious groups, kinsmen, and neighbors understand the people's problems and try as much as possible to help with the little they have. However, the court and farmers club do not understand because of bribery."

A woman in Kawangu, Indonesia comments on how institutions must properly understand community problems in order to tackle them:

> *What is most important about an institution's activities and*
> *assistance is their usefulness to the people. Assistance does*
> *not have to be in the form of cash or goods. Even when an*
> *institution provides a large sum of money, it cannot be consid-*
> *ered effective when it does not address the problems the com-*
> *munity is facing.*

Access, Closeness and Contact

> *Cadres should work closely with the masses to understand*
> *their concerns and aspirations.*
> —A resident of Ha Tinh, Vietnam

Poor people value ease of access to institutions and consider it a key aspect of effectiveness. While ease of access may be enhanced by physical proximity, poor people speak about the importance of being visited by or being able to visit and talk to officials, politicians, or other sources of physical, emotional and spiritual solace wherever they may be located. Musanya villagers in Zambia rate institutions based on the extent to which they have regular contact with them. The Member of Parliament (MP) is "mentioned in negative terms because he does not visit them, and to them this means he is not effective, supportive, and worthy of trust.... The men did not even consider

Parliament an institution worth mentioning." The women, note the researchers, rate the councilor as ineffective as "they could not see his work and just like the MP he does not visit them. The first women's group thought that he might misuse the money the MP gives, though they were not sure."

In villages in Bihar, India frequency of visit and contact comes up as the second most important criterion after usefulness of the institution. Poor people view the Manjhar village postman and watchman as important because they are both approachable and provide many valued services. The postman, for instance, writes and reads letters for others, and the watchman helps resolve quarrels. In Ruamsamakee, of Bangkok, Thailand the "community defines accessibility as being able to call for aid in times of need and receiving constant assistance…. They said the Sor Sor (MP) only comes during election time, which is not considered accessible."

In Genengsari, Indonesia poor people consider shops and kiosks the most important institution because at "any time" any of the villagers can turn to them for goods on credit or small loans. The Village Credit Bank also scores well because its procedures are said to be simple and loans up to Rp 200,000 can be extended instantly. Elsewhere in Indonesia, moneylenders also score well because of their accessibility. Youth groups in Pegambiran say they especially value the head of the neighborhood associations *(rukun warga)* because he routinely approaches the youth and his presence makes them feel that their aspirations are being taken into account.

In Search of Character

Poor men and women value particular qualities in an institution that define its essence or character. These character qualities affect how poor people perceive how well institutions function. The same institution may get high ratings for importance and effectiveness and low ratings on participation, trust, listening or respect. What emerges is that, despite the global efforts to create institutions that serve the poor, many of these institutions created by outsiders—whether from the state, civil society, the private sector, or international organizations—often do not have the character poor people value. Only when all these institutions embody the characteristics laid out by poor people will they make a sustained difference, a difference that matters in poor people's lives. Poor people want institutions they can participate in and that they can trust to be relevant, to care and to listen. The standards for good institutions set by poor people in Gowainghat, Bangladesh could stand as a model:

- ▸ Stand beside people in their evil days.
- ▸ Give attention to and listen to the problems of poor people.
- ▸ Have consistency in word and deed.
- ▸ Do not do such things as may create loss to the people.
- ▸ Do not get involved in any corruption.
- ▸ Do not indulge corruption.

- Do not discriminate between Hindus and Muslims.
- Give honest and good suggestions at the time of adverse situations.
- Do not give special favors to the rich.
- Give fair verdicts.

Can we rise to this challenge?

Notes

[1]The discussion of qualities of institutions started with describing what an institution is and listing institutions that play important roles in poor people's daily lives and during crises. Local terms were used without making distinctions between organizations and institutions. Researchers made lists of institutions. The discussion then focused on qualities deemed important in institutions. In some countries participants assigned scores from a maximum of 50 or 100 to rate characteristics or institutions. In Eastern Europe participants sometimes became angry when asked to rate formal institutions and in a few places refused to participate further in the discussion.

Chapter 10

Governance:
Poor People's Scorecards

Summary

From the perspective of poor people worldwide, there is a deep and wide-spread crisis in governance. While the range of institutions that play important roles in poor people's lives is vast, poor people are excluded from participation in governance. State institutions, whether represented by central ministries or local government, are often neither responsive nor accountable to the poor; rather, the reports detail the arrogance and the disdain with which poor people are treated. Poor people see little recourse to injustice, criminality, abuse and corruption in their interactions with institutions. Not surprisingly, poor men and women lack confidence in these state institutions even though they still express their willingness to partner with them under changed behavior and rules.

In the presence of dysfunctional state institutions, poor people turn for help to institutions of the private sector or civil society. In the private sector, local shops and moneylenders emerge as the unlikely heroes because, although they may sometimes be "bloodsuckers," they are present when needed and quick to respond.

Civil society institutions, including NGOs, help poor people survive. They do not, however, help poor people develop bargaining power with more powerful state institutions, politicians, local government and the rich who control jobs, factories, plantations, trade, credit and other livelihood sources. There are few examples of beneficial partnerships among poor people, NGOs and the state.

Poor people depend primarily on their kin, their own informal networks, religious organizations and community-based organizations for support in surviving. However, these are mostly disconnected from the resources of the state or of other civil society or private sector institutions.

Introduction

We give our voice to the people closest to us.
—From a group discussion participant, El Gawaber, Egypt

When they assist you they treat you like a beggar...but we aren't...we pay taxes....There must be transparency in government actions, tax money has to be well employed....They invent these useless constructions and grab our money.

—Participant, discussion group of poor men,
Vila Junqueira, Brazil

There are four dragons: law court, prosecutor's office, khokimiat [highest state authority], and head of police. Nobody can get anything until they are satiated.

—Participant, discussion group of poor men and women,
urban Uzbekistan

Given power differences and the dependence of poor people on those with wealth and power, poor people's lives and decisions are governed by the behavior and decisions of local and distant elite—be it as individuals or in institutions—in the government, in the private sector and in civil society. Informal and formal institutions mediate their access to resources and opportunities. Hence, for them governance is not a matter just of the state, but rather involves all those individuals and institutions from the private sector and civil society whose rules, actions and behaviors affect poor people's choices, security, safety and livelihoods.

The findings in this chapter draw from small group discussions about institutions.[1] The chapter is organized in four sections: institutional ratings; governance and accountability of state institutions; paying the price, private enterprise; and governance and accountability in civil society.

Given the recurrent messages of disempowerment and disenchantment with a broad range of institutions, we decided to undertake further systematic quantitative analyses of poor people's overall ratings of importance, effectiveness and ineffectiveness of institutions. Ratings of institutions vary with the criteria being considered. Thus, an institution like a school or hospital may be considered very important, but may be scored low in effectiveness because of poor performance or limited access. Since the questions were open-ended and asked separately for each issue, the number of institutions listed as important, effective and ineffective varies.

The ratings on importance are based on how frequently the institution was mentioned among the top five most important institutions in each community where the exercise was conducted.[2] The ratings on effectiveness and ineffectiveness are based on whether an institution was mentioned as effective or ineffective. Discussions were lively in most places; however, not every group completed the ratings on effectiveness and ineffectiveness. The pattern of institutional ratings confirms the detailed analysis of how poor people described their interactions with institutions. The message from poor people is sobering.

Institutional Ratings

> *The neighborhood association is the only institution that really*
> *strives to solve the problems...it is the only institution that tells*
> *us the truth and operates any day, any hour...the association*
> *is close to us, knows the problems.*
>
> —Participant, discussion group of men and women,
> Vila Junqueira, Brazil

Poor people's descriptions and ratings of their relationship with state, private and civil society institutions yield important information for all concerned with making institutions of the state, markets and civil society more propoor. Overall, while a range of state, civil society and private sector institutions emerge as important in poor people's lives, more civil society institutions—particularly poor people's own informal and formal community-based organizations but also NGOs, religious organizations, local leaders, and kin and family—emerge as effective than do state institutions. State institutions, however, dominate in poor people's pick of ineffective institutions (see figures 10.1 and 10.2).

Overall, in poor people's judgment, 45 percent of important institutions in their lives are state institutions, 33 percent of effective institutions are state institutions, and 83 percent of ineffective institutions are state institutions.[3] By contrast civil society institutions constitute almost 50 percent of important institutions, 60 percent of effective institutions, and only 15 percent of ineffective institutions. Private enterprises make up 7 percent of both important and effective institutions and practically disappear from poor people's lists of ineffective institutions.

Important Institutions

Participants first discussed and identified institutions they consider "important." They identified a range of state, private, and civil society institutions that play a significant role in their lives. These are reported for urban and rural areas in figures 10.1 and 10. 2. Overall, in urban areas, 47 percent of the institutions considered important are state institutions, 45 percent are civil society institutions and 8 percent are private enterprises. The most frequently mentioned important institution in urban areas is health services, 15 percent of the time, followed by community-based organizations and kin or family, 12 percent. While the overall distribution between state and civil society institutions is not very different in rural areas, the differences among the institutions in terms of how frequently mentioned, are not as sharp as in urban areas. Thus, in rural areas, community-based organizations, municipalities or local government, religious organizations and health services receive more or less equal ranking. In rural areas local leaders emerge as important more frequently than in urban areas.

Effective Institutions

The pattern of results changes, however, when the discussion focuses on effectiveness. In urban areas only 31 percent of institutions identified as effective are state institutions. The majority of institutions identified as effective are civil society institutions, 60 percent, primarily community-based organizations, kin or family, religious organizations and NGOs. Private enterprises constitute 9 percent of most effective institutions (see figures 10.1 and 10.2). The pattern of results is very similar for rural areas.

Ineffective Institutions

The most dramatic difference between the distribution of state and civil society institutions emerges in rating of ineffective institutions. In urban areas, of all institutions identified as ineffective, more than 81 percent are state institutions (see figures 10.1 and 10.2). The most prominent among these are the police, municipalities and a range of government ministries. There is almost no mention of private enterprises as ineffective in urban areas. The pattern is similar in rural areas, with 90 percent of all institutions rated ineffective being state institutions. Very few private enterprises are rated as ineffective, while NGOs feature among ineffective civil society institutions at a rate of 5 percent in rural areas.

Governance and Accountability of State Institutions

If someone gets "chopped up" or sick, or if they were burnt by fire, the health clinic is one of the quickest to respond to the need.
> —A discussion group participant, Duckensfield, Jamaica

Poor people have no access to the police station, bank, government offices, and the judge of the village court. The rich people dominate these institutions.
> —A village in Bangladesh

Despite the trend toward formal democratization and decentralization, poor people by and large do not experience local government or local representatives of central state institutions as either enfranchising or responsive to their needs and priorities. Rather, what poor people report in detail is often unrestrained abuse of the power of the state. Reports of

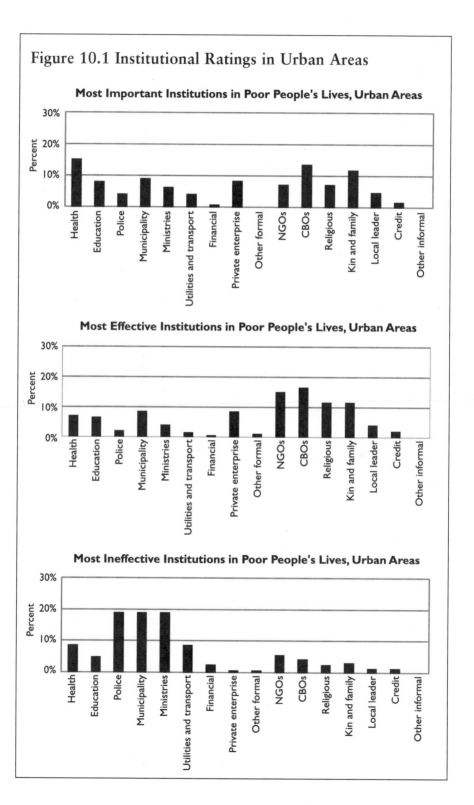

Figure 10.1 Institutional Ratings in Urban Areas

Most Important Institutions in Poor People's Lives, Urban Areas

Most Effective Institutions in Poor People's Lives, Urban Areas

Most Ineffective Institutions in Poor People's Lives, Urban Areas

Figure 10.2 Institutional Ratings in Rural Areas

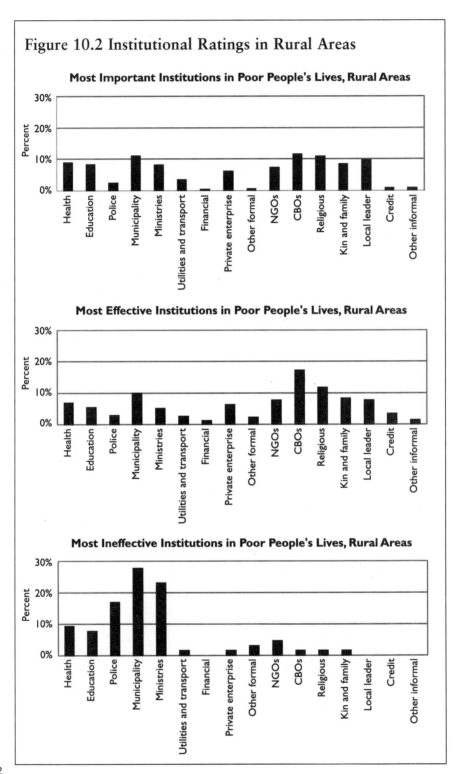

public officials using their positions for economic gain are common across countries, and poor people feel powerless to take action. There are exceptions, especially as related to municipalities, schools, health centers, courts and police in some places. This section discusses issues of accountability; responsiveness; documents, rights and power; decentralized governance; and empowerment and partnership.

Accountable to Whom?

I heard rumors about assistance for the poor, but no one seems to know where it is.
—A discussion group participant,
Tanjugrejo, Indonesia

The municipality collects donations, and then they share it among themselves.
—A discussion group participant, urban
Bosnia and Herzegovina

The ruling of the court is unpredictable and influenced by bribes, hence 20 scores out of 50. The Malawi Mudzi Fund and Farmers Club were supposed to help when people need it, but since they are not understanding and exclude us most of the time, they don't help, 10 scores out of 50.
—Participant, discussion group of poor men,
a village in Malawi

In the past, children used to be beaten to learn; now they are beaten to get money from their parents to pay for special group lessons.
—Discussion group, Dahshour, Egypt

The village head is very important. He is involved in deciding who gets loans. He can help you.
—Discussion group participant, Tra Vinh, Vietnam

In community after community poor people report that state institutions—whether delivering services, providing police protection or justice, or making political decisions—are either not accountable to anyone or accountable only to the rich and powerful. In the face of dependency and little recourse to justice, poor people remain silent even when confronted with gross abuse of power.

Poor people frequently describe encounters with public officials as frustrating and humiliating. The efforts to obtain social assistance illustrate the point. While study participants in Eastern Europe and Central Asia often mention pension, disability, child support and other programs as very important sources of support, many poor people from these regions indicate that major reforms to the safety net system over the past decade have not kept pace with increased need and have created serious hardships. In a city in Russia a woman characterizes the officials of the social assistance department as "impolite and even crude with ordinary people from the village. I go there for my social benefit for my children. I have to wait for two hours; they treat me very badly. If I cry and shout that my child is ill, they'll give me something. But it happens seldom."

Extortion by officials exploiting their power appears to be widespread. Extortion by forest department staff, for example, is reported from both Bangladesh and India. In a village in Bihar, India many women in the poorer communities collect and sell wood for fuel. On alternate days, women make their living by selling wood in town. Daily income from the sale ranges between Rs 20 and Rs 30. But the forest guard charges a cut of Rs 5 at the checkpoint for every headload of wood carried out of the village.

Although exceptional individuals can be found everywhere, by and large poor men and women encounter the rich as obstacles to their struggles for a livelihood. In a village in Bangladesh, for example, poor people say they do not experience any social exclusion in the village in terms of caste, religion or profession. However, they point out social exclusion in terms of social classes or wealth. They equate wealth with power and their poverty with exclusion.

In one city in Uzbekistan poor people speak bitterly about the power of the rich to buy their way to services even when poor people may be more desperate and first in line. A 36-year-old security guard recounts,

> The president said that for people with anemia medicines are
> for free. Not long ago my wife was put in the maternity home.
> I brought her medicines for 7,000 som, borrowed the money.
> Over four days they gave her four Novocaine injections and re-
> fused to give the remaining shots. The rich ones, naturally, can
> easily part with their cash. Their wives are well looked after. I
> went into the office of the lady in charge and said that if some-
> thing happened to my wife, I would kill her. After that they im-
> mediately gave the rest of the shots.

A 22-year-old man from a city in the Kyrgyz Republic made links between inequality, greed, the law, lawlessness and discrimination:

> Our current poverty level is caused by poor performance of
> municipal authorities. Municipal officials have stolen and sold
> out everything of value. They are greedy and never stop.
> Poverty is also caused by lack of law and order and lack of
> equality. It looks like laws are written for the poor only, and
> the rich do whatever they please.

Eight women and two men in a discussion group in Esmeraldas, Ecuador describe their helplessness in the face of abuse and unfair treatment by the mayor and municipal staff: "Some receive us, others don't. It's awful....They are abusive....They treat one almost like a dog.... The municipality only serves the high-society ones....The mayor even slapped a woman who asked for help...."

The police are the least accountable institution. The police often play such a negative role in poor people's lives that they add to poor people's insecurity rather than alleviate it. In Bihar and Andhra Pradesh, India the researchers note that "the police as an institution draws very bad responses from poor people across the two states, and most groups believe it to have a bad impact on people." In Ozerny, Russia a participant says, "When they raided the cellars, nothing was done, no one was found. I was robbed clean. I made a statement. Then I see the policeman drinking with the guy who robbed me."

Poor people also indict their elected representatives severely. The ineffectiveness of political pressure through elected representatives is reflected in the striking cynicism of poor people on every continent. People especially disparage elected officials for turning their backs on campaign promises to deliver much-needed services. "When he did want the vote, we did see him, but since we have already given him the vote, we have not seen him again," says a group of men from Bower Bank, Jamaica. Young Roma men in Bulgaria say, "All they do is promise. They take turns...then come election campaigns, and they start making big promises; we give you this, that, and the other; you'll have jobs, food, we'll repair your dwellings. Then—nothing. They've lined their pockets and couldn't care even if we starved to death."

In El Gawaber, Egypt poor people tell researchers that elected officials "can be re-elected regardless of what the poor want or need. In addition, the poor themselves realize that they cannot influence the decisionmaking process." Exceptions to the systematic low ratings of politicians were noted in some communities in Brazil, Ghana, India (Andhra Pradesh) and even Russia.

Lack of Responsiveness

> *Why should a person ask for taverns and condoms in parliament? He should have been coming here to listen to people's problems....Can we eat condoms?*
> —Discussion group of men and women, Mbwadzulu, Malawi

> *It is hard to get to the right person in the municipality, and when you do he says, "I'm sorry I am not able to help you."*
> —Discussion group of poor men and women,
> Zenica, Bosnia and Herzegovina

The worst institution listed was the state school...it used to be good but nowadays it is falling apart; there are whole weeks without a teacher, no director or efficient teachers, no safety, no hygiene.
—Discussion group of women, Vila Junqueira, Brazil

Poor people value involvement in decisionmaking that affects their lives. Every hour spent in meetings, however, is time lost in the struggle for survival. When they do participate in government-called discussions, they see few benefits from such participation, or they don't even believe they are heard. In Indonesia poor people in several villages say that although meetings are held, their voices are never reflected in any decisions taken. In the province of Ha Tinh, Vietnam poor people express frustration with commune-level decisionmaking meetings to which they are invited but at which, as Mr. G observes "no ordinary people can discuss."

Apart from time, poor people also mobilize and contribute their own precious resources to government-managed communal efforts. People give many examples of absconded funds. In Los Juríes, Argentina, for example, poor women complain that municipal authorities held a festival to raise funds to repair the road. While funds were gathered, the roads were never fixed, "nor have we seen the money that we ourselves contributed." To many poor people, despite physical proximity, government programs often seem uninformed by their needs and difficult to access. In Razgrad, Bulgaria a 72-year-old widow complains about the terrible timing of special assistance for coal in which funds are received in April: "They said they will give us money for heating. That's good, but we are not citizens with central heating to pay each month. We buy coal once a year, in autumn." In Sekovici, Bosnia and Herzegovina, discussion groups say they avoid seeking assistance from the municipality and local health-care and social services because although one may be able to "get something...the road between the entrance door and the assistance received is a very hard and rocky one."

Throughout the world, state-managed health services are valued but often considered ineffective, as discussed in chapter 5. In Khaliajuri, Bangladesh participants say that doctors are an effective institution only for those who are "well off" in the society because doctors only go "to the houses of those people who have money for treatment, respect them, and put importance on their opinion." However, there are exceptions in many places, where participants praise individual programs, clinics and staff.

Schools emerge as the most important institution in many places, but they are often not rated effective, honest, trustworthy or receptive to poor people, particularly women. In Netarhat Panchayat, Bihar, India the school emerges as the most important institution in poor people's lives, followed by the bank, post office, and *panchayat* (village council). While recognized for its importance, the school receives very low ratings in efficiency and good work; very low ratings on community control over school; and low ratings on trust and honesty and on extent of women's participation. Poor people report that the "teacher in the coeducational primary school is very irregular and hardly comes to the school for more than two days a week."

Poor people find it almost impossible to access formal banks for savings and credit. Collateral requirements, payment schedules, distance, lack of information and bribes all exclude poor people from banking services.

In rural communities of Latin America problems with lack of access to credit for agriculture and to banking services are widespread. A woman from Chota, Ecuador says that "poverty results from the absence of loans.... No one has the resources to plant.... This is the only reason." In Guadalupe, Bolivia participants also say that credit is available only from neighbors because banks require land titles.

Participants in Malawi recount many problems with credit programs. In the village of Mbwadzulu, while a few families have benefited from credit provided through the Malawi Rural Finance Company, participants generally feel that deposits, collateral, interest rates and repayment terms are excessive, given local conditions. Another hurdle is the restriction that only one group at a time is eligible to receive a loan in the community. Similarly, participants in a small group from Phwetekere say, "So many lending institutions have emerged, but their operations are hardly transparent. People do not know how to access them. Those who have tried have been let down by high levels of collateral demanded."

Similar sentiments are echoed elsewhere. "To give me a loan they cripple me," reports a participant from El Gawaber, Egypt when considering problems with the local loan programs. In one city in Egypt poor men and women are knowledgeable about three credit schemes that are operated by the city's Social Services Department, a voluntary association, and the Social Fund for Development. As one researcher notes, poor people cannot take advantage of these credit systems, however, because of "nepotism in the Social Services Department, high interest rates on small loans in the case of the voluntary association, and collateral for the Social Fund in the form of two employee salaries."

In Vietnam rural communities rate the official credit program highly, but poor people mention with some frequency problems with lack of information, very limited coverage and favoritism in distribution. In Ha Tinh Province a poor man says, "Loans have been given at the subjective decision of the hamlet leaders who provided the loan to the person he liked."

Where banks exist and are accessible to poor people, they often appear on the discussion groups' lists of valued institutions. In Mohammadpur, Bangladesh two women's groups give a fairly high score of trust in the local bank because they can deposit their savings and withdraw money at will. On the grounds of efficiency, however, much lower ratings are given because poor people have difficulties obtaining "checkbook, passbook, and deposit book in time." Also, the women say the bank provides loans only to wealthier groups when crises arise. Some groups give extremely low scores to the bank because of concerns that its staff takes bribes for approving loans and that there are no opportunities for voicing complaints to the bank.

The Power of Documents

He could not get unemployment allowance—so many documents to collect!

—A 39-year-old man, fired for ill health, and unable to afford surgery, Olmalyq, Uzbekistan

If I had had an identity card, the police wouldn't have been able to throw me out.

—A displaced slum dweller, Hyderabad, India

Documents required by the state become instruments of power. They can confer rights. Ration books in India, for example, entitle their holders to subsidized commodities. The need for documents also renders poor people vulnerable. Those without the proper documents cannot claim their rights. To obtain them can cost much in time, humiliation, fees and bribes. Poor people find documents difficult to keep safe: they can be damaged, lost, burned, mislaid or stolen. Many holders cannot read or understand them. Those who have documents find they can be demanded, confiscated, torn up or returned only on payment of a bribe. Papers play their part in the harassment, exclusion· and powerlessness of the poor.

Those who control the issue of documents are well placed to extract payments. Bribing someone to get documents is often the norm. As a middle-aged man from a discussion group held in a city in Bulgaria explains,

> For each paper I have to ask how to fill it out and to give a packet of coffee to the woman in the mayor's office. And the Gypsies they do not even ask; they know already. When they are told that there is some paper to fill out, they come with a chicken in the bag in order to save time; they give the chicken and they go back home even without asking what the paper is for.

While other participants in this discussion group feel the man exaggerated a bit, they also say, "But he is right." In Bosnia and Herzegovina, some say the process of verifying and certifying the documents for a service could cost more than the assistance provided is worth.

Those who lose documents lose their rights and entitlements. A landless and very poor widow in Dorapalli, India was forced to buy rice on the open market "though the price is exorbitant" because she lost her ration card, which would have provided her with subsidized rice.

Poor people also often lack the documents, such as land titles, needed for obtaining loans or for other purposes. Obtaining documents is difficult. In Vares municipality in Bosnia and Herzegovina researchers were told that the authorities "are extremely unapproachable, and when you ask for some documents they say they can't find them, but they don't even look, and they say that you have to collect them again, but then the next time they say that they found them." In Indonesia, in a village the poorest reported difficulties in obtaining health cards needed for free treatment.

New migrants into cities, as in Vietnam or Russia, may need residents' permits. Those without them can be arrested. And those with them can have the permits confiscated or torn up. Refugees in a Russian city who live in culvert cylinders and garbage areas stay in hiding because the police have confiscated their registration papers. They say, "Our life is a prison. Russians do not respect us. We are in hiding from the police. They tear up our registration certificates and say we don't have any rights...."

Decentralized Governance: Municipalities, Councilors and Mayors

Government has let us down, too many promises—never
fulfilling them. Look how these roads stay. They never have
to drive upon our street. They look after their streets. And
they try and find helicopters. We need a government of God.
—A 30-year-old unemployed mother,
Thompson Pen, Jamaica

Those in the municipality care only about their salaries and
themselves, and not at all about others.
—A resident of Vares, Bosnia and Herzegovina

"It [local government] is nonexistent."... "They do not give
you any results." "They must get involved in the areas they
rule; they must look at the small part of Argentina under their
scope and fulfill their role, and they don't do it."
—Comments from women in a discussion group,
La Matanza, Argentina

It's the mayor who makes the decisions. If he doesn't like
somebody, there's no social assistance for them. The mayor
makes the lists.... Last year he decided that those who had live-
stock won't be entitled to welfare; yet in some case one goat
didn't qualify as livestock, and in others it did.
—Participant, discussion group of women,
urban Bulgaria

Decentralization of resources, finances, capacity and authority to local governments and councils in both rural and urban areas is a growing trend in an effort to create more effective, responsive and representative governance and delivery of basic services to citizens. One major impact of decentralization is the potential for supporting democracy at the local level. In many countries, decentralization efforts have been given major impetus by changes in the legal framework.

Three countries in the study (Bolivia, India and Vietnam) have recently made innovations in the legal framework aimed toward decentralized grassroots democracy. The Law of Popular Participation in Bolivia (1993) devolves resources and authority to the municipalities and empowers people's local organizations to serve as vigilance committees, both in decisionmaking and in monitoring municipal action. In India the Panchayati Raj devolves budgets and decisions to the communities and requires that one-third of the *panchayat* (village council) leaders be women. And in May 1998 Vietnam introduced Grassroots Democracy Decree 29 to bring democracy to the communes. The decree is centered on four key categories of participation—*"People know, people discuss, people execute, and people supervise"*—and aims to bring democracy and economic development to all (steering committees were created in the first year, although not a single one was headed by a woman). However, whether or not decentralization makes a difference in poor people's lives depends on many factors, including the strength of poor people's organizations.

In rural areas, the municipality or local government emerges as among the most important institution in poor people's lives: 11 percent (figures 10.1 and 10.2). Although municipalities in urban areas are mentioned with nearly the same frequency (9 percent) as they are in rural areas, they are only the fourth-most frequently mentioned important institution by urban participants. While municipalities do figure in poor people's pick of effective institutions (9 percent), they dominate in poor people's pick of ineffective institution at 19 percent.

In the former Soviet bloc countries, in particular, municipalities are the most frequently mentioned ineffective institution; they score low in most discussion groups. In Orgakin, Russia participants say municipal and district authorities do not visit their village for months at a time.

In Russian towns and communities where mayors are mentioned, more often than not, poor people rank them among the most ineffective institutions. In a town in Russia people express great anger toward the mayor and his association with "the blacks," a derogatory term for "rich ethnic minorities from nearby areas," perceived to be engaged in shady deals in collusion with officials.

In Vila Junqueira, Brazil the city's legislature is considered the worst institution, a group of poor men observe, "The municipal Congressmen are all thieves...they do not solve anything, there are no schools, no health care. They do not vote issues that interest the people." Discussion groups in Isla Trinitaria, Ecuador feel they have little influence over government authorities unless they happen to know someone within a government agency who could provide some help.

In Bangladesh local government representatives receive largely negative reviews, with the exception of some favorable reports on their relief work after the 1998 floods. The members and chairman of the *union parishad* (the lowest administrative unit of government) are considered important but largely inaccessible to the poor, and particularly to women. In all but two communities, the local chairmen are judged to be corrupt in distributing relief. In the Dhaka settlement, ward commissioners are not well perceived because poor people think they show bias toward wealthier residents in delivering infrastructure.

There are instances in which the municipal authorities are well regarded, particularly in responding to crisis. In Isla Talavera, Argentina participants praise the municipality for providing support during floods. A participant from Nuevas Brisas del Mar, Ecuador said that she was desperate after losing her home from El Niño until she received a new home from the government: "They gave me this house. I thank God even if it is small. We are somewhat uncomfortable, but at least I am not renting."

In Indonesia's rural areas the lowest level of village government, the neighborhood level, is rated highly particularly for helping out during the recent economic crisis. In one community, a poor man says, "We could not imagine how we would be able to eat during the crisis. Our crops were destroyed by disease and pests; there was no rain, and it was difficult to sell our woven cloth. Luckily, there was the *padat karya* [food or cash for work] project for road rehabilitation from the Ministry of Manpower, solicited by our village officials." Other assistance during the crisis came from the *puskesmas* (health center) in the form of health funds. However, the group feels the distribution of this assistance was not fair or equitable.

Similarly in Kaoseng, Thailand four out of five discussion groups consider the municipality crucial in assisting the community in time of crisis: "the municipality gives more respect to the community—not rejecting to serve or regarding the community as invaders like in the past."

In Brazil change in governance rules has enabled ordinary citizens to participate in the budgeting process of local government. In some communities, community representatives have become involved in this citywide participatory budget-planning process.

There are also a few examples of caring mayors, who establish the potential for change. Participants in Zawyet Sultan, Egypt say, "The people in the northern side of the village, they referred to him as the only one who helps. As for the people in the southern side, they said that he doesn't care about anyone and that he only serves those who are near him." In Nova Califórnia, Brazil the mayor received favorable mention in one women's group when they were asked about who helps in an emergency situation. In Vila Junqueira, Brazil a woman indicates that "things have improved a lot in the last eight years. It was the mayor that started these improvements. The community helped a lot with the labor. Everybody helped and thank God now we have a proper neighborhood." In another area, a poor man proudly takes out the telephone number of the mayor, signifying direct access and caring.

Empowerment and Partnership

> When asked about their opinion of the local village council, the women laughed and responded that it was "men only."
> —Research team, El Gawaber, Egypt

The schools in Vares were always strong. The school is the carrier of everything—everything revolves around it. Here we organize various events and entertainment, sporting competitions.... Vares has always had a lot of spirit, and we are trying to maintain that spirit.

—A resident of Vares, Bosnia and Herzegovina

Poor people know their needs, problems and priorities. However, they almost always state that they need partnerships with governments to solve many livelihood and community problems. Despite disillusionment about government interest, skills, behavior and commitment, poor people want to work in equal partnership with their governments. Equality, however, does not translate into doing half the work, but rather a partnership of mutual respect, with each partner contributing resources appropriate to particular problems and contexts.

Despite problems, there are promising examples of partnerships between governments and community groups. While governments have started to reach out to community groups, they have yet to focus on investing directly in the organizational capacity of poor people to manage resources themselves and to keep decentralized governments accountable. Changes in the legal structure, such as those undertaken in India and Bolivia, designed to empower local organizations now makes this a possibility. However, in the absence of special efforts to include women, they will continue to be passed over.

In several countries decentralized governments have reached out into communities. In some of the *favelas* of Brazil, partnerships with sanitation authorities stand out as promising ways to improve infrastructure in poor communities. A group from Padre Jordano, Brazil states, "If it were not for the help of the politicians supplying the construction materials, so that we could fix the sewers, the number of diseases here would be much higher." In Indonesia the neighborhood associations (below the level of village associations and village chiefs), which are actually an arm of village-level government, are considered very important, effective and trusted institutions everywhere, by everyone except rural women. Rural women, by and large, feel excluded by the head of the neighborhood association, usually a man. The heads of these associations issue identity cards and certificates of good conduct that help in obtaining jobs, and identify families in need of social assistance. In the community of Harapan Jaya a discussion group of men say they turn to their neighborhood chief first when problems arise: "He is responsible for getting aid from the *kelurahan* [village] office allocated for our neighborhood. He has lived in the area all his life and is a known and trusted person who puts common funds to productive use for the benefit of all residents."

While unknown under the previous regime, in the last two years neighborhood groups in Indonesia are beginning to demand accountability of village chiefs. In Tanjungrejo when there were problems with the neighborhood chief who embezzled funds from the Social Safety Net program for the poor, the community forced him to resign. In Galih Pakuwon study participants say that while village officials had consulted them about community development activities, they "feel that the activities were not transparently implemented. Examples were the distribution of the basic essential goods that did not reach the targeted beneficiaries, the distribution of asphalt for road repairs, etc."

Poor Thai people credit the Tambon Administrative Organizations with solving community problems and managing local development activities. These bodies are said to "belong to the community" and are also valued for serving as a link with a range of government agencies and for obtaining aid. In the community of Baan Chai Pru discussion groups say that community organizing has increased as a consequence of the economic crisis and the presence of returned migrants who are using "their knowledge and experiences" to help villagers come together to solve local problems.

In Uzbekistan the government delegates to the *mahalla komiteti,* or neighborhood committee responsibility for identifying recipients and distributing some forms of social assistance. Each committee is run by a locally elected chairman, who is supported by a secretary, and both positions are government funded. In some communities these committees appear to be taking on other functions, such as helping to resolve family disputes. In Dangara the committee organized local contributions and labor for a gas pipeline project to all the households.

Effective government and community partnerships have emerged particularly in the management of schools, and in some areas, health services. In Urmaral, Kyrgyz Republic the school is ranked as the most important institution, as well as the most trustworthy one; groups give it 50 points on a 50-point scale. A group of younger poor men say, "We can't live without the school. We have to think about education of our children, and we're grateful to the teachers for their patience and for their hard work." Other groups speak about their high respect for the school "because it keeps working in spite of all difficulties, and gives education to our children." When asked why school is ranked as number one, a discussion group of poor men and women in Urmaral say they "trust the school, can influence its work, resolve the issues related to performance of the school at parents' meetings."

In other countries as well, when communities play an active role in school governance, school performance improves. In Río La Sal, Bolivia the local school board is highly valued for its effectiveness, for being trustworthy, and for offering help, and people "feel they participate in its decisionmaking." As one participant says, "I don't have education and am not aware of many things...my children now can read and they explain to me what I don't know. The school board is our organization; we all participate." Elsewhere, however, and as discussed in greater detail in the next chapter, schools are less than perfect.

An example of government and community partnership in health emerges from Brazil. In Vila União, Brazil the community health program, called PACS (Programa de Agentes Comunitários de Saúde), is rated the most effective because it provides immediate assistance, safety and care even though the program suffers from "clear management problems." PACS is sponsored by the federal government in partnership with municipalities.

Interactions with Private Enterprise

It is hard to participate in something that involves profits.
—Participant, discussion group of women,
El Gawaber, Egypt

Employment is important if you are going to achieve.
—Participant, discussion group of young men,
Duckensfield, Jamaica

We cannot change the situation, the trader controls everything because he has money and I do not.
—Participant, discussion group of kilim weavers, Foua Egypt

Poor people appreciate the employment opportunities provided by private enterprises, the investment sometimes made in community-wide improvements, and the caring sometimes shown by employers during emergencies. However, accounts of exploitation, low wages, and exclusion from any partnership in business are common. Despite problems, work in the formal economy is highly valued; poor people consider these institutions effective because they are often their only sources of income and help in crisis.

The Power of Industry

If only the wages were paid on time, we could as well go and work.
—Discussion group, Andijan, Uzbekistan

Given the difference in power between those who can provide jobs, a place in the market areas, access to buying and selling channels, and poor people who need to survive, private employers in fact often govern the lives of poor people. From large farm landlords to boat owners and mine owners or those who run factories, construction companies, cafés or manage buildings, poor people turn to those who can offer them work. The importance of private enterprise in job creation is mentioned in many parts of the world. However, to create market opportunities that benefit the poor, the nature of poor people's interactions with the private sector needs to be understood. In addition the informal overlap between those who work in state institutions and those in the private sector at each level needs to be understood. Poor people understand well how these linkages make it even more difficult to earn a living. A discussion group of men in Bulgaria explain, "So where's all the money? The revenue from the market is 800 million a month, and he has 20 stalls in the market place.... They're buddies with the market manager and the mayor, great buddies. They've teamed up...they own warehouses, eateries, while us folk, we are ostracized."

Poor people often have detailed knowledge of local markets and their links to external markets, but face severe constraints in entering markets. The following example about the business of breeding pigs reflects detailed knowledge about costs, risks and profit margins for business enterprises common in their area. In Etropole, Bulgaria a group calculated the costs of breeding pigs for external markets as higher than for the local market, taking into account the probability of illness and the pigs being "poor eaters" and falling prices. "Breed pigs for the local market because there is some profit in it. A swine needs some 250 kg of grain fodder to weigh 70 kg before it can start breeding. Then you have to wait three months, three weeks and three days of pregnancy. A normal swine delivers 2 to 8 piglets which could be sold in the neighboring village for breeding; there is a good market for them; but year before last the average price of a 12–15 kg pig was some 40,000–50,000 leva, and the last year, some 25,000–30,000 leva.

In Oq Oltyn, Uzbekistan the *sovkhoz* [collective farm] emerges as important across most communities because it is the main job provider and also distributes land plots among households. Here are a few of the many examples of assistance:

> ▸ If you have money in the *sovkhoz* cash office, our director would never deny you help.... Last year the *sovkhoz* helped me to solve the problem of my sister's education; she entered a school as a contract student. He remitted 57,000 som to the school where my sister is enrolled. This amount is even bigger than what I earned in *sovkhoz*, which means that now I am indebted to the *sovkhoz*.
> ▸ It helped me in a funeral; I had been given a sack of flour and some oil for free. True, it was ten years ago.
> ▸ It is difficult to make savings in the *sovkhoz*. For working one hectare of land they pay 400 som a month [the price of 5 kilograms of flour]. You must go to the field every day, regardless of whether there is work or not.

Poor people highly value factory jobs. In Olmalyq, Uzbekistan it is considered prestigious to have a job at a local factory. According to many participants, while everyone wants a job at the factory not everyone can afford it as large bribes are needed ("up to 100 U.S. dollars"). People also call the factory's general director the "mightiest" in the city and part of the business and political elite.

In parts of Jamaica plantations emerge as important institutions. Participants rank Tropicana Estate, Eastern Banana, and Fred M. Jones very highly as they have provided jobs for community members over the years and contribute to the infrastructure of the community. Residents of Duckensfield, for instance, receive a wide range of social services and utilities, including electricity, water and telephones, and people think the presence of plantations helped bring these to the community.

Poor people know well that there are clearly more poor people looking for work and business opportunities than there are opportunities. This simple fact leads to their widespread experiences of abuse, exploitation and discrimination. Many of these issues have been highlighted in chapter 3, which describes poor people's struggles for livelihood, their lack of connections in getting any jobs, their inability to protect themselves from lawlessness on the job or even to ensure that they get paid when the work is done. Chapter 4 establishes how hungry people are offered less pay by employers who are well aware of their desperation. Chapter 8 describes how corruption and collusion between the police and the better-off results in further exploitation of poor workers and their helplessness in the face of injustice. Ethnic minorities and in some contexts women experience discrimination and harassment (see box 10.1).

Prejudice against the poor seeps down to the lower level employees in the private sector. In Brazil discussion group participants said they are harassed by surveillance and security guards in shops, supermarkets and banks. In the supermarkets, "when we go there to buy something, we see the movement of the security guards talking to one another. Once I got fed up and asked the guard, 'Why are the poor discriminated against and harassed when they come here? You'd better know that my money is cleaner than that of the rich.... It was gained with a lot of work and not from fishy business.'" In Foua, Egypt some who worked as casual laborers complain that their employer would not stand by them during times of ill health and that "the owner of the business puts us under his feet and walks on us."

Shops and Moneylenders

The moneylender and the pawnshop are like husband and wife. One month we borrow from the moneylender and pay the pawnshop. Next month we borrow from the pawnshop and pay the moneylender.
—Participant, discussion group of women, Indonesia

Shops or kiosks are the first place to go for community members any time they are short of what they need.
—A discussion group participant, Genengsari village, Indonesia

Poor people frequently turn to shopkeepers, pawnbrokers and moneylenders to borrow funds, buy goods on credit or sell off personal property, and they often rate these institutions quite high on importance. With little access to formal credit channels, these resources prove critical to the survival strategies of poor people almost everywhere. Poor people report that they need credit not only to cope with crises but also to manage daily expenditures in lean times. In Netarhat Panchayat in Bihar, India the shop is systematically rated the highest on almost every criterion considered important: importance and usefulness, efficiency, good work, and trust and honesty. As a researcher notes, shops receive such high ratings because they serve multiple functions:

> *Many people in the village are in the habit of purchasing household consumables on credit from the local shop, and the credit facility is considered to be a useful service. The shop also serves as a local selling point of farm produce from many villagers.... No villager is ever known to have accessed any loan from the bank, although people are aware of such provision.*

In Russia the local shop is commonly regarded as a very important institution that supports people during a crisis. Poor people call the shop owner of Orgakin one of the most respected people in the village. She makes goods widely available on credit and arranges special assistance for poor families in need. With many villagers facing wage arrears from employers or delays in the payment of pensions, poor people greatly appreciate the opportunity to buy goods on credit.

In Genengsari Village, Indonesia shops and kiosks are considered very important in the daily lives of people. In addition to purchasing goods on credit, people say they can "borrow cash, although only a small amount and only when it is available." Three out of four groups rate the shops as providing the greatest benefit to the community. Participants say the shops are the most effective local institutions because they are the easiest places to go for help, they offer help to whoever is in need, and they provide assistance at a meaningful level. Similar findings emerge in Jamaica.

Local moneylenders appear with surprising frequency on poor people's lists of institutions of local importance, but, here again, views on whether they play a positive or negative role vary widely. In Kebele, Ethiopia a group of young males rank the local moneylender as the most important institution in their community because it is their only hope for starting a small business some day by buying and selling food items.

Despite calling them "bloodsuckers," a reflection of high interest rates and dire consequences for nonpayment, poor people appreciate the speedy service and flexibility that moneylenders provide: they often extend loans on the spot without collateral requirements and allow payments to be made in kind, with cash, or through the provision of labor.

Governance and Accountability in Civil Society

> *Jimpitan is when every participating family contributes one cup of rice every month. The collection has been used for helping poor families that really needed help and should be repaid. For rice given to old disabled people, no repayment is required.*
> —Participant, discussion group of men and women,
> Galih Pakuwon, Indonesia

There is no unified community, there is no unity, when they have to speak with authorities the people feel afraid.
—Discussion group of poor women, Isla
Talavera, Argentina

Civil society institutions encompass a range of institutions from very informal networks based on friendship, kinship and interest, to local leaders, religious organizations and NGOs. These institutions play important roles in the lives of poor people during crises and in their daily lives. This section discusses the role of community-based organizations, local leaders, religious organizations and NGOs.

Community-Based Organizations

Poor people living in urban and rural communities are rich in social networks and local institutions. There are innumerable examples of poor people helping each other to overcome survival, safety and social problems. Nonetheless, communities often lack unity. Poor people's informal networks and organizations by and large have not been able to strengthen their bargaining power with states, private enterprises, traders, or NGOs. In the study communities, only a few cases of poor people's networks have transformed into people's movements.

The most important institutions in poor people's daily lives are their own community-based groups and other local people. Community-based organization refers broadly to both formal and informal membership-based organizations. In rural areas community-based organizations are most frequently mentioned as both the most important and most effective institutions. In urban areas community-based organizations receive the most frequent mention as important institutions after health-related institutions and are the front-runner as the most frequently chosen effective institutions (figures 10.1 and 10.2).

Local groups, such as community councils and neighborhood associations, engage routinely in helping families avoid destitution when crises hit. In the villages of Achy and Kok Yangak, Kyrgyz Republic, for example, the local councils of elders promote mutual support within the community by collecting money toward needs such as funeral expenses or road repairs.

In Brazil neighborhood associations with locally elected leaders have emerged as important community-based organizations. Most of these organizations have their origins in land struggles. In communities where the neighborhood association is strong, it has successfully brokered resources and partnerships with municipalities to improve infrastructure and attract health and education resources to the community. Neighborhood associations have united across communities to form federations, with their own newsletters, resources and mobilization activities.

Neighbors in Plovdiv, Bulgaria are good contacts when one is searching for a job. In Buq, Somaliland a group of women meets weekly to recite religious verses, discuss economic and health conditions, and collect food for needy families. In Egypt credit groups known as *gameya* are common. In Wewala, Sri Lanka informal credit groups run by women provide death benefits to cover burial costs in addition to credit.

Poor people value their own community-based organizations and informal networks because within them they feel they can be heard and make a difference. The researchers from Nakorn Patom in Thailand explain that the local community group is the most valued institution because "they feel that they have a say in the decisionmaking process.... The institutions that the villagers cannot participate in are the government organizations, such as the post office, electricity, health station and police. The market is also another institution that the villagers cannot participate in."

To overcome lack of bargaining power with buyers and sellers, poor people in a few places have organized into trade unions of tailors, dressmakers and bulk purchasers. In Togdheer, Somaliland, for example, women, and particularly young women, highly rate business networks involved in trade and small businesses. The women value these networks for information about markets and for access to credit all over the region and country. One young woman says, "When things get difficult the first people I consult are my credit network, and they either provide the support I need or advise me on how proceed."

However, lack of unity within the community emerges as a particular obstacle to resolving local problems. In Accompong, Jamaica a group of young women observed that some "keep malice and are of a bad mind and hold grudges," and the researchers suggest that this has reduced cooperation and "collective enterprise." In Las Pascuas, Bolivia a youth says, "If we unite we can do more together than can each on one's own." Problems of community discord extend well beyond Latin America. In Wewala, Sri Lanka the existence of a Rural Development Society (RDS) was acknowledged as existing "in name only." The Secretary of the RDS, said the group never meets because "the powerful people do not want to do anything good in this village." Similarly, in Mulipothana village people question the workings of the local RDS, which has collected membership dues, but probably is not holding "bona fide meetings" as required.

In Vietnam researchers note problems created by leaders co-opting mass organizations: "In some places, certain mass organizations were thought to be unhelpful beyond the immediate family circle of the leader. In other locations, the same mass organization would rank highly for poor households.... Much seemed to depend on the personality of the individual leader in each location."

Local Leadership

> *The president of the community [is most trusted] because he*
> *is permanently helping us. He is the strong arm of the commu-*
> *nity and in the school, because if the parents complain about*
> *a teacher, it has to change, and we have this power.*
> —Participant, discussion group of men,
> Novo Horizonte, Brazil

Local leaders, whether formal or informal, play important roles in poor people's lives, particularly in rural areas.

In Bower Bank, Jamaica a discussion group of poor women identify Sister Janet, who runs a local charity, as an effective leader. Poor people say that in any crisis she is always available: "In times of sickness at any hours of the day or night we can knock, Janet is always here...Janet is always willing to help and always here.... When we have an important letter to write she writes it for us." Similar sentiments about turning to local individuals when in need are echoed by members in a youth discussion group. "Michael, the people say, has helped them when they had to go to an interview and had no bus fare, when they had no baby milk, or shoes; he 'helps keep us off the road' and always encourages them 'to do good.'" In some communities in Bihar, India educated young men who have returned to their villages to live are identified as leaders.

In Khwalala, Malawi the village headman and grandparents emerge as the most effective local leaders:

The village headman was identified by all the groups. He is important because he provides leadership, settles disputes, and fosters unity. He is always there for them. He always makes himself available in times of need. Grandparents were only identified by the mixed group and were ranked first. The group pointed out that they are "helpful" because they facilitate and support the process of socialization. They, among other things, provide free advice, impart culturally sanctified manners, and teach about religion and community history that passes on from one generation to another.

In rural Africa some village chiefs emerge as trusted leaders because they continue caring for people despite a lack of contact with the formal authority structures. In Nigeria many village heads receive low ratings, but the village head of Jimowa is considered the closest institution people know and is thereby ranked the highest. The researchers found that

...both the men and the women groups indicated the extent of his helpfulness, enthusiasm, and readiness to assist. He is considered to be a magnanimous person who puts other people's interests above his own. He is acknowledged to usually put aside some money and food, to assist any family in the community in distress. And when he loans out money or seeds he is prepared to wait till the next harvest to collect what he loaned out. He does not collect interest on such payments. He trusts his people and his people trust him. He works extra hard to try to answer as many requests as possible and relates very well with his court as well as the other community members. According to the women's group, "he is the only government we know."

In Ho Chi Minh City, Vietnam a retired government officer took action to reduce flooding in the community. He met with neighborhood leaders and shared a plan to redirect the existing paths and sewage system with each of the residents. The plan was financed by all the local families, and the researchers reported that "people agreed to make contributions because they knew that nobody else would solve the problem for them. The work was done as planned, with the result that there is now no flooding at all in some places, and much less than before in others."

Churches, Mosques, Temples, Shrines, Trees, Stones and Rivers

> *The mosque is our court, school, and lawyer.*
> —A 51-year-old poor man, Urmaral, Kyrgyz Republic

> *The church is fast in dealing with things like diseases and funerals, but when it comes to keeping secrets we can't trust it.*
> —Participant, discussion group of men,
> Chitambi, Malawi

Faith-based organizations emerge frequently in poor people's lists of important institutions. They appear more frequently as the most important institution in rural areas rather than in urban ones. Spirituality, faith in God and connecting to the sacred in nature are an integral part of poor people's lives in many parts of the world. Religious organizations are also highly valued for the assistance they provide to poor people. However, the role that religious or faith-based organizations play in poor people's lives varies from being a balm for the body and soul to being a divisive force in a community. In ratings of effectiveness in both urban and in rural areas, religious organizations feature more prominently than any single type of state institution, but they do not disappear completely when ineffective institutions are specified.

In Baan Pak Wan, Thailand researchers note that "the Buddhist monks were supporting the villagers as much as they could, and the abbot even found donors from another province to build the *ubosod* [the Buddhist ritual ceremony place] on the temple's ground without collecting any money from the villagers."

In Kajima, Ethiopia the *Erethca*, or holy tree (which literally means "wet straw" in the local language), together with the Coptic Church, is the source of spiritual strength and faith. Explaining its importance, the community report reads as follows:

> *There is a huge tree at the bank of one of the seven crater lakes in the area. People go to the tree on a Sunday after* Meskal *[a church festival] with wet straw in their hands. The wet straw symbolizes the desire to have "wet land," "wet hands," etc. Wet things are supposed to stand for prosperity and wet land*

allows growth. The main purpose therefore is to pray to God to make the land wet with rain. People said, "We believe in it and it works; we get together and pray when we need something desperately; we go and pray for our children's health."

In Brazil the church emerges as more effective than the municipality in many communities. In Vila União, Deus é Amor, a Protestant church, was regarded as a reliable, effective and trusted institution that helps deprived families. A participant comments, "I always go to church to pray or if I need something, I ask for it." In Argentina, Brazil and Ecuador poor people single out names of particular pastors or ministers as always being kind and trying to be helpful. But in Mtamaba, Malawi, together with the government, the church scores low in trust, 10 out of 50, because "they do not assist people equally. They tend to favor others so we cannot trust them fully."

The dismantling of communism in the former Soviet countries has led to the emergence of a range of faith-based organizations. In Etropole, Bulgaria discussions were lively. Participants there agree that the Pentecostal Church is more efficient than the Orthodox Church, which is said to provide "moral help." The Pentecostal Church is reputed to be the "Gypsy Church" and is singled out as helping poor people and those who were ill; its pastors go out into the community to be with poor people despite the fact that they have their own children to feed. A middle-aged poor man declares, "The pastor goes to the houses every day to speak with the stupid women...and they receive American money; everybody knows that."

In Jamaica the church seems more important to women than men and to the elderly than to the young. In Freeman's Hall, for older women,

> *...the church provides fellowship and a point of interaction with each other; they sing hymns, read scriptures, and pray together. The church is within walking distance of their homes, and for them possibly the only place to go when not at home. The same would be true for older men. However, there was one man who was vehemently against the church who commented, "The church sells clothes given to them by the [Salvation Army]. They are just sharks for money. The church is money grabbers...they just want to baptize." He felt the pastor was running a racket and profiting from the church.*

A different picture of churches emerges among the Maroons in Accompong, Jamaica: "The Maroons are more interested in the churches that provide expression for their cultural heritage, the Myal religion and which permit the playing of the traditional *gumbay* drums." One of the more popular churches in the community, the Zion Church, keeps alive some of the Maroons' spiritual rituals.

In Madaripur, Bangladesh the mosque is at the top of the list of important institutions:

> The mosque is useful to the villagers as they can perform
> their prayers in the mosque. There is also an arrangement in
> the mosque to teach the Arabic language; it is extremely use-
> ful in social ceremonies such as marriage and death. However,
> women clearly stated that they had no participation in any
> decision about the mosque or decisions taken from the
> mosque.

In Kok Yangak, Kyrgyz Republic poor residents consider the local mosques important even though they describe some mullahs as being too greedy; despite this, in most communities the mosque did not feature in the top 10 institutions. In Urmaral, Kyrgyz Republic the mosque serves multiple functions. Participants there say,

> The mosque is our court, school, and lawyer, while the village
> council is of no support, and policemen just provoke disorder.
> If something is stolen, the police do not search for the thieves,
> and, even if the thieves are caught, no further action is taken.
> All this does is a favor to thieves, they go on stealing and be-
> come still more impudent.

Nongovernmental Organizations

> Had it not been for PUSH [NGO], we would be dead.
> —A poor villager in Linda, Zambia

NGOs, where present, play important roles in poor people's lives. Poor people's analysis of NGOs provides some striking findings. NGOs have stepped in to fill important gaps created by the breakdown of government-provided basic services to poor people, but have limited presence. While deeply appreciated in many places, NGOs do not receive systematically high ratings on criteria considered important by poor people, who would like to be involved in decisionmaking in programs that NGOs manage. There are also as yet few examples of strong partnerships between poor people, NGOs and governments. And NGOs rarely invest in local organizational capacity that would let poor people's organizations lobby for better provision of all services and a better environment for entrepreneurship and private investment.

In both rural and urban areas, NGOs represent 7 percent of the most important institutions in poor people's lives (figures 10.1 and 10.2). They feature more prominently, however, as effective institutions in urban areas at 15 percent, and less so in rural areas, 8 percent. Approximately 5 percent of institutions identified as ineffective are NGOs.

NGOs Step In to Serve the Poor

*If it were not for Karitas we would have gone hungry, naked,
and barefoot. Whatever we needed we turned to Karitas and
they never turned me back empty-handed. Anything they had,
they gave out.*
—A mother with a family displaced by war, Capljina, Bosnia
and Herzegovina

*Our village is forsaken by God and our administration. After
disintegration of the USSR no one has visited to find out how
we live. We are very thankful to Counterpart Consortium,
NGO Assistance Center.*
—A 58-year-old man, Tash-Bulak, Kyrgyz Republic

Without the work of NGOs helping poor people who are struggling to stay alive, there is no doubt that the suffering of many poor families would increase. NGOs are reaching out and working with households and communities to distribute food and medicines to poor families, widows, refugees and the disabled. NGOs are in the forefront both in times of peace and during massive dislocations caused by war, working to improve the environment, education, health, productivity and community life.

In Kebele 30 in Ethiopia poor people identify what appeared to be the lifetime work of one woman as the most important institution:

*The most important institution in this community is the one
known as Sister Jember's NGO. There are many reasons for
saying that: First, as a result of the effort of this institution,
children who never would have had the chance to go to school
have received schooling free of charge. Second, virtually all the
houses of the disabled and weak people in this community
have been renovated free of charge by the same institution.
Third, all the poor and mostly weak people have received food
and clothing from Sister's NGO. It is mostly geared to help the
most vulnerable section of the community, like those who are
old and disabled. They feed and give them hope.*

In Bower Bank, Jamaica adult men and young men rank Food for the Poor as number one in importance:

*All groups spoke of Food for the Poor as an important source
of assistance to the community providing them "with a start."
Another valued group in the country was the Negril Coral Reef
Preservation Society (NCRPS) in Little Bay. The NGO helps to
clean up the community, especially the beaches, and this helps
protect the coral reef, which increases fish breeding. The*

*women of Little Bay especially expressed gratitude to the
NCRPS for helping community members to take pride in their
community.*

In Bosnia and Herzegovina NGOs receive both frequent mention and
mostly high praise. For the Croat residents of Vares, researchers note,
"Karitas is their savior, and it is noticeable that they live better and are better off." In Bratunac, an elderly poor woman praised the Red Cross: "The
Red Cross is the only organization we got something from concretely, unlike
the other organizations, and that is why we trust them." Similarly in Sekovici
poor people say, "Only the Red Cross gave us flour, sugar, and oil. That is
the only institution that has helped us in these years of misery."

In India, some local NGOs were consistently praised and trusted. In
Sohrai of Bihar, India the NGO SSVK, also known as Lok Shakti, figures at
the top in the ratings of the institutions:

> *The villagers say the NGO was the organization that mitigated
> their sorrow when their village was submerged in the flood of
> 1993. For months they were sheltered in tents provided by the
> NGO and given khichdi [a porridge of pulses and cereals].
> Later they were also provided plastic sheets for roofing. It is
> the NGO Lok Shakti therefore which is believed to be the vil-
> lagers' succor in times of distress and crisis.*

In Baan Ta Pak Chee, Thailand NGOs emerge as the most trustworthy
and sincere in providing help without expectations of return. The researchers
report

> *...the housewife group trusts the NGO because the NGO
> has offered help as needed to the villagers for a long time.
> When there was a shortage of cows and buffaloes, the NGO
> lend cows and buffaloes to the villagers and will get them
> back when they have calves. Also, the NGO offered succes-
> sive help and conduct the evaluation for other project imple-
> mentation.*

The Issue of Scale

> *Ak Bairak NGO has created 10 jobs for mothers of disabled
> children and organized a kindergarten group for the disabled
> children.*
> —Research team, At Bashi, Kyrgyz Republic

> *No NGOs or charity organizations have helped this school.*
> —Participant, discussion of a group of parents,
> Munamalgasvewa, Sri Lanka

NGOs hardly existed that provided technical support for organizational or institutional strengthening in the neighborhoods.
—Research team, Florencio Varela, Argentina

Given the huge scale of the poverty problem and the small scale of most NGO activities, it is important to recognize that they still have limited presence, particularly in the communities in Africa and in the former Soviet countries and in Latin America.

As in some parts of Asia, the NGO presence in Latin America is quite diverse in communities. In an institutional mapping exercise performed by participants in Ecuador, NGO activity was described as follows: "Inside the circle we find Help by Actions, who has done a lot for us. It has helped us in health and infrastructure.... DRI-Cotacachi is helping with a pork project. It helps the community and mixed associations.... INNFA is helping everyone in the community with education for children 0 to 2 years old, and 6 years old."

NGO activity in Eastern Europe is recent but growing. Not surprisingly, with some exceptions, poor people mention NGOs less frequently than other institutions. Even one person being helped, however, is better than nobody being helped. In At Bashi, Kyrgyz Republic NGOs distribute humanitarian aid and provide clothes to the poor. Another NGO, Chynar Bak, was created in 1998 to support orphans and women who adopt orphans. It has 12 members and offers free lunches for orphans in one of At Bashi's canteens with money contributed by local traders and businesspeople.

In Thailand the NGO Soun Mechai, in addition to providing assistance with large water jars, toilets and interest-free loans, provides scholarships to poor but deserving students: "At present, Soun Mechai grants students' scholarships to intelligent but poor students in the entire district of Baan Pai." Both men and women groups give the maximum scores for most criteria to this NGO, except for a score of seven for effectiveness by the women.

One example in the communities of a large-scale effort by an NGO is Proshika in Bangladesh. Proshika provides a wide range of services, credit, schools, latrines and awareness of rights, and works with associations of poor women or men, called *samities*.

Accountable to Whom?

They [NGOs] give resources; they undertake research, but there were other negative views because some are covers for businesses.
—Participant, discussion group of women,
La Matanza, Argentina

The work of the Red Cross is little known to the villagers. Those who went were outraged to see that clothes were not given, but sold there, or according to some information, admission is not free.
—A discussion group participant, Ozerny, Russia

The only institution that was said to allow community participation in decisionmaking was the Mabonde Women's Club, a community-based organization. This is a women's club aimed at income-generating activities, such as farming and knitting, to improve the livelihoods of their members.
 —A discussion group participant, Muchinka, Zambia

Not every poor person seeks to be actively involved in NGO management. But the lack of accountability of NGOs to poor people did surface in many places. This situation is particularly striking in cases such as one in Bangladesh where an NGO is praised highly on all criteria, but criticized for not involving people in its decisionmaking. Lack of accountability is evident from reports of lack of information about NGO activities, and researchers heard some reports of corruption, nepotism, rudeness and irrelevance. These findings, however, should be viewed against the backdrop of overall positive ratings on effectiveness given to NGOs by poor people.

In Khaliajuri, Bangladesh participants express rather strong dissatisfaction with an NGO working on credit:

The staff members of the NGO misbehave with group members if they fail to repay loan on time for family wants. The NGO never extends the time limit for loan repayment though there are definite and acceptable reasons. Moreover, the NGO gives very little importance on the opinion of participants in the other group-related activities.

Researchers note participants' feelings that

...if they had more control or influence over NGO, staff members of NGO would attach more importance on their opinion and poor people would have got rid of the problem of loan repayment; the poorest of the poor would have had the opportunity to make themselves members of the NGO and would have been able access the credit market.

In the former Soviet countries poor people expressed ambivalence and suspicion toward some NGOs because of their lack of accountability. In Muynak, Uzbekistan, a young man comments:

The workers of the NGO cut away the labels and distribute it instead of the humanitarian assistance, which they divide between themselves. They laugh at us, when they give us the boots of different sizes or big soldier's trousers. The boots are rather heavy and the soldier's trousers are big—it would be better if they gave us foodstuff.

When asked about other NGOs famous for their activity on Aral Sea and Pre-Aral Territory protection, the participants of Muynak declare, "We did not hear and see the representatives of the Union for Defense of the Aral Sea and Amu-Darya, and we do not know anything about the NGO."

Poor people in the Kyrgyz Republic have little contact with NGOs, and their role does not seem very important. In Bosnia and Herzegovina a researcher notes,

> *Several Catholic relief organizations focus their attention on providing help for their co-religionists, although several participants commented that Catholic Relief Services was notable for providing help to everyone.... Some Catholic and Muslim participants criticized the tendency of religious organizations to focus on rebuilding churches and mosques when people are still going hungry.*

In Sarajevo, Bosnia and Herzegovina researchers note, "Many people don't like or trust local NGOs or the people who work in them because they believe that they keep things for themselves which are intended for wider distribution." One resident spoke of how

> *...an Italian organization donated bathroom fixtures, but no one who needed them got them, only some crumbs. The municipality received 40,000 DM to fix people's homes, and they took it all for themselves. They even sold my stove from the UNHCR. What they were supposed to hand out to people they took for themselves and sold later. Since the humanitarian aid stopped a year ago, nobody has given out anything.*

In Ruamsamakee, Bangkok poor women say NGOs are not accountable to poor people but rather cater to the needs of the better-off. One comment on how, during a crisis, different groups have different opportunities for assistance is especially telling. A group of poor women say, "The rich women's group seeks help from rescue agencies and foundations while the poor female group has to solve the problems by themselves with maybe some aid from relatives."

In the city of Foua, Egypt poor people do not consider participation in decisionmaking as a criterion. This is not because they think it is not important, but because they have given up hope that anyone will listen to them. The researchers write, "This is related to the fact that the poor are very clear about who has the power to make decisions. They feel that institutions responsible toward them are particularly the public and voluntary sector. However, making these institutions accountable to them requires heavy transaction costs that they cannot provide."

Community, NGO and Government Partnerships

> *The leaders coordinate with the government institutions and
> NGOs to procure services for the village. As a result they were
> able to get tube wells to the village and three tanks and village
> roads rehabilitated.*
>
> —A researcher, Munamalgasvewa, Sri Lanka

There are few powerful examples of successful, large-scale partnerships
among communities, NGOs and governments. In Little Bay, Jamaica one
positive institution identified by members of the community, particularly by
younger groups, is the Negril Area Environmental Protection Trust (NEPT).
The group was launched in 1994 by 16 organizations that joined forces to
protect the conservation area.

In Bangladesh the large NGO Proshika, plays a brokering role with local
government, intervening on behalf of villagers. This relationship appears to
depend on the individual contacts of Proshika staff. For instance, the local
samities (organizations of poor women or men who are involved with NGOs)
have yet to evolve into a network of poor people's organizations that have
systematic representation in government-managed programs. Despite these
limitations, Proshika made vital contributions to Ulipur during the floods of
1998:

> *To the men in all villages, Proshika is the most important insti-
> tution; women at Hatya also supported the view of men al-
> though they put a similar importance on a* dewan *(a landed
> man having some influence on the power structure). The im-
> portance of Proshika was shown in terms of its officers' close
> relationships with the villagers. The men at Aminpara placed
> high confidence on a development officer of Proshika. The offi-
> cer not only performs his duty but also helps them in various
> ways. If they need any help in the* thana *administration or in
> the* thana *court, he assists them. Women at Hatya received all
> kinds of assistance and sympathies from Proshika officers dur-
> ing the flood [in] 1998. In the flood their tube well and latrine
> submerged with their houses. They were living in open air on
> the embankment. Proshika workers managed to install a com-
> munity tube well and a community latrine and relieved their
> sufferings. They explained that when they were being washed
> away by the flood even their own kin did not come forward to
> help them. Besides Proshika, they could only remember the*
> dewan, *who still helps them during illness and other crises.*

One of the most effective collaborations between community groups,
the private sector and government agencies was reported in the *favelas* of
Brazil. The neighborhood associations are regarded as the most important
institutions in 9 of the 10 sites and are the second-most positively evaluated

institution. They are highly regarded for representing community needs to public agencies and for helping residents during crises and in day-to-day life. To illustrate their diverse functions, a group of men and women from Nova Califórnia say they rely on their association "in case of health problems at home, lack of food, lack of housing, and other emergency problems." Participants there also feel they had influence over their association and that they had good access to the city government: "The president of the association has the ability to arrive, to talk, and to lay questions from the community on the floor."

Indeed, the testimony of a resident of Nova Califórnia suggests an intertwining of governmental, community and nongovernmental and private sector institutions:

> *In the case of sickness in the home, when I can't solve it, I turn to the president of the Neighborhood Association...and if the problem remains...I have Saúde em Casa [Health in the Home], the ambulances.... I look for help from the president of the Neighborhood Association, or the local government.... If the president can solve it, we talk with her; if she can't, we have to look for other means...outside of the neighborhood. The president of the association goes to the Citizenship Committee of the Bank of Brazil to solve problems that surpass her capacity, such as when the association doesn't have money to do what we have to do, be it medicine, basic food baskets.... Whatever is needed of them, they are there, and give.... We trust them.*

Potential NGO Roles in Changing Local Governance

> *The NGOs should monitor the performance of these [state] agencies and should try to be impartial in the community's internal issues.*
> —A discussion group participant, Entra a Pulso, Brazil

> *We want someone from the local village council to collaborate with us.*
> —Participant, discussion group of women, El Gawaber, Egypt

> *But they [traders] charge high prices for their goods and do not allow us to bargain.*
> —Participant, a discussion group of women, Madana, Malawi

Poor people find it difficult to organize and apply political pressure on their own. A big part of the problem is risk: the risk of offending patrons and powerful officials, and incurring loss of work, fines, violence or other penalties.

Another part is poverty of time and energy. A Sri Lanka report notes, "The very poor rarely attend meetings. They have to forgo a day's casual labor to do so."

The presence of local leaders and civil society institutions, including NGOs, that support local organizational capacity can make the difference in helping poor people overcome exclusion and exploitation as well as sheer fear of reprisal. Yet in our studies there seem to be few examples of NGO activities that increased poor people's participation in local governance or increased the accountability and transparency of local government decision-making.

Conclusion

Poor people's experiences call out for the reform of all institutions engaged in serving them: governments, NGOs, religious organizations and community organizations as well as private enterprises, banks and other civil society organizations. Very few institutions created by outsiders fulfill poor people's desire to have institutions that "stand by them in their evil days."

In an era of rapid decentralization, poor people's low ratings of local government in urban and rural areas should give pause. As local government stands as the only institution that can reach the majority of the poor, who are often scattered in remote communities, ensuring that decentralization serves poor people takes on even greater urgency. There are four areas for action. First, funds need to be directed to poor people's organizations through community-driven programs where community groups manage resources and make decisions. Second, investment is needed in organizations created by poor people and accountable to them. Third, these associations need to be linked to each other beyond the community level and to local governance structures. And, fourth, local government should be held accountable to empowered local associations of poor men and women. Special efforts will need to be made to ensure that poor women are included in governance.

While NGOs are greatly appreciated, poor people would like NGOs to respond to their needs and poor people would like to be involved in NGO decisionmaking. There is little evidence from the study that NGOs have had an impact on local governance. Religious institutions are respected and play key roles in poor people's lives, but poor people have criticized even these institutions for their lack of fairness and their role in reaching out only to their flocks, thus sowing the seeds for disunity.

Poor people depend on each other for survival. Friends, neighbors, and both formal and informal community-based organizations play critical roles in poor people's lives, in their daily struggles as well as during emergencies. The resources of these groups are limited, and community fracturing and the pressures of daily survival prevent them from organizing more effectively. Although there are striking examples of mobilization, poor people's organizations are by and large disconnected from each other and from other support organizations outside the community.

One of the biggest challenges to poverty reduction is the design and management of propoor institutions and investment in networks of membership-based organizations of poor men and women.

Notes

[1]Groups of poor men, women, seniors and youth discussed the institutions that were important in their lives. In some cases lists of institutions were written or drawn on cards or paper. People then discussed criteria to rate institutions. Once criteria were identified and agreed upon, groups rated institutions on these criteria. Scoring of institutions was done with pebbles, beans or other local material. In some countries the scores were simply written on sheets of paper. In some communities, particularly in Eastern Europe and Central Asia, discussion of performance of state institutions unleashed such anger that participants refused to engage in further discussion.

[2]The data were analyzed based on both ratings and descriptions of institutions. The percentages for the top five most important institutions are based on how frequently an institution was mentioned in each community across all discussion groups. The analysis is based on data from 21 countries, 183 communities and 1,254 discussion groups. Sri Lanka and Vietnam were not included in this analysis because the methodology used in conducting institutional analyses was different in these countries. The regional distribution was as follows: Africa, 451 discussion groups; Asia, 208 groups; Eastern Europe and Central Asia, 358 groups; and Latin America and the Caribbean, 237 discussion groups. When the analysis was repeated using a weighting system that took into account ranking of the institution, there was no shift in the pattern of results.

[3]It cannot be assumed that if, for example, health institutions make up 10 percent of effective institutions, they make up 90 percent of ineffective institutions. The percentages represent distribution of the five most frequently mentioned institutions across discussion groups. The ratings on effective and ineffective were queried separately in free-flowing discussions.

Chapter 11

Powerless, Trapped in a Many-Stranded Web

Summary

Poor people often feel powerless, trapped in a web of linked deprivations. Earlier chapters describe nine of the dimensions that anchor the web. A final dimension, personal incapabilities, or lack of information, education, skills and confidence, is explored in this chapter. Poor people frequently describe problems with accessing information about government, market and civic activities, particularly outside their communities. Often this is due to geographic isolation, lack of communication and social exclusion. Though many see education as a means to upward mobility, costs and difficult access often deter or prevent them from sending their children to school. Poor people often lack practical skills that would help them earn a livelihood. Their lack of ability to provide for their families and belong to society leads to low self-confidence and self-worth.

Some escape the many-stranded web of disadvantages. For others, the shocks to which they are vulnerable make them poorer and more powerless. Powerlessness leaves most poor people having to choose between one bad thing or another. In the face of agonizingly constrained choices, poor people are remarkable for their tenacity, resilience and hope. For them, the will is there, but often not the opportunity. The challenge for development professionals, and for policy and practice, is to find ways to weaken the web of powerlessness and to enhance the capabilities of poor women and men so that they can take more control of their lives.

Trapped and Tied

[Poverty is] like being in jail, living under bondage waiting to be free.
> —A young woman, Thompson Pen, Jamaica

We are left tied like straw.
> —A discussion group, Dibdibe Wajtu, Ethiopia

Many poor people feel they are trapped: kept poor and made poorer by multiple disadvantages. Their experience suggests these disadvantages are more comprehensive and more tightly interwoven than much professional and sectoral analysis recognizes. Several metaphors illustrate the condition of powerlessness, poverty and illbeing. Poor people themselves use the metaphors of a trap, of prison and of bondage.

While each of the individual dimensions of poverty is important, it is even more important to understand that the dimensions form a powerful web. They interlock to create, perpetuate and deepen powerlessness and deprivation. It is this interlocking that makes it difficult for the poor to escape poverty and easy to fall back into poverty after clawing their way out. It is this multifaceted nature of powerlessness that makes it difficult for poor people to organize and makes successful cases of organization even more remarkable.

This chapter consists of two sections. Part I explores the last of the 10 dimensions that comprise the interlocking web: personal incapabilities. Part II then explores the nature of the multifaceted web as experienced by poor people. This section first reports on how the many-stranded web keeps poor people powerless through multiple causes of deprivation and multiple impacts on deprivation. It then highlights how the interlocking dimensions of deprivation and powerlessness add to the precariousness of poor people's climb out of poverty and how series of shocks and stresses throw them right back into poverty. Finally, it highlights how this multidimensionality of deprivation painfully limits poor people's freedom to choose and act. It constrains their choices. Their powerlessness forces them to select between two agonizing choices, two losing propositions—such as whether to have food or send children to school—further limiting their own and their children's chances of success in the struggle for a better life.[1]

Part I. Lack of Capabilities

If they [children] can't eat, how can they learn?
—A woman, Kebele 11, Ethiopia

Poor people are disadvantaged by lack of information, education, skills and confidence. Many factors contribute to limited personal capability, including physical isolation, being cut off from the powerful and wealthy, lack of access to media and limited schooling. All these contribute to limited confidence, and together they reinforce powerlessness and voicelessness and marginalization in society.

Lack of Information

We do not know anything.
—A middle-aged man on rights and the law,
Razgrad, Bulgaria

Opportunity is a contact.
—Discussion group participant, Vila Junqueira, Brazil

Poor people are acutely aware of their lack of information and lack of contacts to access information. Across countries, poor men and women discuss how these put them at a disadvantage in their dealings with public agencies, NGOs, employers, traders and lenders, and contribute to their feelings of powerlessness. Prejudice and discrimination add to physical isolation and combine to further isolate people from information and new economic opportunities.

Not knowing about services, rights and meetings or about how to gain access to them is another deprivation of the poor. The many impacts of the lack of information on poor people's lives can be seen from exploring their experiences in one country, Vietnam. In two districts in the Tra Vinh region of Vietnam physically isolated people cite lack of information and poor access as their biggest constraints. In one area isolated and remote households report that they do not hear of impending credit program services, and those who benefit most tend to be family and friends within the leaders' social networks. In other remote areas, poor families say that lack of information about when government workers will be near the area means that they miss accessing much-needed services. In one commune, poor people say they miss free vaccinations for their children because they miss the health worker's visit.

Lack of information about planned government actions often leaves people angry, further deprived or confused. In a village in the district of Duyen Hai farmers said that they had not been consulted before irrigation canals for shrimp farmers were constructed across the village farmland. This led to waterlogging and made much of the land useless. Researchers write, "Farmers claimed that they were not forewarned; rather they were invited to attend a meeting and informed that the decision had already been made. Since land-use certificates have not been issued in this village, no compensation will be paid for lost land, as local farmers have no legal claim to it." In another village, women indicate that they feel vulnerable because of lack of information, not knowing about government decisions and having no say in community issues. Mrs. C., whose family lost 4 *cong* of land, said, "What can I say? I did not complain about losing the land because they are the government and I am a citizen and we don't dare stir things up or challenge anyone."

Isolated people also often find out about meetings after they have happened. A woman from another community says, "I have lived here for 10 years and never been called to a meeting of any kind." In Ha Tinh, Vietnam a participant says, "I live quite far from other people.... By the time I hear about things, the opportunity has passed." Not knowing and being out of touch also affect poor people in cities and towns. The researchers in Ho Chi Minh City, Vietnam found in the three urban districts they visited that the poorer people are, the less they know about the welfare services in their area.

Poor people in Bulgaria report similar experiences. Participants in Plovdiv complain of lack of information about humanitarian aid from the Red Cross: "Who has the right to get this aid? Well, those who happen to be in the hospital the same day, for example, for taking medical tests, are more eligible." Discussion group participants in Razgrad state that the mayor controls the social assistance rolls and the police. They feel that municipal services could improve if they had more control over the mayor and had somebody to explain to the people what the law is, what they are they entitled to, and to whom they could make complaints against the mayor.

In Isla Trinitaria, Ecuador there is a lack of awareness of various public institutions and NGOs that work in the area. People say lack of publicity about the activities of organizations prevents them from reaching the majority of people in the settlement. A discussion group states that they feel uninformed, "we are trying to see how we are fooled." Their overall despair with lack of information about government action that affects their lives, and over which they have little control, can be summarized by a discussion about the president of a district committee: "We don't know anything about him"; "we know that once he brought medicines"; "we don't know anything"; "he works on water affairs." A leading issue of concern to them was the possibility of eviction, of being removed from an embankment even though "the people are not informed about what is going to happen." Other groups used stronger language to express their vulnerability and growing despair fueled by lack of information about proposed government action. According to one participant, "I feel insecure, I am in the hands of the mayor...what can we do, to whom should we turn?... I would like to have a machine gun to kill them, the first one who gets into my house...working for the right [to a house] and losing everything is very sad. Leave it to God. He will be coming very soon...."

Telephones, Media and Information Technology

The well-off have telephones, car...computers, access to services, live on the labor of others and have leisure.
—A poor woman, Morro da Conceição, Brazil

Poor people's isolation from information is compounded by lack of access to communication and information technology, including telephones, Internet, radio, printed material and television. The degree of isolation varies across regions.

More in some parts of the world than in others, poor people talk about the importance of telephones to increase their connectivity to information, such as the market prices for their goods and other knowledge about the outside world. In Millbank, Jamaica the need for telephones was mentioned by several discussion groups. The researchers write:

The community feels very strongly that the market exists for their enterprise and the road and telephone would lead to the creation of an economically viable industry. However, they ranked telephones as more important as they believe these will provide income earning opportunities and a faster response time to health or other emergencies that may arise in the community.... The lack of telephones was a recurring theme, possibly derived from a sensed of alienation through the remote location. Aside from the telephone, the young men and women have a craving for information technology, and are well aware of the Internet, seeing enterprise opportunities for marketing their products in the area.

In other discussion groups in Millbank, women equate the telephone to the local bridge across the river. In one group, a woman declares "this is the year 2000, the age of technology; it is full time that we get a telephone." In Little Bay, Jamaica lack of telephones and post offices is a problem identified by all discussion groups. Discussion groups say that while poor road conditions lead to their isolation, the lack of telephones make their problems even more acute. This is seen as contributing to the high unemployment among women as they are unable to respond to job advertisements in newspapers. In Bower Bank, Jamaica a young woman again highlights the need for telephones, and suggests that calling people anti-technology is a way of teasing them as backward. A few older men in this community had cellular telephones and were seen using them in public.

In the Kyrgyz Republic as well, telephones receive frequent mention as a way of solving problems, accessing timely emergency health assistance and information about prices. In Turusbek, people say they are ill informed because of bad roads and no telephones or newspapers. In Bedsa, Egypt women await the installation of a new telephone facility to put an end to their isolation. In Binh, Somaliland poor people say that in the absence of telephones, messages are still carried over long distances by runners. In Mtamba, Malawi poor people report great difficulties with placing a telephone call to the hospital to request an ambulance when someone is very sick.

Newspapers are valued as sources of information even where literacy is low. A program in Lao Cai, Vietnam to distribute radios to remote H'mong households is much appreciated.

The power of computers and computer-related skills to generate new employment opportunities, as well as increasing access to information, is mentioned by some parents, but primarily by young people in Eastern Europe. In Uchkum, Kyrgyz Republic parents complain that teachers are not teaching their children modern computer skills because there are no computers in schools. In Tiekovo, Russia while the employment bureau is rated low for not having paid employment benefits for three years, young girls speak favorably of their launching new computer training courses.

Lack of Education

> In Nigeria, if you are not educated, you cannot get a job,
> and no job determines position in the society. Our parents
> did not go to school, and so we are poor today. Education
> can change this.
> —Participant, a group of youths, Dawaki, Nigeria

> I dreamt that I was sending them to university, that they may
> be somebody but I am afraid that secondary school is as far
> as they can go.
> —A mother, Bratunac, Bosnia and Herzegovina

> They sentenced me to death when they did that.
> —A woman from El Gawaber, Egypt speaking of being
> forced by her parents to withdraw from school

Poor people make distinctions between literacy and education. For reading and using documents, for checking prices, and for avoiding exploitation, they see basic literacy as a key ability. Lack of literacy and numeracy makes poor people vulnerable, and minority groups seem especially exposed. Participants from indigenous communities in Ecuador mention that their illiteracy makes them "an easy target for fraud by businesses." In the words of an indigenous woman from Asociación 10 de Agosto in Ecuador:

Because we had no schooling we are almost illiterate.
Sometimes we cannot even speak Spanish; we can't add. Store
owners cheat us, because the Indians don't know how to count
or anything else. They buy at the prices they want and pay less.
They cheat us because we are not educated.

Many poor people emphasize the importance of literacy for accessing jobs. A 51-year-old man from Tabe Ere, Ghana tells the researchers that he is blind, meaning that he is illiterate, and this is why he and so many others in his village can never get a job in the nearby town. In Bangladesh and India high levels of illiteracy are widely viewed to be key reasons for underemployment. A participant in a women's discussion group in Little Bay, Jamaica says, "If we could read we could go to Negril to get good work."

Poor people in community after community indicate that they value education highly as a key to a better future for themselves and especially for their children. In Ha Tinh and elsewhere in Vietnam, men, women and children are all very concerned about education and see it very clearly as one of the few means to break the cycle of poverty "because it is very hard to live on agricultural production." Nevertheless, the poor identify many barriers to education. The high costs of school even when school is "free" is perhaps the most pressing obstacle that poor people raise when discussing education, but problems of distance, the need for children's labor, and the quality and relevance of the schooling also figure in many discussions.

The Strain of Costly and Distant Schools

Even though my two daughters are of age to go to school, they
don't go because I have no money to send them. The big one is
six and should go to primary school but I can't find the money
to buy a uniform, shoes or bag. My other daughter used to at-
tend Millbank Basic School but had to stop because I can't af-
ford the $500 for school fees. My son will be ready for school
in September but I can't see how I'll be able to send all three of
them to school.... I want to learn to read and write, get good
work so that I can send my children to a good school, so that
they will not have to farm but will be able to get good work.
—A poor woman, Millbank, Jamaica

There are wrenching testimonies from all regions in the study of poor families that struggle with difficult decisions of whether to invest in their children's education. For the poorest families, sending a child to school can imply very serious costs related both to income lost and to school fees, clothes, supplies and other expenses like payments to teachers, building and furniture funds and so on. Where parents do manage to send and keep their children in school, they often make tremendous sacrifices. A poor man in

Duckensfield, Jamaica with seven children explains, "I use most of my pay to school the children so that makes it impossible for me to build a good house."

In Ho Chi Minh City in Vietnam one poor women explains that "her son just plays all day instead of going to school" because she is unable to raise the fees that must be paid at the beginning of the school year. In some study sites in Vietnam teachers reportedly humiliate children in front of the class by discussing how their parents have not yet paid their fees. Children prefer to withdraw from school rather than face this humiliation.

Reports from Zambia and Nigeria also are full of stories about profound difficulties with covering school fees and being forced to withdraw children from school. An elderly woman from the village of Tash Bulak, Kyrgyzstan shares her stark choice of only being able to educate her sons:

> When our children were small, it was easier to take care of them. Now they need to go to school, which means they need clothes, and shoes, and school supplies. We don't have enough money, so only two of our children, two sons, attend school, and our daughters stay at home, because they have no shoes and the school is located very far from here, 6 kilometers. The boys walk this distance. Occasionally some driver would pity them and give them a free ride.

In some regions the hardship of covering fees is a relatively new phenomenon. In Indonesia study participants report that only recently have they been unable to afford the fees due to the economic crisis. In Pegambiran, some discussion group participants expressed concerns that many families who needed special assistance with school fees were not covered under the existing safety net programs. In the former Soviet Union, the cost of schooling is a leading concern because in the past education was free. As a man from Dimitrovgrad, Bulgaria shares,

> I have to pay a fee of 23,000 leva for the kids. Where on earth am I supposed to find this money? I simply don't have it! So I tell them that I can't afford it. "Then take your kids home!" So who's to look after them at home.... Now tell me how am I supposed to find this money? ... How could I raise this money...pay day-care fees, go and pick the kids up from the day care—how? This means I'm forced to start stealing—I'm a 50-year-old man.

Researchers from Kyrgyz indicate that education has become an "acute" problem due to the "constant need of parents to contribute their money for needs of the school" and for books in both rural and urban areas. Similarly, in Egypt fees for education are new, and many express difficulties with payment.

In addition to educational costs, small group discussions about schools frequently raise concerns with the long distances that children must travel to reach school. In some villages this seems to pose a more formidable barrier than the problem of costs. In rural Ghana both men and women stress the lack of educational facilities as an issue. In Bangladesh all the study areas identify the lack of school facilities as an important problem and view the traveling required to attend distant schools as a key constraint for not sending children to school. In Gowainghat, adolescent girls often do not go to secondary school because young boys tease them in the road.

In Bosnia, where schooling was interrupted by the war, access to education is a serious concern in discussion groups of youth and women of all ages. In Somaliland people note a simple lack of educational facilities due to the war. In some war-affected areas of Sri Lanka it is reported that the poor do not send children to schools in outside villages due to security concerns, despite the poor quality of local schools.

By contrast, satisfaction with improved access to school is mentioned in a discussion group from the Chemusa, Malawi: "In the past schools were very far, about 5 km away. These days our children are just walking 2 km to Mbayani for their school." The communities visited in Malawi consistently mention education as a relatively low priority, although often still among the top 10. This may reflect the satisfaction with the government's policy of free primary schooling in addition to opening new schools and the urgency of other needs.

Children's Labor Needed

> *At times of disaster...children are taken out of school and are sent to towns to be employed as servants and requested to send money to their parents in the farmlands.*
> —Poor young men in Dibdibe Wajtu, Ethiopia

As a teacher from Nuevas Brisas del Mar in Esmeraldas, Ecuador explains, parents find it difficult to keep their children in school because they are often needed in more immediately productive activities: "Children have gone... Many have to shine shoes for a living.... We started out with 30 students and finished with 20. There is a desertion of five to ten students per level." In Freeman's Hall, Jamaica, it is common practice for parents to keep children away from school on Fridays to reap crops for the main market on Saturday.

In Dimitrovgrad, Bulgaria some children "dig for scrap instead of going to school," meaning that they steal wires and any other metal that is available. In Ethiopia researchers write that in rural areas children between the ages of 6 and 12 are more likely to tend cattle than attend primary schools. When they attend, they are taken out at times of crisis to help the family.

Problems of Quality and Relevance

> *This school was ok, but now it is in shambles, there are no teachers for weeks. It lacks competent principals and teachers. There is no safety and no hygiene.*
> —Discussion group, Vila Junqueira, Brazil

In many communities, problems of educational quality and relevance come to the fore. In India people mention teachers who only come to school two days a week. Discussion groups in the *favela* of Vila Junqueira, Brazil express frustration with both the staff and security. Participants in Samalankulam, Sri Lanka speak of shortages of both teachers and classrooms. The researchers who visited Cañar, Ecuador report that discussion groups felt that "high school graduates are not well prepared ... they don't teach well."

Problems of abuse and corruption also touch schools. In villages in Egypt, participants report that parents may be forced to pay special tutoring fees lest their child "is made to fail." In the Kyrgyz Republic, discussion group participants say a university diploma used to be more prestigious "because now people can buy diplomas."

Some poor people also raise deep concerns about the relevance of schools to employment prospects. Many express bitterness that education does not necessarily bring a better future. As an older women from Duckensfield, Jamaica explains,

> *My husband and I make all the sacrifice to send our children to school out of our very small wages and because of that we couldn't build a proper home up until now...how my husband and I spend all of our little earnings on education for the children and two of my children can not get work to support us and we are old people now.*

Similarly in Egypt, Ethiopia and Ghana people voice frustration because even with education finding jobs is extremely difficult. In Egypt, even technical schools are criticized for being overly theoretical and not opening up the job market. In Samalankulam, Sri Lanka the researchers note that youths who complete their education "are forced to take up agriculture as they cannot find employment to suit their educational background."

Among study participants who managed to escape poverty, education is indeed mentioned but with strong regional differences. A 57-year-old shopkeeper from Nova Califórnia, Brazil credits hard work and education for helping him overcome the "precarious nature" of life: "I always worked a lot and have my degree. Today I have my business here, and it is enough to live quietly."

Lack of Skills

A bad life is when you cannot find employment and have no money and no useful knowledge.
—A poor man, Kebele 30, Ethiopia

I live in the hope that things will be better for the children, that they will complete school, learn some trade.
—A poor woman, Sarajevo, Bosnia and Herzegovina

Poor people don't know how to manage a business, and so they can't improve their situation.
—Discussion Group of elderly men, Ho Chi Minh City, Vietnam

Although I live with my mother, right now I am on my own. I have been kept back from society. There is no training center in this community nor employment for me as an unskilled young man.
—Poor youth, Little Bay, Jamaica

In many parts of the world poor people speak about the importance of learning practical skills to enable them to make a livelihood. Participants in Las Pascuas, Bolivia link unemployment to lack of schooling and training: "If they are trained, they have greater knowledge, and they are able to get work doing whatever." The importance of skills acquisition also emerges strongly from life stories of people who have escaped poverty. Informal apprenticeships with relatives and learning by observation are cited for agricultural and livestock jobs as well as for crafts, small manufacturing and trading. Two different life stories follow:

Ali Karibo of Adaboya, Ghana was the first son of eight children. His father was a poor farmer who had no cattle but a few sheep and goats. The piece of land he had bought was very rocky so he did not do much farming. Ali had no formal education but according to him, his father taught him how to farm on rocky land. " My father fitted a hoe and gave it to me." His father died when Ali had not reached a marriageable age and the mother was too weak and poor. At that early age of 14 years he saw that he had no help but God. He said he worked hard on the rocky soil to remove the rocks. This has brought him fame and peace of mind. Those who know him use him as an example to encourage their children.

As a farmer, Ibu T of Kawangu, Indonesia does not own any rice fields. She owns an unirrigated field to plant tomatoes,

*cowpeas and mung beans. Eighty percent of the yield is sold in
the market. She said, "I used to be poor but things have
changed. My life is better off because I worked hard such as
planting vegetables and weaving cloth to be sold."*

Young people in particular are aware of their lack of skills as limiting
their income-earning opportunities. But it is rarely only lack of skills that is
limiting. A poor 20-year-old young man in Jamaica said, "I would like to see
some major improvements towards youth in the community skills training
and a market for produce...I would like skill in woodwork, furniture building, art or carving." When asked why he wasn't doing carving or woodwork
right now, he responded: "do I have tools and money to start? But if we as
youth have skills training, that would help and some financial help as well so
I could help myself to better my life."

Sometimes however, even those with skills report difficulty in finding
jobs. Men in Cassava Piece, Jamaica observe that there are few opportunities
even for those with masonry, carpentry, and tiling skills.

Low Self-Confidence and Self-Worth

*When I had nothing, everybody neglected me. The boss scolded
me for any kind of silly mistakes. However, now I am not
working as a day laborer and so everybody respects me.*
—A poor man, Khaliajuri, Bangladesh

A human being without roots doesn't have meaning.
—Community leader, Bode, Recife, Brazil

*Poverty demoralizes us, I feel humiliated. Therefore, I never
leave the village.*
—A sick woman, Tash Bulak, Kyrgyz Republic

Lack of confidence is frequently mentioned as a result of poverty. Sometimes
this poverty is the result of loss of confidence, especially from having been
unemployed for some time. In Bosnia the inability to find a job makes people feel worthless to themselves and their families. Low self-confidence can
lead to self-isolation. Young men in Bower Bank, Jamaica rank absence of
self-confidence as the second biggest impact of poverty:

*Poverty makes us not believe in ourselves. We hardly leave the
community. Not only are we not educated, but we also don't
have a street-wise education. Some people don't know how to
behave when they go beyond their community because they are
so frustrated, locked up in the house all day. They don't have
an understanding and therefore can't relate. Some would say
that ghetto people don't know how to behave.*

Poverty, illness, disease, loss of livelihood sources and discrimination all combine to deplete poor people's confidence to continue with the struggle. A 27-year-old girl from a village in Ethiopia in which many people were lepers says: " Yes, most of us who reside in this village are lepers. Even though at present I am not suffering from leprosy. My mother was a leper. So everyone knows that I am the daughter of a leper's family. Even though the community has not excluded me officially, there is no attempt to accept me as being part of this society. And I also feel so." A blind man in Doryumu, Ghana said, " no one recognizes me. I have a big name only when I move in the streets with children following me. That is all the recognition I have, with the children. No one has even invited me to any meeting."

Lack of hope and being unable to see a way out does for some result in madness and suicide. Giving up and being overwhelmed is described as "dying on your feet" by a man in Kebele 30, Ethiopia; " being on the edge of madness, going crazy" by a woman in Krasna Poliana , Bulgaria; " people do not smile, they look sad" by a woman in Tash Bulak, Kyrgyz Republic; "not seeing the light of happiness" according to an older man in Khaliajuri, Bangladesh; and finally "hanging oneself" by a poor man in Jalal Abad, Kyrgyz Republic.

A community leader named Pedro in Bode, Brazil started community cultural work to counter the sense of alienation and sense of worthlessness among youth. His understanding of the social and psychological consequences of poverty started with his own life experience and observing as a young child his single mother who had to constantly "fight a lot and had to sacrifice herself as a washerwoman." For Pedro, the only way to improve the quality of life in the community is through classes in arts and vocational courses.

Part II. Keeping Poor People Powerless: The Many-Stranded Web

No one cares about us. We have no rights whatsoever.
—Men's discussion group, Krasna Poliana, Bulgaria

Poor people are held down not by one deprivation but by multiple deprivations. This section first presents the many-stranded web of powerlessness based on analyses of poor people's experiences. It then provides one illustration of poor people's descriptions of multiple linkages and is followed by data on shocks and sequences of events that lead to the downward slide into poverty. The final section highlights the agony of choosing between two losing propositions.

The Many-Stranded Web

The dimensions of deprivation are multiple. Their connections are also interwoven. Not every deprivation applies all the time. The combination of deprivations is specific to people, households, social groups, communities, regions, countries, climates and seasons. What poor people have in common is how often and how strongly the dimensions combine to keep them powerless and poor.

Poor people's experiences seem to converge primarily around 10 dimensions that add up to lack of freedom of choice and action, to powerlessness. These have been highlighted throughout this book and are summarized in figure 11.1. The dimensions of powerlessness and illbeing that emerge from the analysis are described below.

Precarious Livelihoods with Few Assets. Precariousness is compounded by limited ownership and access to assets—physical, financial, human, environmental and social. Hunger is not uncommon. Poor people survive through a patchwork of low-paying, temporary, seasonal, often backbreaking and sometimes illegal activities (chapter 3).

Isolated, Risky and Unserviced Places of the Poor. Not only do poor people live in areas that are geographically isolated—remote rural sites or urban slums lacking transportation—but they also live in areas that are poorly serviced by basic infrastructure and that can be physically dangerous, unhealthy and unsanitary, or prone to natural disasters. Vulnerability is exacerbated by stigma, as poor people often find it hard to find jobs when their address is known (chapter 4).

Hungry, Exhausted and Sick Bodies. The poorer people are, the more likely their livelihoods depend on physically demanding work—often involving long hours, dangerous conditions and meager returns. Those who are hungry and weak and who look bad are often paid less and less reliably. Poor people also report difficulties accessing medical care due to high costs, corruption in fees and preferential treatment for those with influence and money. They frequently mention being asked to wait a long time and being treated with rudeness and indifference by medical staff (chapter 5).

Unequal Gender Relations. Exclusion of women from social, political and economic life limits their choices and increases their vulnerability when they are on their own. Violation of deeply entrenched roles of men as "breadwinners" and women as "caretakers" has created turmoil and domestic violence against women. Domestic violence against women remains widespread (chapter 6).

Isolating Social Relations. Social isolation includes the experience of being left out, looked down upon, pushed aside and ignored by those more powerful at all levels, with an impact on poor people's access to resources and opportunities. Poor people often face discrimination based on ethnicity, gender, caste, material poverty, age and the community where they live (chapter 7).

Figure 11.1 Dimensions of Powerlessness and Illbeing

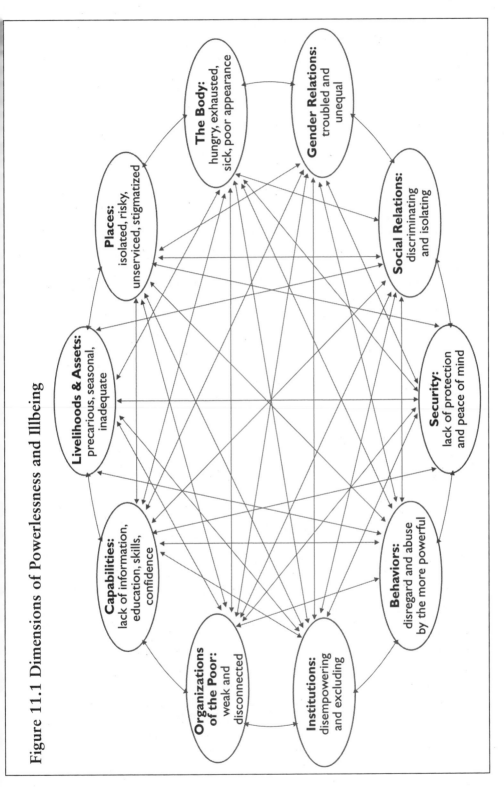

Insecurity and Lack of Peace of Mind. Poor people feel that they are more insecure and vulnerable today than 10 years ago. They lack connections, the ability to bargain for fair treatment or fair wages, access to capital, and protection by police and under the law. Breakdown of traditional social support systems with increased economic hardship adds to this stress. For women, widowhood invariably brings on destitution and social and physical vulnerability (chapter 8).

Abusive Behavior of Those More Powerful. Poor people often experience those who have more power over them as abusive, rude and uncaring. These include people upon whom they depend for livelihoods and services. Being forced to submit to such behavior compounds their lack of self worth and sense of powerlessness (chapter 9).

Disempowering and Excluding Institutions. From the perspective of the poor, there is a crisis in governance. Poor people's contact with a range of state, private sector and civil society institutions is experienced as disempowering and excluding. Poor people recount countless incidents of humiliation, corruption, lying and cheating. Not surprisingly, poor people lack confidence in these institutions. As a consequence, many primarily depend on their own informal networks (chapter 10).

Weak and Disconnected Organizations of the Poor. Poor women and men participate in a range of informal and formal local networks and organizations, although by and large these groups are limited in number, resources and leverage. These groups and networks rarely connect with other similar groups or with resources of the state or other agencies. Isolated and disconnected, poor people's organizations have difficulties shifting their bargaining power with institutions of the state, market and civil society (chapter 10).

Poor in Capabilities. Poor people are often isolated from information about jobs, economic opportunities, credit, as well as information on how to gain access to government services and their own rights as citizens. They also struggle with schools that are costly, distant and of mixed quality. Combined with poor education, lack of skills and lack of connections, poor people often lack self confidence. This compounds their helplessness when faced with hunger or exploitation (chapter 11).

Poor People's Descriptions of Linkages

The multiplicity and interlinkages of the causes and effects of poverty are graphically illustrated in the visual analyses carried out by poor people. Again and again participants show their awareness of a whole range of causes and effects. Figure 11.2 is an analysis of the causes and effects of poverty by a group of women in Dobile Yirkpong, Ghana. It illustrates themes such as poverty of time and energy ("sleeplessness" and "always busy and no time to rest"), inability to pay school fees leading to a high dropout rate from school and illiteracy, and "inability to unearth potentials." As else-

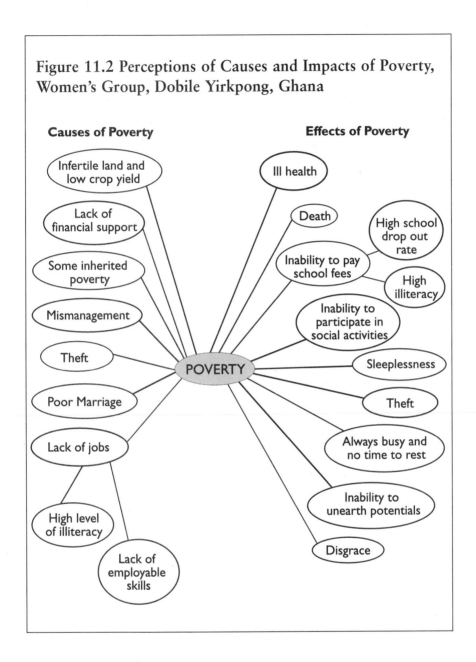

Figure 11.2 Perceptions of Causes and Impacts of Poverty, Women's Group, Dobile Yirkpong, Ghana

Causes of Poverty

- Infertile land and low crop yield
- Lack of financial support
- Some inherited poverty
- Mismanagement
- Theft
- Poor Marriage
- Lack of jobs
- High level of illiteracy
- Lack of employable skills

POVERTY

Effects of Poverty

- Ill health
- Death
- High school drop out rate
- Inability to pay school fees
- High illiteracy
- Inability to participate in social activities
- Sleeplessness
- Theft
- Always busy and no time to rest
- Inability to unearth potentials
- Disgrace

where with other factors like ill health, the analysis indicates a circularity of causation, in this case with theft, which appears on both sides.

To a striking degree many of the strands of the web of powerlessness can be seen to have multiple links and circles of causality. A discussion group of women in Freeman's Hall, Jamaica shows this circularity of causality and with education.

Poorness causes education, particularly of children of sec-
ondary school age, to be cut short. Leaving school early at
maybe 14 or 15 years old means you can't manage a job and
contributes to some early parenthood. It was considered that
early parenthood led to more babies because of the resultant
lack of a job. So the cycle continues with children having chil-
dren and remaining poor so that they in turn cannot afford to
send their kids to school.

Similarly a group of women in Los Juríes, Argentina described the circularity of deprivation:

There is a lack of food and there is malnutrition because
parents can't buy the food necessary to live...many kids
don't even get the minimum. Being poor, they don't get the
vitamins and because of this kids get ill.... Poverty brings
illness from malnutrition or because they get wet out in the
fields.... There is so much hunger and a child can't go to
school; has no shoes; doesn't have equipment; and being
poorly fed, doesn't learn well.

Shocks, Stresses and Sequences

When you sow you hope to harvest at least the minimum,
but unfortunately my efforts were in vain. I had to feed
children and so I sold some cattle to buy wheat and clothes.
There are six of us in the family. One sack of flour will last
us for 20 days. So, we had to sell one sheep every month to
buy flour, and in the end we had no sheep left. One can patch
torn clothes, but how can one patch an empty stomach?
—A farmer, Tash Bulak, Kyrgyz Republic

Powerlessness and vulnerability compound each other. How shocks and stresses can knock and press poor people or households down is captured in individuals' life stories. In each community research teams conducted one open-ended interview with a woman and another with a man who had always been poor or who had fallen into poverty. These case studies bring to life how shocks and stresses, often combined and in sequence, keep poor people poor and make them worse off, reducing even what limited control and choices they have.

A content analysis of shocks that triggered and stresses that contributed to their downward slides was conducted for 125 of these case studies. Figure 11.3 shows the triggers or shocks and stresses that precipitated an individual's drop in wellbeing.[2] The focus is on negative change, such as loss of land or a job or a decline in wages, rather than on more static conditions of

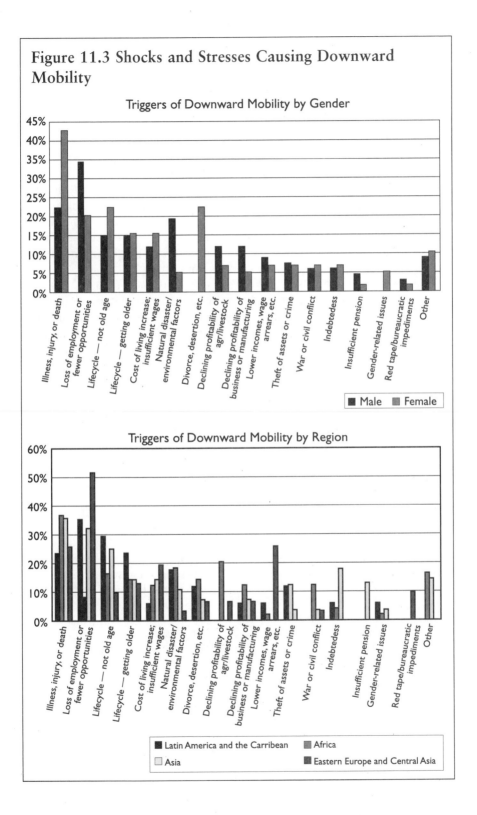

Figure 11.3 Shocks and Stresses Causing Downward Mobility

Triggers of Downward Mobility by Gender

Male   Female

Triggers of Downward Mobility by Region

Latin America and the Carribean   Africa
Asia   Eastern Europe and Central Asia

poverty, such as "lack of land," "unemployed" or "low wages." It is precisely because these women and men had so little that they were so vulnerable when misfortune occurred.

In these 125 case studies, sickness or injury of a family member was the most frequent trigger for a downward slide. There are gender differences, however. This is primarily due to social practices that can lead to loss of social status, property and children as soon as a woman is widowed. Divorce and desertion are cited by almost 25 percent of the women as a cause of destitution, but are not cited by any men.

The second most frequent trigger or stress causing downward mobility was loss of employment or a decline in temporary and seasonal wages. This was reported more by men than women. In Eastern Europe and Central Asia people attribute rising unemployment to the closure of factories and businesses, layoffs, and the dismantling of collectives, with wage arrears, lack of pay, falling wages, or being paid inkind also important.

Life-cycle changes unrelated to old age refer to the added burdens of raising young children, the direct and indirect expenses of sending children to school, and the often very high toll of dowries and wedding ceremonies. Women in the case studies spoke somewhat more often than men about these impacts. Both sexes said old age and related problems of increasing physical weakness and vulnerability to illness figure prominently as causes of deepening poverty. Men mentioned natural disasters and deteriorating environmental conditions more frequently than did women. In Tash Bulak, a man from Kyrgyz Republic describes how three years of drought wiped out his savings, including his cattle, sheep and his peace.

Box 11.1 Sinking in the Trap: An Old Man in Khaliajuri, Bangladesh

He is 60 years old. He has four daughters. His economic status is declining year after year. Eight years ago he worked as a sharecropper. He had physical capacity and so could get loans from moneylenders. But as his physical strength declined, he could no longer get loans. He sold all his movable assets to give his daughter in marriage. Now he works as a day laborer in the fields or on a fishing boat. However, because of his physical condition, people are less willing to give him work. On average he earns Tk 20 to Tk 25 per day, less in the rainy season. If he fails to get work even for a single day, he has to collect food by begging. Due to unavailability of work, each member of his family had only one square meal throughout the preceding week. On the day when he gave the interview, he earned only Tk 12 working as a day laborer on a fishing boat. He bought 1 kilogram of wheat for Tk 11. It was to be the only food for the six-member family for that night. They had been without food for the rest of the day.

Impoverishment often occurred in these 125 cases through sequential and combined misfortunes and stresses. One mishap could make a person more stressed and less able to cope, and so more vulnerable to further shocks. The case study in box 11.1 from Bangladesh of a 60-year old man shows how sometimes a set of conditions or an incident brings several of the dimensions and connections into play.

Agonizing Choices

To have my friends and son not following in my footsteps—to hell with everything else....I'd risk anything.
                                        —A young urban criminal from Bulgaria

Powerless as they are in many respects, poor people face options that are often exceptionally constrained. In making choices, the best they can do may be to look for the least negative, the least damaging. They have little cushion against mistakes. They have to choose with care, for example, among different sources of cash or credit for daily needs or for an emergency. They are forced, again and again, to trade off one bad thing against another. The examples that follow illustrate both strategic choices and commonplace daily decisions.

These agonizing decisions take their toll. People cope by focusing on one day at a time, becoming indifferent, apathetic or hovering near losing their mind. Michael Akoese, a 46-year-old man living in Adaboya Ghana, confides to the researchers that he sold most of his property and assets, including his beloved motorcycle, to take care of his family's needs. Unable to cope, he said he became mentally disturbed because he had too many things to think about at the same time. He remained indoors for many days before taking the decision to accept his fate and live on.

Violent Abuse or Public Humiliation?

In the Kyrgyz Republic women who suffer from domestic abuse are said to believe it is better to be beaten by their husbands than to raise children alone and that humiliation, which cannot be seen by other people is better than the status of a single woman. One woman says, "Very few women go to the health-care center if they get beaten by their husbands. If there is an apparent trace of beating on a woman's face, she would rather invent some story than admit she was abused."

Go Hungry or Miss School?

A widespread and agonizing tradeoff, sometimes faced by poor families daily, is between education and food. This may be especially acute where it is socially normal for children to go to school. In Viyalagoda, Sri Lanka many poor families restrict their expenditures on food to meet the education and clothing expenses of their children; as one housewife comments: "Even without filling our stomachs, we spend for the schooling of our two children. Nobody sees what we eat." The community report from Bedsa, Egypt notes that the poor struggle constantly to find their daily bread and to secure opportunities for their children through education: "We deprive ourselves from food, and we tear from our flesh so that we can find money to pay for the children's education." Even when poor children attend school, they may learn little if there is hunger in the household. A mother in Ha Tinh, Vietnam says: "My children are so hungry they cannot learn in school."

Many others are below the threshold where sacrifices can secure schooling. A 62-year-old man in Ethiopia who works as an office guard is very bitter about his inability to feed his family. With all the expenses entailed, he says he cannot even think about sending his children to school.

Suffer Sickness or Go Without?

A repeated dilemma is to suffer from illness or starve. The tradeoff is between, on the one hand, pain, disability, and perhaps death, and, on the other hand, loss of productive assets to pay for treatment, leading later to less food and income, stinting, and even starvation (see box 11.2). The choice is stark—to feed some family members or buy medicine to treat

---

Box 11.2 Pigs and Pain

A woman in Lao Cai, Vietnam is the only laborer supporting herself and seven other family members: her 70-year-old mother-in-law, her sick husband, and five children, aged 10, 8, 6, 4 and 1. Their precarious livelihood is breeding and selling pigs. They have one breeding sow and two piglets. Her husband looks young, but frail. He walks very slowly and is hunched over, although his present condition is an improvement from the days when he could not walk at all. Not taking the fluctuating symptoms seriously at first, the family used traditional medicine to try to cure his ailment for one year. The pain continued to increase, and he finally went to the village health station. They bought some medicine, but this failed to work. They were advised to go to the district hospital but stated that they didn't have enough money. When asked why the family didn't sell their piglets to raise cash for treatment, the husband responded that the piglets were necessary for them to manage their food security. Eventually he could not move his shoulders and legs, but with continued use of traditional medicine, he has been able to walk again for about one year. His back still hurts now, and he is only able to do minor work inside the house, such as sweeping the floor.

The husband's suffering and disability are part of a livelihood strategy. His pain saves the pigs.

those who are sick. A pensioner in Sekovici, Bosnia describes his dilemma. His pension has dropped from DM 250 to DM 45. He is unable to produce enough from working the land to have any produce left over to sell as he and his wife are elderly and physically frail. What little extra is produced they "push" their children to accept. He said: "Today I received half a pension and I am wondering what to buy first—medication for the old woman, which is 18 DM, or a bag of flour, which is 14 DM—but I cannot buy both."

Poverty or Danger of Death?

Those who join armed forces where there is active fighting risk death. In rural Ethiopia a discussion group of men and women report, "Life in the area is so precarious that the youth and every able person has to migrate to the towns or join the army at the war front in order to escape the hazards of hunger escalating over here."

The team report from Ihalagama village, Anuradhapura, Sri Lanka says,

> Forty-five youths have joined the armed forces. They have passed their GCE Ordinary Level and Advanced Level examinations. Because they have not been able to find suit-able jobs, they have joined the forces. They feel that their jobs will be safe as long as the war prevails. However, there is uncertainty as to how long they will be able to survive. "Every time there is an operation in the north-east, we are scared stiff until we know what the outcome is," some said. The villagers said, "Joining the army means certain death. You are trained and sent to the battlefront. In 45 days, everything is over." Another villager said, "Poor boys join the army. After all, do any from the wealthy class ever join the army?" However, the salaries are good and quite enough to lead a good life. Money the soldiers send home is used for the education of their siblings and to buy food. The job is good as long as you survive.

Conserve Energy or Go to Work?

Many in the former Soviet countries face the choice of staying home and in bed to conserve their energy and thus need less food or going out to do jobs unsure if they will get paid at all at the end of the day. A woman in Sekovici, Bosnia explains, "The pension is low, 39 KM or 200 dinars (17 DM). We get one part in marks and the other part in dinars, and it is not enough to eat normally for a month, let alone cover electricity and water and buy firewood for the winter. One cubic meter of firewood is 15 DM, and I need three or four meters to see me through the winter." She like many others stays home to conserve energy.

Isolation or Shame?

Poverty can pose a choice between isolation and shame. Torn clothing and the appearances of being poor can isolate and exclude. The research team in Khaliajuri, Bangladesh writes, "Due to poverty...they cannot buy clothes for their family members; their wives and daughters cannot go out of their houses because they feel shy. They cannot participate in any festivals. They cannot give their daughters in marriage. At that time a person goes mad and wishes to commit suicide." In Bosnia, unable to afford even small gifts, women isolate themselves at home. "I can't socialize as wherever I go I need to take at least 100 grams of coffee and I cannot afford it. March 8 [International Women's Day] passed and I did not knock on the door of a single woman, nor did anyone visit me."

Child Neglect or Penury?

Women face acute tradeoffs between income and child care:

> In Indonesia, [a young woman's] husband...left and
> went abroad. She looked after their boy and girl.... She...
> wanted to dedicate her attention to them. She used to
> work, once, weighing junk. Her children were neglected
> and looked malnourished. She quit her job. That was her
> dilemma: if she did not work she would not have enough
> money; if she did, her children would not get due atten-
> tion. After quitting her job, she frequently had a problem
> meeting her daily needs. Often she had to walk to the pawn-
> shop to borrow money, depositing her still good clothes
> as security.... Because she often pawned her clothes and
> other belongings, and was unable to buy them back, she
> had only a few clothes left. She only went to the money-
> lender when she was really forced to because of the
> exorbitant interest rate of 20 percent a month.

In Ak Kiyi, Kyrgyz Republic:

> The baby was wrapped in Gulaim's scarf and kept crying.
> Gulaim, the baby's mother, suffered from depression.
> When we entered the room, the baby was on the floor
> next to an electric heater that had in all likelihood been
> made by Gulaim's husband. One would receive an electric
> shock if the device was touched carelessly. When asked
> whether she was not afraid that her children would touch
> the heater and get an electric shock, Gulaim said indifferently,
> "Well, we can't heat the house otherwise. I tell the children
> not to touch it. Yesterday my relative, a school teacher who

lives in the school dormitory, left her children locked up at home and left for work, and when she came back, she found her boy...."

Migration: The Woes of Home or the End of the Family?

Children cry when they cannot get their meals in time. The wife quarrels with her husband when he fails to bring in the necessary money and grain for the family. The young ones migrate to the cities. This way many families have dispersed and marriages have been broken.

> —An elderly woman in Mitti Kolo Peasant
> Association, Ethiopia

Migration has positive aspects. But in both India and Sri Lanka poor people say it is better to be at home and poor than rich but with the family separated. A case study in Geruwa, Bihar, India records that despite her misery, a poor woman has neither allowed her husband to go out of the village in search of work, nor ever migrated herself: "The woes of home are far better than the comforts of an alien land," she says. In Banaran village in Indonesia a poor woman wants to work abroad but does not have the heart to leave her children, apart from not having the money to go. The decision, though, often goes the other way. A woman in Wewala, Sri Lanka says, "Yes, we go, but it is the end of the family."

Be Cheated or Starve?

Poor people know when they are being cheated or offered unfair prices for their produce. Having little surplus or access to credit and faced with hungry children, they find themselves selling their produce at low prices or accepting low wages. In Freeman's Hall, Jamaica discussion groups state that the middlemen pay the farmers after they have sold their produce. So in effect the poor farmer subsidizes the middleman. Short of cash, the poor farmer is then unable to plant as much as he would like.

Mina lives in Teikovo, Russia. After being laid off from her factory job she took on a job as a street cleaner in her district. For nearly three years her payments have been irregular and meager. Usually she gets about 100 rubles ($4) per month. She cleans a vast area near a big apartment building. Her boss sometimes fines her for her faults in sweeping or in clearing ice and snow. Mina is often hungry and eats mostly the cheapest pasta, drinks tea from dried raspberry leaves and eats bread and salt when she can get it. She jokes about her old TV set: "it is feeding me every evening. I take a program instead of my supper. Then I go to bed." Her precarious four-dollar-a-month job is the only sliver between her and total starvation.

The Challenge of Powerlessness

*An uneducated man can be dominated just with bread
and water. The educated man does not want this; he wants
citizenship.*

—A poor man in Isla Trinitaria, Ecuador

*I teach others now. I am proud of my job. Work is now my
capital, work adds more value to my life. Before I worked, my
life was empty.*

—An illiterate woman who learned hairdressing,
Foua, Egypt

*I love my job in the soup kitchen...I do not earn anything
but I feel happy, important...I am helping the children here to
have a feeling of union...to know how to share with others in
the future...I believe that you have everything when you help
people. It is very good to give hope, to give happiness...I feel
peace in it. I know what it is to live without having something
to eat, what it is live in deprivation....*

—A volunteer who is a widow and domestic worker,
Borborema, Brazil

Poor people are caught in a web of multiple and interlocking deprivations. Together these combine so that often even when asked to "participate" and express their opinions or report on wrongdoing, they remain
silent. Despite the imbalance in power and being overtaken by shocks and
mishaps, many poor people retain their hope and grit to persist. Many
emerge out of destitution to reach out and help others. What is remarkable
is the resilience that so many show and how they battle against the odds to
gain a better life for themselves and their children. A young widow of
Geruwa, India speaks for herself and many others when she says, "Even in
times of acute crises, I held my nerves and did not give in to circumstances.
My God has always stood with me."

The challenge for outsiders is to build upon poor people's initiatives,
hard work and resilience in the face of seemingly insurmountable problems
of accessing market opportunities, government services and civil society resources. The challenge for policy and practice is to empower the powerless in
their struggles to find a place of dignity and respect in society. It is to enable
poor men and women to enhance their capabilities and claim their rights. It
is to increase their access to opportunities and resources. It is to enable them
to take more control of their lives and to gain for themselves more of what
they need.

Given the web of powerlessness and voicelessness, the questions change:

- How can development polices increase poor men and women's access to opportunities and resources and their freedom of choice and action?
- How can poor women's and men's own efforts and organizations be supported?
- How can networks and federations of poor people's organizations (women and men) be heard and represented in decision-making that affects their lives at the local, national and global levels?

Notes

[1] The findings about lack of information, education, skills and confidence are drawn from discussions on wellbeing, security, risks and opportunities, social exclusion, priority problems and concerns, and the quality of poor people's interactions with institutions. The findings on the "web of disadvantages" pool together information from all of the study topics and methods, including discussion groups' analyses and diagrams of the causes and impacts of poverty.

[2] The *Methodology Guide* asked research teams at every site to obtain insights into the lives and life histories of five individuals or households. These were to include one poor woman and one poor man who had always been poor or one poor man or woman who had fallen into poverty. The account was to include major events or shocks—as recalled by them—in their lives. A subset of 125 life stories was selected based on completeness of information.

Chapter 12

A Call to Action:
The Challenge to Change

Summary

The call to action and change is compelling. It is to define development as equitable wellbeing for all, to put the bottom poor high on the agenda, to recognize power as a central issue, and to give voice and priority to poor people. It is to enable poor women and men to achieve what they perceive as a better life. These basics underpin efforts to transform the conditions poor people experience, empowering them with freedom to choose and act.

The multiple dimensions of deprivation demand multiple interventions. The agenda for change requires actions to make the following shifts:

- *From material poverty to adequate assets and livelihoods.*
- *From isolation and poor infrastructure to access and services.*
- *From illness and incapability to health, information and education.*
- *From unequal and troubled gender relations to equity and harmony.*
- *From fear and lack of protection to peace and security.*
- *From exclusion and impotence to inclusion, organization and empowerment.*
- *From corruption and abuse to honesty and fair treatment.*

Three other transformations are indicated: professional reorientation to starting with poor people's realities, institutional reorientation from dominating to facilitative behaviors, and personal commitment to bring about change in poor people's lives. Whether Voices of the Poor makes a difference depends on the actions or inaction of all touched by this study.

Introduction

The people who read this book have the power to make a difference. Most of us are neither powerless nor poor. We can influence thinking, policy and practice. To a degree denied to the poor, we are free to make choices and changes. What should those changes be?

In writing this book we have tried to keep faith as messengers and interpreters, reporting and representing what participants said and shared. Our dilemma has been how much further to go. We believe that the poor women and men who participated in the study would want us to point to practical implications. Accordingly, in this final chapter we draw on poor people's recommendations as well as our own experience. Throughout this chapter we have illustrated the text with examples of poor people's recommendations, but make no attempt to cover every topic. We set out two major challenges and an agenda for action, which identifies seven themes.

The Challenge to Reflect: The Meaning of Development

Reflecting on the experiences of poor men and women has driven us to revisit the meaning of development. What is significant change, and what is good? And which changes, for whom, matter most?

Answers to these questions involve material, physical, social, psychological and spiritual dimensions. Historically many development professionals have given priority to the material aspect of people's lives. Important as this is, poor people's views of wellbeing, as we have seen, span wide and varied experiences and meanings. The words of a poor woman in Ethiopia illustrate some of the range and balance: "A better life for me is to be healthy, peaceful, and live in love without hunger. Love is more than anything. Money has no value in the absence of love." To encompass multiple dimensions, and to make space for poor people's own ideas of the good life means working toward wellbeing for all.

A key measure of development then becomes the enhanced wellbeing of those who have it least. Defined in their own terms, poor people have shown us how much a small change can mean to those who have very little. The increments in wellbeing that would mean much to the poor widow in Bangladesh—a full stomach, time for prayer, and a bamboo platform to sleep on—challenge us to change how we measure development. Basing the calculus of development on equity and wellbeing demands giving heavy emphasis to the bottom end of poverty. This argues for a reorientation of development priorities, practice and thinking. It reinforces the case for making the wellbeing of those who are worse off the touchstone for policy and practice.

The bottom poor, in all their diversity, are excluded, impotent, ignored and neglected; the bottom poor are a blind spot in development. In many places, especially in Africa, their numbers are seen to be increasing. They are often difficult to reach and help. They find it difficult to help themselves. In Bangladesh they "hardly receive any help from neighbors." Often they are untouched by government and NGO programs. They are not creditworthy. They do not have documents. They fall through safety nets. They are frequently sick. They cannot afford medical treatment. They are chronically short of food. They are exceptionally vulnerable and insecure. In urban areas they fear and hide from the police and officials who hound them. They subsist or die on the fringes of society.

The Challenge of Power: Whose Voice Counts?

> Do people live equally here? Look at my fingers. Are they equal?
> —A discussion group participant, Kajima, Ethiopia

> A dog won't betray its master.
> —A poor man, Ulugbek, Uzbekistan

Poor people lack voice and power. They do exercise agency but in very limited spheres of influence. In describing illbeing and the bad life, poor people, and especially women, often express powerlessness vis-à-vis employers, the state and markets; their inability to get a fair deal; their inability to take a stand against abuse, lying and being cheated; their inability to access market opportunities. To stand up against those on whom you and your family depend is risky and can even be a matter of life and death. Differences in power between women and men and between the poor and the nonpoor affect opportunities and outcomes in countless interactions.

The voices that count most are those of the powerful and wealthy. It is they who make, influence and implement policy. To make a difference poor people must be able to make their voices heard in policy and have representation in decisionmaking forums. This implies changes in power relations and behavior. Organizations of the poor become very important means to changing power relations. Investing in poor people's organizations requires shifts of mind-set and orientation among professionals and institutions. The inspiring examples of champions who serve the interests of the poor show what individuals can do to ensure that the voices of the poor are heard and acted upon. In today's "wired" world the opportunities for sharing the realities of poor people's lives, for changing mind-sets and for ensuring that poor people's voices are heard have never been greater. Coalitions representing poor people's organizations are needed to ensure that the voices of the poor are heard and reflected in decisionmaking at the local, national and global levels.

The Agenda for Change

A person doesn't have the strength or power to change anything, but if the overall system changed, things would be better.

—A poor man, Sarajevo, Bosnia

This study's starting point is poor people's own analysis. Their priorities differ and are specific by group and context. These differences underscore the importance of participatory analysis by diverse groups of poor people and decentralized action to fit their varied priorities. At the same time, poor people have much in common, pointing to more widely applicable policies and practices.

The dimensions of wellbeing and illbeing are many. While priorities vary by location, the study gives added weight to poor people's voices crying out against the agony of hunger and sickness, the deprivations of lack of work, the anxiety of insecurity, the injustice of discrimination, the frustrations of powerlessness, the denial of opportunity to children and much else. The questions are what should be done and who should do it. Here poor people provide some guidance.

Poor people call for access to opportunities, decent wages, strong organizations of their own and a better and more active state. They call for systemic change. They want more government, not less—government on which they have influence and with which they can partner in different ways. They look to government to provide services fundamental to their wellbeing. Poor people's problems cut across sectoral divides. They challenge us to think and plan beyond narrow disciplinary boundaries while still remaining responsive to local realities. This requires institutions that are more decentralized, facilitative and accountable to poor women and men.

In reviewing what poor people explicitly called for, as well as our own analysis, we have identified seven themes for change. Practical measures for implementing change will depend on national and local contexts, but progress across these themes is an urgent priority for poor people around the world. They are:

- From material poverty to adequate assets and livelihoods.
- From isolation and poor infrastructure to access and services.
- From illness and incapability to health, information and education.
- From unequal and troubled gender relations to equity and harmony.
- From fear and lack of protection to peace and security.
- From exclusion and impotence to inclusion, organization and empowerment.
- From corruption and abuse to honesty and fair treatment.

1. From Material Poverty to Adequate Assets and Livelihoods

Poverty and destitution are part and parcel of our lives.
—Participant, discussion group of women, Kowerani
Masasa, Malawi

Every day there are more unemployed; every day one sees more men around the neighborhood.
—Participant, discussion group of men and women,
Moreno, Argentina

There is great insecurity now. You can't make any plans.
—Participant, discussion group of men and women,
Kalofer, Bulgaria

In defining poverty and insecurity, poor people speak about hunger, their precarious lives, lack of assets, their limited ability to cope with shocks and their lack of access to loans and capital. Even where poverty has decreased, as in Vietnam, poor people say their insecurity has increased. With some exceptions, poor people report that their economic opportunities have declined in the 1990s. Many blame governments for mismanaging the economy, for privatization, high taxes, and inflation; for declines in affordability of agricultural inputs; for distant markets; for lack of cheap credit; for corrupt services; or simply for lack of care for the poor.

In this environment, poor people's livelihood strategies are largely in the informal economy and frequently consist of a patchwork of low-paying, risk-prone and often back-breaking work. Poor people offer many recommendations specific to their contexts (see box 12.1). Moving away from poverty to a life that includes assets and livelihood security will require three sets of actions: fuel the economy from below; support producer organizations of the poor and provide social protection; and enhance access to savings, credit and venture capital services.

a. Fuel the Economy from Below

Many participants feel that economic opportunities have bypassed them. In Indonesia and Thailand in particular, they are acutely aware of the ill effects of macroeconomic decline. Proper macroeconomic policies and programs are clearly essential, but stronger links are required to the micro level where poor people live and work. Poor people propose nurturing the local economy through a variety of ways including building access roads; having better and fairer access to markets for rural producers; building village food-storage barns; stopping the practice of giving rich people rights to buy or use common property resources; ensuring minimum crop prices until the economy stabilizes (former Soviet countries); redistributing land; removing oppressive rules governing the urban informal sector; and encouraging rural small and large-scale industries and factories (see also box 12.1).

b. Support Producer Organizations of the Poor and Provide Social Protection

> *As individuals we cannot do a thing.*
> —From a discussion group of poor kilim weavers,
> Foua, Egypt

The informal sector is cut-throat, fragmented and extremely diverse. In rural economies, poor farmers are often isolated from each other. Membership-based organizations of the poor that build solidarity among informal workers, small farmers and other producers may improve conditions for the poor. By working together, poor people's associations can obtain better prices for goods, buy in bulk, share information, and organize to influence municipal and state regulations affecting vending, public transport and so forth. Examples of people organizing include farmers' groups, fishermen's groups, tailors' associations, marketing cooperatives and credit associations.

Most informal sector workers are casual workers with no direct access to government-provided social security even where it exists. Innovative micro-insurance schemes are needed to protect poor workers.

c. Enhance Access to Savings, Credit and Venture Capital Services

While much has been learned about microcredit lending systems, they still do not reach many poor people. Access to credit can be difficult due to collateral requirements, rigid repayment schedules, loan amounts that are too small, and corruption among lenders. Shopkeepers and money-lenders, despite their high interest rates, are greatly valued for giving loans for consumption, for not having bothersome procedures, and for allowing payments to be made in kind, including in labor. Participatory research is needed to guide institutional innovation to channel credit through appropriate mechanisms to fit local requirements. To establish such microcredit lending programs may require retraining field workers and changing incentives so that the programs' success is judged by the quality of their interactions with the borrowers as well as by collection rates.

Poor people often point out that they lack access to capital to start new business ventures. There is a need for venture capital funds for poor people.

Box 12.1 Poor People's Recommendations for Improving Livelihoods and Building Assets

Develop local industries and services to reduce unemployment

Participants from Nampeya Village, Malawi have many suggestions for bringing jobs into their areas including rice milling and packaging, tobacco handling centers and sugar making plants; and loan schemes for minibuses so the village can be connected to urban centers more reliably. They say that such changes would mean that they might "at least be employed as either guards, cleaners or moppers."

In Munamalgasvewa, Sri Lanka the poor want help to start businesses in mat making and other reed handicrafts, and for repair shops for radios, televisions, motorcycles, bicycles and two-wheeled tractors.

Change municipal regulation to reduce difficulties in street vending

Women in many countries speak about municipal regulations that made vending trade difficult. Women recommend organization and joining hands to fight municipal authorities. In Kaoseng, Thailand a woman community leader who learned about community organizing a decade earlier at the threat of house demolitions and evictions organized to protest municipal parking regulations that affected access to their fish markets and their sales.

Invest in people's organizations

"We want to form our own organization; our own, protecting our own rights," says a Roma group from Krasna Poliana in Sofia, Bulgaria.

Expand access to formal credit

In Jaffna, Sri Lanka poor people say that "to improve the future living standards of the village, they expect the two lending institutions, the United Currency Society and the Social Development Center...to extend a helping hand by encouraging savings and giving loans when necessary."

Act on many fronts

In Dibdibe Wajtu Peasant Association, in Ethiopia, people say that opportunities would improve

> ▸ *"...if there is the chance for employment...*
> ▸ *"...if there are credit facilities, the farmer can use them to increase production and improve his life."*
> ▸ *"...if the widowed and landless women are given some sort of vocational training, they can make it a means of living."*
> ▸ *"...if the farmer is given some sort of training in the use of money he can save some of his earnings to use it in days of difficulty."*
> ▸ *"...if people who suffer from dense settlement were able to move and settle in fertile, unsettled areas."*

Provide day care

In Novo Horizonte, Brazil participants ask for day care because "it is very important, especially for the mothers who have to work. It also could be a source of leisure for children."

2. From Isolation and Poor Infrastructure to Access and Services

If we get a road we would get everything else: community center, employment, post office, water, telephone.
— Participant, group of young women,
Little Bay, Jamaica

The lack of capital is related to the road condition that does not allow people to sell farming products.
— Participant, group of poor women, Waikanabu, Indonesia

The authorities never come here.
— A woman, Asociación 10 de Agosto, Ecuador

We can solve some of the problems ourselves, such as the problem of the dirty streets, but how can we solve the potable water and lake problems?
— A youth, El Mataria, Egypt

Poor people are frequently disadvantaged in where they live and work, and in access to basic services. Often they are geographically isolated, whether in slums or remote rural areas, with roads, transport, telecommunications, lighting, access to information and markets that are inadequate or lacking altogether. Schools, clinics and hospitals are far away and of low quality. Shelter, water, sanitation and fuel are inadequate and unsafe. Many farm families seek livelihoods on marginal lands. Many, both urban and rural, are insecure in their tenure of land and the plots on which they live. And they are exposed to environmental hazards, such as floods, droughts, fires, pollution and epidemics.

These conditions exacerbate poverty. It takes poor people longer than others, and often very much more energy, to fetch water, wash, find and collect fuel, maintain their shelter, get to market to buy and sell, get information, gain access to government offices, contact friends and relatives, get treatment for sickness or accidents, and in slums even to go to the toilet. Conversely, reliable, convenient and accessible infrastructure reduces time and energy required. Those who benefit are likely to be disproportionately female because of gender responsibilities of running households and, increasingly, meeting household expenses as well. Not surprisingly many poor people's recommendations focus on improving their physical environment (see box 12.2).

a. Assign Greater Priority to Basic Infrastructure

Reliable housing, water, roads, sanitation, and energy provide critical foundations for households and community development. The contrast between slums and more prosperous parts of many cities is acute. The major benefits from adequate infrastructure have been stressed many times, as by this group of poor men in Ethiopia: "If we had received government assistance in the areas of water and electricity, it would have created a great deal of opportunity for us to improve our lives." As the many examples across countries show, poor people make valiant efforts to solve their problems, but often with limited long-term success resulting in poor people paying more than the rich for services. Provision of sustainable basic services requires new working and financial partnerships between governments and poor communities. Encouraging investments in improving infrastructure services by poor people requires giving poor people security of tenure.

b. Reduce Seasonal Risks; Strengthen Environmental Management

Many poor people and poor communities are located in environmentally vulnerable areas, such as steep hillsides, floodplains, arid lands, and unhealthy, polluted areas—all of which are more vulnerable to extreme weather. Poor people often live and work in such places because better lands are unafford-able. Where other options are limited, measures to protect against floods, fires, riverbank erosion, landslides and many different forms of pollution are needed, along with interventions to foster better conservation of soils, forests, sources of water and fish stocks.

Community-based processes are needed to guide land and resource use planning and regulations so as to bring meaningful benefits to poor communi-ties. For example, in Khaliajuri, Bangladesh people propose that if the govern-ment or NGOs would build a permanent embankment, erosion would slow and livelihood opportunities would increase. In Kaoseng, Thailand participants recommend that the government should enforce its bans on illegal fishing equipment and reduce the release of wastewater from processing plants.

3. From Illness and Incapability to Health, Information and Education

> Before, everyone could get health care, but now everyone
> just prays to God that they don't get sick because everywhere
> they ask for money.
> —A discussion group participant, Vares,
> Bosnia and Herzegovina

> It is difficult to take the children to and from the clinic. It's
> costly and stressful; sometimes it takes a whole day.
> —A woman, Little Bay, Jamaica

> Because we've had no schooling we are almost illiterate....
> Store owners cheat us, because the Indians don't know how to
> count or anything else. They buy at the prices they want and
> pay less. They cheat us because we are not educated.
> —Participant, discussion group of woman,
> Asociación 10 de Agosto, Ecuador

Physical incapabilities include hunger, weakness, illness, exhaustion and disabilities, and they exacerbate poverty of time and energy. Other incapabilities are lack of information, education, literacy and skills. On the positive side, wellbeing includes health, strength, education and skills, all of which empower.

The importance to poor people of access to good and affordable health care would be difficult to exaggerate. The body is a poor person's main asset. Yet it is those who most need strong bodies for work who are most exposed to sickness and accidents and least able to obtain or afford treatment. Illness, injury and death stand out as causes of poverty. Innovative means of provid-ing protection during health and other income-related shocks is greatly need-ed. Some of poor people's recommendations are reflected in Box 12.3.

Complementary interventions that help poor people overcome time and energy poverty will also protect the poor people's most important energy system—their own bodies.

Literacy, gaining skills and education are valued and seen as a means out of poverty. Skills training is stressed for starting micro and small businesses. Education is less valued when an economy is in trouble, and more when it is prosperous. Despite their belief in the potential value of education, the poor struggle with its cost and question its quality, language of instruction, and relevance to future livelihood.

a. Expand Access to Curative Medicine

Preventive medicine is important, but it is curative medicine that the poor emphasize. Catastrophic illness devastates. Poor people know the effects of being sick and unable to work, when the body flips from asset to liability, and of the costs of getting good treatment. Poor people need low-cost health care,

---

Box 12.3 Poor People's Recommendations for Health Services

Be kind
"The doctors should be kind and polite; they have taken a special oath, this is their business. They have to be welcoming and to talk with everybody, to listen to one's problems. But they are not. Most of them are quite rude; they make the people wait for several hours...."
— A discussion group of men and women, Plovdiv, Bulgaria

Ethics, traditional healers and citizen monitoring of hospitals
"Hospital staff should stick to their professional ethics and values. They are no longer reliable. Drugs and essential equipment are in short supply. We hear the government has sold off some of the public enterprises. The money realized from this exercise could be used for procuring drugs for our hospitals. The government should consider strengthening links with traditional healers who could be an alternative, but their practices are unhygienic. Finally, the government should consider the involvement of the public in day-to-day management of these hospitals. We should be able to offer our views...if we are granted this opportunity, we shall not heap all the blame on government for substandard services in our hospitals.
— Discussion group, Kowerani Massasa, Malawi

Expand poor people's access to health care
In Ha Tinh Province, Vietnam, participants propose that the government provide health insurance for farmers, health examinations free of charge for poor and elderly people, education about health care and family planning, and free family planning services. People also express a need for more sufficient stocks at commune health stations.

---

while the poorest cannot afford even low costs. Improving access to curative services, minimizing travel costs, reducing waiting times, and making treatment affordable for poor people would prevent much impoverishment.

Rather than preferential treatment for the rich, participants in Ha Tinh, Vietnam probably speak for many in urging "preferential treatment for poor households to help promote access to health services...."

Poor people resent and are deterred by the rude and callous way health professionals often treat them. Sri Lanka may be a source of lessons, standing out as a country where poor people, with few exceptions, speak with appreciation of government hospitals, good and polite doctors, and free hospital treatment.

b. Provide Health Insurance

In Vietnam poor people say farmers should receive health insurance. Similarly in Borg Meghezel, Egypt poor people consider an efficient health insurance system as critical. Health insurance for the poor is an area for learning from current practices and for innovation.

c. Support Access to Information

It would be good if we had a telephone here in the collective center or at least if we could phone from the post office....
—Discussion group, Bratunac, Bosnia and Herzegovina

Over and over again, poor people mention their isolation from information; information about programs of assistance, their rights, job contacts, how banks work; government plans that affect their lives directly—for example, plans to move people from an embankment; prices; NGO, village government and local government activities.

In addition to information dissemination through mass media, poor people's connectivity to each other and to sources of information can be greatly enhanced through access to communication and information technology. Rural information technology centers, cellular telephones and Internet access can change poor people's negotiating power even while deep structural inequities exist.

d. Make Education Accessible and Relevant

Both government and NGOs can arrange better education systems ... both for functional as well as technical education.
—A discussion group, Chittagong, Bangladesh

In ranking community priorities, poor people in community after community indicate that they value education and technical training as keys to a better future for themselves and especially for their children. In many countries, and particularly across Africa, school-related costs and the distance to schools are serious and sometimes insuperable problems. Quality and relevance of education are also issues. Eliminating direct costs of schooling, including costs of school supplies and uniforms, and offsetting indirect costs, such as loss of children's labor through scholarships, would encourage many more poor families to send their children to school. Implementing such propoor measures in a resource-constrained environment requires creative context-specific solutions. Across different contexts, poor people said participation in school management made teachers show up for work.

4. From Unequal and Troubled Gender Relations to Equity and Harmony

Many men have been retrenched, are jobless, and do not have any steady source of income. As a result, women have assumed the role of breadwinner in many households.
—Research team in Kowerani Masasa, Malawi

Before, it was clear that the woman is to keep the house and take care of the family, while the man was earning the daily bread. Now the woman buys and sells stuff irrespective of the weather and earns the income for the family, while the man is sitting at home and takes care of the children, fulfilling the traditional women's work. This is not right; this is not good.
—An elderly man, Kenesh, Kyrgyz Republic

It's because of unemployment and poverty that most men in this community beat their wives. We have no money to look after them.
—A man, Teshie, Ghana

Exclusion based on gender remains widespread and entrenched despite changing laws in some countries. This is evident in gender roles at the household and community levels and in poor women's unequal access to livelihood resources and services. With some exceptions, men are viewed as the major decisionmakers in community affairs.

At the household level, however, people perceive major changes to be under way in gender relations. With increased economic hardship and a decline in poor men's traditional livelihood strategies, more poor women have had to make their way into the informal economy, primarily in low-paying and often menial work. In many societies, for women to work outside the home violates social norms; it is a source of tension and shame, especially when the primary reason is men's unemployment. These sweeping changes are placing enormous stress on households.

Poor people mention domestic violence in many forms with great frequency. Physical abuse of women in the household remains widespread. While it is in decline in some communities, in other communities, physical violence is reported to be increasing. This increase is linked to women's work outside the home, a violation of traditional norms, and a threat to men's sense of masculine identity. The decrease in domestic violence in some areas is linked to women's greater income-earning ability and willingness to walk out of abusive relations and support themselves, awareness raising done by NGOs and churches, and occasionally police support. Many communities also report harassment and abuse of girls and women at the community level and in the workplace. Examples of poor people's recommendations are reported in Box 12.4.

Existing gender relations in society and in the household affect poverty interventions. This fact needs to be part of the calculus of design and evaluation of policies and programs. Improvement in gender relations within households and in society can result in enormous gains in wellbeing. Achieving such improvement requires change in social norms, a gender approach to development, psychological support to both men and women, support to women's groups and appropriate legal reforms.

a. Launch Campaigns on Gender Relations

There may be no other domain than gender relations that suffers such neglect by governments, international agencies and the private sector as gender relations. Mass media campaigns are needed to change social norms

---

Box 12.4 Poor People's Recommendations to Reduce Gender Inequity

Increase legal action against domestic abuse

A group of women from the poor urban community of Twashuka Shanty Compound in Zambia propose that the government should provide police to deal with murders, wife-batterings, sexual abuse of female children, wife-killings, rape and assault. They say "the police should stop being corrupt" and take seriously the problems of sexual abuse of female children.

Strengthen awareness about dowry

Participants from Khaliajuri, Bangladesh feel that legal measures alone cannot end the practice of dowry and they recommend campaigns to raise public awareness on the devastating problems it creates. They suggest that the government should broadcast awareness programs through different media, for instance, illustrating dowry problems with real cases. Rather than broadcasting the different punishments for taking dowry, they should indicate how a poor father becomes landless by giving dowry.

for better and more adaptive gender relations and to help boys and men to redefine masculinity. Such campaigns would entail actively encouraging men, where appropriate, to adapt to and enjoy new domestic roles. Prominent, powerful and popular men can and should set examples as role models.

b. Mainstream Gender-Sensitive Approaches

Over and over again women have been left out of programs of assistance—and influence over design of programs—from agricultural extension to government-provided loans or training. In addition women are participating less in community activities as they take on new income-earning roles. The backlash against women's small and painful gains, and the struggles, depression, and frustration felt by men, call for a gender-sensitive approach to move out of textbooks and into the practice of development. By implication, then, all interventions must take into account the intermeshing of women's and men's lives and the impact of interventions on equity and peace in the household.

Social roles and identity are closely intertwined. Rapid changes exact an emotional and psychological toll with economic and social consequences. Both men and women, in separate and mixed groups, need physical and social space to gather and talk about themselves, their society, and their loss and grief to enable them to function more effectively in a changing society.

c. Support Women's Groups

In some countries women's groups (for example, the *samity* women's group created by NGOs in Bangladesh) stand out as making a difference in poor women's struggles to earn a living in dignity. Depending on the cultural context, women's groups are powerful ways of reaching poor women, building confidence and establishing economic security.

d. Undertake Legal Reform

Discrimination against females and denial of their human rights are still widely embodied in both law and custom. Legal reform, where it has not taken place, to establish equal rights of inheritance for women, including rights to land and other property, must be a high priority. Equally important is extending legal aid to women. The customary despoliation of widows, their humiliation and impoverishment, cry out for both legal and social redress. The limitations of the law are evident, though, from India, where dowry is illegal but widely practiced. The way dowry impoverishes poor families who have daughters, and reinforces discrimination against females throughout their lives, is again evident from case studies. The many efforts to change such customs and their severely discriminatory effects deserve support.

5. From Fear and Lack of Protection to Peace and Security

The police have become the rich people's stick against common people.

—Discussion group of men and women,
urban Uzbekistan

I do not know whom to trust, the police or the criminals. Our public safety is ourselves. We work and hide indoors.

—A woman, Sacadura Cabral, Brazil

Even before the war, there was plundering and theft, but that was a herald to the war. Before the war, places were well lit. People worked and had money...those most in need were protected, but now nothing.

—Discussion group, Sarajevo, Bosnia and Herzegovina

We are dying from these greedy people who are stealing our food.

—A man from the Serenje District of Zambia

Security is peace of mind and the possibility to sleep relaxed.

—A woman, El Gawaber, Egypt

In many countries in both rural and urban areas poor people report a decline in social connectedness together with increases in crime, lawlessness, selfishness and violence. Although there are differences in scale and intensity, the problem of declining public safety as an element of increasing insecurity is mentioned in almost every country, in both rural and urban areas. Breakdown in social cohesion is reflected in conflict and violence within the home as well. Many of the poor link these trends to decreases in economic opportunities, increased competition for resources and poor government policies. In Eastern Europe and Central Asia the decline also is linked to the political and economic transition.

As a result of economic stress and erosion of traditional family support and government safety nets, poor people feel less able to protect themselves from shocks and stresses. These include natural disasters, crime, theft, illness, price fluctuations and unemployment.

The police emerge not as sources of help and security, but rather of harm, risk and impoverishment. While there are some exceptions, including in Ethiopia, Sri Lanka and Zambia, in many places the police are considered a necessary evil, vigilantes and criminals. Poor people's recommendations focus in different ways on enhancing safety, security and peace (box 12.5).

Civil wars based on clan rivalries and ethnicity in several countries have brought untold suffering to the poor, and even after years of peace, life has not returned to prewar standards. In Bosnia, Somaliland and Sri Lanka poor people speak of very slow and difficult recoveries and lingering tensions.

a. Invest in Building Social Cohesion

Every society has processes of building social cohesion through a variety of mechanisms: celebrations, community sports, community works, conflict resolution councils, the village headman in Malawi, the Community Council and Age Groups in Nigeria, and the Save the Town Association in Kok Yangak in the Kyrgyz Republic—all are examples of ways local organizations take action to make life more livable. In rural Malawi and Zambia, people have organized neighborhood watch groups to curb crime. In communities in Eastern Europe and Central Asia, opportunities to collectively grieve over sudden and large losses may be particularly helpful in easing the cost of moving forward. The case here is for encouraging processes that support community solidarity and bridging social capital or social interaction across social groups.

b. Invest in Social Protection

Living on the edge, despite hard work, poor men and women have little resilience to bounce back after disasters hit. A social protection approach broadly defined should focus on building assets of the poor and increasing their reserves and resilience in the face of crisis. There is need for programs that protect poor men and women from the effects of human-made and natural crises and the effects of life-cycle changes.

c. Undertake Police Reform

The crisis in police brutality, with "protectors" becoming the problem, calls out for solutions. Poor people need and want the police, but good police. In some areas poor people feel that the police are not to blame for their failure to deal with criminals. They point out that the police are poorly paid, their lives are at risk when tracking criminals and these risks become higher each year as criminals become better armed.

One option is community policing, where the police discuss and agree with community residents on a common protocol for police action. This approach has transformed community-police relations and has brought down crime in some urban neighborhoods. Another tactic may be to increase women police: in Jamaica the only police officer mentioned who was accessible to the poor was a woman; in Brazil the poor speak highly of some women's police stations, while others are reported to be underfunded. Other measures to encourage and enable the police to protect—not persecute—the poor could include systems of police accountability, better pay and backup from the criminal justice system. Yet other solutions should be sought from experience gained with police reform wherever this has taken place.

d. Strengthen Conflict Mediation and Resolution

After civil war or riots have ended, rebuilding infrastructure is relatively easy. Mourning loss, healing deep hatreds and wounds, and building collaboration across social divides are, however, extremely difficult. Building peace at all levels requires skills and expertise in conflict mediation and resolution as well as counseling. While reforming the judiciary is important, in many countries where government has little presence in rural areas, traditional forums for dispute resolution play critical roles. In Somaliland the *Guurti*, a forum to resolve disputes between clans, is ranked highly by most people and credited with bringing and maintaining peace to communities. In the Bihin area a committee of elders, which formed following the signing of the Peace Charter in 1993, regulates water sharing during the dry season and resolves disputes over land use.

Solving community problems through joint action across previously warring ethnic lines is difficult. In Bosnia and Herzegovina NGOs are working through the Center for Civil Society in southeastern Europe to build cooperative relations across community groups, among traditional leaders, and with local authorities. Community-based projects across ethnic and social groups, as well as conflict mediation efforts and skills training, need to be supported. In some countries, the ability to resolve conflicts is cited as an important criterion in rating institutions. In Egypt poor people speak of the ability of traditional councils to resolve disputes; in Ethiopia the *omda* (the traditional mayor) is valued for skills in dispute resolution so that "only if the matter is very serious, like a murder" is it referred to the police.

6. From Exclusion and Impotence to Inclusion, Organization and Empowerment

> We all know that if you are at the bottom, you will be the object of aggression, and we are afraid of those on the top. The people cannot gather together and put them in their place.
> —Discussion group of men and women, Etropole, Bulgaria

> The responsibility for the problem is 90 percent on the government, but we vote badly, we do not monitor, we don't demand our rights, and we are not active to demand a correct action by the government.
> —Discussion group of men and women,
> Morro da Conceição, Brazil

Poor people's evaluations of institutions show that by and large they are excluded from participation in decisionmaking and in equal sharing of benefits from government programs as well as from those of NGOs. The poor want desperately to have their voices heard, to make decisions, and not to always receive the law handed down from above. They are tired of being asked to participate in government projects with low or no returns. Some of their suggestions are reflected in box 12.6.

Organizations of poor people at the local level are critical if they are to influence decisionmaking at the local, national or global levels.

a. Create the Legal Framework for Participation

The framework for grassroots democracy, the right to participate, must be enshrined in law. This has to include rules about public disclosure of information; freedom of association, speech and the press; freedom to form organizations; and devolution of authority and finances to the local level. Institutional rules and incentives are needed to translate laws into effective governance structures. The challenge is to create propoor government institutions accountable to the poor.

While legal frameworks create the space for action, whether or not laws are effectively put into practice depends on many factors, including the local capacity to organize and mobilize around the new rights enshrined by law. In Horenco, Bolivia the implementation of the Law of Popular Participation is complicated by divisions within the community. In Ha Tinh Province of Vietnam, in one commune participants say, "All decisions are top-down. For example, decisions on contributions, fees, taxes, and the like. All the people could do is what they are required to do as informed by the village manager." These examples underscore the point that while a legal framework may be necessary, it is not in itself sufficient. A key precondition is organized communities that can participate in devolved authority structures and keep local governments accountable.

b. Support Local Organizational Capacity

If we aren't organized and we don't unite, we can't ask for anything.

—Participant, discussion group of women, Florencio
Varela, Argentina

Quite often poor people feel that they are "made to participate" in government programs. They often express the general sentiment, "We are asked to attend meetings, but our participation makes little difference." When programs are implemented, the poor once again are left out. "In the end they would see and feel that the activities were not transparently implemented," say the researchers from Galih Pakuwon, Indonesia.

In many countries the study found that people trust their own solidarity groups and associations to be most responsive to their needs and priorities. In Somaliland clan elders resolve conflicts between clans; in Nchimishi, Zambia a neighborhood health committee "swings into action once there is an outbreak of dysentery." These organizations provide the foundations for mobilization and active participation in grassroots democracy. Organizations of the poor need to be strengthened to participate effectively in local governance. This capacity building is critical if laws are to be translated into human dignity and freedom for the poor. NGOs and the private sector have important roles to play, provided it can be ensured that they are accountable to the poor. Local organizational capacity is a key element in building grassroots democracy, but without "bridging social capital" to link similar social groups across communities, or groups with complementary resources (such as NGOs, the private sector, or the state), organizing local groups by itself is unlikely to move poor people out of poverty. Organizational capacity building requires long-term commitment and long-term financing; otherwise, outsiders are liable to take over local priorities and leadership.

7. From Corruption and Abuse to Honesty and Fair Treatment

> *There is much bitterness, especially in the thought that any op-*
> *portunities that may come will be taken by the rich and they*
> *could never find a* wasta, *or middleman, to enable them to find*
> *a better or more permanent job. If they have a right, they can-*
> *not take it because they cannot afford a lawyer. If the poor go*
> *to the police station to accuse a richer man, he is afraid: "My*
> *accusation may turn out in the favor of the rich and against*
> *me. But if we are equal, I may have justice."*
>
> —Researchers, Dahshour, Egypt

> *The municipality collects donations, and then they share it*
> *among themselves.*
>
> —A discussion group participant, Bosnia and Herzegovina

The problems of corruption, "connections," and violation of basic human rights with impunity is voiced over and over again by poor peo- ple in many countries. They experience corruption in their daily lives: cor- ruption in the distribution of seeds, medicines and social assistance for the destitute and vulnerable; in getting loans; in getting teachers to teach; in customs and border crossings; in the construction of roads; in getting per- mission to move in and out of cities or stay in certain areas; in street and market trading; and in identity cards. Even humanitarian assistance is often reported to be waylaid. For many, access to justice and courts is a distant dream because of lack of information, distance from the courts and a strong belief based on experience that only money buys justice. Poor peo- ple's suggestions are reported in box 12.7.

a. Recognize Corruption as a Core Poverty Issue

Societal norms about corruption being expected and tolerated must change. While tackling the problem on a sectoral basis is important, societal norms about corruption must shift to the expectation of honesty and justice. No sin- gle agency can tackle or resolve the issue, but seeds must be sown widely to create global and local social movements against corruption, large and small. The moral authority of the religions of the world can be a powerful means to bring honesty and justice back into public and private life.

b. Provide Legal Aid and Build Awareness of Rights

> *There are four dragons: law court, prosecutor's office,*
> khokimiat *[highest state authority] and head of police. Nobody*
> *can get anything until they are satiated.*
>
> —A discussion group of men and women, Uzbekistan

Poor men and women need legal assistance and need to be educated about the law and their rights. Legal assistance and legal education have to be made available at the local level and on a long-term basis for poor people to have confidence in justice without fear of repercussions. Poor people will need protection to ensure that those who first dare to claim their rights in courts do not have to pay a high price in terms of their own lives, destruction of their property, or harm to family members. A woman in Uzbekistan, who taught herself about the law to get her son released from jail, says, "I am not afraid of anybody. If you know the law, you are secure."

c. Invest in Civic and Media Monitoring

Transparency through right-to-information movements, including transparency about budgets, combined with use of the media, has a key part to play. Change in this arena will entail investment in television, radio and other media; training and support to journalists; publicity of corruption statistics; creation of citizen "scorecards" on corruption in particular agencies; support to allies and activists at the local level; and use of information technology to publicize specific cases of corruption and to make heroes of "clean" traders, officials and politicians. In Russia, in the city of Magadan, local media are viewed as a force to battle corruption: "They trust those reporters who make local news. They revealed the facts of corruption among the municipal offices, they told of the money from the local budget that was spent by the mayor on his own needs." To gain legitimacy and protection, broad-based coalitions across communities and countries can deepen change and support local initiatives.

d. Create Downward Accountability

Some of the best institutional performance was reported where there was downward accountability to community groups. In education, when given the opportunity through parent associations, poor parents demand value for their money and hold schoolteachers accountable for their performance. When health workers are accountable to communities and there are mechanisms for feedback, delivery of health care improves. In Nova Califórnia, a *favela* in Brazil, the city initiative Saúde em Casa [Health in the Home] provides health services such as dentists, clinics and psychologists in mobile offices to communities. It emerges as one of the three best and most important institutions. Saúde em Casa is considered an institution with good service, as much because it is in the community as because it solves health problems or refers them to be solved by other institutions. When asked which institutions the community has greater control over, the people said, "We have more control over the Association...over Saúde em Casa...the community has the telephone number, the cell phone, the home phone number, and can complain from home in case of bad care from the Saúde em Casa doctors."

e. Campaign and Make Heroes of Honest and Caring Officials

Campaigns against corruption should be combined with acknowledgment and appreciation for honest and caring officials. Find and publicize those who behave well, especially those who improve conditions by cleaning up corruption and those who are outstanding in their spirit of service. Make them role models for their peers. Reward them. Promote them. Publicize performance standards and inform users, so service performers can be held accountable.

In the *favela* of Novo Horizonte, Brazil participants describe desperate living conditions, but when asked which institutions they trust, a man says, "What makes me trust in one institution is when I knock on its door, it is open to me. Look...this prefecture is so nice that I have the mayor's private phone number. He is a mayor who does not close the doors to the community, and it is the same with the secretary of social development." Another example that warrants particular attention is the praise given by a group of poor women to the superintendent of the Constant Spring Police Station in Cassava Piece, Jamaica. A group of poor women had praise for the police officer: "Anybody can have access to the superintendent in charge of Constant Spring Police Station. If you have a complaint you just walk in and ask to see her and they just send you upstairs to see her. She will call up the officer and deal with him."

Examples abound elsewhere. A sheikh in El Gawaber, Egypt distributes *zakat* (alms) during the night so that nobody notices who is getting it, and the dignity of the poor is preserved. A community health worker in Chief Kabamba, Zambia, although short of medicines, serves everyone without discrimination. The village head in Duyen Hai, Vietnam, though from a majority group in a minority community, has won the hearts of the villagers and helps everyone. A nurse in Ozerny, Russia never turns anyone away. A principal in Dimitrovgrad, Bulgaria raises money from the affluent to keep the children of the poor in school. A priest in Isla Trinitaria, Ecuador, considered the most important person in the community, provides medicine and food, organizes health services, and makes links with other institutions. A poor man in Vila União, Brazil struggled against the odds, became a community worker, was elected community leader, and now works to help street girls who have been victims of violence. A *Samurdhi* (government program for the poor) officer in Thirukadallur, Sri Lanka goes everywhere and nobody has anything bad to say about him. Women throughout Somaliland were the peace mediators between warring clans.

f. Build Institutional Character

Poor people are often badly treated by officials, by service providers, particularly those of the state, and by traders, with behavior that is crushing, cruel, humiliating, taunting, angering and frustrating. Corrupt and bad behavior comes in many guises, even in the extreme forms of violence, imprisonment and extortion. Pervasively poor people report rudeness, arrogance, insensitivity and lack of respect from those in authority. Together these deter poor people from contact with outsiders and in seeking services.

Institutional design efforts must include defining the character, qualities and the behavior desired of all those who are affiliated with the institutions. What poor people want are staff who are accessible, who listen, and who are patient, polite, sensitive and committed. They indicate the huge difference it means to be treated with respect, not to be kept waiting longer than others and not to be looked down on because of old clothes and shabby appearance. At little additional cost, the wellbeing of poor people can be dramatically improved by changes in service providers' attitudes and behavior. An attitude of service, respect and caring even when help is not available is profoundly appreciated.

In addition to appropriate incentives, mind-set shifts can be facilitated by the following:

▸ *Share good practice.* Champions like those above can inspire and help others, spreading their practices through learning visits, secondments, and peer-to-peer training. They can be rewarded through the recognition and prestige attributed to good practice.

▸ *Train for changes in behavior and attitudes.* Make behavior change the core of curricula in training institutions and programs. Reinforce this especially in the training of service providers, such as police, teachers, doctors, nurses and extension workers who have direct contact with poor people. In training institutions and programs, introduce training modules, exercises and self-critical reflection to encourage sensitive listening and learning, nondominating facilitation, and a spirit of service, with the style of training itself participatory.

▸ *Involve staff in poverty immersions and participatory appraisals.* Provide opportunities for open-ended learning from poor people. The study demonstrates the powerful impact participatory appraisals can have on those who facilitate them. The potential here is to make direct experiential learning available to those in international agencies, governments, corporations and civil society. Staying in poor communities for even short times and serving as field facilitators in participatory poverty studies create experiential opportunities to listen and learn face-to-face from poor people.

The Challenge to Change

Listening to voices of poor people is a beginning, but only a beginning. At worst, it may only lead to a change in rhetoric. It sounds good to have elicited the voices of the poor. Quoting their striking statements as we have done in this book may make an impression. But the crux is deeper change. Poor people can be heard, quoted and written about without the harder step of changing policies. And policy can be changed without the even harder step of changing what actually happens on the ground. The voices of poor people cry out for change. Commitment to deep change demands a lot. Three domains for change stand out: professional, institutional and personal.

The *professional* change that is required is a paradigm shift. It concerns professional concepts, values, methods and behaviors in development. It entails modifying dominant professional preconceptions with insights from participatory approaches and methods. It implies starting with the realities of the poor. To do so is not to deny the validity of other approaches and methods.

It is, rather, to introduce a different starting point and point of reference that other approaches and methods can complement. It demands that professionalism include reflection on the implications of decisions and actions for poor men and women.

Institutional change is cultural and behavioral. To the extent that organizations reward domineering behaviors, they are antithetical to the sensitive, responsive and empowering approaches needed to give the needs and interests of poor people priority. These behaviors are dictated by the norms, rules, rewards, incentives and values implicit in organizations. Organizations that affect poor people's lives include donor agencies, governments and their departments, the private sector, NGOs, universities and training institutes.

Personal change is fundamental to the other two. Changes that are professional and institutional and changes in policy and practice all depend on personal commitment and change. The self-evidence of this statement should not detract from its force, for eventually it is individuals who make a difference, including individuals who behave and act differently even when surrounded by rot, corruption and indifference.

The need and opportunity to act and to change are greatest for those who are wealthy and powerful and who never come in direct contact with poor people. For them it can be hard to know the effects of their actions and inactions. It can be easy and tempting not to know. Few politicians, policymakers, senior bureaucrats, staff of international agencies and the influential elite have had the chance to learn from poor people. This book is no substitute for direct experience, but we hope that, however modestly, it will help to bridge this gap. Those who speak through these pages were generous in the time they gave to the study. They shared their experience. Many have suffered traumas of war, violence, hunger, sickness, debt, exploitation, exclusion, harassment, pain and fear. Many wondered whether anything they said would make any difference.

Will *Voices of the Poor* make things better for those poor people who took part or for the hundreds of millions of others like them or their children? The answer is that it depends. It depends on the vision, courage, and will of all touched by this study. It depends on us all.

APPENDICES

Appendix 1
    Study Team and Acknowledgments

Appendix 2
    Study Countries and Sites

Appendix 3
    Overview of Study Themes and Methods

Appendix 4
    About the Authors

Appendix 1. Study Team and Acknowledgments

This book draws on the work of many people who were involved in different phases of the *Voices of the Poor* study. The *Voices of the Poor* study was led and managed by Deepa Narayan, Lead Social Development Specialist in the World Bank's Poverty Group, Poverty Reduction and Economic Management Network. Patti Petesch, Consultant, provided overall coordination. Meera Shah, Consultant, provided methodological guidance and training to several study teams. Robert Chambers and colleagues, with the Institute of Development Studies (IDS) at the University of Sussex, provided advisory support. Ulrike Erhardt, Ben Jones and Tiffany Marlowe provided administrative and research assistance.

The research was made possible through the generous financial support of the U.K. Department for International Development (DFID), numerous departments within the World Bank, and the Swedish International Development Cooperation Agency (SIDA). IDS support was financed by DFID, SIDA and the Swiss Agency for Development and Cooperation. Several of the country studies were partially or fully financed by NGOs. These included Proshika, Concern and ActionAid in Bangladesh; Praxis and ActionAid in India; ActionAid in Somaliland; ActionAid, Oxfam, Save the Children, the Vietnam-Sweden Mountain Rural Development Program, and the Vietnam Sweden Health Cooperative Program in Vietnam.

The study would never have been undertaken without the support of Ravi Kanbur, who was Director of the World Development Report until May 2000, and Mike Walton, who was Director of the Poverty Group of the World Bank until September 2000. Several people contributed to the early discussions framing the study. They included participants at a workshop held at the World Bank in New Delhi in August 1998, a second workshop at IDS in December 1998, and a workshop held in January 1999 at the World Bank in Washington, D.C. involving over 100 participants.

A methodology guide was developed and piloted in four countries led by Chamindra Weerackody in Sri Lanka, Anchana Naranong in Thailand, Fernando Dick in Bolivia and James Mascarenhas in India.

The 23 country studies on which the book is based were conducted by local research teams. Below are the team leaders and members.

Argentina: The study team was led by Daniel Cichero, Patricia Feliu, and Mirta Mauro and team members included Silvia Fuentes, Hernán Nazer, Blanca Irene García Prado, Héctor Salamanca, Mariano Salzman and Norberto Vázquez.

Bangladesh: The study was coordinated by Md. Shahabuddin, and the fieldwork was led by Rashed un Nabi, Dipankara Datta, Subrata Chakrabarty, Masuma Begum and Nasima Jahan Chaudhury. The study team also included Mostafa Zainul Abedin, Shukhakriti Adhikari, Dil Afroz, Selina Akhter, Zaed Al-Hasan, Khodeja Begum, Morzina Begum, Hasibur Rahman Bijon, Pradip Kumar Biswas,

Lipi Daam, Nikunja Debnath, Bijoy Kumar Dhar, S. M. Tozammel Haque, Emarat Hossain, Tariqul Islam, Iqbal Hossain Jahangir, Roji Khatun, Shohel Newaz, Moshfeka Jahan Parveen, Rajia Pervin, Amjad Hossain Pintu, A. K. M. Azad Rahman, Ashekur Rahman, Mizanur Rahman, Abdus Salam, Shofikus Saleh, Mezbah Uddin Shaheen, Afroza Sultana and Al-Haz Uddin.

Bolivia: The study team was led by Fernando Dick and included El Departamento de Gestión Rural de la Universidad Nur. Study team members included Freddy Chávez, Desiderio Choque A., Pablo Cuba, Gualberto Jaramillo, Pilar Lizárraga A., Daniel Moreno, Ligia Muguertegui, Q. Hermis Quintana, Policarpio Quiroz, Mirela Armand Ugon, Carlos Vacaflores R., Daniel Vacaflores and Martha Vargas.

Bosnia and Herzegovina: The study team was led by Dino Djipa, Mirsada Muzur and Paula Franklin Lytle, and also included Dado Babic, Vesna Bodirogic, Sanja Djermanovic, Fuad Hegic, Milos Karisik, Maida Koso, Elma Pasic, Marko Romic and Mladen Vidovick.

Brazil: The study team was led by Marcus Melo and also included Denilson Bandeira, Josineide Menezes, Mirna Pimentel, Flávio Rezende, Rosane Salles, Ana Flávia Novaes Viana and Ruben Vergara.

Bulgaria: The study team was led by Iliia Iliev, Petya Kabakchieva and Yulian Konstantinov, and also included Kristina Andonova, Gyulbie Dalova, Vera Davidova, Dimitar Dimitrov, Milena Harizanova, Toni Mileva, Raitcho Pojarliev, Ivan Popov, Dessislav Sabev, Venelin Stoichev, Vesselin Tepavicharov and Milena Yakimova.

Ecuador: The study team was led by Alexandra Martínez Flores and also included Milena Almeida, Elizabeth Arauz, Santiago Baca, Pablo Cousín, Nicolás Cuvi, Oswaldo Merino, Eduardo Morcillo, María Moreno and Edith Segarra.

Egypt: The study team was managed by the Center for Development Services in Cairo. Members included Ali Abdel-Aal, Redah Nagi Abul-Magd, Iman Amin, Bellah, Areeg Bahie El-Deen, Ihab Saad El-Mashaly, Hisham El-Rouby, Ashraf Gaballah, Sameh Fayez Guirguis, Mohamed Ahmed Abdek Kader, Marlene Kanawati, Maher Mahmoud, Nermine Mitry, Fatma Mossalam, Mohamed Naguib, Rasha Youssef Omar, Alaa Saber, Mohamed Sami, Mohamed Samy, Reda Hassan Radwan and Ali El Zafarany.

Ethiopia: The study team was led by Dessalegn Rahmato and Aklilu Kidanu and also included Alemayehu Abebe, Gillilat Aberra, Solomon Alemu, Belisumaa Assazenew, Meron Bekele, Mekonnen Bekureyesus, Gezahegne Belay, Begasshaw Direse, Tesfaye Kassa, Fitsum K. Mariam, Muluka Nuru, Aberra G. Tsadik and Yemistarch Zena.

Ghana: The study team was led by Ernest Kunfaa, Tony Dogbe, Heather J. Mackay and Celia Marshall, and included Harriet Adjapong Avle, Bright Asare Boadi, Philip Acheampong, Michael Tsike, Godfred Fosu Agyem, Adjapong Avle,

Nana Awuku, Richard Basadi, Solomon Yaw Fordjour, Victoria Kumi-Wood, Joe Lambongang Aba Oppong, Prudence Seeninyin and Victoria Tuffour.

India: The study team was led by Somesh Kumar and also included V. C. S. Bahadur, Bhartendu, Anindo Banerjee, Ronnie Barnard, B. Rama Devi, Shirsendu Ghosh, S. S. Jaideep, H. K. Jha, N. J. Joseph, Madhumati Katkar, Somesh Kumar, Jyotsna Kumari, Neelam Kumari, P. S. Lalita Kumari, Kumari Mridula, G. Muralidhar, K. S. N. Murthy, Nagendra, Murali Krishna Naidu, Amitabh Pandey, Harshavardan Patnaik, K. J. Prabhavati, Anamika Priyadarshini, B. Saroja Rajashekhar, D. Rajeshwar, Netala Rajeshwari, R. Venkata Ramana, V. V. Ramana, V. Paul Raja Rao, E. S. Rathnamma, M. Rajashekhar Reddy, N. Laxmi Narsimha Reddy, Surendra Sain, Shailesh Kumar Singh, Shipra Singh, Neelam Sharma, Surisetty Sreenivas and C. Upendranadh.

Indonesia: The study team was led by Nilanjana Mukherjee and also included Alma Arief, Ratna I. Josodipoero, Sita Laksmini, I. Nyoman Oka, Amin Robiarto, Setiadi, Joko Siswanto, Ronny So, Devi R. Soemardi, Suhardi, Nyoman Susanti, Herry Widjanarko and Susi Eja Yuarsi.

Jamaica: The study team was led by S. Jacqueline Grant and Toby Shillito and also included Hugh Dixon, Paulette Griffiths-Jude, Ivelyn Harris, Glenroy Lattery, Cecilia Logan, Genevieve McDaniel, Oswald Morgan, Steadman Noble, Michelle Peters, Vivienne Scott and Karen Simms.

Kyrgyz Republic: The study team was led by Janna Rysakova and also included Bakhtiyar Abdykadyrov, Janyl Abdyralieva, Gulnara Bakieva, Mariam Edilova, Takhir Hamdamov, Sagyn Kaimova, Esenkan Osmonaliev, Nurmamat Saparbaev, Nurdin Satarov, Turdububu Shamuratova, Lira Tantabaeva and Kunduz Ukubaeva.

Malawi: The study team was led by Stanley W. Khaila, Peter M. Mvula and John M. Kadzandira, and also included Moreen Bapu, Blessings Chinsinga, Augustine Fatch, Annie Kumpita, Brenda Mapemba, Dennis Mfune, Esnat Mkandawire, Slyvia Mpando, Ndaga Mulaga, Rodrick Mwamvani, Judith Mwandumba, James Mwera, Edward Kwisongole, Lilian Saka, Grace Thakwalakwa and Susan Tuwe.

Nigeria: The study team was led by James Zacha, D. Shehu, T. Odebiyi, N. Nweze, G. B. Ayoola, O. I. Aina and B. Mamman, and overall coordination was provided by Foluso Okunmadewa, Olukemi Williams and Dan Owen.

Russia: The study team was led by Alexey Levinson, Olga Stouchevskaya, Oxana Bocharova and Anton Lerner, and also included Lyubov Alexandrova, Vera Gromova and Yulia Koltsova.

Somaliland: The study team was led by Sam Joseph and included Ahmed Adan Mohamed, Haroon A. Yusuf, Omer Edleh Suleiman and Robin Le Mare. All field work, initial analysis and reporting were conducted by members of community-based organizations from Sanaag and Togdheer.

Sri Lanka: The study team was led by Jayatissa Samaranayake and Chmindra Weerackodi and included Chitra Abeygunasekera, Neil Armstrong, Wimal Dissanayake, S. Ganesh, M. P. Jayathilake, Menaka Kandasamy, S. Karthikiyini, R. M. C. Kumarihamy, N. R. Liyanage, Iranganie Magedaragamage, P. S. Muthucumarana, K. K. Ranjan, Samaraj, D. P. L. Walter Silva, M. Sumanaweera, S. Sureshwaran, Chandra Sureshwaran, Lionel Thilakeratne and Ranganathan Umakanthan.

Thailand: The study team was led by Srawooth Paitoonpong and included Sureeratna Lakanavichian, Watthana Sugunnasil, Anchana A. Naranong, Bantorn Ondam, Thippawan Keawmesri and Prinyarat Leangcharoen.

Uzbekistan: The national study team was led by Alisher Ilkhamov and also included regional team leaders Dulya Gulyamova, Arustan Joldasov, Khasan Nazarov and Igor Pogrebov. The regional team members included Erkin Alimjan-uly, Mavlyuda Ashtuhtarova, Muqaddas Azizova, Hayat Bahromov, Shamurad Bahromov, Salimash Baimagambetova, Sara Beares Comeau, Nigar Davletbayeva, Zainiddin Khodjayev, Suyun Muhammedov, Sali Sadykov, Munisa Sharipova, Theresa Truax, Saken Zhulamanov, Sanym Zholdasova, Tamara Zhulamanova and Sadriddin Yadgorov.

Vietnam: The study was led by Carolyn Turk and included ActionAid Vietnam, Oxfam (Great Britain), Sweden Mountain Rural Development Programme and Save the Children Fund (United Kingdom). Other collaborators included the People's Committees for the study of wards, communes, districts and provinces; Hanoi Research; Training Centre for Community Development; the Long An Community Health Centre; Social Science Institute; the Social Development Research Centre; the Youth Research Institute; and the Open University.

Zambia: The study team was led by John Milimo and included Mukwangule Chikama, Fusya Y. Goma, Membe S. Ian, Mable Milimo, Mutinta Mudenda, Chikama Mukwangole, Angela Mulenga, Felix Mulenga, Sikazwe Mulenga, Zyongwe Nancy Mutinta, Edward Mwanza, George Nkhata, Mulenga C. Sikazwe, Willnoad Sunga and Nancy M. Zyongwe.

Others who participated in methodological discussions and provided assistance with identifying country researchers, administration, training and other support included Maria Lourdes Abundo, Nisha Agrawal, Nilufar Ahmad, Graciela Hernández Alarcón, Joachim von Amsberg, Katherine Bain, Mark Baird, Nicole Ball, Bhuvan Bhatnagar, Jeanine Braithwaite, Karen Brock, Sudarshan Canagarajah, Sandra Cesilini, Joelle Chassard, John Clark, Atreyee Cordeiro, Anis Dani, Monica Das Gupta, Tony Dogbe, Nora Dudwick, Peter Rhodes Easley, Janet Entwistle, Lionel Demery, Ghada El-Mootaz, Sarah Forster, Vicente Fretes-Cibils, George Gattoni, John Gaventa, Hafez M. H. Ghanem, Agnelo Gomes, Gita Gopal, Christiaan Grootaert, Isabel Guerrero, Peter Harrold, Norman Hicks, Indrawati

Josodipeoro, Kamal Kar, Jubran Paul Kanaan, Eyerusalem Kebede, Ramesh Khadka, Ron Kim, Jeni Klugman, Valerie Kozel, Reider Kvam, Edwin Lim, Kinuthia Macharia, Mwajuma Masaiganah, William Maloney, Kofi Marrah, Katherine Marshall, Alexandra Martínez, Jimmy Mascarenhas, Kimberley McClean, Deborah Newitter Mikesell, Mohinder Mudahar, Neela Mukherjee, Miranda Munro, Martien van Nieuwkoop, Andrew Norton, Thomas O'Brien, Gillermo Perry, Jessica Poppele, Lant Hayward Pritchett, Caroline Robb, Jorge Uquillas Rodas, Peter Rundell, Alaa Saber, Ritika Sahai, Mallika Samaranayake, Ron Sawyer, Kinnon Scott, Shekhar Shah, Andrea Silverman, Alice Sindzingre, Kamal Singh, Surjit Singh, William James Smith, David Steel, Roger Sullivan, Magdalena Syposz, Laura Tagle, Rajesh Tandon, Pamornrat Tansanguanwong, David Tuschneider, Zafiris Tzannatos, Shizu Uphadya, Per Egil Wam, Anna Maria Wetterberg and Ellen Wratten.

The process of global synthesis began at a workshop held in New Delhi in June 1999, which brought together the team leaders from 20 of the study countries for a week of intensive discussions. Team leaders shared their draft national reports and field experiences, which helped to start the analysis of global patterns and findings.

At the World Bank supporting research and content analysis were conducted by Dina Mesbah-Khavari and Rachel Wheeler and research assistance was provided by Sarah Guroff, Kristin Hirsch, Chia-Hsin Hu, Jennifer Nelson, Veronica Nyhan Jones and Talat Shah. At IDS supporting research and content analysis were conducted by Karen Brock and research assistance provided by Katherine Pasteur, Anna Robinson-Pant, Damien Thuriaux and Kimberly Vilar.

Valuable feedback on an earlier draft was given by participants in a review workshop hosted by DFID in London. Detailed written comments were provided by Stephen Devereux, Claudia Fumo, Jacqueline Grant, Arjan de Haan, Jeremy Holland, Robin Le Mare, Rosemary McGee, Ian Scoones, Toby Shillito and Howard White. Valuable written comments were also received from Anthony Bebbington, John Blaxall, William Easterly, Alisher Ilkahamov, Ernst Lutz, Nilanjana Mukherjee, Susie Orbach, Carrie Turk, Norman Uphoff, Michael Walton, and Michael Ward.

Several people played invaluable roles in the final editing of the book. They included John Blaxall, Jeff Porro and Audrey Liounis. Copyediting was done by Kristin Rusch and Rebecca Kary. The conference version of the book was formatted by Barbara Harrick. The production was managed by the Office of the Publisher at the World Bank.

Finally, and above all, no acknowledgment or recognition can be adequate for the thousands of poor people who sacrificed their time to share their experiences and whose voices are represented here. It is therefore to them that this book is dedicated.

Appendix 2. Study Countries and Sites

REGION AND COUNTRY	CRITERIA FOR SAMPLE SELECTION	SITES AND NUMBER OF DISCUSSION GROUPS

Africa and the Middle East

Egypt	Nine sites were selected with high levels of poverty and to cover different geographic, environmental and livelihood conditions.	**Urban:** El Mataria (Dakahliya Governorate); Foua (Kafr El Sheikh Governorate). **Rural:** Bedsa (Giza Governorate); Beni Amer (Minya Governorate); Borg Meghezel (Kafr El-Sheikh Governorate); Dahshour (Giza Governorate); El Gawaber (Dakahliya Governorate); Sidkia (Aswan Governorate); Zawyet Sultan (Minya Governorate). 9 Sites, 44 Discussion Groups
Ethiopia	Ten sites were selected from three different regions of the country, based on agroecology (high or low land), proximity of site to a main road and whether the area was urban or rural.	**East Shewa, Oromia Region.** *Urban:* Kebele 11 (Debre Zeit Town, Wereda 2). *Rural:* Dibdibe Wajtu; Kajima; Kukura Dembi. **Addis Ababa, Region 14.** Urban: Kebele 23 (Wereda 11, Zone 4); Kebele 30 (Wereda 3, Zone 1). **Dessie Zuria, Debub Wello Zone, Amhara Region.** *Urban:* Kebele 11. *Rural:* Gerardo; Kalina; Mitti Kolo. 10 Sites, 78 Discussion Groups
Ghana	Nine sites were selected based on poverty and geographic criteria, and where the researchers had previously worked or had contacts to facilitate entry into the community.	**Coastal Ecological Zone.** *Urban:* Teshie (Accra). *Rural:* Doryumu (Dangbe West District). Middle Belt. *Urban:* Atonsu Bokro (Kumasi). *Rural:* Twabidi (Ahafo-Ano North District). **Transition Zone.** *Rural:* Asukawkaw (Kete Krachi District); Babatokuma (Kintampo District). **Northern Savannah Zone.** *Rural:* Adaboya (Bongo District); Dobile Yirkpong (Regional Capital); Tabe Ere (Lawra District). 9 Sites, 56 Discussion Groups

REGION AND COUNTRY	CRITERIA FOR SAMPLE SELECTION	SITES AND NUMBER OF DISCUSSION GROUPS
Malawi	Ten sites from 10 districts were selected based on agricultural history and livelihood sources. In each district, actual sites were selected after consulting with district development officers, district commissioners and agricultural officers.	**Urban:** Chemusa (Blantyre); Masasa (Mzuzu); Phwetekere (Lilongwe). **Rural:** Chitambi (Mulanje District); Khwalala (Nkhata-Bay District); Kowerani Kuphera (Dowa District); Madana (Ntcheu District); Mbwadzulu (Mangochi District); Mtamba (Chiradzulu District); Nampeya (Machiga District). 10 Sites, 70 Discussion Groups
Nigeria	Sixteen sites were selected purposively on the basis of regional, ethnic-cultural, religious and geographic diversity, and the possibility of program or project follow-up.	**Urban:** Ayekale Odoogun (Kwara State); Dawaki (Gombe State); Elieke Rumuokoro (River State); Gusau (Zamfara State); Ikara (Kaduna State); Mbamoi (Adamawa State); Umuoba Road-Aba Waterside (Abia State); Ughoton (Delta State). **Rural:** Atan (Oyo State); Bagel (Bauchi State); Bamikemo (Ondo State); Bonugu (Federal Capital Territory) Ikot Idem (Akwa Ibom State); Jimowa (Sokoto State); Okpuje (Enugu State); Tse-Akiishi (Benue State). 16 Sites, 132 Discussion Groups
Somaliland	The communities were selected to include a diversity of urban and rural sites, geographic and natural resource conditions, agricultural activities (pastoral, agropastoral, different species of livestock, farming), clan composition and social services.	**Sanaag Region.** *Urban:* El Afweyne; Erigavo. *Rural:* Bihin; Buq; Daanweyne; Dagaar; Marawade; Sufdhere. **Togdheer Region.** *Urban:* Burao; Daami; Yirowe. *Rural:* Ali-Esse; Duruqsi; Eil-bil-ille; Haqayo Malaas; Kaba-dheere; Qoyta; Yo'ub-Yabooh. 18 Sites, 401 people included in Discussion Groups in Sanaag, 29 Discussion Groups in Togdheer
Zambia	Based on poverty data, the study was carried out in 12 of the poorest areas in the country.	**Lusaka (urban):** Kanyama; Linda; Ng'ombe Compound. **Luanshya (urban):** Roan Mpatamatu; Mikomfwa; Twashuka Compound. **Chinsali District (rural):** Ilondola; Mundu; Musanya. **Serenje District (rural):** Chief Kabamba; Muchinka; Nchimishi. 12 Sites, 60 Discussion Groups

Eastern Europe and Central Asia

Bosnia and Herzegovina	The selection of sites was based on geographic distribution and the need to balance rural and urban areas. Researchers also sought to include medium-size towns in which a specific industry (now closed or at reduced capacity) had dominated the area and employment options. In addition, refugees were represented either through the choice of sites or through special groups.	**Federation.** *Urban:* Sarajevo; Mostar West; Vares; Zenica. *Rural:* Capljina; Polje bijela. **Republika Srpska.** *Urban:* Bijeljina. *Rural:* Sekovici. Refugee Camp: Bratunac (Glogova). 9 Sites, 72 Discussion Groups
Bulgaria	Site selection focused on geographic distribution, ethnicity and poverty levels. Nine sites were selected to include three villages, three big cities and three relatively small towns. Each region is characterized by high levels of unemployment.	**Villages:** Razgrad (Municipality of Lom); Kalaidzhi (Lovech District); Sredno Selo (Lovech District). **Towns:** Dimitrovgrad; Etropole; Kalofer. **Cities:** Jugen (Plovdiv); Krasna Poliana (Sofia); Varna. Special Groups included: Roma heroin users in Varna, Nurses in Sofia and Homeless in Sofia. 9 Sites plus 3 Special Groups, 121 Discussion Groups
Kyrgyz Republic	The three poorest regions were selected for the study. Two of the regions are in the north (Talas and Naryn) and one is located in the south (Jalal Abad). Eight rural and two urban sites were selected based on location of markets and roads, population (to include big, medium and small villages), levels of poverty, presence of NGOs that could support the study team, and geographic diversity.	**Jalal Abad Region.** *Urban:* Bishkek City; Kok Yangak. *Rural:* Achy; Tash-Bulak. **Naryn Region.** *Rural:* Ak Kiya; Bashi; Uchkun. **Talas Region.** *Rural:* Beisheke; Kenesh; Urmaral. 10 Sites, 90 Discussion Groups

REGION AND COUNTRY	CRITERIA FOR SAMPLE SELECTION	SITES AND NUMBER OF DISCUSSION GROUPS
Russia	The sites span seven regions and were selected based on poverty levels and to ensure geographic and urban-rural diversity. The research team also visited a refugee community in Moscow.	**Urban:** Dzerzhinsk (9th District); Ekaterinburg (El'mash Municipality); Ivanovo (8th District); Magadan (3rd District); Novy Gorodok (Kemerovo Region); Teikovo (Ivanovo Region). **Rural:** Belasovka (Semyonovsky); Orgakin (Kalmykia); Ozerny (Ivanovo Region). Special Group: A refugee community in Moscow 9 Sites plus 1 Special Group, 75 Discussion Groups
Uzbekistan	Sites from three regions of the country were selected based on geographic and ethnic diversity and poverty levels. In addition, small group discussions were held with three special groups: students and female daily wage workers in Tashkent and Roma in Qoqand City.	**Tashkent City and Province.** *Urban:* Olmalyq; Ulugbek. *Rural:* Oitamgaly (Oqqurghon District). **Karakalpkstan** (an autonomous republic within the territory of the Republic of Uzbekistan). *Urban:* Muynak city. *Rural:* Takhtakupyr; Turtkul. **Ferghana Valley.** *Urban:* Dangara (Ferghana Province). *Rural:* Dilqushod (Andijan province); Oq Oltyn (Andijan province). 3 Special Groups: Tashkent: Students, and Female *Mardikorlars* (daily wage laborers); Qoqand city: Roma (Gypsies) 9 Sites plus 3 Special Groups, 75 Discussion Groups

Latin America and the Caribbean

REGION AND COUNTRY	CRITERIA FOR SAMPLE SELECTION	SITES AND NUMBER OF DISCUSSION GROUPS
Argentina	Selection of the municipalities and communities was based on poverty indicators and geographic distribution. All five urban sites and one of the three rural site are from the Province of Buenos Aires, which contains roughly a quarter of the country's population.	**Santiago del Estero Province.** *Rural:* Los Juríes (General Taboada District); Villa Atamisqui (Atamisqui District). **Buenos Aires Province.** *Urban:* Barrio Sol y Verde (José C. Paz Municipality); Dock Sud (Avellaneda Municipality); Florencio Varela (Florencio Varela Municipality); La Matanza (La Matanza Municipality); Moreno (Moreno Municipality). *Rural:* Isla Talavera (Zárate Municipality). 8 Sites, 714 people participated in Discussion Groups

REGION AND COUNTRY	CRITERIA FOR SAMPLE SELECTION	SITES AND NUMBER OF DISCUSSION GROUPS
Bolivia	Eight sites were selected based on poverty indicators, ethnicity (more than 60 percent of Bolivia is indigenous) and geographic diversity.	**Urban:** Barrio Las Pascuas (Tarija); Barrio Nuestra Señora de Guadalupe (Cochabamba); Barrio Universitario Ario Alto (Cochabamba). **Rural:** Collpapucho (Aroma Province); Fuerte Santiago, (O'Connor Province); Horenco (Cercado Province); Río la Sal (O'Connor Province). **Rural-Urban:** Las Gamgas (Departamento de Santa Cruz). 8 Sites, 29 Discussion Groups
Brazil	All of the sites are urban. The selection was influenced by the World Bank's ongoing projects and development of an urban strategy. The sites were selected from three Brazilian cities based on geographic diversity, unemployment and poverty levels, and the level of community organization. All sites are or were *favelas*, or squatter settlements.	**Recife:** Bode (Pina); Borborema; Entra a Pulso; Morro da Conceição; Padre Jordano; Vila União. **Itabuna:** Nova Califórnia; Novo Horizonte. **Santo André:** Sacadura Cabral; Vila Junqueira. 10 Sites, 80 Discussion Groups
Ecuador	Nine sites were selected on the basis of geographic diversity, poverty indicators, and ethnic groups.	**Urban:** Atucucho (Quito-Pichincha); Barrio Nuevas Brisas del Mar (Esmeraldas-Esmeraldas); Isla Trinitaria (Guayaquil-Guayas). **Rural:** Asociación 10 de Agosto (Napo); Caguanapamba y el Juncal (Cañar); La Calera (Imbabura); Tumbatú/Tablas, Chota (Imbabura); Voluntad de Dios (Sucumbíos). **Rural and Urban:** Paján (Manabí). 9 Sites, 537 people participated in Discussion Groups

REGION AND COUNTRY	CRITERIA FOR SAMPLE SELECTION	SITES AND NUMBER OF DISCUSSION GROUPS
Jamaica	Nine sites (five rural and four urban) were selected based on geographic diversity, levels of poverty and, where possible, linkages with ongoing projects and research to ensure follow up. Further site selection was influenced by context-specific poverty problems such as land tenure, housing, isolation and unemployment.	**Urban sites:** Bower Bank (Kingston); Cassava Piece (Kingston); Railway Lane (Montego Bay); Thompson Pen (Spanish Town). **Rural Sites:** Accompong (Maroon State); Duckensfield (St. Thomas Parish); Freeman's Hall (Quashie River Sink); Little Bay (Westmoreland); Millbank (Portland). 9 Sites, 1,265 people participated in Discussion Groups

South and East Asia

Bangladesh	The selection of 10 sites was done purposively on the basis of geographic diversity, sociological and environmental factors, poverty levels, and the presence of NGOs that could facilitate the research and follow-up. The sample includes eight subdistricts and two urban slums.	**Urban:** Chittagong City (Bastuhara Slum, Chittagong District); Mohammadpur (Battala Slum, Dhaka City). **Peri-Urban:** Dhamrai (Hiranadi Kulla Slum, Manikganj District). **Rural:** Char Kukri Mukri-Charfession (Bhola District); Dewangonj (Jamalpur District); Gowainghat (Sylhet District); Khaliajuri (Kishoreganj District); Madaripur (Madaripur District); Nachol (Chapai-Nababganj District); Ulipur (Kurigram District).
India	The study was conducted in the states of Bihar and Andhra Pradesh. Sites were selected on the basis of social, demographic, occupational and environmental characteristics. An overriding criterion was to select places that offered the possibility of program or project follow-up.	10 Sites, 50 Discussion Groups **Bihar.** *Urban:* Patna (State Capital). *Peri-Urban:* Geruwa (East Singhbhoom District). *Rural:* Manjhar (Gaya District); Netarhat (Palamu District); Sohrai (Jhanjharpur District). **Andhra Pradesh.** *Urban:* Hyderabad (State Capital). *Peri-Urban:* Konada (Vizianagaram District). *Rural:* Dorapalli (Kurnool District); Jaggaram (Khammam District); Pedda Kothapalli (Srikakulam District). 10 Sites, 59 Discussion Groups

REGION AND COUNTRY	CRITERIA FOR SAMPLE SELECTION	SITES AND NUMBER OF DISCUSSION GROUPS
Indonesia	Twelve sites were selected based on geographic distribution, environmental factors and poverty levels. Focus was on the island of Java because it has the largest number and highest concentration of the country's poor and is the region hit hardest by the economic crisis. In order to have some representation of the rest of the country, the Nusa Tenggara islands were selected. They have livelihood patterns and geoclimatic features that are very different from Java.	**West Java Province.** *Urban:* Harapan Jaya (Bekasi District); Pegambiran (Cirebon District). *Rural:* Galih Pakuwon (Garut District); Padamukti (Bandung District). **Central Java.** *Urban:* Semanggi (Surakarta District). *Rural:* Genengsari (Grobogan District). **East Java.** *Urban:* Tanjungrejo (Malang District). *Rural:* Banaran (Ponorogo District). **Nusa Tenggara Barat.** *Urban:* Ampenan Utara (Mataram District). **Nusa Tenggara Timur.** *Semi-Urban:* Kawangu (Sumba Timur District). *Rural:* Renggarasi (Sikka District); Waikanabu (Sumba Timur District). 12 Sites, 57 Discussion Groups
Sri Lanka	A purposive sample was chosen from the main agro-ecological zones of the country, namely dry, intermediate, wet highland, wet lowland and the coastal zones. To capture the poverty conditions in the war-affected areas, four villages were chosen from the government-controlled parts of the North and East.	**Rural:** Aswedduma (Kurunegala District); Elhena/Ganegoda (Gampaha District); Ihalagama (Anuradhapura District); Kagama/Katiyawa (Anuradhapura District); Kehelpannala (Kegalle District); Kohombana (Ampara District); Kotiyagoda (Moneragala District); Mahanagapura (Hambantota District); Meegahagoda (Galle District); Munamalgasvewa (Puttalam District); Samalankulam (Vauniya District); Thrikadallur (Trincomalee District); Udayatharakai (Jaffna District); Vellur (Trincomalee District); Viyalagoda (Ratnapura District); Weerapandiyana (Puttalam District). **Semi-urban/Coastal:** Sisilasagama (Hambantota District); Thiruneetukerny (Batticaloa District); Wewala (Galle District). 19 Sites

REGION AND COUNTRY	CRITERIA FOR SAMPLE SELECTION	SITES AND NUMBER OF DISCUSSION GROUPS
Thailand	Sites were selected based on economic, geographic and sociological indicators, poverty levels and the existence of government projects for helping the poor.	**Bangkok and vicinity.** *Urban:* Ruamsamakee. *Rural:* Nakorn Patom (Bang-auh Village, Bangsen District). **Central Region.** *Rural:* Baan Kang Sadao (Wang Namyen District); Baan Ta Pak Chee (Khao Chakan District). **Southern Region.** *Urban:* Kaoseng. *Rural:* Baan Chai Pru (Pak Payoon District). **Northeastern Region.** *Rural:* Baan Pak Wan (Ban Pai District). 7 Sites, 42 Discussion Groups
Vietnam	Study sites were chosen to capture the views of poor households in a range of circumstances, which included: an ethnic minority upland area (Lao Cai), a poor coastal area (Ha Tinh), poor communes in the Mekong Delta (Tra Vinh) and poor communities in Vietnam's biggest city (Ho Chi Minh City).	**Ho Chi Minh City:** Binh Thanh District; District 6; District 8. **Ha Tinh Province:** Cam Xuyen District; Can Loc District; Ha Tinh District; Huong Son District; Ky Anh District; Thach Ha District. **Tra Vinh Province:** Chau Thanh District; Duyen Hai District. **Lao Cai Province:** Bao Thang District; Muong Khuong District. 40 Sites were visited in the districts indicated above, A minimum of 180 Discussion Groups took part in the study.

Appendix 3. Overview of Study Themes and Methods

The study is organized around four main themes. Each theme is briefly explained below and is followed by a matrix that provides a checklist of study issues and methods for fieldwork. This is based on the *Methodology Guide* that was used by the local research teams. The full document reviews the principal methods used in the study and is available on the *Voices of the Poor* Web Site at http://www.worldbank.org/poverty/voices.

Exploring Wellbeing

The concept of wellbeing is broader than poverty. Researchers were asked to explore the concept of wellbeing, particularly to understand poor people's definition of wellbeing, the kinds of factors they include in their definitions of wellbeing, and their understanding of the concepts of vulnerability, risk and social exclusion. Three broad questions are explored:

a. How do people define wellbeing or a good quality of life and illbeing or a bad quality of life?

b. How do people perceive security, risk, vulnerability, opportunities, social exclusion, and crime and conflict? How have these changed over time?

c. How do households and individuals cope with decline in wellbeing and how do these coping strategies in turn affect their lives?

Priorities of the Poor

This study aims to explore poor people's perceptions of their problems and concerns along with their prioritization. Issues include:

a. What problems are faced by the different groups (according to age, gender, social hierarchy and economic wellbeing) within the community? What problems are faced by the poor?

b. How do the different groups prioritize their problems in terms of the most pressing needs?

c. Have these problems changed over the years or have they remained the same? What are people's hopes and fears for the future?

Institutional Analysis

The purpose is to understand the role that different institutions play in different aspects of people's lives. Issues include:

a. Which institutions are important in poor people's lives?

b. How do people rate or assess these institutions?

c. Do people feel that they have any control or influence over these institutions?

d. Which institutions support people in coping with crisis?

Gender Relations

This thematic focus attempts to understand whether there have been any changes in gender relations within the household and the community. Specific issues include:

a. What are the existing gender relations within the household? Are women better or worse off today (1) as compared to the past and (2) as compared to men?

b. What are the existing gender relations within the community? Are women better or worse off today (1) as compared to the past and (2) as compared to men?

c. Are there differences in gender relations among different groups within the community?

Methods Used to Explore Study Themes

A mix of participatory verbal and visual techniques were used to facilitate group discussions and interviews with the community members. The *Methodology Guide* provides detailed explanations of the tools as well as illustrative examples of how they can be used. Table A3.1 (which draws from pages 9–15 of the *Methodology Guide*) lists the methods and topics used to facilitate discussion and analysis by the study participants.

Table A3.1 Checklist of Issues and Methods

THEMES AND ISSUES

1. EXPLORING WELLBEING

Methods: small group discussions, wellbeing ranking, scoring, cause-impact analysis, trend analysis, in-depth interviews with individuals or households.

1.1 How do people define wellbeing or a good quality of life and illbeing or a bad quality of life?

▸ Local definitions of wellbeing, deprivation, illbeing, vulnerability and poverty. Since these terms do not translate easily in local languages, it is better to start by asking the local people for their own terminology and definitions that explain quality of life. *Local terminology and definitions must be included in the analysis.* Different groups within the same community could be using different terms or phrases for the same subject. All these need to be recorded.

▸ A listing of criteria on the basis of which households or individuals are differentiated and placed in different categories.

▶ Different wellbeing groups/categories of households/individuals, as identified by the local people. Allow the community to come up with their own categories. Do not impose ideas. There is no fixed number of categories that a community can come up with. Usually these vary between three to six categories, but there could be more. Characteristics (or criteria) of individuals/households in each of these categories should be clearly recorded.

▶ Proportion of households/individuals in each of these categories. This could be exact numbers or indicative scores (out of 100, or any predetermined fixed maximum score). This will give an idea about the proportion of poor or deprived people in a community.

1.2 How do people perceive security, risk, vulnerability, opportunities, social exclusion and crime and conflict? How have these changed over time?

Having discussed people's definition of wellbeing and poverty/illbeing, explore the following themes:

▶ Risk, security and vulnerability
▶ Opportunities and social and economic mobility
▶ Social exclusion
▶ Social cohesion, crime, conflict and tension

The following themes and issues need to be explored in depth to understand the different aspects of wellbeing:

a. Risk, security and vulnerability

▶ Does security or insecurity figure in people's definition of wellbeing?
▶ How do people define security?
▶ Are some households secure and others insecure? How do they differentiate between the two?
▶ What makes households insecure or at greater risk?
▶ Has insecurity increased or decreased? Why?
▶ What are the main kinds of shocks that people have faced?
▶ Are some individuals/households more insecure than others in the same community?
▶ Are some people better able to cope with sudden shocks to sources of livelihoods? Why and how?

b. Opportunities, social and economic mobility

▶ Do people feel that opportunities for economic and social mobility have increased? Decreased? Why and for whom?

▶ What are the consequences of these changes?

▶ Who or which group(s) has benefited the most? Which groups have been unable to take advantage of opportunities or have been negatively affected? Why?

▶ Is it possible for people to move out of poverty?

▶ What is needed to enable people to move out of poverty?

▶ What needs to change for the poor to have greater economic and social opportunities? Is this likely?

c. Social exclusion

▶ Are some people/groups *left out* of society, or looked down upon or excluded from active participation in community life or decisionmaking?

▶ Who gets left out, and on what basis? Why?

▶ What is the impact of such exclusion or being left out?

▶ Is it possible for those excluded to ever become included?

▶ What determines the likelihood of this change?

▶ Are there differences in power between those included and excluded?

▶ What makes some people powerful and others not?

d. Social cohesion, crime, conflict

▶ How do people define social cohesion?

▶ Is there more or less of social unity and sense of belonging than before? Why?

▶ Is there more or less crime and conflict than in the past, or has it stayed the same? Why?

▶ Are there conflicts between groups in the community? Which groups? Why?

▶ Have intergroup conflicts increased or decreased? Why? How?

▶ Does anyone benefit from the increased violence? Can the situation be changed? How?

1.3 **How do households and individuals cope with decline in wellbeing and how do these coping strategies in turn affect their lives?**

▶ Whether there have been any changes in the number and types of wellbeing categories, and/or whether the proportion of people/households in each of them has increased/decreased over the last 10 years.

▶ Whether the criteria for determining the categories have changed over the years.

▶ What has changed? What caused the changes? How has it affected the lives of the people? Have people become better or worse off? Is there a "typology of deprivation"—sudden, seasonal, structural, cyclic, chronic?

▶ How have people coped with these changes?

▶ Are there any foreseeable changes in the future? What and how?

1.4 **Individual case studies**

In-depth discussion/interviews with

▶ One poor woman.

▶ One poor man.

▶ One woman and/or man who has fallen into poverty.

▶ One woman and/or man who used to be poor but has moved out of poverty.

2. PROBLEMS AND PRIORITIES

Methods: small group discussions; ranking, scoring, listing, trend analysis.

2.1 **Listing of problems faced by the different groups within the community, and their prioritization.**

2.2 **Are there differences in problems and priorities being experienced by different groups of people within the community (e.g., according to age, gender, social hierarchy and economic wellbeing)? Identify the problems faced by the poor.**

2.3 **Have these problems changed over the years or have they remained the same? What are poor people's hopes and fears (visions) for the future?**

2.4 Which of these problems do they think they can solve themselves and which require external support?

3. INSTITUTIONAL ANALYSIS

Methods: small group discussions, listing, scoring, ranking and two mini-institutional profiles.

3.1 Which institutions are important in poor people's lives?

a. What are the most important formal, informal, government, nongovernment and market institutions within or outside the community that affect poor people's lives positively or negatively? Why are these judged to be important? Are there any gender differences?

b. Which government and nongovernment institutions have the most positive or negative impact on men and women? Why? Give examples of poor people's experiences. Are there any gender differences?

3.2 How do people rate these institutions?

a. How do poor people rate these institutions in terms of trust and confidence that they place on them? Why? Give examples of why people rate particular institutions high or low. Are there any gender differences?

b. How do they rate the effectiveness of these institutions? What factors do they consider to judge effectiveness? Give examples. Are there any gender differences? Explain.

3.3 Do poor people feel that have any control or influence over these institutions?

a. Which institutions do poor people think they have some influence over?

b. Which institutions would they like to have more control and influence over?

c. Do some people/groups have some influence over these institutions and others are left out? Who gets left out?

d. Profile two institutions in some depth.

3.4 Coping with crisis

This issue deals with understanding safety nets, informal or formal insurance, or availability and outreach of government programs.

a. During times of financial/economic crisis, because of loss of property, jobs, or livelihood, poor crops, disease, environmental crisis, or poor health or death, how do poor people cope? What do they do? How do these affect their lives?

b. What institutions, formal or informal, do poor people turn to during times of financial crisis?

c. Do they mention any government programs? Give details.

d. Are these programs reaching them?

e. What are their recommendations for change or improvement or for new programs if none exist?

f. What features should this program have?

g. Do they mention any NGO programs?

h. Do they mention any informal social networks?

i. Are there any gender differences?

j. If almost everyone in the community is affected by some event (e.g., floods, droughts or earthquakes), how does the community cope?

4. GENDER RELATIONS

Methods: small group discussions; scoring and trend analysis.

4.1 Are poor women better off today as compared to the past?

Are there any changes in

a. Women's and men's responsibilities within the household? Why?

b. Women's and men's responsibilities in the community? Why?

c. Women's and men's role in the decisionmaking process within the household? Why?

d. Women's and men's role in the decisionmaking process in the community? Why?

e. Violence against women within the household? Why?

f. Violence against women within the community? Why?

g. Do women feel they have more/less power today (with their definition of *power*)? Why?

4.2 Are there differences in gender relations among different groups within the community?

a. Are some women better off than other women in the same community (with their definition of *better off*)?

b. Have the changes in gender relations been different for different groups of women in the community?

Appendix 4. About the Authors

Deepa Narayan is the Lead Social Development Specialist for the World Bank's Poverty Group in the Poverty Reduction and Economic Development Network. She has spent 25 years working on poverty policies, research and programs. She has lived in communities in Africa, South Asia and East Asia working with civil society, national governments and international organizations. She has written extensively on participatory development, community-driven development and social capital. Her recent publications include *Voices of the Poor: Can Anyone Hear Us?*; *Bonds and Bridges: Poverty and Social Capital*; *Participatory Development Toolkit*; and *Design of Community Based Development*.

Robert Chambers is a Research Associate of the Institute of Development Studies at the University of Sussex, United Kingdom. Much of his practical and research experience outside the United Kingdom has been in East Africa and South Asia. His books include *Managing Rural Development: Ideas and Experience from East Africa, Rural Development: Putting the Last First, Challenging the Professions,* and *Whose Reality Counts? Putting the First Last.* His main current work is on the development and spread of participatory approaches, behaviors and methods, and on perceptions of poverty, illbeing and wellbeing.

Meera K. Shah is a development consultant and trainer. She is involved in developing and promoting participatory approaches and processes in natural resources management, local institutional development, postconflict and disaster rehabilitation, policy research and advocacy, gender analysis, and monitoring and evaluation. Previously she worked with the Aga Khan Rural Support Programme (AKRSP), India, where she helped pioneer, with others, participatory rural appraisal methodology. Shah has co-edited *The Myth of Community: Gender Issues in Participatory Development* and *Embracing Participation in Development: Wisdom From the Field*; and authored *Listening to Young Voices: Facilitating Participatory Appraisals on Reproductive Health with Adolescents.*

Patti Petesch freelances for foundations, think tanks, NGOs and international development organizations. She has published studies and conducted evaluations on aid effectiveness and coordination, the poverty and environment nexus, civil society participation, and NGO campaigns to reform the international financial institutions. Petesch was previously a staff associate at the Overseas Development Council with responsibilities for research and outreach on environmental and poverty issues. She is the author of *North-South Environmental Strategies, Costs and Bargains* and co-author of *Sustaining the Earth: The Role of Multilateral Development Institutions.*